MW00835396

Reimagining Indian Ocean Worlds

This book breaks new ground by bringing together multidisciplinary approaches to examine contemporary Indian Ocean worlds. It reconfigures the Indian Ocean as a space for conceptual and theoretical relationality based on social science and humanities scholarship, thus moving away from an area-based and geographical approach to Indian Ocean studies.

Contributors from a variety of disciplines focus on keywords such as *relationality, space/place, quotidian practices*, and *new networks of memory and maps* to offer original insights to reimagine the Indian Ocean. While the volume as a whole considers older histories, mobilities, and relationships between places in Indian Ocean worlds, it is centrally concerned with new connectivities and layered mappings forged in the lived experiences of individuals and communities today. The chapters are steeped in ethnographic, multi-modal, and other humanities methodologies that examine different sources besides historical archives and textual materials, including everyday life, cities, museums, performances, the built environment, media, personal narratives, food, medical practices, or scientific explorations.

An important contribution to several fields, this book will be of interest to academics of Indian Ocean studies, Afro-Asian linkages, inter-Asian exchanges, Afro-Arab crossroads, Asian studies, African studies, Anthropology, History, Geography, and International Relations.

Smriti Srinivas is Professor of Anthropology at the University of California, Davis, USA.

Bettina Ng'weno is Associate Professor of African American and African Studies at the University of California, Davis, USA.

Neelima Jeychandran is a Postdoctoral Fellow and Research Associate in African Studies and Asian Studies at the Pennsylvania State University, USA.

Routledge Studies on the Indian Ocean and Trans-Asia
Series Editors: Smriti Srinivas and Neelima Jeychandran

Reimagining Indian Ocean Worlds
Edited by Smriti Srinivas, Bettina Ng'weno, and Neelima Jeychandran

Reimagining Indian Ocean Worlds

Edited by Smriti Srinivas, Bettina Ng'weno, and Neelima Jeychandran

Routledge
Taylor & Francis Group

LONDON AND NEW YORK

First published 2020
by Routledge
2 Park Square, Milton Park, Abingdon, Oxon OX14 4RN

and by Routledge
52 Vanderbilt Avenue, New York, NY 10017

Routledge is an imprint of the Taylor & Francis Group, an informa business

© 2020 selection and editorial matter, Smriti Srinivas, Bettina Ng'weno, and Neelima Jeychandran; individual chapters, the contributors

The right of Smriti Srinivas, Bettina Ng'weno and Neelima Jeychandran to be identified as the authors of the editorial material, and of the authors for their individual chapters, has been asserted in accordance with sections 77 and 78 of the Copyright, Designs and Patents Act 1988.

All rights reserved. No part of this book may be reprinted or reproduced or utilized in any form or by any electronic, mechanical, or other means, now known or hereafter invented, including photocopying and recording, or in any information storage or retrieval system, without permission in writing from the publishers.

Trademark notice: Product or corporate names may be trademarks or registered trademarks, and are used only for identification and explanation without intent to infringe.

British Library Cataloguing-in-Publication Data
A catalogue record for this book is available from the British Library

Library of Congress Cataloging-in-Publication Data
A catalog record has been requested for this book

ISBN: 978-0-367-34453-5 (hbk)
ISBN: 978-0-429-32591-5 (ebk)

Typeset in Times New Roman
by Wearset Ltd, Boldon, Tyne and Wear

Contents

List of figures   viii
List of maps   ix
List of contributors   x

Introduction: many worlds, many oceans   1
SMRITI SRINIVAS, BETTINA NG'WENO, AND
NEELIMA JEYCHANDRAN

**PART I
Proximity and distance**   23

1 **The ends of the Indian Ocean: notes on boundaries and
   affinities across time**   25
   JEREMY PRESTHOLDT

2 **Indian Ocean ontology: Nyerere, memory, place**   42
   MAY JOSEPH

3 **The littoral, the container, and the interface: situating the
   dry port as an Indian Ocean imaginary**   58
   ISHANI SARAF

4 **Seasons of sail: the monsoon, kinship, and labor in the
   dhow trade**   73
   NIDHI MAHAJAN

PART II
Landscapes, oceanscapes, and practices 87

5 Elsewheres in the Indian Ocean: spatio-temporal
encounters and imaginaries beyond the sea 89
NETHRA SAMARAWICKREMA

6 Dicey waterways: evolving networks and contested
spatialities in Goa 103
MAYA COSTA-PINTO

7 Improvising Juba: productive precarity and making the
present at the edge of the Indian Ocean world 118
CHRISTIAN J. DOLL

8 Displacemaking with *shutki:* living with dead, dried fish as
companions 133
BIDITA JAWHER TITHI

PART III
Memory and maps 147

9 Memory, memorialization, and "heritage" in the Indian
Ocean 149
PEDRO MACHADO

10 Shorelines of memory and ports of desire: geography,
identity, and the memory of oceanic trade in Mekran Coast
(Balochistan) 165
HAFEEZ AHMED JAMALI

11 The ship and the anchor: shifting cartographies of affinity
and belonging among Sikhs in Fiji 180
NICOLE RANGANATH

PART IV
Methods and disciplines 195

12 Bibi's *uchungu*: eating, bitterness, and relationality across
Indian Ocean worlds 197
LAURA A. MEEK

13 *Marfa masti*: performing shifting Indian Ocean geographies   212
    PALLAVI SRIRAM

14 Exploring the "unknown:" Indian Ocean materiality as
    method   227
    VIVIAN Y. CHOI

    Index   243

Figures

I.1   Family at Pangsau pass, India–Burma border, 1969   3
I.2   Bettina Ng'weno on the *dhow Shukran*, Kilifi, Kenya, 2015   7
I.3   A street in Kuttichira, Kozhikode with the old Juma Mosque
       and traditional homes of Muslim mercantile communities,
       Kozhikode, 2018   9
I.4   A traditional *kaavu* or sacred grove with consecrated stone idols
       of Kappiri and other local deities, Vypin, Kerala, 2013   11
I.5   The South Asian global guru, Sathya Sai Baba, 1980s   14
I.6   Nairobi City Park, performance for *Nai ni Who?* celebration
       of the Nairobi neighborhoods, 2013   16
2.1   Author in Mnazi Mmoja Park, Dar es salaam, 1967   51
3.1   A view from ICD Baba's shrine   68
4.1   *Vahans* (*dhows*) docked at Jam Salaya during *aakhar* in
       August 2017   76
5.1   Firaz's father, Firaz, and Firaz's young son sort through an
       old collection of gems while Faisa captures the moment with
       her camera   97
6.1   A casino at night, Mandovi river, Goa   108
7.1   Coffee, tea and shisha being sold in a partially completed tower
       near Juba International airport, Juba, South Sudan   125
8.1   *Shutki* drying on scaffolds at Nazirartek, Bangladesh   133
9.1   Kramat Shaykh Yusuf, Macassar, Cape Town   152
10.1   Nakhuda Noor Muhammad reminiscing about Omani rule
       in Gwadar   168
11.1   Memorial for the cremated Sikh holy books, Lautoka
       Gurdwara, 2017   189
12.1   Bibi with her great-granddaughter   203
13.1   "An African Lyre Player" (recto), calligraphy (verso)   215

Maps

1.1 Map of the Indian Ocean region demarcating the British
colonial sphere at the beginning of the twentieth century.
Published in C. P. Lucas, 1906. *A Historical Geography of the
British Colonies, Second Edition, Volume I: The Mediterranean
and Eastern Colonies*. Oxford: Clarendon Press   32

14.1 Route outline of Cruise 3 of the United States vessel Te Vega,
as taken from their cruise reports   232

Contributors

Vivian Y. Choi: Assistant Professor of Anthropology, Department of Sociology and Anthropology, St. Olaf College

Maya Costa-Pinto: Asia Institute, Sidney Myer Asia Centre, University of Melbourne

Christian J. Doll: Postdoctoral Teaching Scholar, Department of Sociology and Anthropology, North Carolina State University

Hafeez Ahmed Jamali: Advisor, CPEC Center of Excellence, Balochistan University of Information Technology, Engineering, and Management Sciences (BUITEMS), Pakistan

Neelima Jeychandran: Postdoctoral Fellow and Research Associate in African Studies and Asian Studies, Pennsylvania State University

May Joseph: Professor of Global Studies, Pratt Institute

Pedro Machado: Associate Professor, Department of History, Indiana University, Bloomington

Nidhi Mahajan: Assistant Professor, Department of Anthropology, University of California, Santa Cruz

Laura A. Meek: Assistant Professor, Centre for the Humanities and Medicine, University of Hong Kong

Bettina Ng'weno: Associate Professor, Department of African American and African Studies, University of California, Davis

Jeremy Prestholdt: Professor, Department of History, University of California, San Diego

Nicole Ranganath: Assistant Adjunct Professor, Middle East/South Asian Studies, University of California, Davis

Ishani Saraf: PhD Candidate, Department of Anthropology, University of California, Davis

Nethra Samarawickrema: PhD Candidate, Department of Anthropology, Stanford University

Pallavi Sriram: Assistant Professor of Dance Studies, Department of Theater and Dance, Colorado College

Smriti Srinivas: Professor, Department of Anthropology, University of California, Davis

Bidita Jawher Tithi: Independent Scholar, Project Lead, Youth DataLab, DORPAN, Dhaka, Bangladesh

Introduction

Many worlds, many oceans

*Smriti Srinivas, Bettina Ng'weno, and
Neelima Jeychandran*

Crafting arrival

This volume charts several pathways – intellectual and methodological – that are
intertwined with the multiple places that we as authors, our interlocutors, and
our communities inhabit. In what follows, we describe how, as editors, we came
to participate in and craft this volume. The narratives below are dialogical and
memoir-like in their texture and emphasize the ways in which where we live or
have lived – as women of color – are formative of how we think and carry out
our work in contemporary Indian Ocean worlds. They reveal how our journeys,
training, or conceptual paradigms create Indian Ocean worlds that intersect but
are also unique. We share this multi-vocality and intersectionality with the other
authors in this volume. Indian Ocean studies has been largely historical in its
content and this significance of history inflects our disciplinary sites of departure
(anthropology or cultural studies, for example) with greater depth than has been
common recently. At the same time, the study of the Indian Ocean, for the most
part, has tended to attract male scholars so that the overwhelmingly female
voices in this volume constitute a real departure for the field. Its study has also
not been especially concerned with the contemporary, ethnographic, or ontological in the ways that anthropology, cultural studies, or literature have been.
We believe that an awareness of these lacunae and creating tracks between these
disciplines is intellectually vital. Many of the authors in this volume try to
address these lacunae through feminist perspectives, fieldwork methods,
memoirs and travelogues, through a focus on the body multiple, invisible histories, non-human actors (marine lives, *djinns*), and subaltern voices, cast in
spatial, material, somatic, mnemonic, and digital registers.

Smriti Srinivas: Hanif Latif (a pseudonym), my car's driver on a visit to
India's west coast in 2019, is a soft-spoken elegant man, who spent 20 years in
Saudi Arabia driving trailers. Commenting on racialized labor conditions in
Saudi Arabia, he was glad to be home in Mangalore upon retirement. There was
nothing particularly unusual about his story, more or less different than the thousands of other men from Kerala to Gujarat, who have worked in the Gulf in
recent decades. What distinguished Hanif was the manner in which the details of
his own biography were cast against the canvas of Indian Ocean worlds: born of

Malayalam-speaking Muslim parents from a border region between Kerala and Karnataka, Hanif grew up in a small town on the South Kanara coast where he went to a local Kannada and Konkani language school studying Sanskrit from Class 6 onwards. Performatively reciting some Sanskrit verses, he told me he had married a Byari woman from the Mangalore area and learnt Byari.[1] In Saudi Arabia, he gained linguistic competence in Arabic, Bengali, Hindi, Urdu, and English bringing the total number of languages he knew to nine. This created an opening to talk politics, about the Bharatiya Janata Party's (BJP) sweeping victory in the 2019 Indian Lok Sabha elections, what it meant for someone like him and me.

Hanif's life seemed to echo myriad other crossings – including mine – over a vast swathe of time. Like Hanif, my life has unfolded across multiple cultural landscapes and political borders, reckoned with displacements and returns, many homes and affective communities, and their loss. Perhaps that is why I felt such kinship with him as he chose to narrate a life-story of multilingual dexterity cast against the precariousness of his position as an Indian Ocean Muslim in the context of recent political events in India. The stakes were high: his sense of self offers a contrast to statist-infrastructural narratives of the Ocean, for instance, by India and China today. And the kinship or friendship enacted between us perhaps betokens ways of being, living, acting that are not usually part of Indian Ocean studies. In what follows below, inspired by Hanif and by Amitav Ghosh's travelling, multi-temporal ethnography (Ghosh 1993) of Egypt, India, and worlds before European hegemony (Abu-Lughod 1989), I offer a map of my phenomenological knowledge of Indian Ocean worlds. While spatial, this map is not cartographic but shares with other scholars (e.g., Amrith 2013; Green 2011; Gupta et al. 2010; Ho 2006; Machado 2014; Prestholdt 2015) the sense of the Indian Ocean as imagination or method, its view obtained through mobilities, processes, and crossings. That is to say, I understand space less as a surface to travel on, a stage for cultural practices, or an enclosure for multiple life-worlds, and more of a *place crossed by pathways of life, remembrance, and openings to the future.*

I come to anthropology via a peripatetic life. My first six years were spent in postcolonial Assam; I retain vivid images of jeeps and winding roads, a mile-stone on the India-Burma border, tea plantations, and our bamboo home in Dibrugarh near the Brahmaputra. In 1971, we moved across the Bay of Bengal to Kuala Lumpur. Seen across the ocean, plantations become ways to connect the coolie, labor conditions and extractive economies in the colony and post-colony: the Assamese plantations bore striking resonances to Malaysian rubber plantations. Farmers largely abandoned rubber by the 1990s but the Malaysia I knew predated the decline of plantation life associated with working class Tamils or the growth of a neoliberal Malay Islamic modernity that increasingly negated certain Indian Ocean pasts (see Willford 2014).

My Southeast Asian sojourn prepared me for Hong Kong, which seemed very much like Singapore and Penang – the port city typology (Broeze 1989) seemed to work for the 1970s – but it did not prepare me for the radical shift in sensory, political, and cultural life as I crossed borders into China in 1974. Blue and green uniforms; thousands of bicycles on Beijing's streets; the smell of cooked cabbage in the commune near our socialist style apartments; furious ice-hockey between Soviet and rest-of-the world teams (watched by their respective Cold War embassy blocs) on a large frozen lake; watching endless re-runs of *Sparkling Red Star* (1974) on state TV while eating dumplings; Tiananmen Square. Mao's China complemented the many socialisms and postcolonial projects proliferating in Indian Ocean worlds from Vietnam to Tanzania offering a counterpoint to other utopian, non-state imaginaries – Gandhian, non-Brahmin, or Buddhist (see Geetha 2011; Geetha and Rajadurai 1998; Queen 1996).

Our family returned to post-Emergency India in 1977; we moved to south India for many years. My undergraduate education at Madras Christian College brought the Indian Ocean into close focus again: within two weeks of classes beginning in 1983, the college shut in protest against anti-Tamil violence in Sri Lanka. Thousands of refugees lived in camps close to my college for years

Figure I.1 Family at Pangsau pass, India–Burma border, 1969.
Image credit: personal collection of Smriti Srinivas.

after while those in my Young Women's Christian Association (YWCA) hostel became friends. My Sri Lankan experience is one reason that my South Asia anthropology classes read Shyam Selvadurai's *Funny Boy* (1994), which evocatively weaves together issues of space, intertextuality, sexuality, and communalism with questions of friendship and agency.

I entered the Delhi School of Economics' Department of Sociology as a graduate student in 1986. "D-School" began soon after Indian independence and was known for its world-class social-science research (see Kumar and Mookherjee 1995). My department refused to separate anthropology and sociology because the classificatory apparatus of colonial/Eurocentric knowledge informed its separation. Given the longue durée of Indian civilization, this made no cognitive or social sense: for e.g., forests and cities have been mutually constitutive at least since the Sanskrit epics if not earlier. I invoke D-School to highlight my ambidextrous and historical social science training that sets it apart from many US anthropology departments; thus, for me, Indian Ocean studies is imbricated with the project of decolonization and the study of South Asian cities is located within a dialogical encounter – temporal, spatial, intellectual – rather than within area studies. However, although Indian cities were being culturally and spatially transformed through transport networks, urban restructuring, or migration in the 1980s and 1990s similar to other Indian Ocean cities (for e.g., Ali and Rieker 2009; Goh 2002; Huyssen 2008; Kusno 2000), in Asia and Africa, the urban was still not an active anthropological field. My doctoral dissertation, thus, focused on two Himalayan villages in Ladakh, Muslim and Buddhist identities, and spirit possession on the contested borders between India, China, and Pakistan. It has in common with my other work the concern with crossings, bodies, and spatiality.

My "urban" engagements began after moving to Bangalore in 1993. With about 13 million persons today, the city has been a high technology research and production center since the 1990s – "India's Silicon Valley" (see Heitzman 2004). As an urban site, however, its historical connections stretch back to the last great South Indian empire in the sixteenth century and, although in the heart of the Deccan, include significant Indian Ocean connections from the eighteenth century onwards; more contemporaneously, it is constituted by regional migrations, hardware and software circuits, and placed within a global economy. Religious performances, somatic practices, and place-memories weave through these histories. In *Landscapes of Urban Memory* (Srinivas 2001), I focus on the city's central civic ritual – the annual "Karaga" performance dedicate to a goddess rooted in a vernacular Mahabharata epic – and several other religious sites in the city to highlight the relationship between the sacred and the civic. The book focuses on non-elite communities who regard themselves as legitimate subjects of history and who produce the metropolis through spatial, ecological, and ritual practices that provide counter-imaginations of the city.

The considerations emerging from my Bangalore research demanded a transdisciplinary, comparative approach tying embodiment, the social, several spatial scales, and temporalities. Thus, I turned to a global religious movement centered on the famous Indian guru, Sathya Sai Baba (1926–2011): *In the Presence of Sai Baba* (Srinivas 2008) tracks the movement in India, the US, and East Africa linking regimes of spatial, somatic, and symbolic production to analyze affinities, differences, or refabulations between sites. *A Place for Utopia* (Srinivas 2015) triangulates utopian designs and practices in South Asia from the early twentieth century to the early twenty-first century with American and European ones. It connects cities such as Indore, Madras, Bangalore, and Los Angeles, religious movements such as Theosophy and American Vedanta, urban planners, pilgrims, migrants, devotees, and ordinary city-dwellers. These books were also the outcome of movement institutionally and spatially in the last two decades: I moved from a position in sociology in Bangalore to a position in anthropology at the University of California via stopovers in New York City, Washington D.C., and Columbus as an urbanist and scholar of comparative religion. In the midst of these movements, I returned several times every year to South Asian worlds. This type of urban, comparative, mobile, interdisciplinary engagement on my part (see also Hancock and Srinivas 2008, 2018) and on the part of some other African and Asian scholars (see, for e.g., Arif 2016; Bayat 2010; Robinson 2006; Simone 2010) at the level of theory and practice are responses to the need for a transcultural and contemporaneous intellectual project. Given my journey, approaching the Indian Ocean through the lens of cities and spatiality, registers/practices (utopian, mnemonic, material, or religious), and contemporaneity, was inevitable. At the same time, this return to Indian Ocean worlds references a shift from an individual sense of the Ocean to an intellectual project bringing together the sensorium and memory of childhood or young adulthood, the lived, the embodied, and the understood, a journey to a wider conceptual terrain that clarifies phenomenological experiences.

Bettina Ng'weno: In preparation for my sister's wedding in 2006 I jokingly ask my male cousins and my dad if they will come in *kanzus* for the wedding. Some laugh and others say they will come in *kanzus*. My dad refuses, saying that is not his tradition. On the day of the wedding itself, all but one male cousin is outfitted in a *kanzu* and a suit jacket, as is my uncle. And my father chose his tradition as internationalist third world solidarity in the form of a Kaunda /Nehru /Mao suit. The *kanzu*, a long white tunic reaching the ankles and the somber dark jackets gave weight to the occasion. Seeing all my tall stately cousins in *kanzus* and jackets, I am reminded of the photos of my parents' wedding some 50 years ago. There, my grandfather is dressed the same, in clothing reserved for the most important occasions – weddings, but also of funerals. A sign of dignity and distinction. Of Indian Ocean connections.

Here in the middle of Nairobi grouped together as people whose grandparents moved from the shores of Lake Victoria to the big city, with, but in the opposite direction of, the railway, and who share cultural clothing habits with their neighbors in Uganda, Catholics staunch and lapsed, young and old, here my relatives, like so many before them, condensing a world of movement into traditional Samia wedding attire. This world of movement consisted of the movement of people, things and ideas across the Indian Ocean. We combined and recombined these items taking them in historical succession, keeping some, discarding others. Retaining meanings and changing meanings. Bearing witness to Indian Ocean connections and creating Indian Ocean worlds. And yet so far from that Ocean on the shores of an inland sea.

On return to Kenya after my B.Sc. in Agricultural Science and Management from the University of California, Davis, I first worked for the Indigenous Food Plant program of the National Museums of Kenya and later for African Center for Technology Studies (ACTS). These two institutions greatly shaped my intellectual trajectory by questioning central assumptions around knowledge, property, and citizenship. Here I established an enduring obsession with property regimes and global dynamics of power. I sought to understand the dynamics of power that relate systems of resource distribution to knowledge production about the way the world works. I turned to anthropology for alternative perspectives and to provide methodology to analyze power at the most global and most local level.

I started fieldwork for my masters at Stanford University in 1993, which was a difficult year for Kenya. It was the first major devaluation of the shilling in the context of Structural Adjustment programs, liberalization and multiparty elections in the midst of Islamic Party of Kenya activism and ethnic land clashes at the coast and inland. It was also the rise of privatization. I looked at the inheritance of land in coastal Kenya to contextualize identity, citizenship, and law.

The changing Digo practices in the inheritance of land illuminated maps of memory and layered understandings of self that incorporated Indian Ocean influences along with colonial and postcolonial ones. Rather than a teleology of property regimes ending in private property, inheritance practices demonstrated the tensions and ambivalence inherent in dealing with neighbors, governments, clans, and changes in religion across oceans and across regimes of power (Ng'weno 1997, 2001). It was not just an issue of post-coloniality, of oceanic connections, of nationalism, or of custom or law (Berry 1992; Hall 1997; Willis 1993). Rather it was an issue of all these combined in the specific logics of this time and place.

I decided to use the opportunity afforded me by doing a Ph.D. at Johns Hopkins University to look at community claims to territory during privatization in Colombia. Here I was interested in thinking spatially in new ways by looking at people supposedly out of place – African descent communities in the Andean region of Colombia. How did their claims reconstitute the state? This led me to interrogate not just ways of thinking citizenship, territory and belonging in Latin America (Ng'weno 2007) but also the silencing of the African presence more generally (Trouillot 1995). In 2003 I took up a position in the department of African American and African Studies at the University of California, Davis. My move from agriculture to anthropology had made visible biases in both science and social sciences. My new position made more visible the hidden power dynamics of both.

As it became harder to travel to Latin America as an African passport holder, and as I also grew weary of living in diaspora far from my parents as they grew older, I decided to return to the Indian Ocean to work closer to home. Yet in returning "home" to carry out research I had to engage what it means to return to a place and look at things differently – differently now as an anthropologist but also differently bringing the perspective from Latin America and the Caribbean. In so doing, I grappled with questions about how one might conceive of regions, what ideas of diaspora and oceans give us pause when looking at different parts of the world, how is space thought differently, and which stories are silenced and why.

I brought with me insights from scholars of the Caribbean and Latin America who pay attention to both historical process and local transformation through global connections (Trouillot 2003). Michel-Rolph Trouillot argues that universals such as development, progress, democracy or nation-state do not just "describe the world; they offer visions of the world" (2003: 35). Yet the vision and the world they claim to describe are contested, negotiated and resisted. The fact of heterogeneity does not belie hierarchy (Mintz 1986; Trouillot 1995). Rather than a free-floating cosmopolitanism, creolization demands attention to mixture in the context of extreme global and local power dynamics. At the same time, people who move, or were moved, have lasting effects on the societies into which they enter and the world further afield (Scott 2004). I use these insights to think oceanographically and spatially about Indian Ocean worlds.

Figure I.2 Bettina Ng'weno on the *dhow Shukran*, Kilifi, Kenya, 2015.
Image credit: Pauline Groom.

In 2011, I took a two-year leave of absence to join the planning team of Aga Khan University (AKU), Faculty of Arts and Sciences to design the social sciences and humanities curriculum for their Arusha campus, whose mandate was to think of East Africa as part of the Indian Ocean. In constant awareness of our connections to the AKU campus in Karachi, and the University of Central Asia, we imagined a curriculum that could both speak to the specificities of the five countries of the East African Community (Burundi, Kenya, Rwanda, Tanzania, and Uganda) as well as across the ocean. This process meant asking what it meant pedagogically to be bound to ocean as well as continent. To imagine no center. To readdress and work through layered contentious histories. To consider how not to center something else in replacing Europe. It meant a (re)turn to works like Abdulrazak Gurnah's (1995) *Paradise* to think the Indian Ocean also from the point of view of East Africa – and an East Africa that was not just coastal. Since then I have done fieldwork in Pakistan, Indian, Sri Lanka, as well as coastal Kenya and Tanzania and inland Kenya, especially the city of Nairobi (Ng'weno 2018).

While working in Nairobi for AKU I did community work with Friends of City Park. This work at Nairobi City Park brought in new Indian Ocean conversations entwined with the city of Nairobi and the history of Kenya and made visible in the surrounding housing, the cemeteries within the park, the export of plant varietals to parks in Asia and the people working to preserve and maintain the park. These stories and connections form part of my investigation into my spatial and temporal analysis of the city of Nairobi as I grapple with the place-making of long-term residents in a city of migrants (Ng'weno 2018).

Fueled by these intellectual trajectories and places, but particularly rooted in East Africa, my Indian Ocean work asks: What is at stake in the way we tell stories about our place in the world today? As such, it seeks to understand how these placemaking stories constitute forms of power through which the conditions for action, knowledge, and life are organized and negotiated. At the same time, it investigates the practices that illuminate the dreams and imaginaries of place that constitute Indian Ocean worlds.

Neelima Jeychandran: Growing up, my grandparents have told me countless tales about us belonging to one of the "prominent" *tharavadu* (home or household) in Calicut or Kozhikode. As an important port city of the Indian Ocean world, itinerant travelers, Hadrami traders, scholars such as Ibn Battuta, Zheng He and his Ming fleet, and later Vasco da Gama, all made their stopovers at Calicut. This cultural significance of Calicut as an Indian Ocean port retold by historical literatures on trade and exchanges for me was a depersonalized history of my hometown. For me, this discourse on Kozhikode or Koyikode as the locals pronounce it, does not reveal the many flavors of the Indian Ocean that can be experienced through Kozhikode's culinary cultures and other intangible heritage. So, what histories of Kozhikode, a city that represents the fusion of many Indian Ocean cultures must I choose to tell here? I wish to narrate a sensory history of Kozhikode, a past that can be engaged with through affective interactions – a history that is still palpable in this Indian Ocean port city. For instance, upon entering the area of Kuttichira with mosques from the fifteenth century and ancestral homes of Muslim trading communities, one witnesses the material blending of traditional Hindu style design and Islamic architectural features (see Shokoohy 2003). While such material cultures visibly showcase the fusion of aesthetic practices, often other everyday customs remind me of the many ways in which people retain and absorb this Indian Ocean transcultural exchanges.

A perfect example of this cultural consumption is Kozhikode's *sulaimani chai*, an adaptation of the Arabic drink *qahwah* that demonstrates the fine blending of Arab and Indian cultures. This specialty tea of Kozhikode is brewed with spices such as cardamom, cinnamon, cloves, ginger, and *jaggery* (cane sugar), and finally a dash of lemon juice is added to infuse the drink with citrus flavor. Like the *sulaimani chai*, other Indian Ocean linkages are even today savored by the coastal communities of the Malabar Coast, yet the histories of these popular quotidian practices seem to evade the dominant imagination of Indian Ocean cultural traditions. And it is these blind spots in the knowledge of the Ocean that I focus on as a scholar.

Hailing from the spice coast in Kerala, my academic entry into Indian Ocean studies was routed via the Atlantic World. The Indian Ocean in many ways

Figure I.3 A street in Kuttichira, Kozhikode with the old Juma Mosque and traditional homes of Muslim mercantile communities, Kozhikode, 2018.

Image credit: Neelima Jeychandran.

flows into the Atlantic and vice-versa. And, this transoceanic circulation can be traced, for instance, through the historical movement of residents from the Gold Coast to Java as recruits in the Dutch army in the nineteenth century (see Kessel 2002). As a graduate student at the University of California, Los Angeles, a conversation with Allen (Al) Roberts on an interesting and odd Afro-Asian connection opened new portals for me. Before my conversation with Al, I had no knowledge that the Hindu deity Dattatreya was being worshipped in Vodun shrines of Benin and Togo as he was appropriated in recent history as the consort of Mami Wata, the powerful water spirit of the Atlantic Ocean (see Rush 2008). Al, who was the Co-Principal Investigator of the multi-sited Indian Ocean research group in the 1990s, proposed the concept of "Afro-Indianis," in which he notes that if the Atlantic World is treated as a process geography, such analysis must extend to include the Indian Ocean as well (Roberts 2000). What struck me the most about the Mami Wata and Dattatreya story was that although it looked like a random occurrence of cultural appropriation, an in-depth study reveals a complex network of exchanges between the Gold Coast and India that created transaction of knowledge systems and religious beliefs that then get rendered through ritual arts.

Interested in exploring indirect connections and inapparent relationalities, I started examining how the oceanic trade networks establish process geographies of the Atlantic and Indian Ocean worlds, linking peoples and places through cultural, religious, knowledge, and economic transactions. Through multi-sited research projects, I attempt to untangle invisible histories of Afro-Asian exchanges that resurface through embodied practices, memoryscapes, and material cultures. In my dissertation, by taking Elmina in Ghana and Fort Kochi in India as case studies, I demonstrated how these places harbor submerged narratives of migration and cultural exchange and survive as repositories of memory. The cultural geography of both the Atlantic and Indian Ocean worlds is a graveyard of memory in which are buried stories of revolts and resistance, brutalities of the pasts, and the histories of the enslaved, dispossessed, and people lost or buried at sea. Since archival records on many of these fraught pasts are either fragmentary, inconclusive or non-existent, many histories remain unwritten. In order to excavate the marginalized histories of human and non-human beings from beneath the submerged layers of dominant discourse, I often turn to the realm of memory and remembrance practices (see Jeychandran 2016).

The memoryscape of the Indian Ocean prevails as a living counter-archive; these are sites of knowledge preserved by the community – they are held close, lived, performed, and visualized. In my current project, I attempt to excavate forgotten histories and sequestered memories about African presence in western India. I examine how marginalized communities – both of African descent and of Indian subalterns – purposefully refabulate African deathscapes and sacred landscapes to narrate silenced histories of fraught African pasts. I consider two different kinds of geographies of death: Hindu shrines dedicated to deceased African slaves found along the Malabar Coast in southwestern India and Sidi *dargahs* (tombs) dedicated to African Sufi saints and martyrs in Gujarat. These shrines and altars serve as placeholders for remembering the dead through spectral geographies and associated ritual observances, and through various acts of memory-making by marginalized communities – both of African descent as well as Indian subalterns.

Focusing on shrines dedicated to deceased African saints and slave spirits, I review the analytical, mnemonic, and spiritual registers of the Indian Ocean world to understand cultural relationalities (see Jeychandran 2019). Most of the shrines for African saints are found in Gujarat because of the region's extensive trading connections with Africa and as a result of the Arab slave trade network in the Indian Ocean in which Gujarati merchants were involved. As in the case of Gujarat, the sacred sites and practices dedicated to African spirits on the Malabar Coast reveal a history of African migration – in this case during Portuguese and Dutch occupation. In the coastal regions around Kochi, memories of forced African migration are preserved through shrines dedicated to deceased Africans or Kappiris. These far-flung sacred edifices constructed to memorialize African saints and enslaved people serve as sites of memory where lesser-known African and Afro-Indian histories are actively performed and restored. The shrines for African saints and spirits operate at multiple levels, as sacred geographies and mnemonic-scapes that simultaneously make reference to a history of African slave trading in the Indian Ocean.

Figure I.4 A traditional *kaavu* or sacred grove with consecrated stone idols of Kappiri and other local deities, Vypin, Kerala, 2013.

Image credit: Neelima Jeychandran.

The shrines for African slave spirits and mystics in western India presents an interesting conundrum to think about the inapparent cultural circulations between the Atlantic and Indian Ocean and the ways in which Afro-Asian connections are reactivated through the realm of sacred geographies and spiritual practices. An interesting case in point is the Hindu Monastery of Africa in Accra, Ghana, which is one of the most prominent temples in West Africa. The Hindu Monastery of Africa was established by Swami Ghanananda, a Ghanaian *swami*. The caretaker of the Hindu Monastery of Africa emphasized during our conversation that *swami's* name is not indicative of the country Ghana, but rather the knowledge or *gyan* that he had accrued and his name is rightly pronounced as Gyanananda, however, the name Ghanananda seems to have struck. The chromolithographs and icons in central shrine of the Hindu Monastery of Africa for me essayed the cross-pollination of faiths in the Indian Ocean and Atlantic worlds. What one sees in the main prayer hall is an array of icons, images, and chromolithographs of deities from the Hindu classical pantheon and non-classical tradition alongside photographs of Indian philosophers, social-reformers from the Vedanta and neo-Vedanta schools, Sikh gurus, Sai Baba, Vivekananda, and also Gandhi, and images of Jesus and the Virgin Mary. This space prompted me to rethink the circulation of spiritualities in the Indian Ocean and to consider other practices beyond Catholicism or Islam, oceanic crossovers that are eclectic and often refabulated by communities and people.

Keywords for Indian Ocean worlds

Indian Ocean studies has emerged in the last decade as a critical interdisciplinary field for art historians, historians, literary scholars, political scientists and more recently, for anthropologists and geographers. The Ocean has offered a response to the compartmentalization of specific area studies and a template for thinking and writing about interculturalism, globality, and transregional movements without necessarily privileging the West; this has enabled scholars, thus, to critically augment postcolonial frameworks and textual inquiries. Adding to the corpus of academic literature on the Indian Ocean are museum exhibitions and in-situ art installations that probe the historical and contemporary connections between African and Asian worlds through a range of objects and displays. Such formats as the exhibition *World on the Horizon: Swahili Arts Across the Indian Ocean*, the Indian Ocean slavery exhibition at the Msheireb Museums in Doha, Qatar, and the dynamic and iterative art festival of the Kochi-Muziris Biennale have created spaces for artists, curators, and communities to express their perspectives and generate new conversations about the Indian Ocean.

While Indian Ocean studies has expanded to include new spaces, topics, and communities (see Hopper 2015; Machado, Fee, and Campbell 2018; Stiles and Thompson 2015), an analysis of this field, however, reveals that the overwhelming focus is still largely historical with an emphasis on trade, migrations, diasporas, and religious networks, i.e., mobilities across this region (e.g., Alpers and Goswami 2019; Barnes 2012; Moorthy and Jamal 2012; Prange 2018;

Reese 2018). Alongside this emphasis on mobilities, the literature has privileged the geographical limits of the Indian Ocean itself as the framework for conceptualization and analysis with an emphasis on ports, coastal sites, and islands (e.g., Green 2011; Hall 2009; Ho 2006; Kooria and Pearson 2018; Schnepel and Alpers 2018; Simpson 2007). Where the focus has been on the contemporary period, much of the investigation has been unevenly split between some examination of literary practices (memoirs, literary texts, languages and writers in the Indian Ocean world; for instance, Desai 2013; Mugane 2015) and dominant concerns of issues of borders and security (see Dua 2019; Weldemichael 2019; Weldemichael, Schneider, and Winner 2017).

While these works portray the textured nature of exchanges and the complexities of approaching the Indian Ocean and its communities as one unit, questions remain: How do communities and publics in contemporary Indian Ocean milieus themselves imagine and make their place in the world within several contexts and through a variety of practices? How can new units of analysis or keywords shed light on this dynamic oceanic space? What cultural value does this space of study have beyond issues of defense, violence, security, or economics? And finally, how do contemporary Indian Ocean worlds involve layered mappings that are yoked to several renderings of the past, present, and possible future?

This volume aims to chart an epistemic shift in thinking and writing about Indian Ocean worlds by stressing the importance of analyzing the **contemporary and contemporaneous**. While we are interested in the historical, we pay special attention to micro-cultural practices for imagining and simulating spaces and the many ways pasts influence the present or are reclaimed by various actors. We recognize that there are many worlds and plural modes of belonging that constitute the diverse spaces of the Indian Ocean. We are interested in building templates for understanding not only the present of Indian Ocean worlds but also its future through ethnographic, multi-sited, comparative or experimental research. Our volume has four points of departure from previous works and harnesses new keywords.

First, it aims to move the discussion forward from an area-based/geographical approach to Indian Ocean studies to intellectually reconfiguring the Indian Ocean as a space for conceptual/theoretical **relationality** based on social science and humanities scholarship. That is to say, it asks: What are the new limits of the Indian Ocean? It is possible, for example, to make conceptual comparisons between cities like Bangalore, Nairobi or Atlanta that have been forged in the last few decades through global religious movements such as guru-based South Asian movements (see Srinivas 2008) or places across the Indian Ocean and beyond to the Pacific and Atlantic through the transnationalization of yoga practice (Miller 2018). Whether it is the manifestation and intercessions of deceased saints at many sites, the presence of spectral beings, and the circulation of minor sacred paraphernalia and power, different spaces in the Indian Ocean are connected through novel religious geographies (Jeychandran 2019). **Jeremy Prestholdt** (this volume) looks at changes in the effective boundaries, interfaces, and perceptions of the Indian Ocean to offer us regions with unstable, porous

Figure I.5 The South Asian global guru, Sathya Sai Baba, 1980s.

Image credit: Personal collection of Smriti Srinivas.

boundaries that are filled in by relations and imaginations. **May Joseph** examines the process of Africanization in postcolonial Tanzania: written as a travelogue forging linkages between Cochin, Dar es Salaam, and New York through memories, mentalities, and affect, she addresses uneasy pasts that surface within Asian lives in the present. Focusing on an inland dry port in the National Capital Region of Delhi, **Ishani Saraf** expands the limits of the Indian Ocean by imagining a port without a coast and by reformulating the notion of the littoral. **Nidhi Mahajan** shows how older patterns of the monsoon still determine social and cultural lives of seafaring communities in Kutch at many levels even as people no longer use the wind to travel; they determine life and livelihood, credit and debt, government regulations, movement and stasis.

Second, instead of privileging mobilities, this volume also emphasizes **place, placemaking, and quotidian practices** as valuable frames for the study of Indian Ocean worlds. It is possible, for example, to approach the Indian Ocean from places and practices distant from coastal areas or islands such as the conflict between placemaking practices of long-term residents of Nairobi and the dreams of urban planners of the city (see Ng'weno 2018). Spaces/places discussed by the authors in this volume include interior cities, coastal landscapes, heritage sites, mines, capital cities, casinos, museums, shrines, and dry ports. Practices outlined by authors include those that coalesce in the built terrain as religious edifices or domestic abodes, healing, music, techniques of the body, mnemonic practices, urban planning, or culinary practices. Exploring sapphire mines and trade in Sri Lanka, **Nethra Samarawickrema** delves into Indian Ocean spaces beyond its maritime frontiers including mountainous landscapes and their subterranean depths to bring into view connectivities that extend beyond the waters; she argues that not all maps of relationality are based on movement. Through a study of so-called "offshore" casinos that have been proliferating on Goa's waterways, **Maya Costa-Pinto** argues that these sites highlight older and emerging transregional networks (including those in the Lusophone Indian Ocean) while also disrupting and reconstructing urban practices in Panaji. **Christian J. Doll** attends to quotidian practices of urbanites in the South Sudan capital of Juba, who engage regional and international circuits in the city to create new communities and infrastructure that temper the effects of state power and recent violence. **Bidita Jawher Tithi** proposes "displacemaking" as a concept to analyze the connections between the displacement of communities and ecological hazards; she studies the dried fish industry in a semi-permanent coastal settlement in Bangladesh as a socio-material assemblage to explore mobilities and becomings of humans and non-humans in Indian Ocean worlds.

Third, while this volume considers older histories and connections between places in Indian Ocean worlds, it is concerned with **new networks of memory and maps** in lived experiences today. Thus, for example, while trade and the ocean might have linked Mombasa with Kochi historically, we are interested in the fact that today neoliberal policies, new migratory circuits, ecological concerns, or memoryscapes relate cities and places to each other differently in the

Figure I.6 Nairobi City Park, performance for *Nai ni Who?* celebration of the Nairobi
    neighborhoods, 2013.

Image credit: Bettina Ng'weno.

lives of persons and communities (see Jeychandran 2016, 2019). Framed around
ideas of the ocean as a space of migration, slavery, marine extraction, and
mutable sacred geographies, **Pedro Machado** examines, the materiality and
practices of remembering the past in specific locales in East and South Africa
and the Gulf; some of these align with state-sanctioned views of the past while
others transcend them to create alternative forms of community memory.
Hafeez Ahmed Jamali examines fragments that trace an arc of relationality
across the Indian Ocean through memory, nostalgia, and diasporic networks to
understand how these layerings play into contemporary views of a new deepwa-
ter port in Pakistan; these fragments critique national narratives of power, privilege, and mobility. Through memoirs, memories, and built structures, **Nicole
Ranganath** presents a perspective on mobility and stasis in the Indian Ocean by
focusing on the camaraderie sealed by Sikhs during their voyage to Fiji and the
ways in which the Sikh diaspora attempted to create anchorage in places far
away from South Asian worlds.

Fourth, in contrast to much scholarship that has tended to focus on historical
archives and textual sources, authors in our volume are steeped in **ethnographic,
fieldwork, and humanistic methodologies** that examine sources such as dance,

the built environment, media, personal narratives, food/medical practices, labor, everyday movements, scientific expeditions, and memorialization in contemporary contexts to offer new insights into Indian Ocean life-worlds. **Laura A. Meek** uses feminist methodologies to examine the quotidian practices surrounding a woman's ailments in Tanzania to bring out the different understandings of the causes that are "eating" her and their broader connections to family relations, land, place, and food. **Pallavi Sriram** delves into historiographies of *marfa*, an Afro-Arab dance in the space of the Deccan region of India showing how this form is actively reclaimed and reinvented by various communities through digital, urban, and transnational registers to craft Afro-Indian and Afro-Arab identities in the present. By examining oceanographic expeditions, **Vivian Y. Choi** suggests that we see the Indian Ocean as an object of scientific knowledge, care, and concern; she stresses that its changing forms expressed in scientific investigations provide another method of understanding the vitality of the Ocean.

This volume asks about the boundaries of the Indian Ocean, the layered maps that make relationalities possible, the spaces that act as thresholds in and out of worlds, the shifting re-inscriptions of geography and power along lines of memory and knowledge, the contemporary use of history and the force of the ocean itself. We argue for approaches that allow for the study of integration brought about through dispossession, the shifting positionalities that mobility demands, the creation of place both enriching and impoverishing, the refabulation of connectivities, the diversity of earlier histories and temporalities of connection and the pull of the imagined future on both the past and the present. The volume has an interdisciplinary focus, our authors bring many strengths, places, and perspectives into conversation, and the chapters are organized into four sections based on our points of departure: proximity and distance; landscapes, oceanscapes, and practices; memory and maps; and methods and disciplines.

Thinking as process

As editors, we wished to talk across disciplinary and spatial boundaries and times, engage in conversations with a wider collective of scholars, and wondered what new insights and methodologies would emerge out of such engagements. Perhaps this was reflective of the fact that as women scholars – and through our previous work – we were receptive to relationality, we were working with imaginations that were not bound by linear narrations of time or stable spaces (and thus had something in common with women's studies/feminist approaches), and we were trying to do research and write against the grain of depersonalized history.

Smriti Srinivas and Bettina Ng'weno brought together 14 faculty and graduate students from across the humanities and social sciences at the University of California, Davis (UC Davis) as an interdisciplinary Davis Humanities Institute Research Cluster on contemporary *Indian Ocean Imaginaries* (2014–2015). The purpose of the cluster was to create an explicit community of scholars focused on the Indian Ocean, to provide a venue for mentorship of graduate students who worked on different regions of the Indian Ocean, and to be a site for faculty and students to think about Indian Ocean imaginaries together in novel ways.

The *Reimagining Indian Ocean Worlds* Mellon Research Initiative (2015–2019) directed by Smriti Srinivas and Bettina Ng'weno built on this foundation with the aim of producing multi-year interest and capacity at UC Davis for rethinking the scope of Indian Ocean studies (see indianoceanworlds. org). In addition to core and affiliated faculty and graduate students, this brought Neelima Jeychandran as a Mellon Visiting Assistant Professor (2015–2017) to the project. We believed that as a collective, we had the ability to shift the conversation in Indian Ocean studies towards new directions by focusing on relationalities, the contemporary, space/place and practices, new networks/maps, and humanistic/ethnographic methodologies. Our purpose was not only to make UC Davis the hub for an Indian Ocean worlds initiative but one that was intellectually and methodologically cutting-edge in comparison to centers and scholarship worldwide.[2]

Our thinking evolved in process. Our initial symposium on *Indian Ocean Imaginaries* in Fall 2015 brought together a larger group of scholars for intensive interaction and enquiry into new directions for Indian Ocean worlds.[3] Between 2015 and 2018, we also convened a lecture series that brought Edward Alpers (University of California, Los Angeles), Sunil Amrith (Harvard), Nile Green (University of California, Los Angeles), Inderjit Kaur (University of California, Berkeley), Pedro Machado (Indiana University), and Jeremy Prestholdt (University of California, San Diego) to campus.[4] We were also excited to have the opportunity to engage our faculty and graduate students in a campus brunch conversation with Amitav Ghosh in April 2017. Alongside the symposium and lecture series, we ran an Innovation Lab for four years. This was a place where the core group of faculty and graduate students met, exchanged ideas, discussed readings, and presented research in progress with the aim of innovating new perspectives and methodologies for understanding Indian Ocean worlds.[5] In 2016, we hosted an international graduate student conference, *Indian Ocean Topographies, Contemporary Worlds, and Situated Practices*, to extend existing frameworks for South Asian studies.[6] The research from the Innovation Lab was presented in two international fora, *Afrasian Transformations: Beyond Grand Narratives?* at Goethe University, Frankfurt and *Africa-Asia Axis* in Dar es Salaam, and was instrumental in laying steps for a working group on Indian Ocean studies in Zanzibar. We hosted for the first time in the US the exhibition *Re-Imagining Iranian African Slavery: Photography as Material Culture* with Pedram Khosronejad.[7] Our final 2018 intense workshop of select scholars furthered all of these discussions: Our goal was a cohesive publication for a compelling reimagining of Indian Ocean worlds. This book is an outcome of this collective process.

Acknowledgments

We are deeply grateful to all those who supported our activities, the creation of this book, and the coming together of an international network of Indian Ocean scholars between 2014 and 2019. Without the Davis Humanities Institute (DHI), through which the Mellon Foundation funded our multi-year research initiative, none of this would have been possible. We are especially grateful to Molly McCarthy, Associate Director of DHI during our Research Cluster and Initiative, for her steady counsel and support. We also wish to thank the following at UC Davis for their support: the Dean of Social Sciences, the Middle East/South Asia Studies Program, the Department of Anthropology, the African American and African Studies Department, and the *South Asia without Borders* Initiative. We thank all the participants in our activities over the years for their generosity of thought and willingness to experiment and imagine with us. Thanks to our colleagues, Jeffrey Kahn, Vaidehi Ramanathan, Nicole Ranganath, Parama Roy, and James Smith for their support. We wish to especially acknowledge our graduate students (many of whom have gone on to academic jobs elsewhere) – Maya Costa-Pinto, Christian Doll, Justin Haruyama, Gillian Irwin, Ayanda Manqoyi, Laura Meek, Chris Miller, Ishani Saraf, Eveleen Sidana, Bidita Tithi, Anuj Vaidya, Mayee Wong, Xan Chacko – whose convivial engagement and insights emerging from their own research made this project unique.

Notes

1 The Byari/Beary community is an old South Kanara coastal Muslim community that speaks a dialect combining Malayalam idioms, Tulu phonology and grammar, and Arabic.
2 Recognizing the significance of the Ocean, a few new centers for the study of the Indian Ocean have emerged worldwide (e.g., the Center for South Asia and Indian Ocean Studies, Tufts University; the Center for Indian Studies in Africa, University of Witwatersrand; Indian Ocean World Center, McGill University; and the Center for Indian Ocean Studies, Osmania University).
3 Participants from outside UC Davis included Gaurav Desai (Tulane), May Joseph (Pratt Institute), Nidhi Mahajan (UCSC), Ketaki Pant (University of Southern California), Jeremy Prestholdt (UCSD), Allen Roberts and Polly Roberts (UCLA), and Martha Saavedra (UC Berkeley); see http://indianoceanworlds.org/conferences/.
4 See http://indianoceanworlds.org/conferences/.
5 The activities of the Lab fed into and intersected with public outreach activities as well as the faculty and graduate student projects.
6 Graduate students from India, Portugal, the UK, the US, Pakistan, and the Netherlands attended (see http://indianoceanworlds.org/satb-speakers/). Our conference was held in conjunction with the Middle East/South Asia Studies Program at UC Davis and as the 5th *South Asia by the Bay* graduate student conference (a collaboration between Stanford, UC Santa Cruz, UC Berkeley and UC Davis).
7 See http://indianoceanworlds.org/2018/05/01/re-imagining-iranian-african-slavery-photo graphy-as-material-culture/.

References

Abu-Lughod, Janet L. 1989. *Before European Hegemony. The World System* A.D. *1250–1350.* New York/Oxford: Oxford University Press.

Ali, Kamran and Martina Rieker, eds. 2009. *Comparing Cities: The Middle East and South Asia.* Oxford: Oxford University Press.

Alpers, Edward and Chhaya Goswami. 2019. *Transregional Trade and Traders: Situating Gujarat in the Indian Ocean from Early Times to 1900.* Oxford: Oxford University Press.

Amrith, Sunil. 2013. *Crossing the Bay: The Furies of Nature and the Fortunes of Migrants.* Cambridge, MA: Harvard University Press.

Arif, Yasmeen. 2016. *Life, Emergent: The Social in the Afterlives of Violence.* Minneapolis: University of Minnesota Press.

Barnes, Ruth, eds. 2012. *Textiles in Indian Ocean Societies.* New York: Routledge.

Bayat, Asef. 2010. *Life as Politics: How Ordinary People Change the Middle East.* Stanford, CA: Stanford University Press.

Berry, Sara. 1992. "Hegemony on a Shoestring: Indirect Rule and Access to Agricultural Land," *Africa*, 62: 327.

Broeze, Frank, ed. 1989. *Brides of the Sea: Port Cities of Asia from the 16th–20th Centuries.* Honolulu: University of Hawaii Press.

Desai, Gaurav. 2013. *Commerce with the Universe: Africa, India, and the Afrasian Imagination.* New York: Colombia University Press.

Dua, Jatin. 2019. *Captured at Sea: Piracy and Protection in the Indian Ocean.* Berkeley: University of California Press.

Geetha, V. 2011. "Social Suffering and Salvation: The Relevance of the Buddha and His Dhamma." In *Religious Faith, Ideology and Citizenship: The View from Below*, edited by V. Geetha and Nalini Rajan, 123–147. New Delhi: Routledge.

Geetha, V. and S. V. Rajadurai. 1998. *Towards a Non-Brahmin Millennium: From Iyothee Thass to Periyar.* Calcutta: Samya.

Ghosh, Amitav. 1993. *In an Antique Land: History in the Guise of a Traveler's Tale.* New York: Alfred A. Knopf.

Goh, Beng-Lan. 2002. *Modern Dreams: An Inquiry into Power, Cultural Production, and the Cityscape in Contemporary Urban Penang, Malaysia.* Ithaca, NY: Cornell University Press.

Green, Nile. 2011. *Bombay Islam: The Religious Economy of the West Indian Ocean, 1840–1915.* New York: Cambridge University Press.

Gupta, Pamila, Isabel Hofmeyr, and Michael Pearson. 2010. *Eyes across the Water: Navigating the Indian Ocean.* Pretoria: University of South Africa Press.

Gurnah, Abdulrazak. 1995. *Paradise.* London: The New Press.

Hall, Kenneth R. 2009. *Secondary Cities and Urban Networking in the Indian Ocean Realm, c.1400–1800.* Washington, DC: Lexington Books.

Hall, Stuart. 1997. "Old and New Identities, Old and New Ethnicities." In *Culture Globalization and the World-System: Contemporary Conditions for the Representation of Identity*, edited by Anthony D. King. Minneapolis: University of Minnesota Press.

Hancock, Mary and Smriti Srinivas, eds. 2008. "Symposium on Religion and the Formation of Modern Urban Space in Asia and Africa," *International Journal of Urban and Regional Research*, 32 (3): 617–709.

Hancock, Mary and Smriti Srinivas, eds. 2018. "Spirited Topographies Roundtable," *Journal for the American Academy of Religion*, 86 (2): 454–553.

Heitzman, James. 2004. *Network City: Planning the Information Society in Bangalore.* New Delhi: Oxford University Press.

Ho, Enseng. 2006. *The Graves of Tarim: Genealogy and Mobility across the Indian Ocean.* Berkeley: University of California Press.

Hopper, Mathew S. 2015. *Slaves of One Master: Globalization and Slavery in Arabia in the Age of Empire.* New Haven: Yale University Press.

Huyssen, Andreas, ed. 2008. *Other Cities, Other Worlds: Urban Imaginaries in a Globalizing Age.* Durham, NC: Duke University Press.

Jeychandran, Neelima. 2016. "Marginalized Narratives: Memory Work at African Shrines in Kochi, India." In *Excavating Memory: Sites of Remembering and Forgetting*, edited by Maria Starzmann and John Roby, 111–130. Gainesville: University of Florida Press.

Jeychandran, Neelima. 2019. "Navigating African Sacred Geography: Shrines for African Sufi Saints and Spirits in India," *Journal of Africana Religions*, 7 (1): 17–36.

Kessel, Ineke van. 2002. "The Black Dutchmen: African Soldiers in the Netherlands East Indies." In *Merchants, Missionaries, and Migrants: 300 Years of Dutch Ghanaian Relations*, edited by Ineke van Kessel, 133–141. Amsterdam: KIT Publishers.

Kooria, Mahmood and Michael Pearson, eds. 2018. *Malabar in the Indian Ocean: Cosmopolitanism in a Maritime Historical Region.* New Delhi: Oxford University Press, India.

Kumar, Dharma and D. Mookherjee, eds. 1995. *D. School: Reflections on the Delhi School of Economics.* Delhi: Oxford University Press.

Kusno, Abidin. 2000. *Behind the Postcolonial: Architecture, Urban Space and Political Cultures in Indonesia.* London: Routledge.

Machado, Pedro. 2014. *Ocean of Trade: South Asian Merchants, Africa and the Indian Ocean, c.1750–1850.* Cambridge: Cambridge University Press.

Machado, Pedro, Sarah Fee, and Gwyn Campbell. 2018. *Textile Trades, Consumer Cultures, and the Material Worlds of the Indian Ocean: An Ocean of Cloth.* SI: Palgrave Macmillan.

Miller, Christopher Patrick. 2018. *Embodying Transnational Yoga.* https://pqdtopen.proquest.com/doc/2191484185.html?FMT=ABS

Mintz, Sidney W., 1986. *Sweetness and Power: The Place of Sugar in Modern History.* New York: Penguin Books.

Moorthy, Shanti and Ashraf Jamal, eds. 2012. *Indian Ocean Studies: Cultural, Social and Political Perspectives.* New York: Routledge.

Ng'weno, Bettina. 1997. "Inheriting Disputes: The Digo Negotiation of Meaning and Power through Land," *Journal of African Economic History*, 25:59–77.

Ng'weno, Bettina. 2001. "Reidentifying Ground Rules: Community Inheritance Disputes Among the Digo of Kenya." In *Communities and the Environment: Ethnicity, Gender, and the State in Community-Based Conservation*, edited by Arun Agrawal and Clark C. Gibson, 111–137, New Brunswick: Rutgers University Press.

Ng'weno, Bettina. 2007. *Turf Wars: Territory and Citizenship in the Contemporary State.* Stanford, CA: Stanford University Press

Ng'weno, Bettina. 2018. "Growing Old in a New City: Time, the Post-Colony and Making Nairobi Home," *City*, 22 (1): 26–42.

Mugane, John M. 2015. *The Story of Swahili.* Athens: Ohio University Press

Prange, Sebastian R. 2018. *Monsoon Islam: Trade and Faith on the Medieval Malabar Coast.* Cambridge: Cambridge University Press

Prestholdt, Jeremy. 2015. "Locating the Indian Ocean: Notes on the Postcolonial Reconstitution of Space," *Journal of Eastern African Studies.* 9 (3): 440–467.

Queen, Christopher S. and Sallie B. King, eds. 1996. *Engaged Buddhism: Buddhist Liberation Movements in Asia.* Albany: State University of New York Press.

Reese, Scott. 2018. *Imperial Muslims: Islam, Community and Authority in the Indian Ocean, 1839–1937.* Edinburgh: Edinburgh University Press.

Roberts, Allen. 2000. "Is 'Africa' Obsolete?" *African Arts*, 33: 1–9.

Robinson, Jennifer. 2006. *Ordinary Cities: Between Modernity and Development*. London/New York: Routledge.

Rush, Dana. 2008. "The Idea of 'India' in West African Vodun Art and Thought." In *India in Africa, Africa in India: Indian Ocean Cosmopolitanisms*, edited by John C. Hawley, 149–180. Bloomington: Indiana University Press.

Schnepel, Burkhard and Edward Alpers, eds. 2018. *Connectivity in Motion: Island Hubs in the Indian Ocean World.* SI: Palgrave Macmillan.

Scott, David. 2004. *The Conscripts of Modernity: The Tragedy of Colonial Enlightenment.* Durham: Duke University Press.

Selvadurai, Shyam. 1997. *Funny Boy.* Harvest Books.

Shokoohy, Mehrdad. 2003. *Muslim Architecture of South India: The Sultanate of Ma'bar and the Traditions of the Maritime Settlers on the Malabar and Coromandel Coasts (Tamil Nadu, Kerala and Goa)*. London: New York: Routledge Curzon.

Simone, AbdouMaliq. 2010. *City Life from Jakarta to Dakar: Movements at the Crossroads.* New York: Routledge.

Simpson, Edward. 2007. *Muslim Society and the Western Indian Ocean: The Seafarers of Kachchh.* New York: Routledge.

Srinivas, Smriti. 2001. *Landscapes of Urban Memory: The Sacred and the Civic in India's High-Tech City.* Minneapolis: University of Minnesota Press.

Srinivas, Smriti. 2008. *In the Presence of Sai Baba: Body, City, and Memory in a Global Religious Movement.* Leiden/Boston: Brill and Hyderabad: Orient Blackswan.

Srinivas, Smriti. 2015. *A Place for Utopia: Urban Designs from South Asia.* Seattle/London: University of Washington Press and Hyderabad: Orient Blackswan.

Stiles, Erin E. and Katrina Daly Thompson. 2015. *Gendered Lives in the Western Indian Ocean: Islam, Marriage, and Sexuality on the Swahili Coast.* Athens, Ohio: Ohio University Press.

Trouillot, Michel-Rolph. 1995. *Silencing the Past: Power and the Production of History.* Boston, MA: Beacon Press.

Trouillot, Michel-Rolph. 2003. *Global Transformations: Anthropology and the Modern World.* New York, NY: Palgrave MacMillan.

Weldemichael, Awet T. 2019. *Piracy in Somalia: Violence and Development in the Horn of Africa.* Cambridge: Cambridge University Press.

Weldemichael, Awet T, Patricia Schneider, and Andrew C. Winner. 2017. *Maritime Terrorism and Piracy in the Indian Ocean Region.* New York: Routledge.

Willford, Andrew C. 2014. *Tamils and the Haunting of Justice.* Honolulu: University of Hawaii Press.

Willis, Justin. 1993. *Mombasa, the Swahili, and the Making of the Mijikenda.* Oxford: Clarendon Press.

Part I
Proximity and distance

1 The ends of the Indian Ocean

Notes on boundaries and affinities across time

Jeremy Prestholdt

The social worlds and littoral affinities of the Indian Ocean region have been amorphous, ever changing, and influenced by broader global currents. Indeed, the region has been defined by its elasticity and porosity. This mutability raises important questions about the spatial boundaries and perceptions of the Indian Ocean as a region: how have the effective boundaries of the region changed over time? How have interfaces with other world regions shaped Indian Ocean relations? How have perceptions of Indian Ocean space changed in consequence of shifting interactions along and beyond regional shores? More precisely, how have these interfaces contributed to the idea of the Indian Ocean as an integrated whole?

To address these questions this chapter traces transoceanic interfaces and changing cognitive maps over several centuries. Referencing Indian Ocean Africa, I consider the disintegrative as well as integrative forces that have defined the region since the early modern era. One conclusion we can draw from this history is that the Indian Ocean's effective boundaries have been remarkably pliant. The region has incorporated other actors into its networks and external forces have played integral roles in shaping Indian Ocean societies. In this context of multidimensional linkage, boundaries of relation have shifted dramatically. To varying degrees, each point along the Indian Ocean's rim has been integrated with a greater diversity of regional and global relations and the Indian Ocean basin has shaped an ever-increasing number of societies along other shores.

This simultaneous connectivity between points within the conventionally defined basin and linkages that stretch well beyond has forged multifocal, layered affinities and contributed to the dynamism of the Indian Ocean as a social concept. Moreover, while *longue durée* patterns of interface often inform historical memory and nostalgia, they have also been discarded in re-imaginings of the region. This phenomenon is particularly evident in the post-Cold War era since affinities have often been tied to metageographical imaginaries rather than specific historical patterns of engagement. Understanding the effective ends of the Indian Ocean as both a geographical field of relation and a concept requires a greater reflection on this history of elastic boundaries and changing perception.

Geography, relation, affinity

The social worlds of the Indian Ocean region have more often been defined by particular interactions, networks, and historical memories than by geography per se (Bose 2006; Bremner 2014). But geography has always played a role in defining Indian Ocean worlds. Ocean currents and the monsoon have offered environmental and historical logics to the Indian Ocean basin (Amrith 2013; Sheriff 2010). At the time of Portuguese arrival in the Indian Ocean, regional vessels had not rounded the Cape of Good Hope, despite Swahili mariners' knowledge that colder waters prevailed to the southwest. In this way, the southern waters of the Indian Ocean acted as a geographical threshold. In the twenty-first century, geographical realities continue to influence definitions of the region, as evidenced by the intraregional effects of the 2005 tsunami and irregularities in the monsoon pattern. Nevertheless, as Kären Wigen and Martin Lewis have suggested, metageographical definitions such as oceans and continents are inherently flawed. If we accept the notion that human relations constitute regions, conventional geographical boundaries can at times limit our understanding of these relations (Lewis and Wigen 1997). Ultimately, the Indian Ocean region has been constituted by specific networks and nodes of interface as well as the perceptions of affinity that these have engendered.

Literature on the Indian Ocean region has generally emphasized its centripetal forces, or those catalysts that have integrated societies and individuals along the rim and thus created affinities. Exchanges, Islam, empires, genealogy, and many other forces have created coherences and concentrations of energy (Alpers 2013; Chaudhuri 1985; Kearney 2004; McPherson 1993; Pearson 2003). These links undergird what Sugata Bose summed up as the "typologies of unity amid diversity" that scholars of the Indian Ocean region have vividly illustrated (Bose 2006: 12). These connections have additionally contributed to perceptions of affinity, including perceptions that postdate the era of sail. Kai Kresse and Edward Simpson astutely summed up regional affinities as the "related but different social worlds" of the Indian Ocean basin (Kresse and Simpson 2010: 1). Moreover, Indian Ocean relationships have been highly localized. Routes of exchange, for instance, have connected specific locales to other locales in particular fashions (Bishara 2017; Simpson 2006). Each locale has evidenced differing configurations of transoceanic relationships since each has had a particular interface profile with other ports. Stronger relationships tend to be proximate, but this is not always so. What is more important are the particular channels of relation that determine interface profiles, channels shaped by, among other things, exchange, religious networks, and empires.

Rather than an Indian Ocean meta-culture, myriad configurations of regional and global interfaces have defined specific locales (Becker and Cabrita 2014). This local constitution of the Indian Ocean region has ensured unstable boundaries, and thus the Indian Ocean has evidenced multiple boundaries of interface – the "hundred horizons" that Bose entreated us to envisage (Bose 2006). Before the late nineteenth century, the region was more a patchwork of intraregional fields of relation than a unified zone. This patchwork and perceptions of it have changed substantially over time. In the postcolonial era, for instance, diverse seas and coasts have gave way to national coastlines and a unified concept of the Indian Ocean.

Regions defined by maritime interactions can be "intrinsically unstable," as Marcus Vink asserted, since their boundaries and meaning are defined by the changing relationships among people along and beyond their shores (2007: 58). Because the particular kinds of human engagements and imagination that create affinity shift over time, Vink, Bose, and others have highlighted the fact that the social boundaries of the Indian Ocean region have been in constant flux (Bose 2006: 6, 2002: 368–369; Vink 2007). Specifically, the Indian Ocean has seen significant expansion and contraction, sometimes simultaneously. This "dual theme of integration and fragmentation," as Vink noted, is essential to understanding the dynamism of the Indian Ocean and its sub-regions (Vink 2007: 53). As many studies of the Indian Ocean suggest, we should remain simultaneously conscious of the micro-boundaries between maritime polities and their hinterland neighbors as well as the macro-boundaries between the regional field of interaction and other oceanic fields. In short, to fully understand the Indian Ocean's fluctuating boundaries we must appreciate the region's porosity and view local and regional circumstances in stereoscope.

Like all maritime zones, the Indian Ocean has been defined by both etic and emic forces, by regional engagements and networks stretching well beyond (Gilbert 2011). Many of the most important relationships that have affected Indian Ocean rim societies have been with actors beyond its shores, including hinterland societies. As I will outline below, etic forces have defined Indian Ocean societies in ways impermanent and enduring. Many of the forces that scholars have highlighted as cohesive elements of Indian Ocean engagement – commerce, belief systems, and empire – have had significant etic dimensions. This dual articulation, or connectivity within the Indian Ocean and simultaneous linkages extending beyond the region, has had myriad permutations, but it is critical to note that extra-regional interfaces have greatly affected the societies of the Indian Ocean for many centuries. And as I will outline in the final section, such interfaces have shaped the popular imagination of the Indian Ocean as a totality.

Connectivity birthed regional socioeconomic relationships and encouraged notions of a unified Indian Ocean. But connections have not always engendered affinities or defined how people perceive space. Moreover, while notions of affinity have historically been rooted in shared genealogy and exchange as well as disembodied practices, including religion and language, this relationship between connectivity, shared experience, and affinity has not necessarily been linear. As I will outline below, emic desires to evoke an interconnected, maritime past that resonates with contemporary concerns has invigorated perceptions of regional coherence and even created new connections.

This chapter reflects on spaces of interaction alongside perceptions of affinity in an effort to outline the effective ends of the Indian Ocean as both a field of relation and a concept. It examines two interrelated phenomena: the boundaries of maritime relation and changing notions of the Indian Ocean as a matrix of affinity. For my purposes, boundaries of relation are those boundaries between zones of significant social, economic, or other interaction. Affinity, on the other hand, refers to perceived continuity between social groups or nations. These phenomena can be complementary or independent. In the Indian Ocean region, interaction has transcended perceived boundaries of relation, and spheres of perceived continuity have not always been defined by interaction. To illustrate these points, in the next section I explore relationships within the Indian Ocean and between the region and distant societies. In the subsequent section, I explore the effect of these diverse relationships on emic imaginations of the region. In the process, I suggest ways in which the popular imagination of the Indian Ocean has both echoed and departed from deeper histories of connectivity.

Shifting boundaries of relation

Maritime and terrestrial links to societies beyond the Indian Ocean rim have long affected the region in ways that complicate conventional definitions of the Indian Ocean. The contemporary geographical definition of the Indian Ocean, reaching from South Africa's Western Cape to the Red Sea and across to Indonesia and Australia, is not only a largely Western and modern concept, but it also obscures substantive historical maritime linkages. At many historical junctures, certain linkages beyond these geographical coordinates have been as important as those within it.

Since antiquity, Southeast Asian maritime linkages with East Asian polities have been vital for both regions (Chaudhuri 1991; Mukherjee 2013). Similarly, mercantile links between the Mediterranean and ports of the Western Indian Ocean were established as early as the second century BCE. These links expanded substantially over the next two centuries (Cobb 2019). As the Indian Ocean became linked to the Atlantic, the resulting dual articulation had significant repercussions. Early modern European trade and colonialism facilitated new connections between places within imperial spheres while creating new boundaries between polities. With the introduction of the steamship and the opening of the Suez Canal, transoceanic relationships further intensified. Moreover, the European colonization of the entire Indian Ocean region in the nineteenth century created new conditions of regional extraversion that significantly altered patterns of regional integration. The emergence of new Indian Ocean rim nations from the late 1940s had similarly dramatic effects on global linkages, as have interstate relations in the post-Cold War era.

Eastern Africa offers a valuable case study of the shifting boundaries of relation and the elasticity of the Indian Ocean region. As I suggested above, in the decades before the Portuguese arrival, Indian Ocean networks had a discernable southern boundary. At the same time, Swahili linkages stretched well beyond the Indian Ocean in other directions, including to China and the Mediterranean. In the early modern era, new multidirectional routes of linkage emerged with the establishment of Portuguese and Dutch colonial empires in the Indian Ocean. The Portuguese, for example, created the first pan-Indian Ocean imperial administrative structure, one that simultaneously conjoined it to the Atlantic.

Along the Eastern African coast, Portuguese aggression forced Swahili polities into a colonial political matrix wherein Lisbon, Goa, and local Portuguese officials impacted the political and economic lives of coastal residents. The Portuguese administrators who governed Swahili port cities attempted to integrate into the structures of regional exchange, but they also constrained economic activities. Ultimately, they diminished the wealth of entrepôts such as Kilwa by displacing Swahili merchants in the lucrative gold trade. Portuguese administrators at Mozambique Island incrementally reoriented trade to the island, encouraging links with Europe, South Asia, and the Americas. Thus, external Portuguese attempts to control continental-Indian Ocean interfaces altered Eastern Africa's oceanic connections, ensuring closures alongside new links with the Atlantic and Western India (Alpers 1975; Machado 2014).

In the Comoros and Madagascar, early modern engagements with Europeans had other diplomatic and economic repercussions. Specifically, new trade routes within and beyond the Indian Ocean offered an important vent for Comorian and Madagascan produce (Hooper 2017). The Comoros Islands' position between markets in northwestern Madagascar and the Eastern African coast delivered wealth to Comorian merchants who transshipped goods and slaves, and from the mid-seventeenth century the Comoros also became a preferred refreshing station for vessels sailing between European and Asian ports. Ndzuwani Island benefited from the needs of these merchant fleets: more than 432 European vessels visited the island and neighboring Mwali in the seventeenth century (Alpers 2001; Liszkowski 2000: 159).

While Portuguese aggression affected the politics of the Indian Ocean region, the emergent Atlantic economy became enmeshed in Indian Ocean exchanges in ways that also effectively expanded the socioeconomic worlds of the Indian Ocean. American silver and gold, for instance, more deeply integrated Indian Ocean societies with wider economic spheres and fluctuations in value (Parthasarathi 2011; Vink 2007). From the Pacific to the Mediterranean and Atlantic, Indian Ocean products reoriented global commerce. For instance, the transatlantic slave trade depended to a great degree on European and Western African merchants' access to South Asian cotton cloth (Kobayashi 2019; Parthasarathi 2011). Greater global interdependence also shaped South Asian production. For instance, in the mid-1660s more than 45 percent of Bengal's export trade was with Europe, while Japan absorbed an additional 40.72 percent (Prakash 1985: 75). The production and aesthetics of South Asian textiles were increasingly shaped by international consumer interests, and they likewise affected tastes across the globe (Parthasarathi 2018; Riello and Roy 2009).

As the societies of the Indian Ocean and Atlantic basins were becoming more interdependent, the Indian Ocean also saw new regional geographies of relation, particularly in the contexts of the slave trade and indenture (Anderson 2012).

The Mascarenes, for example, became creole plantation societies that bore structural similarities to Caribbean colonies, yet the population was almost entirely made up of people forcibly brought to the islands from Eastern Africa and Madagascar. Perhaps no location represents the expansion of boundaries of relation better than Cape Town, which from the seventeenth century became the new threshold of the Indian Ocean world. More than a gateway, Cape Town became a fulcrum of changing relationalities, a space of a great many "horizons." The growth of Cape Town represented a significant extension of the Indian Ocean world into new lands. Not only was Cape Town directly linked to Batavia, but the Dutch East India Company also delivered enslaved Southeast and South Asians to the city from Java, Sulawesi, Bengal, Coromandel, Malabar, and Sri Lanka. Likewise, people from Madagascar and Mozambique were brought to the Cape in bondage and later indenture (Harries 2014; Ross 1983; Ward 2007, 2009; Worden 2016). These groups and their descendants defined the culture and society of the Cape. Islam as well as languages such as Arabic, Buginese, and Tamil were embedded in the Western Cape's cultural landscape and shaped the emergent Afrikaans language, testimony to the remarkable expansion of Indian Ocean social worlds in the early modern era (Jeppie 2011).

On the Swahili coast, the seventeenth and eighteenth centuries likewise saw new boundaries of relation, notably in challenges to Portuguese rule. Firstly, late sixteenth century Ottoman naval incursions created an extra-regional dynamic in Swahili resistance. With this Mediterranean–Indian Ocean alliance, the Portuguese faced a significant challenge (Casale 2010). Portuguese forces prevailed, but Swahili resistance would reemerge with assistance from Oman. The successful overthrow of Portuguese rule on the northern Swahili coast, culminating in the 1698 liberation of Mombasa, led to an effective contraction of the Swahili world since it ended in division with Portuguese-controlled Mozambique. Moreover, the increasingly influential Omani and Hadrami presence in Eastern Africa encouraged a number of new routes of relation that ultimately fixed a strong sense of affinity with southern Arabia (Vernet 2002). After two centuries of Portuguese rule, the only place on the Eastern African seaboard where a sense of affinity with the Lusophone world remained was Mozambique.

By the end of the 1830s, Busaidi Omanis controlled most of the Swahili-speaking world from their capital at Zanzibar. This concentration of economic activity reoriented the Swahili world, facilitating or strengthening ties with the continental interior as well as with Europe and the Americas. Therefore, in the nineteenth-century Indian Ocean, Africa's boundaries of relation expanded once again. The networks of the Indian Ocean extended west through caravan roads engineered by Yao and Nyamwezi merchants. By the late nineteenth century, substantial links between the Great Lakes and the Swahili coast saw regional commodities sold to merchants from as far away as the United States while coastal merchants settled deep in the interior (Biginagwa and Mapunda 2017; McDow 2018).

Indian Ocean rim societies also forcibly integrated an unprecedented number of bonded people in the nineteenth century. Indian Ocean African societies imported slaves from across Eastern Africa and from as far afield as south-eastern Europe. Their labors would create plantation economies and define urban life. Moreover, those drawn from beyond the Indian Ocean's shores shaped the Swahili language since languages of the East African interior, such as Yao and Nyamwezi, affected the vocabulary and phonology of Swahili (Steere 1870: ix). The slave trade from Eastern Africa to the Atlantic world provides other evidence of the changing boundaries of relation. While much of this traffic was between Mozambique and Brazil, slave ships took Eastern Africans as far north as Cuba and the United States (Harries 2013; Hooper and Eltis 2012). The expansion of Indian Ocean networks accelerated dramatically with the opening of the Suez Canal. And the economic development of the sugar economy in Natal, dependent on South Asian labor, integrated yet another region into nineteenth-century Indian Ocean networks (Kaarsholm 2016).

Imports from beyond the Indian Ocean region also illuminate the frontiers of nineteenth-century Indian Ocean engagements with emergent forms of production and consumption. While cotton cloth from Western India had long dominated Eastern African markets, by the end of the 1840s Eastern Africans consumed more US-made unbleached cottons than any other single variety of cloth. The industrialization of cotton textile production in Europe, the United States, India, and Japan resulted in the availability of cheaper textiles in Eastern Africa, which had myriad effects. At the end of the 1830s, a great many American vessels visited Zanzibar. Eastern African ivory, cloves, and sesame found substantial markets in the United States and Europe. This exchange became so important that several Zanzibari sultans sent their own vessels to Atlantic ports. Trade and diplomatic missions to Britain, France, Germany, the United States, and the Ottoman Empire strengthened Zanzibar's interregional economic connections and bolstered diplomatic ties with distant, powerful states (Prestholdt 2008).

With the European colonization of Indian Ocean Africa, regional and interregional relationships again shifted substantially. Colonial states redefined the physical boundaries of Indian Ocean Africa and encouraged new regional and extra-regional linkages. Indian Ocean Africa offers a dizzying example of colonial boundary-making and reorientation: Italian, British, German, and French colonial governments each instituted new borders, programs of economic reorientation, and imperial integration. As a result, empires incrementally pulled colonial subjects into differing spheres of relation. New ports, railroads, and roads more completely integrated the Indian Ocean with the continental interior, encouraging significant migration to the coast. The new ports of the colonial era also attracted shipping from within and beyond the Indian Ocean. For example, by the mid-1920s Japanese steamships linked Eastern Africa to several East Asian ports.

Japanese trade in the region also reveals how Indian Ocean material interests shaped global interfaces. In the early twentieth century, Japanese manufacturers appealed to colonial consumers in the Indian Ocean region by producing low-cost cotton textiles that met multiple niche market demands (Kagotani 1997). As a result, Japanese cotton goods quickly superseded many European and Indian

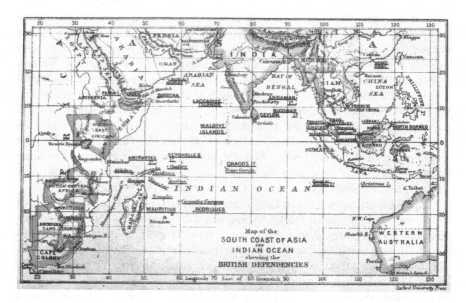

Map 1.1 Map of the Indian Ocean region demarcating the British colonial sphere at the beginning of the twentieth century. Published in C. P. Lucas, 1906. *A Historical Geography of the British Colonies*, Second Edition, Volume I: The Mediterranean and Eastern Colonies. Oxford: Clarendon Press.

Image credit: Wikipedia Commons.

competitors. Despite British attempts to restrict Japanese goods, by the early 1930s Japanese manufactures represented nearly 90 percent of all imported cotton goods in British East Africa. Thus, Japanese goods became central to regional fashion, and this demand ensured the centrality of Indian Ocean societies to interwar Japan's industry (Ampiah 1990; Kitagawa 2006: 164). From the 1950s, Japanese manufactures would again dominate multiple sectors of the Eastern African textile trade, including the vast market for printed *kanga* (Ryan 2013; Suzuki 2018).

This example, along with that of US trade, evidences the diversification of Indian Ocean markets and critical extra-regional interfaces. At the same time, these interfaces illustrate an important point: despite crucial ties to other world regions, such linkages did not create enduring senses of affinity between people along the Indian Ocean's shores and the United States or Japan. The regional boundaries of interaction were elastic, but their expansion and contraction did not always affect the imagination of space.

Shifting imaginations of space

The imagination of the Indian Ocean space has taken many forms as a result of differing interests and in response to regional and planetary circumstances.

Elsewhere I have suggested that perceptions of an Indian Ocean totality are a form of "basin consciousness," a variegated mode of thought informed by historical linkages and perceptions of affinity (Prestholdt 2015). Basin consciousness has myriad underwriting forces, from oceanic travel to genealogy and diplomacy. The cognitive maps of Indian Ocean diasporic communities offer examples of basin consciousness in multiple historical moments with diverse permutations (Alpers 2002; Desai 2013; Ho 2006; Larson 2009). Yet, since at least the 1950s, a common denominator of basin consciousness has been the collective desire to evoke an interconnected, maritime past that resonates with current social, political, or economic concerns. This desire to evoke an integrated Indian Ocean is evident in literature and academic research, political culture, popular discourse, and much else.

The emic language of geography offers a valuable window on changing collective perceptions of oceanic space. Markus Vink has suggested that terms such as the Persian *darya'i akhzar*, or Green Sea, and the Chinese *Nanyang*, or Southern Ocean, reveal cognitive maps of the Indian Ocean and their attendant cultural perceptions. They also evidence divergent understandings of oceanic space. A closer look at regional languages reveals a number of precise reckonings. For example, Arabic conceptualizations of the Indian Ocean rim have operated at two registers: recognition of a unified global ocean and the definition of regional seas (Mukherjee 2011: 63). Arabic-speakers have differentiated among regions such as *bahr al-Zandj* for the western fringe and *bahr al-Ṣīn* for the eastern rim. Historically, Arabic-speakers also employed *bahr al-Hind*, literally "the Indian Ocean," to refer more modestly to the western Indian Ocean (Becker and Dunlop 2012; Hartmann and Dunlop 2012; Mukherjee 2011: 61–65; Vink 2007: 55).

The Swahili language suggests additional geographical conceptualizations. It is particularly telling that Swahili seems not to have had a distinct word for the totality of the Indian Ocean until the end of the nineteenth century. Rather, Swahili speakers conceptualized the Indian Ocean basin as a combination of regional "seas" (*bahari*) and "lands" (*bar* or *bara*). Together, these *bahari* and *bar/a* constituted the Swahili language's primary metageographical designations. Just as tellingly, Swahili often maintained a secondary distinction between the coastland and hinterland, although *bar/a* did not always have clear scalar limits.

In the first comprehensive recording of Swahili geographical concepts – from a dictionary compiled in the first half of the nineteenth century – we see terms such as *bar es suahil* (Swahili coast) and *bar es fars* (the Persian coast under Omani rule) alongside other Arabic-derived terms for coastlands (Krapf 1882: 22). Swahili-speakers supplemented these with thalassic terms such as *bahari el ali* (Persian Gulf) and *bahari ya sham* (Red Sea), though the scales of such "seas" could be quite different. Mombasan Swahili, for instance, referred to the waters around Mombasa as *bahari ya Mvita*, or the "Sea of Mombasa" (Krapf 1882: 306; Madan 1903). At the same time, Swahili-speakers used an overarching term for the global ocean: *bahari kuu*, or the great sea (Krapf 1882: 19; Steere 1894: 252). Thus, before colonial rule the Swahili language had multiple, overlapping registers of oceanic geography, each corresponding to a landmass or polity, with the exception of the "great sea." Yet, as Swahili had no single term for the Indian Ocean region, Swahili-speakers likely perceived the basin a matrix of contiguous seas and coasts rather than a unified field of interaction.

Swahili terminology for oceanic fields began to change at the end of the nineteenth century. In the early colonial period, we see the first evidence of the use of the term *bahari ya hindi*, literally "the Indian Ocean" (Sacleux 1939 [1891]). The extent to which European metageographical concepts of the Indian Ocean were internalized in Swahili perceptions of the region is not clear, but the occurrence of the term *bahari ya hindi* in the early colonial era likely reflects the influence of Western metageographical terminology. Additionally, in the twentieth century, evidence from Swahili dictionaries suggests that the more precise Swahili geographies of seas and coastlands may have been receding. By the late twentieth century, the precise terminologies of the early nineteenth century were largely superseded, at least in popular use, by less precise terms, including the "Indian Ocean."

While the metageographical concept of a unified Indian Ocean gained purchase in Swahili, transcolonial and transregional routes of relation were expanding, and multiple anti-colonial universalisms emerged. Empires created alternative contexts for regional linkages, and the early colonial era saw both the constriction and elaboration of Indian Ocean networks (Bose 2011). More precisely, global empires increasingly framed collective Indian Ocean rim affinities while administratively integrating coastal groups with populations far from the coastal belt. Thus, the context of colonialism engendered overlapping and competing anticolonial universalisms, which both linked Indian Ocean societies and transcended the region.

Multiple strains of thought coalesced in anti-imperial movements from Pan-Islamism to supranationalism (Frost 2010). Ultimately, universalist anticolonial agitation and territorial nationalism ran along converging tracks. Islamic reformism (*nahda*), Arab nationalism, socialism, and the League against Imperialism created transoceanic notions of solidarity, what Isabel Hofmeyr termed "competing universalisms," that were not bound to oceanic space (Bose 2006; Ghazal 2010; Hofmeyr 2010). Concepts of a South Asian political community, for example, transcended particular colonies and indeed the Indian Ocean (Aiyar 2015; Brennan 2012; Hofmeyr 2013;). Thus, the universalisms of the colonial era rarely conformed to the geographical boundaries of the Indian Ocean basin. Moreover, many nationalist movements drew coastal residents into nascent domestic political spheres, which in most cases emphasized a continental orientation.

With decolonization, such territorial nationalisms engendered further contractions of the political and spatial imagination (Gupta 2009). Some political thinkers resisted this boundary fortification by emphasizing a historic maritime orientation. In Zanzibar and coastal Kenya, the era of decolonization saw the popularization of discourses that both celebrated Indian Ocean cosmopolitanism and defended Arab elitism. In Zanzibar, debates around history, race, and geographical orientation seeded election violence (Glassman 2014, 2011). These debates culminated in the 1964 revolution, which would in turn lead to Zanzibar's unification with Tanganyika and a stronger continental orientation. In coastal Kenya, the late 1950s saw the rising popularity of a regional identity fixed on the notion of coastal commonality. Many believed that postcolonial domination by Nairobi would prove disastrous for racial, ethnic, and religious minorities, and this potentially insecure status encouraged political movements that highlighted historical links with the wider Indian Ocean sphere. In the early 1960s, several coastal political parties lobbied hard for separation from Kenya by emphasizing the maritime essence of the coast (Brennan 2008; Prestholdt 2015; Salim 1970). Thus, by the end of the colonial era an amorphous basin consciousness found political expression.

Coastal separatism in Kenya failed, and further nationalist contraction in the postcolonial period saw many states look resolutely inward. In Kenya, the coast became an integral part of the nation. With the dawn of the one-party state, coastal separatism gave way to significant national political engagement. This was true even in areas such as the Lamu Archipelago, where interest in national debates and affinity with Nairobi had initially been limited. The rising political engagement of coastal towns in the 1970s affected and was effected by an emergent identity as Kenyan as well as the notion that such engagement could pay material dividends. Yet, questions of economic opportunity and the position of coastal Muslims as well as other minority communities in the postcolonial nation remained unresolved.

The end of colonial rule also saw new states look outward towards other centers of power beyond the Indian Ocean region, including Washington and Moscow. In the postcolonial era universalist ideologies such as socialism and communism continued to gain traction, and global forums such as the Non-Aligned Movement became important modes of political interface. In this context, maritime traffic continued and even increased, but the political relevance of a maritime Indian Ocean world faded. Most states saw historic Indian Ocean linkages as marginal to their interests. Specifically, state-oriented economic and diplomatic organizations often framed these interests in terms of other geographies or a common experience of colonialism. Just as important, increasing access to radio, cinema, television, and air travel expanded the region's dual articulation, more firmly integrating points along the Indian Ocean rim and far beyond (Brennan 2010; Fair 2018).

The integration of coastal communities into postcolonial states also proved fraught. In Kenya, many coastal people were alienated from the postcolonial economy and suffered a range of ethnic and racial discriminatory practices. Mounting frustrations in the 1980s led to political upheaval in the 1990s. In the context of democratic reforms and the return of multi-party politics, the notion of a coastal cultural entity became a critical political lever. The Islamic Party of Kenya (IPK), for example, relied both on Muslimness and coastal identity as catalysts for political mobilization.

With the end of the Cold War and a reversal of the introverted politics of the early postcolonial era, basin consciousness reemerged. Yet unlike in the early postcolonial era, many nations, not just individuals or movements, began to imagine the Indian Ocean as a coherent sphere. As a result, social groups *and* states reinvigorated historical geographies for the purposes of new social identities, economic relationships, and political calculi (Chari 2015; Gilbert 2011). For instance, in the mid-1990s regional states identified a common set of economic interests. Notably, the Indian Ocean Rim Association for Regional Cooperation aimed to stimulate investment and trade across the basin (Campbell 2003). The confluence of state and popular imaginations of a national maritime identity was initially most evident in places such as Mauritius and Zanzibar. In 1990s Zanzibar, a new tourist economy, with an emphasis on historical preservation, and the return of exiles encouraged the celebration of a cosmopolitan past. Zanzibar's Festival of the Dhow Countries was in many ways a culmination of this reimagination of the island's maritime past (Bissell 2018, 2012).

The end of Apartheid in South Africa also led to reconsiderations of affinity as the descendants of enslaved people at the Cape strongly identified with trans-Indian Ocean genealogies. Many Coloured Muslims put particular emphasis on their Southeast Asian ancestry. So important was this historical link with Southeast Asia that Gabeba Baderoon suggested it came to be seen by many Coloured Muslims as a "sacred geography" (Baderoon 2014). The Indonesian government, in turn, established stronger links with Cape communities and the South African state. Moreover, surging interest in Cape Malay culture and cuisine has seen these promoted by community organizers, museums, and tour companies, thus collectively emphasizing the salience of an Indian Ocean past.

The imagination of the Indian Ocean as a distinct region has only become more important in the twenty-first century. But revivified, layered affinities also evidence tensions. While policy-makers from China to South Africa have sought to reinvigorate regional relations by emphasizing historical affinities, the idea of the Indian Ocean continues to offer an alternative political lever among disaffected groups. Separatism in Zanzibar, Kenya, and the Comoros offers examples of the reanimation of concepts of the region that challenge regional states. For example, though Kenyan officials ultimately crushed the IPK, the party's emphasis on coastal identity buffeted a vigorous public discussion about the history of the coast, its relation to the rest of Kenya, and its interface with the wider Indian Ocean. As the sense of alienation among many coastal residents increased in the new millennium, particularly in consequence of draconian counterterrorism measures and political strife, concepts of coastal commonality once again gained traction. Specifically, in the aftermath of Kenya's contested 2007 election, the Mombasa Republican Council (MRC) gained a wide audience with its call for coastal separation. It employed the imagery of 1960s separatism, challenged the legal foundations of the coast's union with Kenya, and championed the telling slogan, "The Coast is Not Kenya" (*Pwani si Kenya*). While Kenyan authorities proscribed the MRC, it offered a platform for the idea of a distinct coastal identity, utilizing conventional rallies and social media to elicit support. As a result, the notion of a shared maritime, multiracial, and multi-religious past fundamentally distinct from the rest of Kenya became a stronger popular idea – and political catalyst – than at any point since the 1960s (Kresse 2009; Mahajan 2015; Willis and Gona 2013).

Conclusion

One conclusion that we can draw from the evidence presented here is that Indian Ocean networks have not conformed to rigid geographical definitions. Rather, the Indian Ocean region has been constituted to a great degree by its porosity. Interfaces with other world regions became increasingly diverse and important in the early modern era. As a result, the effective ends of the Indian Ocean region have been in great flux for centuries and people along the Indian Ocean rim have remained resolutely multifocal. Another conclusion we can draw is that the Indian Ocean is a dynamic idea that has gained and lost relevance over time. Emic imaginings of the region have been highly variegated, and concepts of Indian Ocean space, including its boundaries, have varied significantly over time. While many of the geographical coordinates of the Indian Ocean have been imagined or imposed by outsiders, and people along the rim have domest-icated many of these etic geographical definitions, they have also reimagined Indian Ocean linkages and their meanings for particular, local purposes. In the post-Cold War era, new spheres of political and economic engagement emerged, which alongside genealogy, tourism, academic research, and much else have encouraged a reimagination of the Indian Ocean region as an integrated whole. Where postcolonial states once posed challenges to regional affinities, many are now keen to develop trans-Indian Ocean relationships. Indeed, the contemporary power and desire of state actors to encourage Indian Ocean engagements and notions of regional affinity is greater than at any point since the colonial era.

The blurred geographical and conceptual boundaries of the Indian Ocean region reveal deep engagements with other world regions and variegated spatial reckonings. They also suggest that a coherent Indian Ocean has often served as a desirable and useful fiction, one elaborated by different actors at multiple historical junctures for many reasons. Tellingly, the perception of the Indian Ocean as a totality is both related to but not confined by the sea. Rather, Indian Ocean basin consciousness has expanded even as maritime connectivity has diminished and multidimensional, extra-regional interfaces have intensified. Therefore, the most powerful and enduring dynamic of the Indian Ocean region may not be the immediate engagements among people along its shores, but rather the projection of sociocultural meaning onto economic relationships, communities of faith, genealogies, and the past.

References

Aiyar, Sana. 2015. *Indians in Kenya: The Politics of Diaspora*. Cambridge, MA: Harvard University Press.

Alpers, Edward. 1975. *Ivory and Slaves: Changing Pattern of International Trade in East Central Africa to the Later Nineteenth Century.* Berkeley: University of California Press.

Alpers, Edward. 2001. "A Complex Relationship: Mozambique and the Comoro Islands in the Nineteenth and Twentieth Centuries." *Cahiers d'Études Africaines* 161: 73–95.

Alpers, Edward. 2002. "Recollecting Africa: Diasporic Memory in the Indian Ocean World." *African Studies Review* 43, no. 1: 83–99.

Alpers, Edward. 2013. *The Indian Ocean in World History.* New York: Oxford University Press.

Ampiah, Kweku. 1990. "British Commercial Policies against Japanese Expansionism in East and West Africa, 1932–1935." *International Journal of African Historical Studies* (23/4):619–641.

Amrith, Sunil. 2013. *Crossing the Bay: The Furies of Nature and the Fortunes of Migrants.* Cambridge, MA: Harvard University Press.

Anderson, Clare. 2012. *Subaltern Lives: Biographies of Colonialism in the Indian Ocean World, 1790–1920.* Cambridge: Cambridge University Press.

Baderoon, Gabeba. 2014. *Regarding Muslims: From Slavery to Postapartheid.* Johannesburg: Witwatersrand University Press.

Becker, C.H. and D.M. Dunlop. 2012. "Bahr al-Zandj." In P. Bearman, Th. Bianquis, C.E. Bosworth, E. van Donzel, W.P. Heinrichs, eds. *Encyclopaedia of Islam.* Accessed 12 February 2018 http://dx.doi.org/10.1163/1573-3912_islam_SIM_1066

Becker, Felicitas and Joel Cabrita. 2014. "Introduction: Performing Citizenship and Enacting Exclusion on Africa's Indian Ocean Littoral." *Journal of African History* 55, no. 2: 161–171.

Biginagwa, Thomas J. and Bertram B.B. Mapunda. 2017. "The Kilwa–Nyasa caravan route: the long-neglected trading corridor in southern Tanzania." In Stephanie Wynne-Jones and Adria LaViolette, eds. *The Swahili World.* New York: Routledge, 541–554.

Bishara, Fahad Ahmad. 2017. *A Sea of Debt: Law and Economic Life in the Western Indian Ocean, 1780–1950.* Cambridge: Cambridge University Press.

Bissell, William. 2012. "From dhow culture to the diaspora: ZIFF, film, and the framing of transnational imaginaries in the western Indian Ocean." *Social Dynamics* 38, no. 3: 479–498.

Bissell, William. 2018. "The Modern Life of Swahili Stonetowns." In Stephanie Wynne-Jones and Adria LaViolette, eds. *The Swahili World.* New York: Routledge.

Bose, Sugata. 2002. "Space and time on the Indian Ocean Rim: theory and history." In Leila Fawaz and C.A. Bayly, eds. *Modernity and culture: From the Mediterranean to the Indian Ocean.* Berkeley: University of California Press.

Bose, Sugata. 2006. *A Hundred Horizons: The Indian Ocean in the Age of Global Empire.* Cambridge: Harvard University Press.

Bose, Sugata. 2011. "Different Universalisms, Colorful Cosmopolitanisms: The Global Imagination of the Colonized." In Sugata Bose and Kris Manjapra, eds. *Cosmopolitan Thought Zones.* 97–111. London: Palgrave Macmillan.

Bremner, Lindsay. 2014. "Folded Ocean: The Spatial Transformation of the Indian Ocean World." *Journal of the Indian Ocean Region* 10, no. 1: 18–45.

Brennan, James R. 2008. "Lowering the Sultan's Flag: Sovereignty and Decolonization in Coastal Kenya," *Comparative Studies in Society and History* 50, no. 4: 831–861.

Brennan, James R. 2012. *Taifa: Making Nation and Race in Urban Tanzania.* Athens, OH: Ohio University Press.

Campbell, Gwyn. 2003. "Introduction: Indian Ocean Rim (IOR) Economic Association: History and Prospects." In *The Indian Ocean Rim: Southern Africa and Regional Co-operation*, edited by Gwyn Campbell. London: Routledge Curzon, 1–41.

Casale, Giancarlo. 2010. *The Ottoman Age of Exploration*. Oxford: Oxford University Press.

Chari, Sharad. 2015. "Africa Extraction, Indian Ocean Critique." *South Atlantic Quarterly* 114, no. 1: 83–100.

Chaudhuri, K.N. 1985. *Trade and Civilisation in the Indian Ocean: An Economic History from the Rise of Islam to 1750*. Cambridge: Cambridge University Press.

Chaudhuri, K.N. 1991. *Asia Before Europe: Economy and Civilisation of the Indian Ocean From the Rise of Islam to 1750*. Cambridge: Cambridge University Press.

Cobb, Matthew. 2019. "Introduction: The Indian Ocean in Antiquity and global history." In Matthew Cobb, ed. *The Indian Ocean Trade in Antiquity: Political, Cultural, and Economic Impacts*. New York: Routledge, 1–14.

Desai, Gaurav. 2013. *Commerce with the Universe: Africa, India, and the Afraisan Imagination*. New York: Columbia University Press.

Fair, Laura. 2018. *Reel Pleasures: Cinema Audiences and Entrepreneurs in Twentieth-Century Urban Tanzania*. Athens: Ohio University Press.

Frost, Mark Ravinder. 2010. "In Search of Cosmopolitan Discourse: A Historical Journey across the Indian Ocean from Singapore to South Africa, 1870–1920." In Pamila Gupta, Isabel Hofmeyr, and Michael Pearson, eds., *Eyes Across the Water*. Pretoria: Unisa Press, 75–95.

Ghazal, Amal. 2010. *Islamic Reform and Arab Nationalism: Expanding the Crescent from the Mediterranean to the Indian Ocean (1880s–1930s)*. New York: Routledge.

Gilbert, Erik. 2011. "The Dhow as Cultural Icon: Heritage and Regional Identity in the Western Indian Ocean." *International Journal of Heritage Studies* 17, no. 1: 62–80.

Glassman, Jonathon. 2011. *War of Words, War of Stones: Racial Thought and Violence in Colonial Zanzibar*. Bloomington: Indiana University Press.

Glassman, Jonathon. 2014. "Creole Nationalists and the Search for Nativist Authenticity in Twentieth Century Zanzibar: The Limits of Cosmopolitanism." *Journal of African History* 55, no. 2: 229–247.

Gupta, Pamila. 2009. "The Disquieting of History: Portuguese (De)colonization and Goan Migration in the Indian Ocean." *Journal of Asian and African Studies* (44): 19–47.

Harries, Patrick. 2013. "Negotiating Abolition: Cape Town and the Transatlantic Slave Trade," *Slavery & Abolition* 34, no. 4: 579–597.

Harries, Patrick. 2014. "Middle Passages of the Southwest Indian Ocean: A Century of Forced Immigration from Africa to the Cape of Good Hope." *Journal of African History* 55, no. 2: 173–90.

Hartmann, R. and D.M. Dunlop. 2012. "Baḥr al-Hind." In P. Bearman, Th. Bianquis, C.E. Bosworth, E. van Donzel, and W.P. Heinrichs, eds. *Encyclopaedia of Islam*. Accessed 12 February 2018. http://dx.doi.org/10.1163/1573-3912_islam_SIM_1060.

Ho, Engseng. 2006. *The Graves of Tarim: Genealogy and Mobility Across the Indian Ocean*. Berkeley: University of California Press.

Hofmeyr, Isabel. 2010. "Universalizing the Indian Ocean." *PMLA* 125, no. 3: 721–729.

Hofmeyr, Isabel. 2013. *Gandhi's Printing Press: Experiments in Slow Reading*. Cambridge: Harvard University Press.

Hooper, Jane. 2017. *Feeding Globalization: Madagascar and the Provisioning Trade, 1600–1800*. Athens: Ohio University Press.

Hooper, Jane and David Eltis. 2012. "The Indian Ocean in Transatlantic Slavery." *Slavery & Abolition* 34, no. 3: 1–23.

Jeppie, Saarah. 2011. "From the Madrasah to the Museum: The Social Life of the 'Kietaabs' of Cape Town." *History in Africa* 38: 369–399.

Kaarsholm, Preben. 2016. "Indian Ocean Networks and the Transmutations of Servitude: The Protector of Indian Immigrants and the Administration of Freed Slaves and Indentured Labourers in Durban in the 1870s." *Journal of Southern African Studies* 42, no. 3: 443–461.

Kagotani, N. 1997. "Japanese Cotton Textile Diplomacy in the First Half of the 1930s: The Case of the Dutch–Japanese Trade Negotiations in 1934." In *Bulletin of Asia-Pacific Studies* 7, 35–44.

Kearney, Milo. 2004. *The Indian Ocean in World History.* New York: Routledge.

Kitagawa, Katsuhiko. 2006. "Japanese Competition in the Congo Basin in the 1930s." In A.J.H. Lantham and Heita Kawakatsu, eds. *Intra-Asian Trade and the World Market.* New York: Routledge, 155–167.

Kobayashi, Kazuo. 2019. *Indian Cotton Textiles in West Africa: African Agency, Consumer Demand and the Making of the Global Economy, 1750–1850.* Cham: Palgrave Macmillan.

Kresse, Kai. 2009. "Muslim Politics in Postcolonial Kenya: Negotiating Knowledge on the Double-Periphery." *Journal of the Royal Anthropological Institute* 15, no. 1: 76–94.

Kresse, Kai and Edward Simpson. 2010. "Between Africa and India: Thinking Comparatively across the Western Indian Ocean." *Zentrum Moderner Orient Working Paper no. 5.*

Krapf, Johannes L. 1882. *Dictionary of the Suaheli Language.* London, Trübner and Co.

Larson, Pier. 2009. *Ocean of Letters: Language and Creolization in an Indian Ocean Diaspora.* New York: Cambridge University Press.

Lewis, Martin and Kären Wigen. 1997. *The Myth of Continents.* Berkeley: University of California Press.

Liszkowski, H. 2000. *Mayotte et les Comores.* Mamoudzou: Editions du Baobob.

Machado, Pedro. 2014. *Ocean of Trade: South Asian Merchants, Africa and the Indian Ocean, c.1750–1850.* Cambridge: Cambridge University Press.

Madan, A.C. 1903. *Swahili–English Dictionary.* Oxford: Clarendon.

Mahajan, Nidhi. 2015. "Moorings: Indian Ocean Trade and the State in East Africa," PhD Dissertation, Cornell University.

McDow, Thomas F. 2018. *Buying Time: Debt and Mobility in the Western Indian Ocean.* Athens: Ohio University Press.

McPherson, Kenneth. 1993. *The Indian Ocean: A History of People and the Sea.* Delhi: Oxford University Press.

Mukherjee, Rila. ed. 2011. "Introduction: Bengal and the Northern Bay of Bengal." In Rila Mukherjee, ed. *Pelagic Passageways: The Northern Bay of Bengal Before Colonialism.* Delhi: Primus, 1–262.

Mukherjee, Rila. ed. 2013. *Oceans Connect: Reflections on Water Worlds Across Time and Space.* Delhi: Primus.

Parthasarathi, Prasannan. 2011. *Why Europe Grew Rich and Asia Did Not: Global Economic Divergence, 1600–1850.* Cambridge: Cambridge University Press.

Parthasarathi, Prasannan. 2018. "Textiles and Silver: The Indian Ocean in a Global Frame." In Pedro Machado, Sarah Fee, and Gwyn Campbell eds. *Textile Trades,* 29–54. New York: Palgrave Macmillan.

Pearson, Michael N. 2003. *The Indian Ocean*. New York: Routledge.

Prakash, Om. 1985. *The Dutch East India Company and the Economy of Bengal, 1630–1720*. Princeton: Princeton University Press.

Prestholdt, Jeremy. 2008. *Domesticating the World: African Consumerism and the Genealogies of Globalization*. Berkeley: University of California Press.

Prestholdt, Jeremy. 2015. "Locating the Indian Ocean: Thoughts on the Postcolonial Reconstitution of Space." *Journal of Eastern African Studies* 9, no. 3: 440–467.

Riello, Giorgio and Tirthankar Roy, eds. 2009. *How India Clothed the World: The World of South Asian Textiles, 1500–1850*. Leiden: Brill.

Ross, Robert. 1983. *Cape of Torments: Slavery and Resistance in South Africa*. Boston: Routledge & Kegan Paul.

Ryan, Mackenzie Moon. 2013. "The Global Reach of a Fashionable Commodity: A Manufacturing and Design History of *Kanga* Textiles." PhD diss., University of Florida.

Sacleux, Ch. 1939 [1891]. *Dictionnaire Swahili-Français*. Paris: Institut d'Ethnologie.

Salim, A.I. 1970. "The Movement for *Mwambao*, or Coast Autonomy in Kenya, 1956–1963." *Hadith 2*. Nairobi: East African Publishing House. 212–228.

Sheriff, Abdul. 2010. *Dhow Cultures of the Indian Ocean: cosmopolitanism, commerce, and Islam*. New York: Columbia University Press.

Simpson, Edward. 2006. *Muslim Society and the Western Indian Ocean: The Seafarers of Kachchh*. London: Routledge.

Steere, Edward. 1870. *Swahili Tales, as Told by the Natives of Zanzibar*. London: Bell and Daldy.

Steere, Edward. 1894. *A Handbook of the Swahili Language, as Spoken at Zanzibar*. A.C. Madan. London: Society for Promoting Christian Knowledge.

Suzuki, Hideaki. 2018. "*Kanga* Made in Japan: The Flow from the Eastern to the Western End of the Indian Ocean World." In Pedro Machado, Sarah Fee, and Gwyn Campbell, eds. *Textile Trades*. New York: Palgrave Macmillan, 105–132.

Vernet, Thomas. 2002. "Les cités-États swahili et la puissance omanaise, 1650–1720." *Journal des africanistes* 72, no. 2: 89–110.

Vink, Markus. 2007. "Indian Ocean Studies and the new thalassology." *Journal of Global History* 2, no. 1: 41–62.

Ward, Kerry. 2007. "'Tavern of the Seas'? The Cape of Good Hope as an Oceanic Cross-roads during the Seventeenth and Eighteenth Centuries." in Bentley, Jerry H., Renate Bridenthal, and Kären Wigen, eds. *Seascapes: Maritime Histories, Littoral Cultures, and Transoceanic exchanges*, 137–152. Honolulu: University of Hawai'i Press.

Willis, Justin and George Gona. 2013. "*Pwani C Kenya*? Memory, Documents and Secessionist Politics in Coastal Kenya." *African Affairs* 112, no. 446: 48–71.

Worden, Nigel. 2016. "Indian Ocean Slaves in Cape Town, 1695–1807." *Journal of Southern African Studies* 42, no. 3: 389–408.

2　Indian Ocean ontology
Nyerere, memory, place

May Joseph

The place of memory, memory as place

Indian Ocean Studies – predominantly the purview of historical and literary inquiry – is only beginning to probe questions of ontology, political mentalities, and sensory ethnography. Carving out the space of trade, navigational networks and their ensuing literary connections, has opened up the possibilities to ask questions about the affective contours of oceanic exchanges. Tracing the histories of commodities such as pepper, nutmeg, cloves, pearls, and cloth, alongside the itinerant histories of human migrations across oceanic connectivities stages the challenge of reconstituting the archive. For those whose lives have been profoundly disrupted, sometimes destroyed, by the vagaries and violence of the region's social histories, the archive of the disappeared, the archive of the unseen, become increasingly persuasive arenas of query. The question of affective tonalities, of the relationships between the human and the non-human, between people and the landscapes that shape their pasts and futures, necessitates an interdisciplinary and experimental approach to the writing of the Indian Ocean sensorium. That space of the emotions where desire for the good life, of forced dispersals through slavery and indentured servitude, of immigration and assimilation, of nationalism and expulsion, produce powerful ontological spheres whose traces are inchoate, intimate, and invisible (see Gupta 2018; Jeychandran 2016; Joseph 2019; Ng'weno 2018; Srinivas 2008). How does one write about the untraceable?

The Indian Ocean is a methodological space, as Isabel Hofmeyr (2010) states. It is a meshed network of multidirectional memory that necessitates multiple narrative strategies in recounting its micro-histories (Rothberg 2009). An implied quagmire when writing the Indian Ocean is the role of memory and the embodied self as tools of inquiry. The deconstructive turn in postcolonial studies led to the incorporation of the Western Enlightenment critique of subjectivity without having the archived production of the self as documented in the archives, museums, libraries, and colonial offices of the West. The ravages of coloniality continue in the postcolonial moment as a second disappearance, where the decolonial self is already outmoded, irrelevant, untheoretical, and indulgent (Kakar 1996). Yet, Europe's excesses in the Indian Ocean over the last

500 years are persistently countered by the pillaged, haunted spheres of the decolonial. The historic burden of legitimacy has meant privileging rigor over experimental forms in order to be heard. The self as a tool of contemporary critical discourse has been theoretically repressed precisely at the time that subaltern voices across the Indian Ocean are raising their critiques (Hall 1996). Through an investigation of the decolonial self, one can begin an itinerary of political mentalities across the Indian Ocean, of which there is very little written by locals, migrants, immigrants, or refugees themselves. Let us enter the space of ontological thought, of sensory history, of probing the political imaginations that fomented Indian Ocean potentialities (Agamben 1999) across generations of migratory displacements.

Sensory histories

The idea of an Indian Ocean ontology is very tactile to me. It is the fleeting feeling here in New York City, at the edge of the Atlantic World, where few have an idea of what the Indian Ocean means, of being woven into the skeins of the Indian Ocean's web through the Dutch East Indian Company's vast networks of over 600 entrepots, of which Batavia (present-day Jakarta) was its most prized, and New Amsterdam (present-day Manhattan) its least valued. Walking along the ghosts of New Amsterdam's contours, hearing Swahili spoken or seeing an image of the Serengeti on someone's T-shirt, a well spring of associations shrink the distance between New York and the East African coast. As the Atlantic swells in all its violent grandeur, I am reminded of a tremulous Indian Ocean past: at once East Africa and Malabar Coasts, Dar es Salaam and Cochin. Sensory histories. Nomadic identities. Here, I excavate what those tangents of political mentalities might mean for an Indian Ocean ontology.

I was born the year of Tanganyikan independence. As a child of African socialism, I grew up under *Ujamaa*, the rallying cry of my childhood. *Ujamaa* was a political experiment that culturally connected me to my parents' communist roots in Kerala of the 1950s. Unbeknownst to me during my Tanzanian childhood, I would come to understand that my South Asian Lusophone identity was another connecting link between Kerala and Tanzania. Portuguese colonization of the Malabar Coast, and the Dutch after them, had shaped the coastal communities my parents were from in Kerala, South India. This was a powerful link that resonated along the East African coast as well. Traces of Portuguese fort remnants at Mombasa and Kilwa. An Omani slave port at Bagamoyo. These forbidding fort constructions left an architectural trace in colonial East African urbanism that was startlingly similar to the anthropogenic destruction of the Malabar region by the Portuguese, Dutch and British. This affective similarity between the fort ruins of Portuguese, Arab and Hadhrami influenced built environments along the Swahili and Malabar coasts presented a shared ontological history. The layered Indian Ocean aesthetics of Arab, Hadhrami and Portuguese influences shaped the visual identities of both the Swahili and Malabar Coasts. They imperceptibly percolated cultural becoming on both sides of the Indian Ocean. However, there was no explicit cultural articulation of decolonial connectivities across these oceanic frameworks outside the narratives of race, citizenship, and immigration during the first years of decolonization in Tanzania or in India. Hence, much of the cultural thickness, the oral, mnemonic, somatic, and lived relationalities that connected contemporary decolonial East African ways of life to the dreams, ambitions, desires, and economic hopes of coastal South Asia from the Malabar Coast to the Rann of Kutch is largely informal, ephemeral, and emergent. It is an amorphous archive that is nevertheless filled with a density of aspirations, feelings, political imaginings.

My early youth was formed through the *Ujamaa* dictum of "education for self-reliance" – an experiment in socialism through villagization (Nyerere 1968). It was a delirium of the now forgotten revolution of feet. Of marching to the ideals of the newly independent African state-Tanzania. This was a pragmatic, socialist African experiment as well as a profoundly Indian Ocean political formation. Caught between the junctures of Second World ideological imaginings, Bandung radicalism, Third World solidarities, and the ontological possibilities of the Indian Ocean, Tanzania under Julius Nyerere embodied a very distinctive Indian Ocean affect. It was a repository of feelings that connected East Africa to the Middle East and South Asia in tactile ways. Tanzanian structures of feeling in the 1970s were shaped by multi-continental encounters: ideologies, music and medicine from Cuba and Latin America; technical knowhow from Yugoslavia and Bulgaria; infrastructural development from China; Soviet military training camps in Tanzania for the Namibians (SWAPO) and Angolans (MPLA) and the African National Congress (ANC). What brought them together was an oceanic sensibility that these influences flowed across the seas, coalescing around Dar es Salaam because of its port city vantage point, at once geopolitical, navigational, and historical.

The first-person narrative of the memoir and travelogue makes it possible to connect Nyerere, New York and the Indian Ocean through micro-histories. The Indian Ocean – with its centripetal and centrifugal forces – necessitates an immersive methodology to come to presence. The subjective turn opens up techniques for such an immersive yet critical approach. It allows a feminist practice of delineating the forgotten, erased, and inaudible voices that otherwise fall out of the visible spaces of the vast, volatile histories of seafaring journeys. The Indian Ocean is a liquid space whose open-ended horizons between the Atlantic Ocean, the Arabian Gulf, and the Bay of Bengal is a merging of memory as place with the place of memory. Deploying a subjective turn enables an investigative, feminist Indian Ocean selfhood to momentarily suture distended geographies – East Africa, India, New York, through the production of a fragmented, illusory self. Montage and juxtaposition of striated time frames activate shards of somatic excavation, at once unstable, open ended, shifting, discursive (Levinas 1987). Traces of the seventeenth century Dutch colonization of Cochin conjoins with embodied memories of seventeenth century colonization of New Amsterdam, through a singular story of arrival from South Asia's Malabar coast to New York, for instance (Joseph 2013). Transoceanic linkages open up mnemonic detours – places embarked and disembarked, places derailed from and rerouted through, to a state of becoming, of belonging, of citizenship. The absence of documentation is folded into forms of rumination, recollection, dreaming, reconstructing minor histories of oceanic placeness. Such techniques of assembling political mentalities allows a narrative space for new affective tonalities. Fabulations of disappeared spaces manufacture accounts of an irretrievable historicity. The rumor, the anecdote, the hearsay, and the archive mesh into the thickness of memory. The old acquires a newness. How one comes to writing its pasts, its displacements, its repressions, and its potentialities, is that space of intimacy we must probe with fierceness. The looking glass of the Indian Ocean is tempestuous and imperfect. Its silences, like the coast of Bagamoyo, or the Malabar – demand multi-genre strategies of writing.

Saba Saba

Its 1 am New York time. I always call mother at this time in Kerala. She lives alone, surrounded by memorabilia from her life in East Africa. Fine bone China and Makonde carvings complement the kitenge wrapped furniture and curtains in her Cochin home. Swahili interspersed with Malayalam structures her vocabulary. I tell her I am arriving 7 July. She says "Ah … Saba Saba … you know Saba Saba? Tanzanian independence day …" chatting merrily into the phone. Whenever a memory or tale from that part of mother's life arises, her face lights up, her voice elated with the unconscious joy her youthful memories evoke in her late octogenarian years. I am startled by mother's Proustian evocation, as it uncannily reinforces my writerly preoccupations with the theme of this section, "Proximity and distance."

Our home was always Tanzanian, for lack of a better term, wherever we were. Dar es Salaam, Doha, Bangalore, Cochin. This slender thread of "Tanzanianess" remained enduring if tenuous. For my parents, being Tanzanian was a placemaking undertaking – of chances taken and lives lived to the fullest. For me, being Tanzanian was a place of childhood and loss – of having walked unfettered through a haven of peace, Dar es Salaam, only to have left as a teenager never returning for reasons that had to do with distance as much as it had to do with painful memories of traumatic leavings. For my American daughter, who has grown up in New York, with a host of digital passwords drawn out of a Swahili vocabulary, Tanzanian city names and lists of East African places to visit one day, Tanzania is a place of the future. A place yet to happen. Through my daughter I have begun to revisit this Tanzanian-ness that continues to percolate my thinking, longing, and now future planning. This Tanzania is an Indian Ocean affect, an aesthetic place of excavation, as much as it is a prospective place of return in a phenomenological sense.

It is that time of year. Summer. Colleagues and friends make plans to travel to research, to vacation. I pack for the long flight to see mother on the Malabar Coast. For most, travelling to Kerala is an adventurous excursion into the Indian Ocean region. Ayurvedic treatments, serene water retreats, and yoga ashrams.

For me, this long haul slowly plays out its drawn-out scenario of the underpinnings of trans-oceanic migration. From East Africa to India to the Middle East to New York, my family's propulsion into modern migrancy embodied all the ambivalences of postcolonial dispersals, along with the optimism of American arrival.

I pack a popup mosquito net as a coming to terms with the reality that I live in the harsh tropics a portion of my life. Clearly, leaving the Indian Ocean was never a simple gesture of severing ties with the old country. This leaving was a series of foldings, or mental ecologies, as Felix Guattari offers (2000). A series of multiplicities that layer into each other, compounding what it means to be of East Africa and India but living in the United States in a state of perpetual engagement with Africa and Asia. This journey is confronting of a different order. It is the assessing of a life that can happen only in the aftermath of the loss of a parent. The effluence that arises is of a particular depth, a raw presence that appears in the absence of the one who has passed. It is an articulation that synthesizes in the wake of a passing. I pack my father's favorite books – two collected volumes of speeches by Julius K. Nyerere, the first President of Tanzania, who was a charismatic public intellectual and formidable orator. Their cover pages torn, the two classic texts have remained an inspiration and constant reminder of my roots in the Indian Ocean.

Cochin

The 21-hour flight from New York to Cochin along with the harsh temperatures alone precipitate a perceptual haziness. The heat, the sweat, the deluge of monsoon rain, the submerged streets from flooding and unmaintained roads, the constant dampness of everything, the persistent stench of mold everywhere during the rainy season, the sheer death-defying effort to cross roads in unforgiving traffic. Despite the chaos, my entire being feels rejuvenated, a certain physiological sensation of well-being immediately envelops my body, wrapping it in a balmy moisturized humid ease. I ease into a sense that I can write, here in Fort Cochin (Kochi). It feels rich and verdant. The rain trees from Brazil canopy the sky and the archipelago sprawls before your eyes – Vypin, Bolgatty, Willingdon Island, Vallarpadam, Ernakulam, and Mattancherry. The hot, fishy smell of the fishing nets along with the clean windswept morning air along Vasco Da Gama Square and the old Fort Manuel seawall reminds one of the layers of history shaping the island city's memories. This to me is the color and visual sense of the Indian Ocean.

I'm here to visit my mother, and to begin the task of unpacking the coastline mnemonically, metaphorically, philosophically. The processes are simultaneous. I wouldn't be in Cochin were it not for my mother. Visiting mother is a process of writing, of inhabiting a certain reality of immigration and unbecoming, of being troubled and immersed in that constant reality of inventing a livable life elsewhere, and painfully forging connectivities around former lifeworlds in the Indian Ocean that are fused into the present. The two tomes of Julius Nyerere in my suitcase remain the anchor against the sharp blue sky and cumulonimbus clouds around me.

Here in Cochin, I am immediately swallowed by the traces of colonialism and the stories of Indian Ocean migration that shaped the Malabar Coast. A string of forts from Kannur (Cannanore), Kochi (Cochin), Thangassery and Attingal along the Malabar Coast, attest to the legacies of Portuguese, Dutch, Arab, Chinese, and British influences. Fort Manuel at Fort Cochin always reminds me of its mirror fort built by the Portuguese in Mombasa much later, Fort Jesus (Joseph 2019). The fifteenth-century Portuguese fort construction's battery walls in Kochi exude that foreboding that is the sentiment that drives me to probe the affective meanings of this place by the Arabian Sea, whose sea-faring histories have so shaped the Indian Ocean littoral (Das Gupta 2004; Malekandathil 2001; Panikkar 2008).

Tanzanianness

Growing up under socialism, school children were prohibited from indulging in identitarianism, ethnic specificity, or sectarianism. The unilateral mood was one of nation building, and the subject of the national project was the socialist, gender neutral citizen, the Ndugu or brother, and eventually, Bibi, or sister. As I now revisit what those early years of decolonial engagement with African citizenship meant, I ask a historically contingent question: what did it mean to be Tanzanian during the first two decades of decolonization? What did Tanzanianness mean for Tanzanian Asians such as myself and my family? We were carving out a political space avant the nomenclature, the political identity, the sociological category of the Tanzanian Asian as citizen subject. Our Tanzanianness was a provisional, precarious, vulnerable political articulation whose legitimacy was constantly under scrutiny, under duress, and the first to be scapegoated. Tanzanian Asians were the expendable community in the project of decolonial reinvention. They were part of the Swahili coast, yet never fully legitimate.

I begin to re-read Nyerere's speeches after nearly forty years:

> 27 May 1958. Sauti Ya Tanu No. 29. We are not afraid of the law.... Colonialism is an intolerable humiliation to us. We shall wage a relentlessly determined battle against it until we are free. We shall use no violence.... We shall not submit to humiliation.
>
> (Nyerere 1968: 59)

I can hear Nyerere's clear passionate voice. I also hear the echoes of one of his influences, M.K. Gandhi.

In one of the earliest unpublished pamphlets written while Nyerere was a student in Edinburgh in the late 1940s, Mwalimu (respected teacher) outlines the rough contours of the colonial landscape in East Africa.

> A world seething in hatred is an intolerable place to live in.... The European official and the European settler rule and maintain their prestige mainly by

hypocrisy, their inner motives would hardly stand examination; the Indian trader makes his living by downright dishonesty or at best by sheer cunning which is hypocrisy; the African clerk or labourer often disregards fulfilling his part of a contract and even a very educated African will pretend to love the European whereas his heart is nearly bursting with envy and hatred....

(Nyerere 1966: 21)

Nyerere's writings in these turbulent anti-colonial 1950s gestures to the real challenges of fighting for sovereignty, independence, and a sense of self, decimated through centuries of colonialism in East Africa. Again, Nyerere:

We appeal to all thinking Europeans and Indians to regard themselves as ordinary citizens of Tanganyika; to preach no Divine Right of Europeans, no Divine Right of Indians and no Divine Right of Africans either. We are all Tanganyikans and we are all East African.

(Nyerere 1966: 29)

This early position of Nyerere's would be reiterated in a speech he gave at the second Conference of Independent African States in June 1960, when Nyerere proposed the notion of a federated East Africa. Formulating a regional identity such as East Africa was highly contentious at the time, coming as it did under the shadow of colonialism and the fight for independence. East Africa was under British rule at the time, and any political theorizing that took away the statist formation of emerging states such as Tanganyika, Kenya and Uganda, was considered suspect. However, for Nyerere, trained in political theory at the University of Edinburgh, the potential for federated states was drawn from instances such as the United States, Canada, and Australia. Nyerere differed from his other East African compatriots fighting for freedom and sovereignty on the future of a federated East Africa. "If we have a chance to bequeath to our children a free and united East Africa, should we treat that chance lightly, or take it seriously as all true patriots should?" Nyerere fully understood the complexities of proposing the idea of a united East Africa but was also wary of perpetuating "the balkanization of East Africa" (Nyerere 1966: 33).

One need only to look at what happened in other parts of Africa and the world to see the truth of this. Separate independence did not help the unity of the subcontinent of India.... The Republic of India is a federation which was brought about at the same time as India achieved her independence. The negative lesson of India and Pakistan I have already mentioned.... The Nigerians wisely and deliberately avoided an India/Pakistan situation.

(Nyerere 1968: 90)

This early articulation of a regional and national identity, at once East African and Tanganyikan, would become anchors of Nyerere's ideological theories, and ones that shaped the atmosphere of public education during the first two decades of independence. What is notable about Julius Nyerere's political strategies of nation building in the precarious early years of postcoloniality, is his understanding of the relationship between landscape, embodiment and inventing a national memory. Fully conscious of the agrarian and rural base of his polity, Nyerere famously applied his pedagogical practice of being a mwalimu, or teacher, to cultivate a lived engagement with nation building. Undoubtedly drawing from the tactile political strategies of Martin Luther King and Mahatma Gandhi, Nyerere adopted an immersive approach to creating placeness in a society decimated by colonial incursion. In his exploration of landscape and memory, the historian Simon Schama writes:

> Historians are supposed to reach the past always through texts, occasionally through images; things that are safely caught in the bell jar of academic convention … but one of my best-loved teachers … always insisted on directly experiencing 'sense of place,' of using 'the archive of the feet.'
>
> (Schama 1995: 25)

Nowhere is this archive of the feet more memorable in postcolonial Africa than in the manner Julius Nyerere used the technique of the long walk to mobilize a sense of Tanzanianness. Nyerere's nod to Gandhi's strategies of non-violence and concept of satyagraha staged through the Salt Satyagraha March from 12 March–6 April 1930 is subtle but present in both Nyerere's public praxis and in his public speeches.

In 1958, Nyerere wrote a memorable document criticizing British colonial officers in the article "Non-violent Methods." One can hear the voices of both Gandhi and Patrice Lumumba in the following excerpt that appeared in *Sauti Ya Tanu* in 1958:

> … we are waging our anti-Imperialism war. Colonialism is an intolerable humiliation to us. We shall … battle … until we are free. We shall use no violence…. We shall not submit to humiliation…. Fellow Africans…. The enemy is losing the cold war…. His only chance is to provoke violence…. Don't be provoked into violence…. The Enemy is bound to lose.
>
> (Nyerere 1966: 59)

This was one year before Tanganyikan independence, and four months after Patrice Lumumba had just been murdered by Mobutu Sese Seko and the C.I.A. in the Congo. Nyerere was tried and convicted for criminal libel because of this article. But the strategies of non-violence and of political praxis through performative acts, such as walking across the state, continued to inform Nyerere's efforts to reach the rural and peasant populations during the first years of the newly independent decolonizing state.

In October 1967, Nyerere undertook a 134-mile walk to Mwanza from Dar es Salaam with rural women, youth, and peasants in support of his manifesto – the Arusha Declaration. This act of walking to invent the idea of socialist belonging, a founding ideology of what it meant to become Tanzanian, left a deep imprint on quotidian daily life in Tanzania. If the Father of the Nation could walk, so could everyone else (Joseph 2013). Nyerere's strategic performance of walking from the metropolitan center to the rural hinterland of the newly independent nation of Tanzania activated a public performance of societal remembering (Connerton 1989). To walk in 1967 was to participate in the historic decolonial act of creating the space of a national possibility, a place of becoming, that walking across the boundaries of the new nation state was pulling together. It was the tactile and sensorial process of producing a new, modern African sensibility, that of "pulling together" as Nyerere called it. Of *Ujamaa*.

I came of age in Nyerere's socialist experiments with *Ujamaa*, of actively inventing a post-independence national identity through walking, marching, dancing (ngomas). It was the space of inventing a new public memory of de-colonial potentialities. This Tanzianness was an emergent structure of feeling in the 1960s (Williams and Orrom 1954. The idea of a Tanzanian identity by the 1970s evoked an emergent national culture with a contentious and cosmopolitan multiplicity incorporating Asian and Arab descent Tanzanians within a decolonizing Indian Ocean imaginary. It was a provisional Tanzanian identity distinctly shaped through Nyerere's political philosophy of cultivating the East African identity he strongly espoused. To be Tanzanian in the 1970s was at once a national and regional identity, at once Tanzanian and East African.

What is distinctive and gets lost within the broader political analyses of African state formations, is that the idea of a Tanzanian identity was uniquely, fundamentally ideological as a socialist utopian project. This notion of a national identity set apart Tanzanian identity formation from neighboring Kenya and Uganda. It also led to a deeper and swifter assimilation of non-nationals, and non-African Tanzanians across the body politic. Swahili was the language of the state, and of communication in public life and education. Race was not the parlance of primary school. Students attending government-run free public schools were all produced as Tanzanians and East Africans during the late 1960s. This national and regional identity was emphatically inculcated in civics classes. *Uhuru na kazi*, independence and work – that was the ascribed grounds for communitas. The emphatic bodily memory of Rousseau's dictum "there is no subjection so perfect as that which keeps the appearance of freedom" very much forged the affective energies of youth life in the late 1960s and early 1970s. Sweeping, marching, planting, self-reliance, were the techniques of socialism. Essentialism was forbidden, sectarianism discouraged in schools, and cultural difference absorbed under the wider rubric of the national socialist project.

Arusha Declaration and socialist belonging

Amidst the maelstrom of revolutionary reinventions unfolding in the Tanzania of the 1960s was what Jacques Ranciere calls the founding narrative of the Festival of Unity. Ranciere's phrase refers to the "new political entity that is at the same time the new object of love, the native land" that emerges in Michelet's *History of the French Revolution.* Ranciere writes "To make possible a history of the age of the masses, one that does not bear on events, we must first speak of that event of a crowd assembled to celebrate the appearance of an incarnated abstraction." (Ranciere 1994) In Dar es Salaam, that abstraction was *The Arusha Declaration* presented by Julius Nyerere at Mnazi Mmoja Park on 5 February 1967.

I have a very intimate relationship to this event of the Arusha Declaration of 1967. My mother was a secondary school teacher at the time. She was at Mnazi Mmoja park with her Form Six students, listening to Nyerere announce the Arusha Declaration. It was an all-day affair that drew students from across Dar es Salaam and involved long hours in Mnazi Mmoja park waiting for the President to arrive. Our 250-square-foot cold water apartment with rats on the

Figure 2.1 Author in Mnazi Mmoja Park, Dar es salaam, 1967.

Image credit: V.L. Joseph.

stairwell faced Mnazi Mmoja park. I grew up with Mother's animated memories of that day listening to Nyerere present the Arusha Declaration and the blueprint for *Ujamaa*. The affective aura of the Arusha Declaration permeated my childhood frolics in the park as Mnazi Mmoja became historic for imagining the new utopian experiment in African modernity. It had the sort of affective power that Washington Square Park has for those who heard Barack Obama give his campaign speech in September 2007 in New York City. Filled with bougainvillea, a serene, green ochre pond with orange fish swimming in it placidly, Mnazi Mmoji embodied the Indian Ocean. Cradled by the sea, it brought the new ideas of modern African citizenship – of socialist becoming and the new ethnicities of Tanzanian identity, into a crucible of foment.

The Arusha Declaration was a policy statement created by Nyerere and his party, outlining a series of legislations that would be implemented to redesign the decolonizing African state into a more viable, sustainable, locally governed state. Its key tenets included the belief that socialism is a way of life whose goal was to build a socialist state where all human beings are equal. A critical aspect was the Africanization of the means of production and exchange away from European and Asian management, to be controlled and owned by peasants through the machinery of the Government and their co-operatives. The ruling party was to be a party of peasants and workers. At least on paper. The range of implementations the Declaration gestured towards included Africanizing all avenues of life including education, business, and economic planning. The impetus for these policy statements stemmed from the oppressive colonial legacies of non-Africans in Tanganyika owning much of the developed infrastructure and real estate of colonial Tanganyika at the time of independence. The challenge to decolonize the pillaged African state led to controversial and uneven policy decisions that dramatically affected non-African Tanzanians by the first decade of post-independence.

Asians being largely mercantile and businesspeople meant that the Arusha Declaration had huge implications for their future in Tanzania. For the commercial and business communities of Asian Tanzanians, the Arusha Declaration meant a drastic realignment of how business and commercial activities would proceed and to what extent Asian Tanzanians could assimilate into the Tanzanian socialist imaginary. For educators like my parents coming from a communist state, Kerala in South India, whose Marxist ideologies and radical socialist projects had generated a broad array of social reforms during their generation, the Tanzanian move towards socialism was less dramatic. My parents were assimilationists, comfortable with the cultural shift towards a Marxist, socialist non-sectarian politics. Mother taught African history and Dad conducted his professional life in Swahili. My entire schooling was in Swahili, with my deskmate being no-one less than Rosemary Nyerere, Nyerere's daughter. Nyerere deliberately sent his children to the most proletarian schools in the nation to prove a point that he was one of the masses. Just a *mwalimu*, or teacher. So much so, he only wished to be addressed as Mwalimu, rather than Sir or Excellency. Schooling under socialism meant classrooms with broken windows. Filthy toilets. Untrained, first generation middle school teachers. First generation students from local communities disempowered by colonialism. The whole nation was an experiment in performing the post-colonial state.

Inauthentic Asians

The question of the role of non-Africans in African citizenship, of Tanzanian citizenship, was foundational in the formation of the new postcolonial African state. It was an Indian Ocean problem. Where did Arab Tanganyikans and Asian Tanganyikans who had been on Swahili shores for centuries, fit in? In "The Principles of Citizenship" speech Nyerere gave as prime minister in 1961, the question as to whether non-Africans can acquire citizenship is raised. (Nyerere 1968). A Citizenship Bill was put forth to the Legislative Council that enabled non-Africans to acquire citizenship by right if they and one of their parents had been born in Tanganyika. Or if they had been registered through other circumstance. In 1961 there was considerable opposition to the bill. "Now, sir, what are we trying to do? We are establishing a citizenship of Tanganyika. What is going to be the basis of this citizenship of Tanganyika?" asked Nyerere at a crowded, rancorous public meeting in Dar es Salaam to a house totally opposed to non-Africans being granted citizenship. "Sir – our own know-nothings, if they got control would say I am sure, that all men are created equal except white people, Indians, Arabs, and Chinamen, who happen to live in Tanganyika" (Nyerere 1968: 126).

Reading this now, 45 years later, pieces of the puzzle begin to fall into place. Father always spoke of the three times he applied for Tanzanian citizenship and was rejected. The first two times the claim was that the application never arrived at the concerned office. The third time was just outright rejection. Buried in the literature on Tanzanian socialism is the suggestion that Asian Tanzanian applications for Tanzanian citizenship were systematically rejected during the 1960s. This has become clearer now. It was surreptitious, ad hoc and rumored during the first decade of independence. Asians were inauthentic African citizens.

In an influential white paper titled "Socialism is not Racialism" the politics of race quickly became embedded in the future of Tanzanian socialism in the form of a negative dialectic. Nyerere was careful to argue against sectarianism, against racialism, against ethnic separatism in the interest of national identity. Yet, even as the argument against race was being made, a delineation of who the inauthentic Tanzanian is, was being articulated. Nyerere notes: "Without ... human equality there can be no socialism.... For it is true that because of our colonial history the vast majority of the capitalist organizations in this country are owned and run by Asians or by Western Europeans" (Nyerere 1968: 258). This challenge of how to fundamentally redistribute the resources of the country in the new postcolonial state, shapes many of the policy statements during this period. Nyerere's caution against dividing up people across race lines in this white paper is prescient for what would unfold in the 1970s.

In yet another of his presidential addresses in 1967, which effectively worked as a policy statement "After the Arusha Declaration," Nyerere explores a number of key issues that would become precipitating issues behind the alienation, marginalization, and eventual eviction of Asian Tanzanians out of East Africa. Given in 1967, the speech begins to raise the tensions between who is a Tanzanian and who can hold positions of corporate power in Tanzania. A key point Nyerere was struggling with was "we do not yet have enough qualified and experienced Tanzanian citizens to do all the jobs which have to be done if the policies we Tanzanians have decided upon are to be implemented" (Nyerere 1968: 385). The second conundrum presented in this key address were the parameters delineating the difference between the citizen, the capitalist citizen and the loyal socialist who might be a trained non-citizen. Nyerere states "… if we are to make progress towards … socialism and self-reliance (we should) get these jobs done instead of indulging our prejudices … of people by skin colour or country of origin" (Nyerere 1968: 385).

By the time anti-Asian sentiments erupted in Kenya and Uganda during the late sixties and early seventies, the tensions that had been carefully avoided by Nyerere through the 1960s became palpable in the Tanzania of the 1970s. The late night worries of my parents of being kicked out of Tanzania still haunt me at times. The winds of anti-Asian sentiment, not unlike the current openly racist ideologies of the US administration's public stance, came to roost in public life. The word "kicked out" captured our experience of leaving Dar es Salaam. The phrase gripped Asian anxiety like a slow decay that swelled and escalated in tension every time one heard of the next Asian acquaintance who had just lost their position on basis of race. It was increasingly an openly accepted sentiment that Asians in Tanzania were not Tanzanian. Neither was there any clear way for Asian Tanzanians to become Tanzanian, regardless of their demonstrated loyalties to the ruling party Tanzanian African National Union (TANU) after 20 years of residency. The public unfolding of socialist ideologies framed in terms of economic nationalism was taking effect alongside the utopian and anti-sectarian ideologies being espoused.

Disinterred

The forced migrations of Asians from East Africa in the mid-1970s was a dispersal that was sensational at the time for its racialized dispersal across the globe (Joseph 1999). It unraveled alongside other global Asian dispersals, such as the genocide refugees of Cambodia and Vietnam, as well as those fleeing famine in Bangladesh. What distinguished the Asian migration out of East Africa was its racially charged staging of the emerging post-war scenario of South–South migrancies and immigrant African citizenship. Most South Asians forced out of East Africa in the 1970s moved to other Western nations, other African states, and for a small demographic, a return to India. Specifically, the city of Bangalore which became an informal *Dar al Islam* or abode of peace – for expatriates and refugees returning to India after a lifetime abroad. 1970s

Bangalore became a tactile East African outpost with Indians from Kenya, Uganda, and Tanzania, such as my family, setting up businesses and building homes in the garden city. A prominent shopping center Shrungar Shopping setting along Mahatama Gandhi Road had a couple of businesses in the mid-1970s, whose proprietors spoke Swahili amongst themselves. Kids like me sang Swahili songs, inspired by Miriam Mackeba, at high school. Ngomas were created at school and college festivals as part of the multicultural fabric generated by African Indians assimilating into the Bangalore milieu. The East African diaspora in Bangalore were a small but distinctive community. Their homes displayed Makonde sculptures, kitenge and kangas for décor, and the music of OssiBisa and Santana, demarcating their African roots vis a vis their new Bangalore life. Wearing safari suits and kitenge designs were particularly striking at the time. It was a chaotic, melancholic, confusing era where the memory of place and the place of memory melded in an Indian Ocean aesthetic that was experiential and informal, but distinctive.

In 1999, a few months before Nyerere passed away, I had the extraordinary chance to see him one more time at the Juan Carlos Center in New York University. He was giving a talk. The strange experience of seeing Nyerere in Manhattan, a place he had rallied against when I was growing up, "we are not in Manhattan" – was poignant. The Indian Ocean past came flooding back. I walked up to Nyerere and told him that I had written a book about him and that I had been his daughter's classmate. Nyerere flashed his famous bright smile. He looked clearly at me and wryly said, "I hope you said some good things about me." Less than a year later, Nyerere was gone. I thought of the two beautiful white ostriches Nyerere kept at the State House in the 1960s. Father would drive us on Sunday afternoons to watch the ostrich elegantly stroll around the grounds. They stood for everything Nyerere need – no heads in the sand, contrary to the adage, they strutted about heads high, curious, arrogant, sharp eyed. I had many good things to say about *Ujamaa* and Nyerere, and if it smacked of Nyerere-ism, it is because history had made it impossible to invent such a potentiality at any other point in Tanzanian history.

The unimaginable scenario, as I try to write this chapter on the Indian Ocean, raises for me the tragic inconsequentiality of migrancy in the Indian Ocean. That peculiar refusal to be anchored down to a place, the hardheaded drive of ambition to keep seeking a better life elsewhere, leading to the eventual reality of belonging nowhere. Writing memory is a practice of making place in the process of placelessness. In the space of migrancy and displacement, writing occupies the weight of presence. It is a vehicle for transacting between the archive and fabulation. Between the policy statements of Julius Nyerere's era and the memories of placelessness produced by historical events.

Writing the self back into forgotten histories, recovering the shards of political imaginaries that lie behind the tenuous reasons why people move across borders, nations, seas, brings agency back into a history of the displaced and the disappeared. It activates a revisiting of the first decades of Tanzanian decolonization in the event of the death of my father. Julius Nyerere's notions of quotidian life and sense of place in the form of *Ujamaa*, shaped the realities of my family. Such meta-narratives of placemaking intersect with the history of displacements and the resulting sense of placelessness that captures the micro-histories of the Indian Ocean. The Indian Ocean foregrounds the intersectionalities between micro-histories, personal histories and the meta-histories associated with placelessness. Across the ecumenical spaces of the Indian Ocean float worlds of disarticulated selves. Forgotten decolonial aspirations. An Indian Ocean methodology entails an experimental interrogation of people, place, and loss. Its form is remembrance.

References

Agamben, Giorgio. 1999. *Potentialities: Collected Essays in Philosophy*. Stanford, CA: Stanford University Press.

Das Gupta, Ashin. 2004. *India and the Indian Ocean World: Trade and Politics*. Delhi: Oxford University Press.

Connerton, Paul. 1989. *How Societies Remember*. Cambridge: Cambridge University Press.

Guattari, Felix. 2000. *The Three Ecologies*. London: Bloomsbury Press.

Gupta, Pamila. 2018. *Portuguese Decolonization in the Indian Ocean World: History and Ethnography*. London: Bloomsbury Press.

Hall, Stuart. 1996. "New Ethnicities." In *Stuart Hall: Critical Dialogues in Cultural Studies*. Ed. David Morley and Kuon-Hsing Chen. New York: Routledge.

Hofmeyr, Isabelle. 2010. "Africa as a Fault Line in the Indian Ocean" in Eds. Pamila Gupta, Isabel Hofmeyr and Michael Pearson, *Eyes Across the Water: Navigating the Indian Ocean*. Pretoria: University of South Africa Press.

Jeychandran, Neelima. 2016. "Marginalized Narratives: Memory Work at African Shrines in Kochi, India." In Eds. Maria Starzmann and John Roby, *Excavating Memory: Sites of Remembering and Forgetting*. Gainesville: University Press of Florida.

Joseph, May. 1999. *Nomadic Identities: The Performance of Citizenship*. Minneapolis: University of Minnesota Press.

Joseph, May. 2013. *Fluid New York: Cosmopolitan Urbanism and the Green Imagination*. Durham: Duke University Press.

Joseph, May. 2019. *Sea Log: Indian Ocean to New York*. London: Routledge.

Kakar, Sudhir. 1996. *The Colors of Violence: Cultural Identities, Religion, and Conflict*. Chicago: University of Chicago Press.

Levinas, Emmanuel. 1987. *Time and The Other*. Translation by Richard A. Cohen. Pittsburgh: Duquesne University Press.

Malekandathil, Pius. 2001. *Portuguese Cochin and the Maritime Trade of India, 1500–1663*. Delhi: Manohar.

Ng'weno, Bettina. 2018. "Growing Old in a New City: Time, the Post-Colony and Making Nairobi Home," *City:* 22(1): 26–42.

Nyerere, Julius K. 1966. *Freedom and Unity/Uhuru na Umoja: Selection from Writings and Speeches 1952–65*. Dar es Salaam: Oxford University Press.

Nyerere, Julius. 1968. *Ujamaa: Essays on Socialism*. Dar es Salaam: Oxford University Press.

Panikkar, K.M. 2008. *Asia and Western Dominance: A Survey of the Vasco Da Gama Epoch of Asian History, 1498–1945*. ACLS History E Book Project.

Ranciere, Jacques. 1994. *The Names of History*. Minneapolis: University of Minnesota Press.

Rothberg, Michael. 2009. *Multidirectional Memory: Remembering the Holocaust in the Age of Decolonization*. Stanford, CA: Stanford University Press.

Schama, Simon. 1995. "Prologue." In *Landscape and Memory*. New York: Vintage Books.

Srinivas, Smriti. 2008. *In the Presence of Sai Baba*. Leiden and Boston: Brill.

Williams, Raymond and Michael Orrom. 1954. *Preface to Film*. Ann Arbor: University of Michigan Press.

3 The littoral, the container, and the interface

Situating the dry port as an Indian Ocean imaginary

Ishani Saraf

Introduction: between limits and possibilities

This chapter draws attention to a particular kind of infrastructural site – a "dry port," and explores the transformatory potential in situating it in the Indian Ocean and in studies of the Indian Ocean. A dry port, as the term indicates, functions like a port but is located inland. This combination of location and function is significant, creating the possibility of imagining a port without a coast. I trace some of the effects this shift holds in re-imagining Indian Ocean worlds, worlds that have in one way or another been tied to a notion of the *littoral*.

The chapter emerges at the convergence of two areas of investigation raised by the organizers of the Reimagining Indian Ocean Worlds Mellon Research Initiative (2014–2019) at the University of California, Davis.[1] The first, a central question of the Initiative, was how to conceive of the "limits" of the Indian Ocean. Reading fictional and non-fictional approaches and accounts of the Indian Ocean through various disciplines, we followed the material, conceptual, and theoretical morphing of the Indian Ocean, into various objects, points of view, interventions, and claims. It emerged that the Indian Ocean was performed, narrated, and related in several ways, making its limits contingent and shifting. The second matter of concern was an exploration of contemporary theoretical possibilities from the standpoint of the Indian Ocean. What knowledge is produced when one is situated in the Indian Ocean? Does this knowledge become relevant only "in context" of the Indian Ocean and so is required to be qualified as such? How do we locate its theoretical contributions, especially if the Indian Ocean can be performed in multiple ways, and its limits are at least blurry and contingent, and at most non-existent? Keeping these two matters of concern in tension with each other, and in conversation with them, I draw on the site of the dry port, a site that emerges at the intersection of various processes, both local and translocal, to understand its implications for contemporary formulations of Indian Ocean worlds.[2]

I "arrived" at the dry port through my interactions with a transnational scrap trader whom I call Mr. Kamal. I met Mr. Kamal through personal connections while conducting fieldwork in one of Asia's large metal scrap and parts markets, which is located in Delhi. In the market, I studied the everyday value-making practices of those who transformed and traded industrial and automotive metallic discards. While some traders in the market did import metal scrap into their shops, Mr. Kamal claimed that he was not as such interested in or involved in "local" (that is, trade within the city or the nation) scrap trade: "one has their own domain of interest," he remarked, when I asked him about whether he was at all connected to the scrap market. Through a company based in Dubai, UAE, Mr. Kamal instead sourced metal scrap from Luanda, Angola and its surrounds, for clients whose factories were placed in the manufacturing zones around Delhi, India. Mr. Kamal's transnational trade in metal scrap illustrated a markedly different (though not necessarily separate) circuit of the circulation and transformation of metal scrap commodities than the market. I was particularly interested in what motivated Mr. Kamal to source metal scrap from Angola to India, and the large scale logistical and procedural infrastructures he mobilized to make this possible. Mr. Kamal narrated to me how it was chiefly the aftermath of Angola's civil war that made the country a resource for him. The country's "destroyed infrastructures" provided a continued source of metal scrap for him to import into India. Describing the imperial logics of an unanticipated form of resource extraction, he claimed that he engaged in a "mutually beneficial" relation with the country, offering a "clean-up" as he recovered resources.[3] In this transnational circuit, the dry port emerged as the site through which scrap metal imports entered the city. "That's easy," he remarked, when I asked him about how he brought scrap so far inland into Delhi. "It comes through the dry port. The shipping company brings it all the way in, and I don't have to worry about it." As scrap entered the city through the dry port, the dry port emerged as a node and a spatial site that placed this particular modality of scrap metal trade within the city's environs, bringing into proximity the places and routes that gathered around the transformation and transport of scrap metal from place to place.[4] It reconfigured, the landlocked city of Delhi, drawing new connections and logics in relation to the ocean.

To situate the dry port in the Indian Ocean, I first discuss the notion of the "littoral" and its relevance for the conceptualization and location of the Indian Ocean in particular studies of the Indian Ocean. I then explore the logics and processes that generate the novel site of the dry port, chiefly through a discussion of the operation of containerization and how it equates land and sea in the domain of transport. This equivalence, I argue, makes it possible to reconfigure notions of the littoral. By drawing on and exploring the site of the dry port, I then explore what this holds for the possibilities of re-imagining Indian Ocean worlds.

Figuring the littoral: land, ocean, port, city

Recent scholarly explorations of Indian Ocean worlds have emphasized the nature and characteristics of the ocean and the oceanic to generate novel ways of conceptualizing area or region-based research. What emerges is an attention to particular material characteristics of water as different from land, to lend conceptual weight to new ways of approaching the Indian Ocean as an *oceanic* region. Further, contrast between land and sea has given rise to creative ways of imagining their meeting, their interface – explored through notions of the littoral. In this section, I consider three texts concerned directly with this approach. The works of Michael Pearson (2003), Shanti Moorthy and Ashraf Jamal (2010), and Edward Alpers (2013) all make a distinction between the materiality of land and sea and provide varying conceptualizations of the littoral and the significance of the littoral in drawing the limits of the Indian Ocean. In bringing together and juxtaposing these perspectives, I set up a field that is generated through the dialogue between them, to demonstrate how drawing attention to the dry port extends the limits of the Indian Ocean by extending the notion of the littoral.

For Pearson, an oceanic history must shift its gaze from the land and "look from the sea to the land, and most obviously to the coast" (Pearson 2003: 5). He argues for an "amphibious history" of the ocean that is able to navigate both land and sea and that is rooted in the "deep structure" of the ocean, including the topography of the ocean, the monsoons, ocean currents, tidal waves, as well as the nature and interactions that occurred on the ocean and its surrounding littoral. He uses the notion of the "ressac," where waves fold upon themselves as they move into and onto land, to describe the relation between sea and land. At the interface between sea and land itself is movement, ambiguity, and the merging of boundaries.

He raises the significant question of how long inland one may go until one would find that the ocean ceases to have any influence on the lives and livelihoods of people, and calls for taking seriously the "fuzziness," "complexity," and "heterogeneity" of oceanic linkages and effects. Pearson points out the presence and intersections of both land routes and sea routes that may emerge through similar or dissimilar political and economic processes, and which may compete or remain separate. However, it is the times that they intersect that become relevant for him: for instance, the contemporary networks of routes developed between railways and container ships. In a way, Pearson's discussion of these routes anticipates the challenge posed by the railways and container ships to the distinction between land and ocean, and the transformation of the notion of the littoral. Still, in searching for a specific idea of the littoral as well as what an ideal "maritime society" might look like, Pearson marks out the distinction between the "port city" and cities that have ports, the former city being one that grows organically around a port (Pearson 2003: 31).

He argues that while all cities have their "umland" and "hinterland," port cities are characterized by also having a "foreland." Here umland is described as "an area which is culturally, economically, and politically related to a particular town and city," often providing food to the city, and acting as a "transitional" between the city and the "pure countryside." The hinterland extends inland from the port city and "begins at the end of the umland." It receives the imports of the port city and contributes to its exports. The foreland is described as the "area of the overseas world with which the port is linked through shipping, trade, and passenger traffic ... separated from the port city by maritime space" (Pearson 2003: 31).

This makes port cities special as they are connected to places that are very far away. Pearson argues, "ports are inclusive, cosmopolitan, while the inland is much less varied, much more exclusive, single faceted rather than diverse" (Pearson 2003: 32). Pearson points to many ports that were and are located and flourished on the banks of rivers, and not just the ocean, pointing out that the relation between a port, the sea, and inland are contingent and complex. However, Pearson argues that "port cities by definition are located on water, whether it be a river, a lake, an estuary, a delta, a harbor or an open coast" (Pearson 2003: 37).

Moorthy and Jamal (2010) focus on the "flux" and "circulation" of the Indian Ocean that make it into a space of "exchange" and "encounter." For them, the Indian Ocean is a space that should be studied in its own right, rather than being seen as an intermediate region between two landmasses or areas. Therefore, rather than seeing the ocean as a border, frontier, or crossing for and between landmasses, they seek to move the structural location of the ocean from the margins to the center. At the same time, they move away from the desire to conceptualize the Indian Ocean as an "alternative to hegemonic northern globalization" (Moorthy and Jamal 2010: 6). Instead, taking on conceptual markers offered by the oceanic, they focus on "movement," "heterogeneity," and "hybridity," while embedding the Indian Ocean in global processes.

In their quest to "humanize" the ocean, not only do they seek to focus on particular social processes that create worlds, but they also point to the "amphibious" nature of humans and the possibility of ocean worlds within them. This orientation to the composition of the human body becomes fundamental for them to posit "the pliability and looseness of the connection" that their edited volume seeks to constitute as the study of the Indian Ocean, one which following and citing Pearson's discussion on the littoral, takes into account the "permeability" and porosity of land and water. Moorthy and Jamal's extension of the littoral to "amphibious" sites like the human body opens up the notion of the limits of the Indian Ocean to various sites and scales. Their extension of Pearson's notion of the littoral is instructive in imagining the littoral as mobile and multi-scalar to address the concerns he outlines.

In delineating the region of the Indian Ocean, Alpers differentiates the oceanic from the landmass, arguing that "oceanic boundaries are, literally, more fluid" (Alpers 2013: 1). The ocean, he argues, cannot conceptually work as a simple substitute for land and is different from land because unlike land it does not have clear-cut boundaries. Studying the ocean would thus require one to change one's orientation significantly. Alpers points to particular material "elements" of the ocean – fish, salt, currents, winds, and the coastlines it may share, as well as the movement of people on it in particular kinds of boats, that combine in specific ways to produce the Indian Ocean through time. He lays special emphasis on the idea of the "littoral," the coastlines that skirt the ocean, "to ensure that only those areas of the surrounding land masses that are effectively connected to the Indian Ocean world are included in its history" (Alpers 2013: 10). In service of that, Alpers too engages with the umland, hinterland, and foreland to describe the interfacing of land and sea through the notion of the littoral. In that regard, Alpers argues that while the umland could be said to be relatively stable and depended on the size of the coastal community, the foreland and hinterland could be viewed as "elastic" entities, depending on the circulation of goods (Alpers 2013: 10). In dealing with questions of the boundaries of the Indian Ocean, he describes how the space, cartography, and imagination of the Indian Ocean have changed not only through time, but also from the perspective of where one is situated in, or in reference to, the Indian Ocean.

In all three approaches, significance is given to the distinction between ocean and land, to the properties of the oceanic contra land, and how these properties may stand in for the kinds of knowledge generated about the Indian Ocean. These draw attention to the meeting place and boundary, or the interface, between land and water. For Pearson (2003), the study of the Indian Ocean requires an understanding of its boundaries from the perspective of a gaze that is situated in the ocean from which it turns to land. This makes central for him the interface between land and water and the dynamics between the two. This interface is ambiguous and diverse with the merging of land and sea, and gives rise to two kinds of problematics, one around the conceptualization of the littoral, and the other related to the influence of and relations between the littoral and what is further inland. These points of concern take him on an exploration of coastal and maritime communities and social lives. In these explorations, the "port city," which is located on water, emerges as one of the exemplary points of reference for the study of the Indian Ocean. Alpers (2013) similarly employs the fluid nature of the ocean to argue for the fluidity of oceanic boundaries. However, he decenters the notion of the gaze from the ocean, arguing that the Indian Ocean is different depending on where one may gaze at it, claiming that both "the reality and the idea of the Indian Ocean have changed over time" (Alpers 2013: 6). Alpers still maintains the significance of the littoral as being "effectively connected" to the ocean, elaborating on the categories of umland, foreland, and hinterland used by Pearson to make the latter two more "elastic". In their engagement with Pearson's notion of the littoral, Moorthy and Jamal (2010) take Pearson's notion of the amphibious further to the physical composition of both humans and oceans constituting the interface itself between land and water as mobile and porous. Therefore, their mission to "humanize the ocean" provides startlingly open possibilities for reimagining Indian Ocean worlds by transforming the littoral figuratively and indefinitely. In the following section, I look to another way the notion of the littoral may be transformed, this time through the process of containerization. By making land and water equivalent in and through the operation of intermodal transportation, I explore how containerization displaces the question of the location of the interface between sea and land from a spatial one to an operational one.

The container

Pearson's (2003) text traces the fate of port cities as entwined with the development of shipping technologies. He outlines the emergence of container ships and the very significant changes that brought to both how goods circulated and the existence of port cities in general. He argues that "ports around the Indian Ocean rose and fell according to how quickly they provided the facilities needed for container traffic" (Pearson 2003: 262). According to him, Mombasa, Columbo, Mumbai, and Singapore expanded significantly to accommodate container traffic, which required infrastructure for intermodal transport. Other ports could not. Pearson thus argues for the gradual demise of "the 'traditional' Indian Ocean port city" (Pearson 2003: 263). In many ways, the port city has been a central feature of Indian Ocean studies – the space of hybrid languages, the coming together of various people from different communities that brought along with them different material-symbolic artefacts, and the fabled "cosmopolitanism" of the littoral. This changed with the coming of the container and its operations. According to Pearson, the mechanization of the loading and unloading of containers resulted in the mass elimination of loading and unloading jobs, and along with the elimination of its large work force, some of the strongholds of trade unions. He adds that, with the speed of travel of container ships, the crystallization of nation-states, and immigration restrictions around the Indian Ocean, the dense circulation and mixing of traders and workers that was characteristic of Indian Ocean port cities declined significantly, making port cities into cities with mere "port functions" attached to them.

The container, Alexander Klose (2015) points out, becomes the means through which intermodal transport is made possible: a detachable and attachable container can be moved across ships, railways, trucks, and so forth, and can move through all kinds of spaces. In this regard, Klose contends that the container is the contemporary "symbol of globalization" (Klose 2009: ix). Klose argues that it is not just the ubiquitous dispersal of containers in all parts of the world that make them thus, but also the fact that they are "modular spaces" and in a sense a material embodiment of a fundamental organizing principle of contemporary life and logistical structure. In attaching itself to all kinds of transport, the container "changes the entire system" of transport, by uniting "the various modes of transport on land and water into a chain" (Klose 2009: 47). More than that, he argues that the container along with its logistical structure transforms the relation between land and sea in fundamental ways as other technologies have also done in the past. For instance, the steamship became an "extension" of the railways transforming the sea into being land-like and dry. The steamship, "transformed the sea into a "system of highways" for the worldwide circulation of goods" (Klose 2009: 95). It became a "smooth surface." With containerization, Klose argues that an additional simultaneous effect of the "liquefaction of land" also takes place, through which flows of "global currents" pass. The simultaneous changing in state of sea and land, Klose argues, "levels the difference between sea and land transport.... Whether one sees the seagoing container lines as extended land routes in a liquid element or surface routes as intracontinental channels between the world's oceans ultimately becomes a matter of per-spective" (2009: 103).

In Klose's narrative, there are two significant points for thinking about the relation between land and sea, their interface, the littoral, and the port city. First, certain processes can remake or reorganize the material effects of land and sea. With containerization, there emerges for particular functions and oper-ations, namely for the transporting of the shipping container, no effective distinction between the material properties of land and water. Second, this lack of distinction between land and water may well be circumscribed by particular functions, in this case transport, and may only be enacted through specific pro-cedures, such as when containers are unloaded from ships and stacked and then loaded onto railways or trucks a few hours later. It does not mean that the rela-tion between land and water is forever changed. Rather, we find that the relation between land and sea becomes contingent upon particular operations and oper-ators, and that the relations have a temporal rather than fixed nature. This suggests that the distinction between the territorial and the oceanic cannot be assumed prior to what is being studied. The distinction (or not) is contingent and emerges through particular kinds of operations.

Thus, if a particular operation or set of operations enables it, the conceptual and physical limits of the Indian Ocean may be expanded or contracted indefin-itely. Further, the suspension of the taken-for-granted distinction between sea and land and their material characteristics makes the interface between the two, if relevant, equally contingent and emergent, requiring further exploration.[5] My argument here is that the littoral, as a privileged site in Indian Ocean studies, can be destabilized in favor of studying particular operations, operators, and inter-faces reconstituting limits and sites of Indian Ocean worlds.

Some examples from studies of the Indian Ocean may help illustrate this destabilization. Haripriya Rangan and Christian Kull's (2010) article begins in the Australian Outback and discusses the presence of the non-native plant *Acacia farnesiana* which was much in abundance before the year 1788, when the first British colony was founded. Rangan and Kull argue that the presence of this non-native species in the Outback makes it possible to critique the notion of the Australian interior as being isolated from the world until 1788 and re-imagine its history as one entwined with oceanic histories of other regions. Stephen Rockel (2014) describes how trade routes, migration, and labor cultures produced a continuity between inland caravan trade in eastern and central Africa and maritime trade on the East African coast. He outlines the various sites and circumstances in which people circulating along these routes encountered each other, finding employment and, also, generating particular modes of sociality and practices. Amitav Ghosh (2010) and Michael Pearson (2010) respectively provide fascinating accounts of languages emerging from the dense circulation of people in the context of working on the ship (Ghosh 2010); and various insti-tutions of cultural brokerage and practices of translation (Pearson 2010) that emerged around circuits of travel. Here, language practices can be seen as emerging from processes of circulation and becoming operators of transactions in their own way. More recently Fahad Bishara's account (2017) shows how the technology of the *waraqa* or deeds that are created with the taking on of debt, spread from Oman not only along the East African coast but also further inland, as well as to other places along the Indian Ocean, bringing with them specific institutions of property, moral notions of obligation, and legal infrastructure. The *waraqas* may be viewed as providing an interface that Bishara calls "connective tissue" that "brought the land to the sea, endowing property and rents with the ability to circulate around the Indian Ocean" (Bishara 2017: 20).

In similar ways, other operations, institutions, and mediations may be identified and imagined, that create particular interfaces[6] between land and sea, or just across different regions and spaces through historical and contemporary explorations of Indian Ocean worlds. For instance, different forms of organizing labor; the production, consumption, and circulation of particular commodities; the travel of religious and political ideas; languages; domestic and kinship relations and their extensions through space and time; maritime and navigation technologies and material cultures; as well as routes and circuits of settlements, both inland and on the shore, could be described as processes and operations in their own right that carve out spaces of continuity which may run through and across sea and land, that construct the relations between them in contingent and particular ways, and that create novel kinds of interfacial entities that bring together, separate, and condition worlds around them.

The dry port

In what follows, I discuss how the operation of containerization and the levelling of the difference between sea and land transport directs attention to a specific spatial entity: the dry port. Situated far inland, and connected to various other ports, both inland and coastal, the dry port takes on significance as part of a network of ports that may traverse a region whether on sea or land. In the light of the demise of the port city as told by Pearson (Pearson 2003), and the mushrooming of dry ports across vast territories, how may we take these together to think through notions of the limits of the Indian Ocean? Further, what kinds of spaces can we imagine when ports are sited on land, inland, and far away from any body of water, in such a way that their proximity to a body of water becomes possibly insignificant?

The dry port as a physical and spatial entity and institution emerges as a result of containerization. According to a United Nations Economic and Social Commission for Asia and the Pacific (UNESCAP) report (2015), "a dry port of international importance refers to an inland location as a logistics centre connected to one or more modes of transport for the handling, storage and regulatory inspection of goods moving in international trade and the execution of applicable customs control and formalities" (UNESCAP 2015: 4). The report states that the functions of the dry port include "customs and other border crossing formalities for traded cargo and to transfer this cargo between the different modes used for transportation between a port origin and an ultimate inland destination, or vice versa" (UNESCAP 2015: 5). According to the same report, an Internal Container Depot or ICD generally handles only containers and container cargo and may often be used interchangeably with the term dry port. In this piece, I will use the term "ICD" to refer to a particular dry port and the term "dry port" when addressing it as a general or conceptual site.

A large network of dry ports exists around Delhi and the northern Indian manufacturing belt. Due to its proximity to factories in the surrounding areas, Mr. Kamal, whom I cited at the beginning of this chapter, imported his scrap shipments to a large and well-connected ICD in Dadri, located in the National Capital Region[7] of India, in the state of Uttar Pradesh. Dadri makes up part of the Gautam Buddha Nagar district created in 1997 and which is described as "one of the largest industrial township[s] of the country" (Directorate 2011: 58). A container could be easily transported right from the ICD to the factories and mills in the surrounding areas by road. Mr. Kamal explained to me how this convenience made it very easy for him to source his materials in Luanda and have it delivered very close to his clients who used the materials to manufacture products.

It took me almost two hours to reach the ICD on road from Delhi, where I was conducting ethnographic fieldwork. I began my journey in a car from north Delhi, and traveled eastward through towns, villages, and other areas that I could not quite characterize, that consisted of high-rise buildings under construction on both sides of the road. These were stretches of spaces that seemed almost unoccupied except by those who were building them and were sometimes dotted by small pockets of agricultural fields. The roads through all these places were big and wide and bordered with the characteristic red soil of the area. At some point the pockets of fields started increasing and turning into a road that was lined with small shops, the boundary line of the ICD became visible, with containers neatly stacked along it.

The ICD in Dadri became functional in 2004 and is managed by the Container Corporation of India (CONCOR), a public sector company and subsidiary of the Indian Railways that is in charge of inland rail transportation of containers (UNESCAP 2015: 24). CONCOR provides an array of container handling, storage, and transportation services and currently handles the largest network of dry ports in the country (CONCOR website). At the time of my visit in 2017, CONCOR had entered into "joint ventures" with other private freight and cargo companies that were also allotted space in the area of the ICD.[8] Built on land belonging to the railways, the ICD was spread over a huge area and comprised of a complex built around railway tracks. The space around the tracks made up the loading and unloading zones. Containers would arrive throughout the day and night. Besides there being loading, unloading, and storage facilities, other processes like custom clearance for imports and exports were also carried out at the ICD in its office complex. From the ICD, containers or goods could be transported further via trucks, trailers, or rail. Trucks and trailers could be seen parked along the wide roads inside the ICD.

At the railway tracks, I met an onsite engineer who was busy repairing a Reach Stacker – a machine that can lift, transport, and stack containers. On one side stood neat lines of containers. Off to another side, an old container stood that had been fitted so that people could rest in it. Next to it stood three other containers equipped with temperature control units for the storage of perishable goods. Showing me how containers are unloaded, he explained many aspects of the complex logistics of the ICD and informed me that its functions would keep expanding in the next few years. He suggested that over the years, the ICD would become an even stronger node in the transport and logistics network that would link coastal and inland ports to airports for the circulation of commodities. The various functions of the ICD that coordinate the timely circulation of goods that come from a vast number of places and go further into an equally if not more varied set of places, makes it a site that primarily negotiates proximity and distance, and embodies these in its operations.

A few minutes away from where we stood, at the boundary of the loading and unloading area, was a shrine. The engineer told me about the strange incidents that had resulted in its continued existence on the grounds of the ICD. While the ICD was in the process of being developed, the shrine was scheduled to be demolished. But whenever bulldozers would come close to the shrine, they would stop working. Currently, it stood in a quiet corner under the shade of a tree, a simple tiled structure with a cement dome-shaped roof. Closed in on three sides, the fourth side had an opening the size of a door and worked as an entrance. The walls of the shrine, both outside and inside were tiled. On the outside walls were four tiles with imagery of Hindu goddesses and auspicious symbols. Along the entrance were also pieces of marble (or a similar stone) shaped like inverted "Vs." These had marigold garlands placed on them. Inside, the main object of veneration was surrounded by more tiled images and icons of Hindu deities. Placed directly across the entrance on a raised tiled surface stood another stone inverted "V." Under it was a lit *diya* or lamp. Upon asking people worshipping at the shrine, I was told that this shrine was of "ICD Baba."

ICD Baba's devotees were varied, including transporters and truck drivers who came frequently to the ICD from different parts of the country, as well as villagers from the surrounding area. A transporter who I spoke to had just finished conducting a ritual at the shrine's premises. His business was in trouble and he hoped that ICD Baba's blessings would effect a turnaround. The villagers from the surrounding areas, I was told, would congregate at the shrine once a year during the festival of Holi. Nested within simultaneous and disparate spatialities and temporalities of operations: of containerization, urban expansion, multi-scalar economies, and local religious practices, ICD Baba and his shrine emerge as novel mediating interfaces. Negotiating proximity and distance and relations between the site of the ICD and the multiple and overlapping local and translocal territories it is located in, ICD Baba and his shrine assembled new social worlds around the infrastructural site of the dry port, incorporating it into the surrounding (trans)local landscape.[9]

Figure 3.1 A view from ICD Baba's shrine.
Image Credit: Ishani Saraf.

Conclusion: contemporary Indian Ocean worlds

A map of CONCOR's various dry ports and terminals found on their website gives a sense of the extensive coverage of the network of ports across Indian territory and, through logistical connections, beyond it. If we are to take Klose's contention that the container is the master sign of globalization, and Pearson's contention that the Indian Ocean may be "studied in and of itself, until roughly the end of the eighteenth century" (Pearson 2003: 287) after which its discreteness becomes suspect due to "external" influences, this map would suggest that these port spaces, both coastal and inland, are over-run by the spatio-temporal ordering of the forces of "globalization," or "zones and corridors of [the container system's] own temporal-spatial organization" (Klose 2015: 58). Klose, however, contends that these zones and corridors can move through spaces where "wholly different principles can assert themselves" at the edges of these corridors (Klose 2015: 58), therefore suggesting the uneven influence of these forces. In this regard, Moorthy and Jamal argue that the Indian Ocean must be approached as being "embedded in the global" (Moorthy and Jamal 2010: 4), taking into account the simultaneity of scales of the Indian Ocean. By shifting attention to operations rather than spatial units, one hopes to further take into account the multiple and constantly changing (trans)local worlds of the Indian Ocean.

Thus, by linking sea and land transport,[10] the container invites the Indian Ocean inland by thousands of kilometers, to the dry port. The emergence of a network of ports along the coast as well as inland redefines the littoral in the Indian Ocean region and Indian Ocean studies, suggesting a transformation of its limits rather than the demise of Indian Ocean worlds. The imperial imagination of China's Belt and Road Initiative, bringing together two massive infrastructural projects called the "Silk Road Economic Belt" and the "Maritime Silk Road" (Johnston 2019) is one, though not only, possible mode of this transformation. The names of the project are themselves revealing for the transformation of the notion of the littoral. For Indian Ocean studies, it suggests that attention must focus on region-making processes and operations, whatever their scale may be, in re-calibrating and re-imagining the scales and boundaries of Indian Ocean worlds.

Rather than view these emergences as a simple narrative of change as a result of the forces of "globalization," situating the dry port in the Indian Ocean means that one has to take into account a plurality of operations to re-imagine Indian Ocean worlds in contemporary times. This plurality of workings may emerge as a result of disparate elements or as concerted force, they may have effects at odds with each other or in tandem, and the duration of these effects too could be varied. Among this plurality of operations, what is the significance of the place of origin of these various disparate elements? What are we to make of Pearson's claim that the Indian Ocean only remains discrete until the end of the eighteenth century after which, due to "external" influences, we may study history *in* the Indian Ocean rather than the history *of* the Indian Ocean? What notions of proximity and distance, inside and outside, make these claims of unity possible? In this regard, Prestholdt's notion of the interfacial constitution and patchwork nature of the Indian Ocean are well taken as are the motivations of "basin consciousness" (Prestholdt, this volume). At the same time, the motivations of identifying the place of origin of various disparate elements suggest particular modalities of narrative and historiography and particular relations of the particular to the universal[11] and the global and the local.

Considering the dry port as part of the Indian Ocean is not to present cases of "competing universalisms" (Hofmeyer 2010), nor to propose an "alternative mode of being in the world that has always been" (Moorthy and Jamal 2010: 4), but rather to think about the plurality and coevality of forces that shape the contemporaneous worlds of the Indian Ocean. Rather than framing the Indian Ocean as the particular to the universal of globalization, or as area to theory, the hope is to disaggregate these unities and discern the ways in which particular operations create formations that require new approaches to locate, imagine, and study them.

Notes

1 I thank the "Reimagining Indian Ocean Worlds" Mellon Research Initiative for funding the research for and writing of this chapter. Thank you to Bettina Ng'weno, Neelima Jeychandran, Smriti Srinivas, and William F. Stafford Jr. for reading drafts of this essay, and my colleagues at the Initiative for engaging with multiple and different versions of this essay.

2 The emphasis on the plural "worlds" in conceptualizing the Indian Ocean is relevant here as demonstrated also by other chapters in this volume.

3 In 2016, Angola banned the export of metal scrap, leading Mr. Kamal to re-organize his business ventures.

4 This approach was inspired by Bettina Ng'weno's description of wooden boats in Gwadar and questioning how far away the nearest trees would have been for these to be built. Similar issues are raised temporally of the city (Ng'weno 2018).

5 See note 6.

6 It is interesting that the notion of the fold or folding have since been used in reimagining interfaces and frontiers on both sea and land. For example, Lindsay Bremner's notion of the "folded ocean" (2014) and Franck Bille's notion of "skinworlds" (2017) both work productively to expand on the spatiality of the interface itself, whether it be on land or water or between the two. In conjunction with Prestholdt's (this volume) description of the various interfaces at work in the Indian Ocean, the expansion and contraction of the interface, as well as its different possible forms provide an interesting avenue of exploration. In this chapter, I consider ICD Baba and his shrine as such possible forms.

7 The National Capital Region (NCR) spills into states surrounding Delhi, allowing for urban and infrastructural expansion.

8 The report has detailed information on the ICD in Dadri including a schematic map of its layout.

9 This has been inspired by Srinivas' exploration of shrines as thresholds (2015) and Jeychandran's narrative of the inscription of the Indian Ocean along the west Indian coast and hinterland (2019).

10 Along with Martin (2013), it is necessary to keep in mind that this levelling of space is not given and that it takes considerable effort and work to enact that levelling.

11 For instance, G Hegel in his Lectures in the Philosophy of World History argues that the only factor that distinguishes European society is its links to the sea (Emmanuel Chukwudi 1997). For him, Asian and African countries do not have this particular relation that accounts for the establishment of the motors of universal history. In the denial of the long history of Indian Ocean worlds, one remembers Susan Buck-Morss' analysis (2009) of Haiti and Hegel, but asks what in fact does the continuation of "universal history" serve.

References

Alpers, Edward A. 2013. *The Indian Ocean in World History*. Oxford, New York: Oxford University Press.

Bille, Franck. 2017. "Skinworlds: Borders, Haptics, Topologies." *Environment and Planning D: Society and Space,* Vol. 36, no. 1, pp. 60–77. https://doi.org/10.1177/02637 75817735106

Bishara, Fahad Ahmad. 2017. *A Sea of Debt: Law and Economic Life in the Western Indian Ocean 1780–1950*. Cambridge: Cambridge University Press.

Bremner, Lindsay. 2014. "Folded Ocean: The Spatial Transformation of the Indian Ocean World." *Journal of the Indian Ocean Region,* Vol. 10, Issue 1, pp. 18–45. DOI: 10.1080/19480881.2013.847555

Buck-Morss, Susan. 2009. *Hegel, Haiti, and Universal History*. Pittsburgh, PA: University of Pittsburgh Press.

CONCOR. N.D. Available at: www.concorindia.com.

Directorate of Census Operations, Uttar Pradesh. 2011. *District Census Handbook: Gautam Buddha Nagar.*

Eze, Emmanuel Chukwudi. 1997. "Race, History, and Imperialism" In *Race and the Enlightenment: A Reader*. Edited by Emmanuel Chukwudi Eze, 109–153, Cambridge, MA: Blackwell.

Hofmeyr, Isabel. 2010. "Universalizing the Indian Ocean." *PMLA*, Vol. 125, no. 3, pp. 721–729

Ghosh, Amitav. 2010. "Of Fanas and Forecastles: The Indian Ocean and Some Lost Languages of the Age of Sail." In *Eyes Across the Water: Navigating the Indian Ocean*. Edited by Pamila Gupta, Isabel Hofmeyer, and Michael Pearson, 15–31. Pretoria: Unisa Press.

Jeychandran, Neelima. 2019. "Navigating African Sacred Geography: Shrines for African Sufi Saints and Spirits in India." *Journal of Africana Religions*, Vol. 7, no. 1, pp. 17–36. https://muse.jhu.edu/ (accessed September 2, 2019)

Johnston, Lauren A. 2019. "An Economic Demography Explanation for China's 'Maritime Silk Road' Interest in Indian Ocean Countries." *Journal of the Indian Ocean Region*, Vol. 15, no. 1, pp. 97–112. doi: 10.1080/19480881.2019.1569326

Klose, Alexander. 2015. *The Container Principle: How a Box Changes the Way we Think.* Translated by Charles Marcrum II. Cambridge, MA: MIT Press.

Martin, Craig. 2013. "Shipping Container Mobilities, Seamless Compatibility, and the Global Surface of Logistical Integration." *Environment and Planning A*, Vol. 45, pp. 1021–1036. doi:10.1068/a45171

Moorthy, Shanti and Ashraf Jamal. 2010 "Introduction: New Conjunctures in Maritime Imaginaries." In *Indian Ocean Studies: Cultural, Social, and Political Perspectives*. Edited by Shanti Moorthy and Ashraf Jamal, 1–31. New York: Routledge.

Ng'weno, Bettina. 2018. "Growing old in a new city." *City*, Vol. 22, no. 1, pp. 26–42. DOI:10.1080/13604813.2018.1431459

Pearson, Michael. 2003. *The Indian Ocean*. London: Routledge.

Pearson, Michael. 2010. "Connecting the Littorals: Cultural Brokers in the Early Modern Indian Ocean." In *Eyes Across the Water: Navigating the Indian Ocean*. Edited by Pamila Gupta, Isabel Hofmeyer, and Michael Pearson, 32–47. Pretoria: Unisa Press.

Prestholdt, Jeremy (2020, forthcoming, this volume) "The Ends of the Indian Ocean: Notes on Boundaries and Affinities Across Time."

Rangan, Haripriya and Christian Kull. 2010. "The Indian Ocean and the Making of Outback Australia." In *Indian Ocean Studies: Cultural, Social, and Political Perspectives*. Edited by Shanti Moorthy and Ashraf Jamal, 45–72. New York: Routledge.

Rockel, Stephen J. 2014. "Between Pori, Pwani and Kiswani: Overlapping Labour Cultures in the Caravans, Ports and Dhows of the Western Indian Ocean." In *The Indian Ocean: Oceanic Connections and the Creation of New Societies*. Edited by Abdul Sheriff and Engseng Ho, 95–122. London: Hurst and Company

Srinivas, Smriti. 2015. *A Place for Utopia: Urban Designs from South Asia*. Seattle/London: University of Washington Press.

United Nations Economic and Social Commission for Asia and the Pacific (UNESCAP). 2015. *Planning, Development and Operation of Dry Ports of International Importance: Report on trends in the development of inland ports and policies underlying their development in selected countries of the UNESCAP region*. Bangkok, November 2015.

4   Seasons of sail

The monsoon, kinship, and labor in the *dhow* trade

Nidhi Mahajan

Flying in the face of the wind

On a sunny morning in September 2017, Ajmal,[1] a *vahan* or mechanized *dhow* owner based in Mandvi, Kachchh in western India began his day as he usually did, by visiting his friend, Narayan, a shipping agent. Ajmal would go every morning to Narayan's office, not because they had business together, but simply to hangout, and more importantly, to use Narayan's computer to check the weather. Like other *vahanvati* or people concerned with the business of *dhows*, Ajmal was accustomed to starting his day by checking wind direction, speed, currents, and the swell of waves in the Indian Ocean on websites such as Windy.com and Storm Watch. Indeed, every *dhow* owner and sailor I knew began his day this way, talk of the weather not being filler in awkward conversations, but at the center of many heated discussions. Despite meteorological services that could foretell the weather, *vahanvati* were always anxious about how the wind, waves, and the current would affect the movement of vessels, their finances, and the safety of people, cargoes, and the vessel at sea.

On that day, Ajmal was busy checking the weather, wind, and waves along the Persian Gulf as his *dhow*, the *Hawa* was voyaging between the UAE, and Yemen. His purposeful browsing was interrupted by the arrival of Amin, the vessel's captain or *nakhwa*. Amin had recently returned to Mandvi from Dubai, not by sea, but by air, another captain sailing the vessel to Nishtoon, Yemen from Sharjah, loaded with cars while Amin was away. As we discussed his travels, I could not help but notice the large model of a *dhow* with a lateen sail that stood framed in the center of the room. Dependent on the sail for movement, *dhow* sailors of yore would have to wait out the monsoon in one part of the littoral. However, nowadays, sailors like Amin could fly in the face of the winds. Yet, the monsoon winds, and the weather continue to shape the itineraries of mechanized *dhows* and the quotidian social and economic life of *vahanvati*.

This leads me to the questions that are at the center of this chapter – how do seasons (especially the monsoon) and weather patterns shape the lives of itinerant *dhow* sailors from Kachchh? Given that the movement of *dhows* is no longer dependent on the monsoons as mechanized *dhows* do not rely on the sail, what valence do historical patterns of seasonal movement have on contemporary *dhow* crews and their families? What role does seasonality play in the economic and social fabric of itinerant *dhow* sailors, owners, and their families? Based on ethnographic research in western India and the wider Indian Ocean world, I examine how seafaring labor is intimately tied to kin relations for *dhow* crews, arguing that a monsoon seasonality structures not just seemingly economic matters, but also social life for seafaring communities in which some people move, and others stay home. Ethnographic research on board vessels at ports as well as in the homes and the domestic spaces of sailors and their families makes these complex relationalities of older trade wind patterns, seasonal calendars, debt, and domestic quotidian transactions visible.

By examining the relationship between *dhow* mobility at sea, and life at home I argue that seafarers of Kachchh have what anthropologist Marcel Mauss has called a "dual morphology" (2004) where social life varies with the seasons. While this seasonal variation was once wrought by natural, ecological factors, I show that despite the *dhow* industry no longer relying entirely on seasonal change for movement, older patterns of seasonality continue to be relevant, even as sailors and vessel owners adapt to ever-shifting conditions – of weather, government regulation, and market trends. This seasonality is deeply embedded in the lives of those at home and those at sea, habituated in quotidian social interactions, rituals, festivals, customs, cycles of debt, labor recruitment, and even government regulation. The monsoon then, is deeply entangled with the temporality of seafaring in the present, this temporality being materialized through a monsoonal financial calendar.

This monsoon temporality that undergirds labor, debt, and kinship relations for *dhow* sailors, *dhow* owners, and their families in Kachchh, has created a monsoonal relationality that shapes exchange and sociality within these communities, ultimately enabling mobility across the Western Indian Ocean, drawing it into a networked space. This transregional relationality comes into being not only through the physical movement of sailors, all of whom are men, but also the women who do not move with them, their capital, and labor enabling this relationality along a monsoon temporality. This monsoon temporality is instantiated in the everyday lives of men who leave and women who stay, and is materialized in cyclical debt and kinship relations that once depended on the winds, and continue to remain in place even as the winds change.

Monsoons at sail

At the center of this chapter then is the monsoon, an ecological phenomenon that is a defining feature of South Asia and the Indian Ocean littoral. From June to September, the monsoon winds blow from the southwest, and from September onward, they reverse direction, blowing from the northeast. The direction of the winds affects rainfall, and hence agriculture in South Asia such that crops are known to be either *kharif* (monsoon crop) or *rabi* (sown in the dry season).

Given that agriculture in South Asia has been deeply dependent on the monsoon, colonial and postcolonial governments have worked consistently to predict and tame the monsoon, aiming to transform the uncertainty of monsoon into calculable risk, as Sunil Amrith has argued (2018a).

The monsoon is not only a pivotal factor for economic life on land, but also at sea. Historians since K.N. Chaudhuri (1985) have understood that the monsoon brought unity to the Indian Ocean as it enabled movement across the sea. The regular seasonal wind pattern was harnessed by early seafarers in the region who used lateen sails, their movement dependent on the monsoon (Agius 2005, 2010; Hourani 1951; Martin and Martin 1978). As sailors moved from one part of the Indian Ocean littoral to another, they would often have to wait in a port city for several months for the winds to change so that they could return home. As Abdul Sheriff has argued, this seasonal movement enabled social interaction between sailors and their hosts, leading to the rise of a cosmopolitan culture across the Indian Ocean (Sheriff 2010).

In much of the literature on South Asia and the Indian Ocean, the monsoon figures as a canvas for history, an environmental pre-condition that enabled the historical movement of people and things (Chaudhuri 1985; Risso 1995; Sheriff 2010). In other accounts, it emerges as an unpredictable, untamable agent, one that state authorities would try to subjugate through meteorology or even hydraulic engineering (Amrith 2018a, 2018b; Roy 2012). Alongside these important narratives that frame the environment as either determinant or as a site upon which the power of state and capital are enacted, there is a need to consider the point of view of farmers, seafarers, and other communities that are most intimately familiar with the monsoon and its effects. After all, for seafarers, life itself is coterminous with the monsoon – deeply entangled in their pasts, presents, and futures.

Sailors and merchants on the west coast of India and the waters beyond had long developed a clear understanding of the monsoon winds. The monsoon pattern has such an influence on trade across the littoral that commerce in Kachchh ran on a seasonal sailing calendar that reflected this dependence on the monsoons. Contracts between merchants were dated based on the monsoon, payment and repayment following the winds along with the cargoes that moved with them.[2] As Chayya Goswami (2016) shows, merchants and mariners of Kachchh divided the year based on the shifting monsoon winds. The calendar indicated that the northeast monsoon or *saji mausam* in Gujarati, began in September, this being the fair season or *mausam khulvi* as vessels would sail from ports such as Mandvi to East Africa (Goswami 2016). The southwest monsoon known as the *aakhar mausam, cheli ghos* or *safar* in Gujarati began in April. For Kachchhi seafarers, the year was divided into *aakhar*, when the southwest monsoon began, and *mausam* when the winds changed. *Aakhar* was a period during which most seafarers would return home, while *mausam* referred to the nine months that they were at sea.[3]

These days, modern Kachchhi *vahan* modelled on the *kotia*, a historic sailing vessel from Kachchh, continue to traverse the old Indian Ocean routes. Yet,

Figure 4.1 Vahans (dhows) docked at Jam Salaya during *aakhar* in August 2017.
Image credit: Nidhi Mahajan.

unlike the *kotia* and other *dhows*, *vahan* and their crews are no longer dependent
on their sails for movement, and run instead on engines. In official terms, these
vahan are known as "mechanized sailing vessels" in India. They are primarily
built in Gujarat, the port towns of Mandvi and Jam Salaya being especially
prominent centers for the *vahan* trade. These *vahan* function as an economy of
arbitrage (Dua 2016), going to minor ports, especially in times of conflict. They
transport rice, livestock, and other foodstuffs from India to Persian Gulf ports
such as Salalah, Sharjah, and Dubai, from where they often then load the vessel
with cargoes headed to Yemen and Somalia, carrying electronics, medicines,
food aid, and even cars. From East Africa, they bring livestock, and, depending
on prevailing international regulations, charcoal to the Gulf. Upon their return to
India, they often bring back dates or used tires from the Gulf, their voyages and
cargoes planned around the vagaries of demand, supply, and government
regulation.

While no longer dependent on the sail, *vahan* can technically fly in the face
of the winds. However, they rarely do so, as it is risky but also because it is an
expensive affair as diesel consumption and hence costs increase as one moves
against the winds. Most vessels thus continue to run with the monsoon, going
from India to the Gulf and East Africa during the northeast monsoon, and

returning home to India or plying routes along the Persian Gulf with the onset of the southwest monsoon. Many vessels remain docked in the UAE through the year, returning to India only if they can expect cargoes to be loaded or if major repairs are needed. Otherwise, vessel owners prefer to save the cost of diesel, and dock their vessels in Dubai or Sharjah, both mid-way points and transshipment hubs between India and East Africa. However, the mobility of sailors themselves is no longer restricted by the monsoon. Most of them now fly back and forth across port cities in the Indian Ocean – especially Dubai and Sharjah – to India on airplanes. Where *aakhar* was once the time of year that sailors would come home, and *mausam* meant that they were away, this seasonal pattern has shifted as voyages and movement are no longer determined by monsoon, even as the monsoon has become more unpredictable.

The monsoon itself has shifted with climate change. Sailors are acutely aware of this as they realize that the rains begin a month later than they once did. This unpredictability is intensified by the increasing frequency of cyclones and tropical storms in the Indian Ocean through the year. However, the old seasonal maritime calendar that divided the year into *aakhar* and *mausam*, still mattered, often in subtle but important ways, seasonality shaping quotidian life of seafarers and their kin, both at sea and at home. This is not only a mnemonic trace or debris (Joseph 2007) of an earlier era where vessels and people were carried by the winds, but is ongoing as Kachchhi seafaring communities continue to have a "dual morphology" (Mauss 2004), even as they quickly adapt to changing conditions – of climate change, weather, labor, capital, markets, governments, and, even, family obligations. Life in the seafaring towns of Mandvi and Jam Salaya still moved with the monsoon, even though the contours of the monsoon itself have shifted.

From *aakhar* to *mausam*: a dual morphology, interrupted?

The towns of Mandvi and Jam Salaya lie on the Gulf of Kachchh, their fortunes linked to the waters that lap their shores. Both towns have a long tradition of seafaring, with shipyards in which vahan are built and run primarily by sailors from the Muslim Bhadala and Wagher communities, alongside some Hindu Kharvas (Varadarajan 1980). Vessels are now owned by members of these communities, or by Hindu Bhatias based in Mumbai. Much of my fieldwork focused on the Bhadala and Wagher communities of two towns – Mota Salaya near Mandvi and Jam Salaya – an hour from Jamnagar. Mandvi has long been an important port town, known for its merchants and seafarers who have connected India to East Africa and Muscat (Alpers and Goswami 2019; Simpson 2006).

Jam Salaya however, is less well-known. Originally settled by Bhadalas and Bhatias from Kachchh, in the nineteenth century it came to be a stop on the railway that extended through Kathiawar. Once a fishing village, it is now famously where *vahan* are built, the village economy being based on seafaring and fishing. Unlike Mandvi which has a mixed population of Hindu Bhatias, Kharvas, Jains, Ismailis, Bohras, Bhadalas (most of whom live in the hamlet of

Mota Salaya), and others, Jam Salaya is predominantly Muslim Wagher, with a smaller community of Bhadalas and about five Hindu families. Despite the differences of history and demography, seasonal patterns of movement in both Jam Salaya and Mota Salaya remain similar, sailors from both towns working on the same vessels, from *aakhar* to *mausam*. It was Shehnaz, the wife of a *vahan* owner from Jam Salaya, who first brought to my attention how life for seafarers is still structured by the monsoon and a calendar divided into *aakhar* and *mausam*.

Shehnaz comes from a long line of Jam Salaya's seafarers. Her grandfather was a sailor on a *vahan*, her father owned a *vahan*, and for the past 35 years, she has been married to Amjad, who is also an experienced sailor, who now builds and runs a *vahan*. He is well-known in the town and amongst *vahanvati* across Western India. When I had arrived for several weeks of fieldwork in Jam Salaya during *aakhar* in 2017, I had assumed that Amjad would be my main informant, as I had known him for a few years. Yet, it was his wife Shehnaz, who became a crucial interlocutor. Although she had never been out to sea, she had an acute sense of the industry's workings in these parts and was Amjad's trusted advisor not only in domestic matters, but also in business dealings. After all, the first vessel that Amjad owned came to him as part of Shehnaz's dowry, and her parents continued to support them as they built and operated *dhows*. Shehnaz's capital, and her "phatic labor"[4] (Elyachar 2010) had made the family's now flourishing *vahan* trade possible. Although she had never moved with the vessels as Amjad once did, she was very much a part of the decision-making process for the family's finances, and was conscious of how the rhythms of life in Jam Salaya and beyond changed as *vahan* rolled in and out of town.

One afternoon, sitting in their home chewing on Iranian dates served by her daughter-in-law, while a Persian cat her son had brought back from Dubai purred at her feet, Shehnaz said to me, "Earlier, our lives were dictated by the monsoon. The year was divided into *aakhar* and *mausam*, but now, these distinctions don't exist. Sailors come and go based on their contracts. They 'sign on' and 'sign off' as they need. Sure, vessels can't leave here between June and September, but then those in Dubai are always running." Amjad, then added, "You're right. No one really thinks in terms of *aakhar* and *mausam* anymore." Shahnaz looked at him thoughtfully, "But then isn't our accounting year still running on that calendar? Salaries are paid when sailors come home during *aakhar*." Amjad, nodded, being stood corrected. Shehnaz then got up and took the Gujarati calendar hanging on the wall and showed it to me. "Look, there are 60 *naroj* (days) during *Akhar*. In *mausam*, there are 300." Shehnaz then explained to me that *aakhar* and *mausam* were marked by Nava Naroj or the New Year, which usually fell at the end of July or the beginning of August. While this seasonal calendar no longer determined the movement of sailors, family finances – for vessel owners and sailors who worked for them – were still dependent on this seasonal calendar, and thus so was social life. Kachchhi seafaring communities continue to have then, what Mauss calls a "dual morphology."

Writing about the Eskimo, Mauss understands social morphology to be a "science whose investigations are intended not just to describe but also to elucidate the material substratum of societies," (Mauss 2004: 19) which includes patterns of residence, volume and density of population, how the population is distributed, and the "entire range of objects that serve as a focus for collective life." (Mauss 2004: 19) In the case of the Eskimo, he suggests that this morphology is a dual morphology that changes based on the seasons. In the winter, social life is intense, as people live closer together, their interactions frequent. During this time, individuals in the group become more aware of their collective identity. In contrast, summer is a time when social bonds become more relaxed as the pace of social life slows down, settlement becoming more dispersed changing how people live, work, and relate to one another. He ultimately argues there are changes in the rhythm of social life not just for the Eskimo, but for any society.

Mauss was arguing against the environmental determinism of his time, and aimed, as Mary Douglas has put it, to "demand an ecological approach in which the structure of ideas and of society, the mode of gaining a livelihood and the domestic architecture are interpreted as a single interacting whole in which no one element can be said to determine the others." (Mauss 2004: 11) Building upon Mauss' work but moving beyond the nature/culture debates, anthropologist Mark Harris (1998) argues for a dwelling perspective of seasonality that emphasizes the periodicity of work, the environment being constituted by the activities of people such that seasonality is intrinsic to people's engagement with the environment and social life more broadly. Indeed, for Kachchhi Bhadalas and Waghers, social life and the environment are deeply entangled, year in and out. People of the coast, their social life too has a dual morphology – split during *aakhar* and *mausam*.

Aakhar is a time of returns. It is when husbands, fathers, and sons come home, their friends and loved ones awaiting their arrival. *Aakhar* is spent in the family home, making repairs to both home and vessel, while contracts for the next year's season are drawn up, and old debts are settled. It is also a time of intense social activity. This is the only time of the year that weddings take place, since the menfolk are present. Yet, as many women and men in Jam Salaya and Mandvi would confess, the intense social activity took an emotional toll, the end of *aakhar* being a relief for many.

When *mausam* began, the villages would be emptied of most seafarers. Those who remained were either ailing or had decided to stay home while other men of the family went off to work. The women would focus on the children, the elderly, and household affairs. Monthly remittances ensured that the household would be running. The men at sea would quickly fall into the routine of work on the vahan, their lives being regulated into six-hour long shifts on board, the roar of diesel engines, waves, and wind at sea replacing the chatter of family members and friends. While some of this has changed as sailors can now travel across the Indian Ocean by airplane, these old seasonal patterns of social interaction remain as the seasonal calendar structures the accounting year, social obligations, cycles of debt, and the organization of labor.

Seasons of work, cycles of debt: labor and kinship for the khalaasi

A *vahan*, like any other ship, functions on a strict hierarchy. Duties and responsibilities of each crew member are clearly defined, movement across the ranks being possible only after years of experience, and apprenticeship (see Simpson 2006). The top rank is of course, the captain or *nakhwa*. The *nakhwa* is responsible for managing all the crew, the loading and unloading of cargo, finances, communication with the vessel owner or *seth*, navigation, and itineraries. He is also the one who deals with port officials, negotiates with traders over freight rates, and buys diesel, and rations. The *nakhwa* is thus the highest paid member of the crew. Not only does he receive a larger monthly salary than anyone on board, but for every trip, he also gets a *baksheesh* or tip from the merchant whose cargo is being loaded. *Nakhwas* are also known to be traders themselves, buying goods in one port and selling them at a higher price at the next. Often, the *nakhwa* might be a member of the owner's family – a son or a nephew. This is preferred by some *vahanvati* as it keeps control of the vessel in family hands, presumably reducing the pilfering of diesel, rations, and freight, and to ensure that the vessel would run as his owner intended.

The second-highest paid crewmember is usually either the *maalim* or navigator, or the *rasoiya, bhandari,* or cook. He is followed by the ship's engineer who maintains the diesel engine, then the *serang* or foreman, the *sukhani* (or the one who steers the vessel's wheel), oilman, and helpers such as the *gherporiya* or watchman. There is usually onboard also a young unpaid apprentice, or *petoriya* who does all the odd jobs. These crew members (apart from the captain) are collectively known as the *khalaasi* or laborers.

All crew members (except the apprentice) receive a monthly salary. This is usually a rather nominal amount, ranging from Indian rupees 20,000 ($289) for the *nakhwa* to 3000 rupees ($43) for a helper. What matters most then, is not the salary but the *hamali* or *majdoori* or labor paid by merchants or the cargo's consigner for each trip made. The cargo consigner typically pays ten UAE dirhams ($2.72) per ton of cargo loaded, this entire amount split between the khalaasi. Typically, on a large *vahan* of about 1200–1400 tons cargo capacity, this meant that each crew member receives around 18,000–20,000 Indian rupees ($260–$289) for each trip or *ghos* they made. This is significantly larger than their monthly salary, and so most sailors think of their financial success or failure in terms of the number of trips they make during the term of their contract. It is the amount earned as hamali on each trip that they remitted to their family, homes running so long as a sailor was laboring at sea. The salaries, however, served a different purpose.

The payment of monthly salaries typically functioned on a cyclical basis – a cycle that followed the accounting year, which in turn, was centered around the seasonal sailing calendar. This seasonal cycle not only regulated salaries, but also debt. Hashim, a retired *nakhwa* in his sixties explained to me how this worked:

See, when you go to a vessel owner, you make an agreement to work for them for 9 months or then 12 months. You then decide if you need an advance so that your house can run even before you get your first installment of hamali. You then take an advance on your salary from the owner. Then you make an agreement with him whether or not the salary should be paid monthly. In Mandvi, they are usually paid every month. But in Jam Salaya, owners make a fuss about this. Salaries for the whole year are typically paid only at the end of *aakhar* – this is when all accounting takes place. Then, if at the end of it, you owe the vessel owner money, you work for that same owner again to pay off the debt, unless another vessel owner is ready to pay your debt and then you are indebted to the next *seth*. And so, it continues. Sometimes, we like that salaries are paid at the end of *aakhar* – it ensures some savings through the year and this is especially helpful of there is a wedding to plan, or house to build. But then you also realize that you invariably end up taking loans from the vessel owner. You always end up indebted to the owner.

His daughter, Shabana, then added, "*Woh apne aap ko girvi kar dete hain.* Think of it in this way – they become bonded laborers. They pawn themselves to the owner." Salaries, paid at the end of the season (at the beginning of aakhar), were therefore intricately tied up with cycles of debt and labor recruitment. Cash-strapped khalaasi and their families invariably looked to *seths* for loans, who in turn, expected sailors to work for them to work off these loans by the next season. This cycle of debt runs based on the seasonal accounting year, which in turn, also determines social life in the village. Yet for most *vahan* sailors, seasonal social obligations to kin motivated them to work at sea, and forced them to take loans.

Most khalaasi I knew deplored the conditions in which they worked. *This is hard work, you're away from home much of the time and you don't even make much money. But there is no choice, we are bound to the vessel owners, and to this industry. We don't know how to do anything else, anyway*, they would say. Apart from the basic need for an income, duties and obligations to kin also ensured that these cycles of debt continued. The timing of these obligations which coincided with the seasonal maritime calendar and accounting year ensured the continuation of these cycles. The fact that weddings only took place once a year in *aakhar*, during the same time that accounts were settled, allowed these cycles to continue. Prior to a wedding in the family, a khalaasi would work to save his salary for wedding expenditures. Unable to fully finance the wedding with his earnings, he would take a loan from the vessel owner during *aakhar*, for the following year. And so, after Nava Naroj, or the New Year, he would again begin working off the debt from the previous year, the cycle continuing.

The cycle of debt, and obligation to kin was best explained to me by Rahim, a *serang* from Mandvi who I met in Sharjah creek in 2017. Rahim was a good natured, middle-aged man. He had worked as a *serang* and *maalim* for many years and hoped one day, to become a *nakhwa*, but also knew that it was unlikely – he didn't have the right family connections. Although he had worked for the same owner for many years now, it was the owner's son, Yusuf, who was the *nakhwa*, and not Rahim. Yusuf was young, and not as experienced as Rahim and so relied on him to run the vessel. Clearly, Rahim had settled for the lesser position because of debts to the *seth* and obligations to kin. As we sat on board the vessel chatting one afternoon, he showed me two videos on his phone and told me, "My daughter was married last year. She's my only girl, so I had told her, whatever you want, you get." The video he shared with me clearly depicted how this promise was fulfilled.

One video panned across his daughter's trousseau – over 70 new, shiny *salwar kameez*, still wrapped in plastic, laid out in a row. Compacts, make-up, hair ties, powder, soaps, shampoos, jewelry – he had brought her everything she might need for many years to come. Another video displayed household goods and furniture for her kitchen and bedroom – a bed, dresser, night table, vases, plastic flowers, stainless steel cooking pots, pressure cookers, knives, cups. He confessed, "I spent over 300,000 rupees ($4300) on her wedding! I of course, had to take a loan from the *seth* for this, so now I'll be working here, paying it off!" Rahim said as I gushed over the video of gifts. "What can I say, she's my only daughter?!" Rahim laughed, sounding both proud and helpless.

Rahim's obligations to his kin did not end there. I asked him about his sister, who had recently bought a new house in Mandvi that I had visited during *aakhar*. Maryam had been widowed when she was very young as her husband, who was also a sailor, had drowned in a shipwreck. She had three young children at the time and was supported by her parents and her brothers while she attempted to find work – making *bandhnis* or tie-n-dyes at home. She had lived with her parents and Rahim for many years, and only now had managed to move into a place of her own. "You liked the house?! I helped her build it!" Rahim said, proudly. He then added softly, "I took a loan from the *seth* earlier for that as well. I'm still paying some of it off. After all, we live by the blessings of women." Maryam took care of their elderly parents and young children, her care work, and phatic labor keeping the family together while Rahim was at sea. Obligations to kin and cycles of debt therefore continued, the timing of repayment and negotiation of these obligations being determined through the seasonal financial calendar. Apart from the accounting year being based on the seasonal calendar, the monsoon continued to play an important role in the *dhow* trade for another reason: the history of government regulation. The mobility of seafarers is not just dependent on weather, markets, and the monsoon, but is also shaped by government understandings of the monsoon since the eighteenth century.

A clash of calendars: regulating the weather and mobility

Even in the age of sail, when the movement of *dhows* across the Indian Ocean littoral depended on the monsoons, other concerns of political economy, the availability of goods, and government regulations shaped the mobility of vessels and the fortunes of merchants. Sailors and merchants needed to maneuver these different factors while planning their voyages across different regions. For instance, writing about eighteenth- and nineteenth-century shipping between Gujarat and Mozambique, Pedro Machado argues that sailing in the Indian Ocean "involved maintaining a delicate equilibrium between meeting the demands of trading seasons in both India and Africa," (Machado 2014: 100) as well as being attuned to the ocean's winds and currents. The maintenance of this balance was further complicated by the Portuguese authorities' regulations between India and Mozambique that sought to restrict movement between India to Africa such that ships should depart Gujarat for Mozambique between November and December to avoid shipwreck and being blown off course, prohibiting vessels from sailing after 31 January. This regulation was opposed by merchants who saw it as an undue interference in their trade. Yet, as Machado shows, sailors and merchants could not ignore the monsoon system and had to abide by a schedule where they sailed for the Delgoa Bay between October–November or January–February, returning between mid-May and mid-June (Machado 2014: 97–98). In later years, British authorities too became familiar with this pattern of movement and the delicate equilibrium that merchants and sailors would maintain, this seasonality also shaping indigenous maritime insurance or *dariyai vima* as insurance claims could only be valid if the trading occurred during the open season (Goswami 2016).

These days, the maritime calendar continues to be followed, the rules about dates of arrival and departure being regulated by the Indian state. In 2015, the Government of India's Directorate General of Shipping restricted movement of sailing vessels to and from India to 15 June–1 September1. Between June and September, no cargo vessels can enter or leave Indian waters. While many assumed that this was to ensure the safety of the crew and the vessel, there is another story that claims that the rule itself came about due to competition between two different vessel owners.

Amongst vessel owners, there is a rumor that two competing vessel owners influenced the dates of sail instituted by the government of India. It is said that in 2015, a *seth*, Altaf, had a cargo of goats that he was to deliver to the UAE. Another *seth*, Hassan, also had a shipload of livestock to transport to the same UAE port. Yet, Hassan's vessel was docked behind Altaf's vessel, which meant that Altaf would have access to the jetty and would depart for the UAE sooner than Hassan. Whoever got there and unloaded first, was likely to do better that season as they would be able to quickly unload the cargo of goats and load other cargo waiting in the UAE, making more trips through the year. Timing was thus, crucial.

Altaf had planned to leave India around 15 August, when the monsoon rains were likely to have ended, the sea being calm again. But Hassan undercut his competitor, by complaining to the local authorities. *How can you allow Hassan's vessel to leave on the 15th? The weather is going to be bad. Anything can happen to the crew.* The government then, to reduce potential losses of life, refused to let Altaf's vessel sail. Instead, the government decided to put a new rule in place. No sailing vessels could leave Indian ports until after 1 September.

Two years later, in 2017, this new rule proved to be a loss-making one for the entire sailing vessel industry. One of the profitable cargoes to transport by *vahan* is livestock, especially goats that are shipped from India to Salalah in Oman, Dubai, and Sharjah. In 2017, however, this business suffered a great loss, simply due to a clash of calendars. Usually, 1 September is a significant date on the seasonal calendar as it is the day of the opening of the season. In 2017, however, it was also significant because it was, on the Islamic calendar, when Eid-ul-Adha was being celebrated. Typically, before Eid, Indian livestock is exported in large numbers to the Middle East. But in 2017, this was not to be as vessels could not leave India and deliver the goats in time for sacrifice for Eid, the government not allowing them to go to sea prior to 1 September.

Vessel owners such as Alam complained about this amongst themselves, as the weather itself had been relatively calm two whole weeks prior to 1 September. The conditions at sea were favorable for a voyage, but authorities would not permit them to depart earlier than the official date. For *vahanvati* attuned to shifting weather conditions, the government's stricter regulations around monsoon patterns was not only an inconvenience but cause for a major financial setback. Yet, they had no choice but to abide by the regulations. Not unlike Vaniya merchants in the eighteenth century, for *dhow* owners and sailors today, what matters is not only the monsoon pattern but also daily changes in weather, markets, competition, and government regulations. These government regulations seek to estimate the monsoon but given the unpredictability of the winds especially in the context of climate change, these inflexible regulations do not account for conditions at sea. Fisher folk, and seafarers, who are accustomed to reading even subtle shifts in the weather are better equipped to guide themselves and their vessels safely through a changing monsoon, government regulation being unable to keep up with these shifts.

From sea to shore: a monsoonal relationality

The monsoon is a defining feature of the Indian Ocean. It has carried people, things, and ideas across the littoral as *dhows* harnessed these changing winds. Historically, the monsoon has been instrumental in creating relationality across the ocean, the quotidian lives of those living across the Indian Ocean being deeply entangled with the monsoon. Seafarers from Kachchh have been intimately familiar with the monsoon: they have sailed with these winds, even though they can now fly in the face of them. Their labor, cycles of debt, rituals, marriage, insurance, and their financial and social obligations have been embedded within a monsoon temporality. They have a dual morphology that materialized through government regulations and cycles of debt. Seasonality is thus part of the habitus of the seafaring men who move across the Indian Ocean, and the women who do not move with them.

Anthropologists and historians have shown how marriage and genealogical ties across the Indian Ocean enabled mobility across the region, especially in the case of creole families (see Ho 2006; Seng 2018). The capital, care work, and phatic labor of women who do not sail with the winds has been central to this monsoonal mobility. While scholarship on the Indian Ocean has often privileged the unique forms of mobility this history of transregional connection has generated, it is as crucial to examine stasis, alongside the vessels, peoples and ideas that travel. The dhow and the home, sea and land, mobility and stasis, taken together open avenues for viewing a monsoon temporality and monsoon relationality that define the lives of those who leave, and those who stay across the Indian Ocean littoral.

Notes

1 Pseudonyms have been used for all people and vessels through this chapter.
2 For example, Bohra Tayabji Budhabai, a Gujarati merchant with business in Zanzibar had a contract whose repayment terms were dated according to the seasons of *mausam* (northeast monsoon) and *demani* (southwest monsoon) in 1933 and 1934. ZNA AA12/19: 581/1876 (Zanzibar National Archives). I am most grateful to Hollian Wint for sharing this document.
3 While seafarers describe winds in many ways, often based on the direction they are blowing, this "*aakhar*" and "*mausam*" distinction is crucial as not only does is describe the general direction of the wind, but more importantly, it is also a temporal distinction that has social meaning. While there are other ways in which winds are described based on their direction and force, for the purposes of the maritime calendar, it is *aakhar* and *mausam* that are significant.
4 Julia Elyachar defines phatic labor as social infrastructure that "produces communicative channels that can potentially transmit not only language but also all kinds of semiotic meaning and economic value" (Elyachar 2010: 453).

References

Agius, Dionisius A. 2005. *Seafaring in the Arabian Gulf and Oman: The People of the Dhow*. London: Kegan Paul International.

Agius, Dionisius A. 2010. *In the Wake of the Dhow: The Arabian Gulf and Oman*. Reading: Ithaca Press.

Alpers, Edward and Goswami, Chayya. 2019. *Transregional Trade and Traders: Situating Gujarat in the Indian Ocean from Early Times to 1900*. New Delhi: Oxford University Press.

Amrith, Sunil S. 2018a. "Risk and the South Asian monsoon." *Climatic Change* 151, no. 1: 17–28.

Amrith, Sunil. 2018b. *Unruly Waters: How Mountain Rivers and Monsoons Have Shaped South Asia's History*. Penguin UK.

Chaudhuri, K.N. 1985. *Trade and Civilization in the Indian Ocean: An Economic History from the Rise of Islam to 1750*. Cambridge: Cambridge University Press.

Dua, Jatin. 2016. "Dhow Encounters." Transition, 119: 49–59.

Elyachar, Julia. 2010. "Phatic Labor, Infrastructure, and the Question of Empowerment in Cairo." *American Ethnologist* 37, no. 3: 452–464.

Goswami, Chhaya. 2016. *Globalization Before Its Time: The Gujarati Merchants from Kachchh*. Gurgaon: Penguin Books.

Harris, Mark. 1998. "The Rhythm of Life on the Amazon Floodplain: Seasonality and Sociality in a Riverine Village." *Journal of the Royal Anthropological Institute*, Vol. 4, no. 1: 65–82.

Ho, Engseng. 2006. *The Graves of Tarim: Genealogy and Mobility Across the Indian Ocean*. Berkeley: University of California Press.

Hourani, G.F. 1951. *Arab Seafaring in the Indian Ocean in ancient and early medieval times*. Princeton: Princeton University Press.

Joseph, May. 2007. "Old Routes, Mnemonic Traces." *UTS Review*, 6: 44–56.

Machado, P. 2014. *Ocean of Trade: South Asian Merchants, Africa and the Indian Ocean, c.1750–1850*. Cambridge: Cambridge University Press.

Martin, E.B. and Martin, C. 1978. *Cargoes of the East: The Ports, Trade, and Culture of the Arabian Seas and Western Indian Ocean*. London: Elm Tree Books.

Mauss, M. and Beuchat, H. 2004 *Seasonal variations of the Eskimo: A Study in Social Morphology*. London: Routledge & Kegan Paul.

Risso, Patricia. 1995. *Merchants and Faith: Muslim Commerce and Culture in the Indian Ocean*. Boulder, CO: Westview Press.

Roy, Tirthankar. 2012. *Natural Disasters and Indian History: Oxford India Short Introductions*. New Delhi: Oxford University Press.

Seng, Guo-Quan. 2018. "The Gender Politics of Confucian Family Law: Contracts, Credit, and Creole Chinese Bilateral Kinship in Dutch Colonial Java (1850s–1900)." *Comparative Studies in Society and History*, 60, no. 2: 390–414.

Sheriff, Abdul. 2010. *Dhow Cultures of the Indian Ocean: Cosmopolitanism, Commerce and Islam*. New York: Columbia University Press.

Simpson, E. 2006. *Muslim Society and the Western Indian Ocean: The Seafarers of Kachchh*. London: Routledge.

Varadarajan, Lotika. 1980. "Traditions of Indigenous Navigation in Gujarat." *South Asia: Journal of South Asian Studies*, 3, no. 1: 28–35.

Zanzibar National Archives. Letter from Bohra Tayabji Budhabhai. ZNA AA12/19: 581/1876.

Part II
Landscapes, oceanscapes, and practices

5 Elsewheres in the Indian Ocean

Spatio-temporal encounters and imaginaries beyond the sea

Nethra Samarawickrema

On the surface, it may seem that to be a person of the Indian Ocean, one must have seen the sea. That one must have glimpsed its clear blue waters, smelt its salty air, and had a whiff of being connected to others elsewhere. In the small coastal town of Beruwala in southern Sri Lanka, such sentiments are palpably true. Near the town's main mosque is a market where gems are traded from across the maritime world. The stones' itineraries are as diverse as those of the men who exchange them: Beruwala's traders are often on the move, going west to Madagascar, Mozambique, and Tanzania, and east to Thailand, Hong Kong, and China. It is through their movements that gems circulate, hand-carried across great distances. For many of Beruwala's traders, mobility is a way of life. To be a trader of Beruwala requires acquiring a deep knowledge of places far away from Beruwala.

To chart the lives and itineraries of Beruwala's traders is to tell a quintessentially Indian Ocean tale. It is a familiar one for those who have learned to "take a view from the boat" (Ho 2004), to discern geographies of relatedness beyond territorial and national categories. For those who work on the Indian Ocean, the nexus of kinship and commerce, the system of trust-based credit, and the centrality of mobility to trade in Beruwala make this town a recognizable part of the Indian Ocean world. These mercantile practices link Beruwala's traders with other littoral communities along the ocean's rim (Bishara 2017; Ho 2006; Pearson 2006; Machado 2014; Simpson 2006)

Yet, are the people *of* the Indian Ocean only those who move *across* the Indian Ocean? Can one be an Indian Ocean actor while living in the mountains, having rarely seen the sea? In the south-central hills of Sabaragamuwa, 80 kilometers away from Beruwala, is the urban center of Ratnapura, known as the 'city of gems.' In nearby villages reside another group of people who also make journeys, not across the sea but into the earth. These are mineworkers, some who have mined for generations and others who mine occasionally in search of a lucky break. For them, the sea is far from sight. Their gaze, instead, is trained underground. It is through their risky journeys underground that the gems first emerge from alluvial deposits deep in the earth. These men too think of mobility; it has multiple valences for them. It includes everyday travels from homes to mines, into tunnels underground, and to temples and shrines where they make offerings to multiple deities for protection. Enmeshed in their work are their aspirations for mobility away from the life of labor. Yet, for many, these dreams are connected to forms of stuckness – arrested journeys, stymied aspirations, and, for injured workers, bodies with reduced mobility. Nevertheless, miners work with a resolute refusal to remain stuck.

Taking their vantage points into account, I ask: What does mobility and connectivity in the Indian Ocean look like from fifty feet underground? In what ways do such perspectives converge or diverge from the view from a coastal trading town? How does the Indian Ocean world, and the sea as a space, appear to the actors who mine and trade gems across it? These questions raise a broader line of inquiry: is the Indian Ocean world the same as the sea, or does it encompass a sphere larger than the water?

To revisit the significance of the maritime returns us to questions posed by early historians of the region as they began to imagine the Indian Ocean world. K.N. Chaudhuri (1985) sought to define the Indian Ocean region as an analytic space, as a world overlooked in state-centric conceptions of geography and territoriality. Pearson (2007: 38), who conceptualized people across the littoral as a distinctive society, asked: do shorefolk have more in common with other shorefolk thousands of kilometers away than they do with their immediate hinterlands? For Chaudhuri, it was the sea itself that enabled such commonalities, for the ocean provided an unbroken means of travel from the beaches of the Suez and the marshes around Basra all the way to China (1983: 3). As merchants were obliged to travel, Chaudhuri wrote, they played a vital role in facilitating these connections (ibid.).

Thus, more often than not, traders have been prominent actors in our accounts, mobile people whose movements have enabled scholars to trace connectivity across this watery world (Aslanian 2011; Das Gupta 1982; Goswami 2011; Ho 2006; Pearson 2010; Risso 1995; Trivellato 2012). They have been accompanied by others in our texts – sailors, monks, saints, financiers, pirates, slaves, mercenaries, and laborers – many of whom have made voyages by sea (Blackburn 2015; Bose 2006; Campbell 2006; Dua 2016; Green 2011; Metcalf 2007; Parkin and Barnes 2016; Tagliacozzo 2009). Indeed, in the difficult task of demarcating and delineating the ocean as a spatial entity, the people whose journeys have helped us conceptualize the Indian Ocean as a world have largely been those who have moved across its waters.

I too began my work on the Indian Ocean starting by the sea. As I conducted fieldwork with gem traders on the coast, I uncovered a recognizable story of a littoral society linked to others across the sea. Yet, I found that to focus only on the maritime was to tell a partial tale. As I followed the gem-trading networks inland to Ratnapura, the perspectives of miners in the mountains reoriented my views, leading me to reconsider where and how we locate the Indian Ocean World. This mountainous vantage point revealed a world larger than the sea itself. Such views are not new. Many of the region's scholars acknowledge that the Indian Ocean has tendrils that extend inland. Historians retracing the steps of migrants, for instance, observe how maritime connections may be found even where the water is absent: "deep in the Malaysian jungle," Amrith writes, "Hindu shrines sprout from the landscape as if washed up by the sea" (2015: 8). At the same time, interior regions occupy an unstable place in Indian Ocean imaginaries. As Verne (2019) observes, in attempting to identify shared characteristics of maritime communities, Indian Ocean scholars have sought features that distinguish littoral societies from those in the hinterlands, resulting in dichotomous views of maritime coasts and terrestrial hinterlands. By doing so, we risk replacing land-bound imaginaries of space with bounded notions of the maritime, portraying the hinterlands as cut off from maritime circuits of exchange, as terrestrial counterpoints to a connected oceanic world (for exceptions, see McKinley 2018; Sivasundaram 2013).

How then do we conceptualize the Indian Ocean World beyond the sea in ways that moves past dichotomous views of coasts and hinterlands? "A history of an ocean," Pearson wrote, "needs to be amphibious, moving easily between land and sea" (2007: 5). This chapter is an amphibious ethnographic account drawing on the spatial and temporal imaginaries of Sri Lankan miners and traders. I distinguish the analytic frameworks developed by Indian Ocean scholars from emic conceptions of space and time in the region. The Indian Ocean world, I found, is not a category that the miners and traders I worked with recognize or use to locate themselves. However, they have their own spatial and temporal imaginaries. I explore their senses of space and time in the Indian Ocean through the notion of elsewheres, which enfolds imaginaries of distant places and pasts that continue to shape their risky pursuits. I follow their attempts to become unstuck from their places of origin and economic conditions through speculative mining and trading. Through this, I examine when and where coasts, hinterlands, and the ocean itself become significant. Following their journeys into the earth and across the ocean, I trace how their movements are shaped by multiple temporalities, some extending into geologic time, prior to the formation of the Indian Ocean. These temporalities form undercurrents that continue to shape their movements and imaginaries.

By attending to emic experiences of time and space in the region, I not only work towards reimagining the relationship between the Indian Ocean world and the sea, but also seek to contribute to conversations amongst anthropologists developing new frameworks to understand the Indian Ocean as an active space today, rather than a lost world. Recent research, for instance, by Nidhi Mahajan, on the shadow economies of the maritime region, reveals how long-standing seafaring networks "do not recede from view in the face of nation-states," but move flexibly across different forms of state sovereignties and regulatory regimes, "charting a new course along old routes across the Indian Ocean" (2019: 416). Ethnographic perspectives, from both the land and the sea, capture the life of the contemporary Indian Ocean world, revising declensionist notions that this world disintegrated as nation-states rose and air travel replaced older forms of seaborne migration and trade.

Dreams of mobility

Rajan had been stuck. Not just for a while but for eight years. Each day, he returned from the mines empty-handed. At first, he didn't make much of it. This time of stagnation had come at the heels of a sudden windfall at a previous mine. Stone after stone had emerged from their panning baskets and each worker had gone home with several hundred thousand rupees in hand. As the foreman, he made a sizable amount, enough to repair the roof and to buy some gold. This was the feeling he had chased after since he tried his luck at an unlicensed mine as a 15-year-old and made 5000 rupees from his first attempt. The last windfall was everything he had dreamed of.

Then, suddenly, it dried up. Years passed. The money disappeared. The pieces of gold jewelry his wife had collected ended up in the bank, where she pawned them to meet their daily needs. At one point, 380,000 rupees worth of gold – everything she had gathered during their life together – was locked in the bank. And yet, he kept going to the mines.

I met Rajan at Sudath's house, where neighboring miners often gathered. Several evenings a week, I would make my way to Sudath's home. I would arrive around 5 pm to meet the men who gathered there after work had ended but before night fell and the heavy drinking began. In those hours, I would sit with Sudath and his neighbors, as they chewed betel and unpacked their days.

It was on one of these days that I first met Rajan. He struck me as unusual, for it was rare to meet a Tamil foreman. Sabaragamuwa is ethnically mixed but mining is mostly done by Sinhalese men. Yet Rajan had worked as a miner all his life and was one of the most skilled foremen around. The night I met him, Rajan was preparing to work at a new mine on a land owned by the Saman Devāle, a powerful regional shrine dedicated to Lord Saman, a deity from whom miners sought blessings each time they descended underground. The day ahead held promise. I could picture it. Baskets of fruit would be offered to the deity at the Saman Devāle. Makeshift shrines would be constructed at the site, facing four directions. As the foreman, Rajan would make the first cut into the earth. The mine owner's wife would prepare a festive breakfast: *kiribath*, rice boiled in coconut milk; *katta sambol*, made of Maldive fish ground in chili and lime; and *kavum*, sweets made from rice flour and jaggery. They would stand around, estimating how deep they would need to dig.

Tonight though, the conversation was not on beginnings but on periods of stagnation. It began when I asked Rajan about the longest period in which he went without making money. Eight years, he said, he was stuck without cash while debt mounted.

"Did you think of giving up mining?" I asked.

"No,"

"What kept you going?" I asked, trying to imagine what it must have been like to spend years leading one crew after another into the earth, digging, tunneling, and panning, to no avail.

He laughed. "Chance," he said. "I was waiting for my chance. You see, what is different about mining is that you are chasing after something unseen. You never know when it will come. But when it comes, it comes all at once. It doesn't go to waste. In other jobs, what you bring home is gone by the end of the day. Not here. You can do something with it."

Rajan's words echoed those of other miners. With mining, periods of bounty are interspersed with periods of scarcity. Miners wait for their chance like they wait for the rains after the April sun has scorched the earth. The reward, in their eyes, if it comes, is an amount of cash substantial enough to transform into tangible, material things – an extra room in the house, a motorbike, gold. Rajan had a few such moments in past decades. "He made it all happen," Sudath told me, "he built a house, he sent his children to school. All from mining." There was shared pride in his voice, not just in his friend, but in the possibilities held open by their labor. A vocational pride.

Yet, I knew that the dream went further. It was not stability that most miners sought, but upward mobility that was rarely within the reach of manual labor. Workers often spoke of their desires to find a winning stone. They described these stones as *"goda ena gal,"* stones that could deliver them out of the muddy pits. Miners dream of finding a winning stone to achieve a kind of transmutation that enables a person to change from one state to the other, to move from one class to another, to become mine owners or landowners.

To embrace the possibility for such mobility meant dealing with prolonged periods of stasis. Listening to Rajan, I realized how dreams of mobility and experiences of stuckness were entangled. These dreams sustained Rajan through eight years without cash. While this may seem hard to comprehend, enough of these aspirations have been realized in Ratnapura to hold open the possibility for such transmutations, however remote (see Walsh 2003 for parallels in Madagascar). Houses, even mansions, have been built. Class and caste oppression, with their crippling constraints, had seemingly been overcome in individual lives through money earned by gems, even though men who achieved such mobility continue to be aware of the stigma of their origins. Newly built manor houses dot the hills, their woodwork replicating the styles of old manor houses belonging to the region's elite in an architecture of aspiration. Upon passing such homes, miners would say to me: "So and so started inside the pits. See what they made of themselves." Tales are told of remarkable feats. They are shared, embellished, and recounted to the point where fact and fiction meld into each other, shaping collective dreams. As Scarry writes, "beauty brings copies of itself into being" (2011: 3). So it is with stories of aspirational dreams realized against the odds. It is these dreams that hover above the diesel fumes, the dreams that hold at bay the terror of a tunnel collapse. It is the hopes of miners of getting unstuck that make it possible for gems to be excavated from archaic riverbeds underneath the mountains before making their way across the sea.

In pursuing their aspirations, miners also unearth other material objects that fuel their imagination. As workers excavate alluvial deposits, ghosts of the past emerge, bringing traces of the Indian Ocean left by strangers from elsewhere.

Elsewheres

I heard it again when I went to the mine that day. *Mukkaru*. Damith, a seasoned miner, pointed to a mound that workers describe as *kunu pas*, waste soil. This was made from the material removed to find the *illama*, an alluvial deposit. Sticking out of the sand were shards of pottery. Damith picked up a piece and tossed it back onto the mound. It must have been an old stove, he speculated. He saw the discovery as an excellent sign. It meant that they had been here before, the people he described as *Mukkaru*. They were Muslims, he said, and had been here long ago, from somewhere abroad. Where, he did not know, but from the Middle East, he mused. They had mined, he explained, for specific stones. The rest, they left behind. "How do you know they were here?" I asked. "They would leave these stones they had drilled holes in – *Mukkaru gal (stones)* – that's how we know." If they had come before, it meant that they took what they wanted and left everything else. Everything else was what Damith was after: blue and yellow sapphires, rare pink padparadschas, shot with orange. These stones held promise, promise and possibilities that lay underneath the ground.

Here in Sabaragamuwa, with no technical means for prospecting, the only option is to dig, searching for clues. As they dig, mineworkers are both tunnel builders and archeologists, looking for traces in the aggregated layers of soil. Like archeologists, they examine the soil, interpreting the shards they find as "writing on the ground" (Dawdy 2016: 40). These fragments tell stories – if there is this, then there must be that. If a remnant of an old tunnel appears, then there lies the possibility of striking the alluvial deposit. While many of these buried tunnels are recent, built within their lifetimes, sometimes older objects appear – such as the small stones with tiny holes in them – that are shards of life from a much older time. It is these clues from the more distant past that workers seek out to imagine the possibilities of finding gems.

Everywhere in Sabaragamuwa, I kept hearing about the *Mukkaru* people and of their pierced stones. Aware that I was researching mining, workers would ask me if I knew where they were from, what they were looking for, and why they pierced the stones. I had no answers. To date, there has been no archeological research to investigate the *Mukkaru* stories, although one study suggests that these shards may have been left by an itinerant bead-making community from South India, which would explain the existence of the pierced stones (Dehigama 2016). What I am most interested here, though, is the significance that the material remnants have for miners today, how these traces fit into miners' imaginaries, and how they bring Indian Ocean connectivities into the mental landscapes of men in these hinterland villages. Such imaginaries provide windows into how wider worlds of connectivity become locally known in mining sites (see Walsh 2004). In Ratnapura, miners' sense of Indian Ocean connectivities come not from looking out at the sea 80 kilometers away but from looking into the earth. Elsewheres are located, buried in fact, underground.

The elsewheres of miners' *Mukkaru* stories speak of places that are distant, unknown, and unnamed, yet linked to them across space and time. These elsewheres are not specific locations in the Indian Ocean that they can name and identify but constitute imagined geographies of connectivity. Strangers from these elsewheres have become familiar to mineworkers through the materiality of the mines. Through years of work, miners have gained an intimate knowledge of that which lies underneath the ground: the layers of soil, silt, and sand, the pockets of gases trapped between layers, the ancient riverbeds that carry gems. With this knowledge also comes a well-honed understanding of the technologies and practices required to tunnel through the terrain. They draw on this knowledge to read the fragments that they find and make inferences about how those who had been there before had mined and what they may have been looking for.

These material traces contain clues and leads to coveted mineral deposits. They provide a means of navigation, of wayfinding underground. In speaking of the *Mukkaru* and in using their traces as routes to alluvial deposits, miners link their present and future to the pasts of strangers who had crossed the ocean. For them, the discovery of a *Mukkaru* stone creates what archeologist Shanon Lee Dawdy (2016) describes as a sense of heterotemporality, where the past, present, and future are experienced together through an accidental encounter with a material remnant from the past. In such encounters, Dawdy notes, drawing on Benjamin's writing on time, the past suddenly lives again, like a haunting, "where what has been comes together in a flash with the now to form a constellation" (Benjamin 1999, cited in Dawdy 2016: 31). For miners, encounters with *Mukkaru* shards also open a pathway to gems that could bring about their much-desired futures of transcending the stuckness of labor at the mines.

Returning to the question of how the Indian Ocean world becomes known to those who live and work within it, the discovery of *Mukkaru* stones enables miners to form senses of themselves as participants in a longer history of trans-local connectivity that the gem trade has enabled. While they see themselves as part of a wider world today, connected by the global circulation of the stones that they find, the knowledge of elsewheres that come through the *Mukkaru* stories has a different spatial and temporal significance – it encompasses imaginaries that speak to an emic sense of geographic connectivity and of historical time. This time is not bygone but continues to appear and is actively sought and engaged with.

Mountains, oceans, and estranged stones

If connections across the ocean become visible and knowable to men in the mountains through the material traces left by those who crossed the seas a long time ago, then how do they appear to those who live on the littoral, growing up hearing the sound of its waves? What kinds of Indian Ocean pasts and futures become folded into these elsewheres? I will explore these questions through the stories of one family in the coastal gem-trading town of Beruwala.

* * *

I didn't know Faisa had a brother until I saw an unfamiliar face in her maternal home. I met her through her husband Ismeth. Ismeth, Faisa, and I would drive south together from Colombo, where they spent their weekdays, leaving on Saturday morning to make it in time for the Beruwala market. Sometimes they would return to Colombo that night, but on most days would remain through the weekend. Such comings and goings were common for women of her age, who moved between their maternal homes in Beruwala, and their houses in Colombo, where they had moved to educate their children. Until recently, it was only the men who moved back and forth, but in her generation, things had changed.

For Faisa's father, husband, and her sons, mobility was a way of life. Home was a place one left and returned to; the weeks and months were shaped by comings and goings. Many of their travels remained within Sri Lanka, as they moved between coastal towns, or between Beruwala, and Ratnapura in the hills. The ocean was never far. The coastal route from Colombo to Beruwala hugged the seashore; between the coconut groves and fishing villages, we could see the turquoise waters extending towards the horizon. For Faisa's family, the ocean constituted an intimately familiar landscape – a place to walk, swim, buy seafood, to glimpse en route between their homes – and yet, not a place to cross. Elsewheres, for them, seemed multiple, but not across the ocean. Or so it appeared until I met Faiza's brother Firaz.

He was seated in an armchair when we arrived that morning, wearing a light-colored shirt and a white sarong. As he sat there, his bare feet tapped the red cement floor. His large hands rattled the delicate porcelain coffee cup. His eyes would wander off even while he had a captive audience. A group of younger men, all cousins, had come to see him, asking him questions, pressing him for more information about East Africa. Everyone seemed a little more animated – his mother's steps were quicker, his father laughed more. Faisa's smile had gained a feisty edge. Surprised to learn they were siblings, I said to her, "I didn't know you had a brother." "He is never here," she replied, waving her hand in his direction with a shake of her head, as though she was chastising a recalcitrant child. He had come from Madagascar. "He comes," she said, snapping her fingers, "and just like that, he's gone. Off to Madagascar, Tanzania, or who knows where."

Dreams of upward mobility had not come easily to her family, despite their multistory house in Beruwala. Her father had started out as a gem cutter. Her eyes grew moist talking about him. He had run away from home at 14, trying his luck in Colombo. When that failed, he had traveled to Ratnapura to work in his brother's shop. This too had not gone well. Strapped for cash, he had approached a Sinhalese businessman and borrowed 1000 rupees to begin trading by himself. This was a sizable sum in the 1970s. Then he had his lucky break. With 600 rupees, he bought a sapphire in Ratnapura and sold it to a trader in Beruwala for 25,000 rupees. He built his business this way, buying stones from gem auctions in Ratnapura and selling them to South Indian traders and other traders from Beruwala. When he told me about it, he pointed to his children – Faisa who was preparing tea in the kitchen and Firaz who was playing with a

Figure 5.1 Firaz's father, Firaz, and Firaz's young son sort through an old collection of gems while Faisa captures the moment with her camera.

Image credit: Nethra Samarawickrema.

neighbor's child – and said: "I sent them to the best schools. Private schools with English education. They both speak perfect English. I didn't finish school, but I educated them. And I gave all my sisters in marriage. All from the money I earned." Seeing his eyes soften as he said this, knowing that he could not converse in English himself, I felt my own throat tighten, realizing how self-making was a multi-generational endeavor for him.

Traveling between the hinterlands and coast brought social mobility for the family, enabling them to move from working as gem-cutters to become traders within a generation. Their trajectory paralleled that of many others in Beruwala. To make this possible, Faisa's father had to leave the coast and turn away from the ocean, traveling inland to source stones. It was through buying from the hinterlands and selling them to Indian traders who crossed the sea that he made his money. The Indian Ocean and the maritime world did not draw him as the mountains did. The small coastal town he grew up in was more a place of entrapment for him as a youth, a place he had to leave. Mobility for him came from traveling to the hinterlands, returning home to sell the stones he purchased. Nevertheless, his mobility was set off by other Indian Ocean mobilities.

Crossing the ocean would require another generation. It was only in the 1970s with air travel that Beruwala's traders began to go abroad frequently. For Faisa's family, such movements came later in the 1990s. It was only made possible by the Madagascan boom. This had made the crucial difference for Firaz. The family had worried about him since he was a teenager. He had not done well in school. He would come home from his private school on the weekends and hang out with his cousins at the gem market. Even then he wouldn't play by the rules. Then one day, he announced he was leaving for Madagascar, a place on the lips of every young man in town. News had spread that there was a sapphire boom, and droves were boarding flights to the island. This was a new departure for them. For Beruwala's traders, sapphires were not stones they brought to Sri Lanka, but stones that they purchased in the island's hinterlands, cut, and polished on the coast and sent abroad. Then, Madagascar boomed. Those who traveled there returned, reporting that the gems they encountered across the sea had an uncanny resemblance to the gems at home; at times it was hard to tell the difference. The stones from Ratnapura were rising in price as sellers from there were traveling abroad. During Madagascar's gem rush, Firaz and other youngsters from Beruwala shifted their interest from Sri Lanka's mines for those in East Africa. Now, he came and went. That was the end of his time in Sri Lanka. He would return with new stones from Madagascar, Mozambique, and Tanzania only to leave again.

Unlike his father's generation, Firaz's journeys required crossing the sea. His elsewheres lay not in the mountains, but across the western reaches of the Indian Ocean in East Africa. While the process of traveling to Madagascar was new for Beruwala's traders, the routes they traveled were old. They flew above maritime thoroughfares traversed by traders, sailors, financiers, slaves, and indentured workers who had moved for centuries between South Asia and East Africa along Indian Ocean trading routes (Bishara 2017; Campbell 2006; Machado 2014; Parkin and Barnes 2016). Moreover, unbeknownst to them, they were retracing the steps of a much older Indian Ocean journey, which extended far back into geologic time, a journey that had shaped the objects they traded.

When Firaz and others noticed that the gems in Madagascar were similar to those in Sri Lanka, they were glimpsing through the materiality of the stones, traces of geologic processes that scientists have been studying for half a century. Through research on plate tectonics, geologists have uncovered that in the Proterozoic Era, a supercontinent named Gondwana formed through a major collision between West Gondwana, comprised of Africa and South America, and East Gondwana, encompassing Australia, Antarctica, and India (Macdougall 2011; Sankaran 2003). Following this collision, known as the Pan-African event, which took place approximately 600 million years ago, before the opening up of the Indian Ocean, Sri Lanka and Madagascar lay side-by-side in Gondwana (Dissanayake and Chandrajith 1999). Not only did this collision bring the islands together, but it also created a continuous mineralization zone that ran through Madagascar, Mozambique, Tanzania, Sri Lanka, the Southern tip of India, and Antarctica (ibid.). Sri Lankan and Madagascan gems were born together through the same tectonic event, which created the same mineral varieties – corundum, spinel, topaz, zircons, and aquamarine – in both islands (ibid.). Strikingly, geologists now hold that the tectonic processes that led to the assembly of Gondwana, which resulted in the genesis of gems in both islands, are fundamentally linked to subsequent tectonic events that later dismantled the supercontinent (Yoshida and Santosh 2018). During the Cretaceous period, as the landmass of East Gondwana broke up, Madagascar began separating from India about 84 million years ago, opening up the Western Indian Ocean (Acharyya 2000). As the ocean was born, Sri Lanka and Madagascar drifted apart, migrating away from each other, taking their identical gemstones with them.

In the 1990s, Madagascar's sapphire boom drew traders from across the world (Walsh 2016). When Beruwala's traders arrived, they were startled to discover the familiar in an unfamiliar land – the stones in Ratnapura had cousins in Madagascar. Amongst the foreign traders who followed the boom, Sri Lankans were able to establish themselves as key buyers of its sapphires, for they could tap into their localized knowledge of Ratnapura's sapphires to trade their estranged cousins in Madagascar. This was particularly lucrative as the uncut Madagascan stones were cheap to purchase, and they had the expertise in Beruwala – from gem cutters who had generations of experience working with Ratnapura's sapphires – to cut, polish, and recirculate the Madagascan gems throughout their Indian Ocean trading network.

Multiple temporalities of movement and connectivity became folded into Firaz's journeys, suggesting new views of mobility in the Indian Ocean. Geology reveals that it is not just the people of the Indian Ocean who have been on the move. On a geologic timescale, the ocean itself has been a restless place: the continental shelves that make up its rim have also been in motion. Places dispersed across the Indian Ocean today were linked in deep time. Sri Lanka, Madagascar, Tanzania, and Mozambique bear the mineral remains of these linkages. In a moment of heterotemporality, of multiple pasts and presents converging, Firaz's search for an elsewhere retraced the steps that the stones themselves had once traveled. Collectively, Beruwala's traders' search for sapphires connected the then and now, their mercantile routes closing a loop in geologic time by drawing together islands that were once adjacent and then drifted apart as the ocean came into being.

Conclusion

To see the Indian Ocean from the multiple vantage points that make up the gem-trading network is to view the region through shifting perspectives. Each perspective – from the bottom of a mineshaft, a mountainous landscape, a coastal town, an airplane flying above an old trading route – provides a different view, changing how one imagines this world. For those who work at each location, pursuing their dreams, Indian Ocean connectivities are experienced and imagined through emic senses of space and time that become folded into localized vocabularies and stories of elsewheres. These elsewheres change, depending on the position from which one looks. For the men from Beruwala, the elsewheres are specific and known through travel and trade, even though the locations change across generations. For Faisa's father, elsewheres lay in the mountains; for Firaz, they were found across the ocean. For Ratnapura's miners, the elsewheres remain significant yet elusive, distant in space and time. For each of them, their ties to other places were made possible through the seaborne movements of others, yet the sea itself lies outside the primary frame of their spatial imaginaries.

However, fueled by speculative dreams of social and spatial mobility, miners' and traders' search for elsewheres link them with people and places of the Indian Ocean world, not just across space, but also across time. Indian Ocean pasts do not lie dormant. They emerge in unexpected ways, intruding on the present, shaping dreams of potential futures. These pasts show up as shards of old stoves, as pierced stones, as imprints left by tectonic collisions, opening pathways to gems that hold the possibility of transmutation, both real and imagined, for those who seek them. Some of these pasts run deep into geologic time. Islands separated at the birth of the Indian Ocean carry material traces of their proximity in gemstones formed together 600 million years ago, traces that produce new Indian Ocean connections today.

These connectivities reveal an Indian Ocean that is not a lost world that disintegrated with the rise of nation-states and the advent of air travel, but one that continues to be made and remade through exchange and movement. While the region's interconnected pasts have been uncovered by the remarkable efforts of its historians, to reimagine it today also requires an anthropology of the Indian Ocean. As archeologists, geologists, and historians of the Indian Ocean have pieced together the region's past through material and narrative fragments in archives, inscriptions, and archeological sites, ethnographic perspectives reveal how traces of these histories shape the aspirations, pursuits, and futures of its denizens today.

In particular, as the gem trade shows, the Indian Ocean remains significant for many of those who are not easily recognized as actors within it, given that they live and work in places that are at the edges of what is often imagined to be the Indian Ocean world. The speculative pursuits and spatial and temporal imaginaries of my interlocuters show it is possible to reimagine the relationship between the contemporary Indian Ocean world and the sea. Their mobilities reveal a world with the ocean at its center yet one that does not end where its waters meet the shores. As it has always folded in many other landscapes of connectivity, for those who live, work, and travel within it, this world linked by the water, and made through seaborne exchange, continues without the ocean as the only conduit for movement. Their work, movement, and imaginaries show that it is indeed possible to be people of the Indian Ocean without having seen, or journeyed elsewhere, by sea.

Acknowledgments

I am deeply grateful to the miners of Ratnapura and traders of Beruwala who shared their stories with me. To protect their privacy, they remain unnamed. I thank Smriti Srinivas, Bettina Ng'weno and Neelima Jeyachandran for inviting me to participate in this publication, and for their feedback. I am indebted to geologist Gregory Dering for explaining the assembly and dismantling of the supercontinents and for helping me see the Indian Ocean with new eyes. Anne Blackburn, as well as members of the Dark Skies Feminist Ethnography Collective – Grace Zhou, Dilshanie Perera, and Allison Kendra – gave invaluable feedback. My thanks also go to David Stentiford, who nudged me towards making a non-human turn and to Sriyanthi and Tilak Samarawickrema for their support. My research and writing were funded by the Wenner-Gren Foundation's Dissertation Fieldwork Grant, the National Science Foundation's Doctoral Dissertation Improvement Grant, the Mellon Foundation's Dissertation Fellowship, and the Stanford SEED Foundation's PhD Fellowship.

References

Acharyya, S. K. 2000. "Break up of Australia–India–Madagascar Block, Opening of the Indian Ocean and Continental Accretion in Southeast Asia with Special Reference to the Characteristics of the Peri-Indian Collision Zones." *GONDWANA RESEARCH* 3: 425–444.

Amrith, Sunil S. 2015. *Crossing the Bay of Bengal: The Furies of Nature and the Fortunes of Migrants*. Cambridge, Mass: Harvard University Press.

Aslanian, Sebouh David. 2011. *From the Indian Ocean to the Mediterranean: The Global Trade Networks of Armenian Merchants from New Julfa*. Berkley: University of California Press.

Bishara, Fahad Ahmad. 2017. "A Sea of Debt by Fahad Ahmad Bishara." Cambridge Core. March 2017.

Blackburn, Anne M. 2015. "Buddhist Connections in the Indian Ocean: Changes in Monastic Mobility, 1000–1500." *Jeconsocihistori Journal of the Economic and Social History of the Orient* 58 (3): 237–266.

Bose, Sugata. 2006. *A Hundred Horizons: The Indian Ocean in the Age of Global Empire*. Cambridge, Mass.: Harvard University Press.

Campbell, Gwyn. 2006. *The Structure of Slavery in Indian Ocean Africa and Asia*.

Chaudhuri, K.N. 1985. *Trade and Civilisation in the Indian Ocean: An Economic History from the Rise of Islam to 1750*. Cambridge; New York: Cambridge University Press.

Das Gupta, Ashin. 1982. "Indian Merchants and the Trade in the Indian Ocean c. 1500–1750." In *The Cambridge Economic History of India*, edited by Tapan Raychaudhuri and Irfan Habib, 407–433. Cambridge: Cambridge University Press.

Dawdy, Shanon, Lee. 2016. *Patina: A Profane Archaeology, Dawdy*. Chicago, IL: University of Chicago Press.

Dehigama, Kanchana. 2016. "Bead Making in Southern Sri Lanka: Some Observations." *Narrations* 1 (2): 6–29.

Dissanayake, C.B. and Rohana Chandrajith. 1999. "Sri Lanka-Madagascar Gondwana Linkage: Evidence for a Pan-African Mineral Belt." *Journal of Geology* 107 (2): 223.

Dua, Jatin. 2016. "Dhow Encounters." *Transition* 119: 49–59.

Goswami, Dr Chhaya. 2011. *The Call of the Sea: Kachchhi Traders in Muscat and Zanzibar, c.1800–1880*. New Delhi: Orient Blackswan.

Green, Nile. 2011. *Bombay Islam: The Religious Economy of the West Indian Ocean, 1840–1915*. Cambridge: Cambridge University Press.

Ho, Engseng. 2004. "Empire through Diasporic Eyes: A View from the Other Boat." *Comparative Studies in Society and History* 46 (2): 210–246.

Ho, Engseng. 2006. *The Graves of Tarim Genealogy and Mobility across the Indian Ocean*. Berkeley: University of California Press.

Macdougall, J.D. 2011. *Why Geology Matters Decoding the Past, Anticipating the Future*. Berkeley: University of California Press.

Machado, Pedro. 2014. *Ocean of Trade: South Asian Merchants, Africa and the Indian Ocean, c.1750–1850*. Cambridge: Cambridge University Press.

Mahajan, Nidhi. 2019. "Dhow Itineraries: The Making of a Shadow Economy in the Western Indian Ocean." *Comparative Studies of South Asia, Africa and the Middle East* 39 (3): 407–419.

McKinley, Alexander. 2018. "Mountain at a Center of the World." Duke. https://dukespace. lib.duke.edu/dspace/handle/10161/16849.

Metcalf, Thomas R. 2007. *Imperial Connections India in the Indian Ocean Arena, 1860–1920*. Berkeley: University of California Press.

Parkin, David and Ruth Barnes. 2016. *Ships and the Development of Maritime Technology on the Indian Ocean*.

Pearson, Michael N. 2006. "Littoral Society: The Concept and the Problems." *Journal of World History* 17 (4): 353–373.

Pearson, M.N. 2007. *The Indian Ocean*. London: Routledge.

Pearson, Michael. 2010. "Islamic Trade, Shipping, Port-States and Merchant Communities in the Indian Ocean, Seventh to Sixteenth Centuries." In *The New Cambridge History of Islam/Eleventh to Eighteenth Centuries Volume 3, The Eastern Islamic World*, edited by David Morgan and Anthony Reid. Cambridge: Cambridge University Press.

Risso, Patricia. 1995. *Merchants and Faith: Muslim Commerce and Culture in The Indian Ocean*. Boulder, CA: Westview Press.

Sankaran, A.V. 2003. "The Supercontinent Medley: Recent Views." *Current Science* 85 (8): 1121–1124.

Scarry, Elaine. 2011. *On Beauty and Being Just*. London: Duckworth Overlook.

Simpson, Edward. 2006. *Muslim Society and the Western Indian Ocean the Seafarers of Kachchh*. London; New York: Routledge.

Sivasundaram, Sujit. 2013. *Islanded*. Chicago: University of Chicago Press. www.press. uchicago.edu/ucp/books/book/chicago/I/bo15506861.html.

Tagliacozzo, Eric. 2009. *Secret Trades, Porous Borders: Smuggling and States along a Southeast Asian Frontier, 1865–1915*. New Haven, CN; London: Yale University Press.

Trivellato, Francesca. 2012. *The Familiarity of Strangers: The Sephardic Diaspora, Livorno, and Cross-Cultural Trade in the Early Modern Period*. New Haven, CN; London: Yale University Press.

Verne, Julia. 2019. "The Ends of the Indian Ocean: Tracing Coastlines in the Tanzanian 'Hinterland.'" *History in Africa* 46 (June): 359–383.

Walsh, A. 2003. "'Hot Money' and Daring Consumption in a Northern Malagasy Sapphire-Mining Town." *AMERICAN ETHNOLOGIST* 30: 290–305.

Walsh, Andrew. 2004. "In the Wake of Things: Speculating in and about Sapphires in Northern Madagascar." *American Anthropologist*. 106 (2): 225–237.

Walsh, Andrew. 2016. *Made in Madagascar: Sapphires, Ecotourism, and the Global Bazaar*. Toronto, ON: University of Toronto Press.

Yoshida, Masaki and M. Santosh. 2018. "Voyage of the Indian Subcontinent since Pangea Breakup and Driving Force of Supercontinent Cycles: Insights on Dynamics from Numerical Modeling." *Geoscience Frontiers*, SPECIAL ISSUE: Frontiers in geoscience: A tribute to Prof. Xuanxue Mo, 9 (5): 1279–1292.

6 Dicey waterways

Evolving networks and contested spatialities in Goa

Maya Costa-Pinto

Introduction[1]

In 2014, an Indian news website noted that floating casinos in Goa, a former Portuguese colony on the West Coast of India, "now dot the picturesque Mandovi River, in whose historic waters once Arab *dhows* and Portuguese galleons anchored for trade in gold and spices" (Nagvenkar 2014). The waterways on the edge of the capital city, Panaji (also known as Panjim),[2] accommodate fishing boats, mechanized fishing trawlers, tourist boats, and passenger ferries. In recent years however, offshore water-based casinos have come to dominate the waterscape. Initially introduced to Goa in the 1990s to attract tourists, over the past few years, a number of casinos have come to occupy the city waterways. These floating casinos employ migrants from other parts of South Asia and the economic and social activities that take place on them, according to the government, produce substantial revenue for Goa. They have also generated significant debates about environmental pollution and urban planning and, residents suggested, irrevocably altered the spatial dynamics of the city. This chapter situates the Goan casino as an ethnographic site that draws upon historical maritime routes and oceanic networks even as it unsettles and remakes the surrounding urban environment. In doing so, it reveals the ways in which oceanic imaginaries and urban landscapes are intimately and integrally connected in contemporary Indian Ocean worlds.

The first floating casino to operate on the Mandovi River, the "Caravela," was named after the first Portuguese vessel to enter Goa in the sixteenth century. Celebrated as the Portuguese "ship of discoveries," the original vessel was known for its maneuverability and ability to withstand turbulent weather and tall sea waves, which made it ideal for long voyages (see Mathew 1988: 280–283). In contrast, the casino Caravela and the casinos that followed were parked in a river and most were considered by residents and experts alike to be largely unseaworthy (see Sequiera 2017). In 2013, the Caravela casino disappeared and re-emerged on the Mandovi in 2016 as "MV Royal Flotel." The vessel – completely refurbished to resemble a "marine mammal coming up for air" (D'Souza 2016: 11) – has been described as a floating hotel that accommodates offshore gaming, although some Panaji residents I spoke with preferred to characterize it as a casino "with a few hotel rooms." Shaped like a dolphin, the casino architecture is such that it "seeks connections" with its watery environment and "distance from the gambling games" (Kingma 2008: 35) invoking a sense of play to suggest that it is not merely a gambling house but also a place for amusement and enjoyment. Other casinos situated on the river are modeled on the classic Mississippi riverboat casinos – the exterior form directly referencing the interior content.

Currently, Goa houses both onshore and offshore (or floating) casinos but live gaming, which includes baccarat, roulette, blackjack, and poker are only allowed in water-based, "offshore" casinos. The first offshore casino was allowed on the Mandovi River in the late 1990s and since then more casinos have appeared on the waterways. Although there have been recent attempts to clarify the meaning of the term, "offshore"[3] was not explicitly defined in legislation and despite promises by the government to "throw the casinos into the sea" (Kamat 2014a), they remain on the Mandovi River, "offshore," but still within city limits.

Casino advertising proliferates around Panaji and land and water-based traffic jams and riverfront parking problems have become increasingly common. Recent reports from the National Institute of Oceanography and the Goa State Pollution Control Board noted that the waterways outside Panaji had "alarmingly high levels of coliform bacteria" and were therefore unsafe for fishing, swimming and other water sports (Botelho 2018: 59; Tare 2017).[4] Over the years, city residents have lobbied to relocate these casinos to the Arabian Sea but their campaigns have met with limited success. "Offshore" in local news articles and official documents in Goa refer to a distance of 12 nautical miles from the shore (see Botelho 2018: 58; Tare 2017). However, many city residents rarely employed these technical, juridical descriptions in daily conversation, the "sea" or "ocean" was understood to be a watery expanse situated a significant distance from the city and "offshore" was equated with "out of sight." Even as many residents are aware of the casino presence on the river, few consider the casinos "offshore."

In general, casino operators do not want to shift to the sea; traveling to the casino and, as one noted, "loading" and "unloading" will be challenging and "risky" especially as there is "no security in the high sea" (Tare 2017) and much of the infrastructure, the labor, and the customers are situated on land. As the push to move the casinos "out of sight" gathers momentum, the casinos have petitioned to relocate live gaming from the water to land. Recently, the government has indicated that casinos will have the option of moving to a "specially designated entertainment zone" on land (Botelho 2018: 59; *Navhind Times* 2017) 'out of sight' for city residents and will therefore likely be "external to much social observation and thus community monitoring" (Cameron and Palan 2004 in Zalik 2009: 557). A land-based location, one casino chairman asserted to the British Broadcasting Corporation (BBC), will enable casinos to grow their market and "create a destination just like Singapore or Macau" (Hashmi 2015).

As the preceding accounts suggest, an ethnographic focus on casinos highlights several contested forms of spatial practice across land and water. This chapter focuses on two intersecting scales of spatial practice: First, it examines various Indian Ocean and Lusophone networks that are emerging and evolving as casinos become sites that reaffirm Goa's transoceanic connections across Asia, while simultaneously facilitating regional connections between Goa and other parts of India through labor and tourism. Second, it explores the multiple ways stationary water-based casinos reconfigure or disrupt quotidian urban practices. Foregrounding these intersections present alternative ways of conceptualizing the urban oceanic interface in Indian Ocean worlds.

Evolving networks and new routes

Goa played a pivotal role in the Portuguese empire of Asia and was the focus of its efforts to concentrate Indian Ocean trade in its ports (Pearson 2003: 135; Subrahmanyam 2011). As an administrative and economic center of Portuguese Asia, it was the "entry point into the Indian subcontinent and a crossing point for the commercial shipping routes between the Indian Ocean and the South China Sea" (Goncalves 2003: 56), and became a hub for merchants from Malacca, Persia and China (among other places). The resulting prosperity earned it the moniker "Golden Goa" (Fernandes [1989] 2002: 65) and historical literature on Goa highlights the importance of transoceanic connections within the Indian Ocean realm and the Lusophone world (Boxer 1969; Pearson 1981). In particular, during the late sixteenth century and early seventeenth century, Macau served as a regular port of call (and occasionally as the final destination) as part of the Goa–Japan route – one of the most important Portuguese shipping routes in Asia (Murteira 2014: 95). In addition, ships would regularly travel between Lisbon and Macau via Goa. Portuguese vessels would depart Macau and travel through Siam, Burma, Timor, Malacca, and Ceylon to reach Goa, carrying silk, porcelain and textiles before journeying to Portugal (Hao 2011: 57). In their travels from Portugal (through Goa) to Macau, the ships would bring sandalwood, silver and other items (Hao 2011: 57). In the twentieth century, new transoceanic networks situated around the export of iron ore were fostered with various parts of Europe and East Asia including Japan (Newman 2001: 13–14).

After Portuguese rule ended and Goa became a part of the Indian nation-state in 1961, tourism and mining came "to represent the foundation of the post-colonial Goan economy" (Trichur 2013: 109). Goa was a "haven" for western travelers and although initially tourist activity was limited to a few areas mainly in North Goa, it caused a significant disruption to local life; by the 1980s, the emergence of charter tourism led to unregulated growth and ecological damage (Routledge 2000: 2649, 2001: 225; Saldanha 2002: 96; see also Alvares 2002). In the 1980s, the Goa government, in an attempt to bring the economy in line with the national economic agenda, advocated for and obtained support from the Indian government for their tourism policy (Trichur 2013: 113). Trichur (2013) notes that since the 1980s, tourism has become the "the growth sector of the Goan economy" (109) as the Indian government instituted a series of incentives and subsidies to draw investment to tourism (113).

In recent years however, there has been a shift towards "cultural" aspects of tourism, which has privileged Portuguese-inspired varieties of music, dance and architecture (Fernandes 2007: 125; Mora 2016: 26).[5] The nostalgic ideal of Portuguese Goa – an ideal that has been supported by public officials in a bid to generate more tourism – has upset some who resent the "representation of Goa as Portuguese" and insist that Goa is part of India (Fernandes 2007: 126).[6] Rather than focus exclusively on Goa's relationship with Portugal, the Goan tourism office and other assorted NGOs have recently sought to revitalize the cultural links between Goa and various former Lusophone colonies with a shared history, such as Macau. In addition to hosting the 2014 Lusofonia Games[7] and participating in various Lusofonia festivals, in 2016, a series of exhibitions was held in conjunction with the Macao Foundation, the Macao Government Tourism Office, and the Lusophone society of Goa at the Central State Library in Panaji.

As mining in the state has declined significantly,[8] the Goan government has increasingly come to rely on tourism to generate revenue. In recent years a steady stream of domestic visitors from the rapidly growing Indian middle class largely sustains the Goan tourist industry and fuels the demand for casinos (see Botelho 2018: 60). Although there is an influx of visitors during the "tourist season" (from October–February), Goa has struggled to attract tourists during the monsoon months when many coastal establishments (particularly in North Goa) close. The casinos, open throughout the year, have sought to fill this void and have positioned themselves as a 12-month tourist destination.

Some residents in Panaji expressed concern that Goa was fast becoming known as the "Las Vegas of India." However, casino developers also drew inspiration from other casino destinations in Asia, particularly Macau. In addition to the close cultural links with Goa, Macau is one of the most popular gambling destinations for Indian tourists: in 2002, there were 5000 Indian tourists in Macau and by 2010, there were 169,000 Indian tourists, many of whom were coming specifically to gamble (Unnithan 2011). This significant increase has been attributed to the International Indian Film Awards held in Macau in 2009, when a large contingent of the Hindi Film Industry traveled there (Unnithan 2011). Macau presents an ideal destination for Indian tourists: there are direct flights to Hong Kong (Macau is a short boat ride away), a tourist visa is available on arrival and, like Singapore (which is also becoming an increasingly popular gambling destination for Indian tourists), it can be a stopover – a regular port of call – on the way to or from another destination. The influx of Indian tourists has also led to the launch of a number of Indian restaurants in both Macau and Singapore (Unnithan 2011).

Given Goa's close proximity to India's major cities such as Bangalore, Mumbai, and Delhi, casino directors note that it has the "potential to catch the throng of gamblers" that usually head to other gambling destinations in Asia (Sharma 2014) especially as patrons are able to make multiple trips in a year. As one regular visitor from Bangalore noted in an interview with the BBC, he previously "used to travel to Macau twice a year, but now I come here [to Goa] every two months" (Hashmi 2015). A number of domestic tourists visiting casinos in Goa would have previously visited casinos in Macau, Singapore, Sri Lanka or Nepal. A *Times of India* article notes that Indian tourist operators emphasize the enthusiasm for gambling, particularly during festivals such as Diwali and divide the casino destinations Indian tourists frequent into four groups (see Kaushik 2016). The first category includes popular domestic destinations such as Goa and Sikkim. The second category comprises travelers who earlier chose Kathmandu but are now opting to travel to Sri Lanka as it has, according to travel companies, replaced Kathmandu as a superior experience for a similar price. The third group encompasses high-income earners who want to travel abroad specifically for gambling. These individuals usually opt for Macau. Finally, the high net-worth luxury travelers "only travel to Vegas" (Kaushik 2016).

The Goan casinos, one representative from a casino company contended to a news source, were not merely gambling hubs but rather an entertainment venue where a "family, a couple or a single person will find more than just gambling" (Sharma 2014). Similar to Macau or Singapore, he noted, visitors expect to "eat well, watch a show, shop or even stay over at an integrated hotel" (Sharma 2014). Casino representatives felt that it made strategic business sense to emphasize "entertainment gaming rather than hard-core gambling," given that the Goan casinos do not "offer the crazy table limits" that casinos in Macau or Las Vegas do; on cruise ship casinos, the table limits were generally also high (Sharma 2014). As one casino chairman noted to the BBC, "we are catering to the mass market, not the high rollers" (Hashmi 2015).

Michael,[9] a Goan in his thirties, characterized himself as a visitor to the Goan casinos but an occasional gambler. This was not unusual as he noted that a number of Goans who visit these casinos do not necessarily go to gamble but rather to enjoy the food and entertainment. Michael emphasized that although the casinos attracted a diverse customer base, most were male Indian tourists who would often come with their friends – casinos in Goa have largely remained a male realm. However, Michael noted that some men would also bring their families, who would stay in a hotel and partake in other tourist activities in Panaji and North Goa, while they gambled. Sometimes, if their relatives showed an interest, tourists would take the entire family to the casino, and casinos had areas for children precisely for this purpose.

The entrance to most of the water-based casinos is situated along the Panaji riverfront and visitors travel to the casinos via "feeder" boats. The interiors of the ships and the experience aboard have been tailored to Indian preferences. In one upscale casino, for example, the gaming tables were made in India and the mirrors were from "Chor bazaar"[10] (Das 2015). Most of the floating casino vessels comprise three or four levels. The first floor of the casino generally hosts a reception desk and a separate playroom for children. Parents could leave their children in this room in the care of the casino staff while they tried their luck in the casino. The food and entertainment area is located on a separate floor. The food, served "buffet style," includes vegetarian and non-vegetarian sections, which incorporates a selection of "western" and Indian dishes. In addition, Goan

Figure 6.1 A casino at night, Mandovi river, Goa.
Image Credit: Maya Costa-Pinto.

casinos generally have an entertainment space that often hosts a musical act along with a series of dance performances to popular Bollywood songs.

The gaming area occupies an entire floor and is specifically designed to suit Indian gambling preferences. In addition to games such as baccarat, roulette, and blackjack these casinos include others that are particularly popular in India such as Teen Patti[11] and Paplu[12] (see Sharma 2014). The gaming tables are usually situated in the center of the room while slot machines line the sides. Table games are much more popular than slot machines in India (see Das 2015) since gambling is treated as a social activity; slot machines, which require minimal, if any, social interaction and are very popular in the United States are therefore barely used.

Most casinos also have a VIP area for serious gamblers who buy a VIP package. Das notes that in the VIP area, guests are served "imported drinks" as opposed to regular customers who drink "Indian-made foreign liquor"[13] and in the upmarket casinos, certain areas reserved for high rollers are by invitation only (2015). These areas provide grander facilities – leather chairs, marble topped tables, private gaming suites as well as superior amenities including butler service and a corporate chef catering to the dietary requests of customers, which can include anything from sushi to Jain food (Das 2015). The aim is, presumably, to create an ambience similar to high-end casinos in Macau and Singapore where some of these guests are regular customers.

The workforce on the floating casinos is diverse. It includes Goans, some of whom have previously worked in the merchant navy or on cruise liners, and a significant number of employees from India's northeastern states (particularly Manipur, Mizoram, Nagaland).[14] There is also a large contingent from Nepal, where the casino industry is on the wane and layoffs occur frequently (Nagvenkar and Rodrigues 2013). The exodus from the northeast to major metropolitan areas in India is well-documented (see Karlsson and Kikon 2017) and many of the migrants from the northeastern states employed by the casinos are women who work primarily as casino dealers (Shetye 2014). A recent article in a local news website interviewed some of these casino dealers about their experiences (see Nagvenkar and Rodrigues 2013). Many female employees emphasized the difficult conditions they endured working in a casino, the judgment that ensued from people they met, the long shifts, and the response from casino patrons. Some had health issues that had resulted from working long shifts at the casino. However, others felt that the casino provided a stepping-stone to a future career within the hospitality and broader tourism industry (Nagenkar and Rodrigues 2013).

In his study of casino spaces in the Netherlands, Kingma (2008: 43) notes that, casinos, with security techniques and measures in terms of monitoring, handling money, and the enforcement of "behavioral norms" function as a "pan-optic space" (see Foucault 1979). In Goan casinos, women noted that they were "being heard and watched (virtually every second)" (Nagvenkar and Rodrigues 2013). One observed that the surveillance cameras throughout the casino, which monitored the behavior of all the guests, provided a safer working environment than some other tourist industries (Nagvenkar and Rodrigues 2013).[15] Indeed, a casino director in Goa argued that this constant surveillance provided safety for the entire family, especially children (Nagvenkar 2014).

The architecture of, and within, the casino vessel stood in sharp contrast to the neighborhood where the land-based entrance to the casino was located. Despite the fact that the casino has been designed with the South Asian customer in mind, the overall aesthetic of the casino interiors conforms to a template of "casino architecture" often inspired by spaces in Macau and Singapore. Jaschke notes that standard features in casinos including mirrors, chandeliers and lighting features produce a "blurred spatiality and immersive atmosphere" that "expanded and internalized the space, redirecting the gaze into the casino" (2003: 124). In addition, the "aestheticized handling of the equipment" by gamblers and dealers suggests "a ritualistic character to the gambling action" (Jaschke 2003: 126). Time spent on the casino constitutes an "easy listening, user friendly imprisonment" with "infinite choice but seemingly no way out" (Klein 2002 in Jaschke 2003: 124). This seems particularly pertinent to the casinos parked on the Mandovi. The interior architecture and ambience of cosmopolitan glamour inside the casino meant that many visitors barely noticed that they were on a waterway, or indeed in Goa, until they were ready to depart the casino and return to Panaji. Occasionally customers had to wait for the feeder boats and would get impatient and slightly anxious if they were in a rush to get to land. For customers who were uncomfortable around water, particularly those from landlocked areas, traveling on the river at night was not very appealing, despite the bright lights of the casino.

Onshore impact

Ambiguously "offshore," aspects of "casino culture" have started to permeate the urban landscape, becoming deeply entangled with the lives of local residents. In addition to land-based entrances situated on the riverfront, casinos have started to advertise in various places around the city including on road traffic barriers and on signs describing heritage structures. Companies that own the casinos have also established a robust corporate social responsibility program often partnering with local NGOs and the city government. Perhaps in order to circumvent the "social and political challenges" that accompany the casinos, these companies have mobilized certain practices and strategies "in pursuit of new markets and novel techniques" (see Dolan and Rajak 2016: 4). One casino group, for example, has introduced a learning institute that offers hospitality courses. In addition, the group has introduced a series of community and environmental initiatives including a compost plant in cooperation with the Corporation of the City of Panaji (D'Souza 2016: 20). To the extent that residents were aware of these programs, some expressed skepticism and noted the irony of casino operators supporting waste-related initiatives.

Much more controversial was a casino company's recent purchase of a 65 percent stake in the local football (soccer) club, FC Goa, which upset some local fans. The "overt advertising" by the company – team jerseys now have the "casino name emblazoned boldly" – has isolated some supporters who were hoping to sidestep the ownership subject (D'Mello 2016). In contrast to many parts of India where cricket dominates, D'Mello notes that football occupies a unique place in Goa and its popularity has transcended linguistic, religious, and socio-political divides. This team's victories were celebrated across the populace and the entire state was "plunged into sadness" when it was defeated (D'Mello 2016). However, many fans, particularly those who vehemently opposed the casinos, felt betrayed by the change in ownership; residents remarked that they found the blatant advertising especially offensive and some fans deserted the team. In the last two years, FC Goa paraphernalia has been conspicuously missing from houses and politicians have joined the chorus of critical voices against the new ownership (D'Mello 2016). Other fans have reluctantly come to accept the ownership change. As the president of a youth football academy observed to a local news website: "We love football, so the ownership does not matter. The earlier owners had passion for the game, so I was disappointed about the change.... But in the end football was earlier supported by mining companies, now by casino companies, so what's the difference?" (D'Mello 2016)

There has also been significant opposition to the casinos from a number of different religious bodies and local non-governmental organizations. In the early

1990s, the Diocesan Service Center for Social Action, an organization connected to the Catholic church, launched a campaign against the introduction of casinos by arguing that they would "deteriorate the moral fabric" of Goan society (Botelho 2018: 59) and recently the Centre for Responsible Tourism, a church-affiliated organization, addressed a letter to the Chief Minister of Goa conveying their concerns regarding a proposed tourism master-plan. In particular, the letter argued that the casinos have "brought a bad name to the State" and entreated the government to abstain from "generating revenue from vices" (Kamat 2014b). Non-governmental organizations such as Aam Auraat Aadmi Against Gambling also claimed that contrary to government reports that casinos have added employment and tourism opportunities, they have only increased "the rate of crime, drunken rage" and facilitated "the rise of escort services" (Gatty 2016).

Many residents in Panaji viewed the casinos as a social evil and/or the basis of an ecological disaster. Yet, even as casinos have been portrayed as "vice dens" (Unnithan 2011) and an "ATM" (*Times of India* 2019a) for the government in political speeches and newspaper articles and opinion pieces, some residents in Panaji and the surrounding areas were more ambivalent. They found the casinos simultaneously frustrating and fascinating: Michael remarked that in his family, the reaction to the casinos differed along generational lines. His parents, who had grown up in North Goa and frequently travelled to Panaji in their childhood, had seen Goa transform from a quiet Portuguese colony to an international holiday destination bringing "undesirable tourists," which in turn generated "unregulated expansion." To them, casinos evoked the worst of tourism excess, in addition to harming Goa's reputation nationally and internationally. However, Michael noted, that a number of his contemporaries viewed the casinos as a form of entertainment. Their discomfort with casinos stemmed from the oil and sewage that, they argued, the casinos were depositing in the river, and which was harming its aquatic ecology. Therefore, while some younger residents were hesitant to visit the floating casinos, they were comfortable occasionally visiting the land-based ones.

Residents who had grown up and continued to live near the heritage districts such as San Tome and Fontainhas were particularly critical of the casinos impact on the Mandovi riverfront. Due to Fontainhas' location on the banks of one of the city's waterways, Ourem creek, it was one of the first areas to be settled in Panjim. Celebrated as "Asia's only Latin Quarter," the area has retained its appearance due to planning and development initiatives (Fernandes 2007: 125–126). Popular with tourists, it has Portuguese street names and houses decorated in ways that are evocative of Portuguese provincial towns (Fernandes 2007: 126). Since the arrival of the casinos, these heritage districts, which are close to some of the land-based entrances, have been plagued by traffic congestion and parking problems. One resident, who, on encountering heavy traffic as he drove along the main road leading to the city late one night, remarked that Panjim must be "one of the few cities where there is a parking problem and traffic jam" in the early hours of the morning.

A number of entertainment venues and restaurants were situated along the riverfront and hosted weddings, birthdays and other events. One urban planner I spoke with observed that the appeal of these venues lay in their close proximity to, and view of, the river. With the advent of the casino vessels, however, the river had become like a "creek between two buildings." Although the urban planner had originally opposed water-based casinos and advocated for their removal, over the years he had very reluctantly begun to "accept" them. He acknowledged that after numerous promises from the government, it was unlikely that the casinos would be relocated in a hurry. A few other residents mentioned that the casino provided jobs for many people in Goa not just for those who worked in the casinos but also for those who worked in the food and beverage industries that supplied the casinos. With the decline of mining, these residents argued, the city had come to rely on tourism revenue. The urban planner echoed this sentiment but cautioned that the challenge moving forward was whether the city could find alternative sources of revenue – "we want to have revenue along with some kind of life in the city."

Casinos "constitute urban space and simultaneously threaten it" (Kingma 2011: 94). Zandonai notes that in Macau, although casinos are "geographically and physically defined entities, somewhat allocated to specific sites," their social, cultural and economic influence extends past areas within which they are assigned to function (2015: 11). While casinos have transformed the urban topography producing "a towering skyline" with "fantastically ornamented" structures, they have also altered areas of the city not in the immediate vicinity of the casinos such that Macau has been rendered "partly unrecognizable" to its inhabitants (Zandonai 2015: 11). In particular, as parts of Macau adapted to the influx of tourists, they have "emptied the urban space from prior social, commercial, and symbolic functions that were more closely tied to the residents' sense of place" (Zandonai 2015: 11). Panaji residents seemed eager to avoid a similar fate. In one instance, incensed that casino advertisements were sharing space with heritage signs – situating "rival or opposing worlds" within the same frame (see Hoek 2016: 82) – activists and residents complained that the casinos were exploiting Panaji's abundant heritage and ensured that the advertisements were eventually removed (Kamat 2017).

Conclusion

Perhaps akin to the ships that once traversed the Mandovi (Nagvenkar 2014), Goan "offshore" casinos constitute a "heterotopic space" that provides "escape from, the everyday worries of land-based responsibilities" (Grant-Smith and Mayes 2017: 1384; see also Foucault 1986; Johnson 2013; MacNaughten and Urry 2000). Casino operators and some residents variously characterized these vessels as a place of fun, relaxation and play that generated significant revenue for the city in order to legitimize their presence on a major waterway. These vessels are spatial enclaves that produce contradictions (Johnson 2013) and residents, bureaucrats and politicians variously portrayed the casinos as a polluter, a place of excess and transgression, but also (often reluctantly) as a site of economic opportunity.

The proliferation of water-based casinos revitalize and reconfigure Goa's long-standing links in the Indian Ocean and Lusophone world while simultaneously generating new spatial networks within South Asia as it accommodates the influx of migrants from various parts of the subcontinent who come to work in the casino industry. Although these vessels remain moored in Panaji and like a cruise ship, "the ship itself, not the sea nor the ports, is promoted as the primary destination" (Steinberg 2001: 163; see also Grant-Smith and Mayes 2017: 1385), they remain deeply connected to, and inspired by, other oceanic destinations. In particular, the design and the ambience of the casino transport patrons to other casino destinations, such as Singapore and Macau, even as they play an outsized role in city life. Macau and Goa, united by their colonial experience and pursuing new avenues for reengagement are now reconnected through new maps by their "reliance on gambling as a way of developing their respective tourism based economies" (Jouhki and Bo Neilson 2016). To some constituencies in Goa, Macau served as an ideal model with a casino culture and economy to be emulated, but to others it exemplified a cautionary tale, a once flourishing urban "place" that had been damaged by casino excess.

The offshore casinos situate the city as a node for various emergent and evolving networks but also unsettle prevailing quotidian socio-spatial orders (Grant-Smith and Mayes 2017) by encroaching onto historic neighborhoods and disturbing forms of everyday spatial practice. In addition to parking problems and traffic congestion, many residents encounter the casinos or their advertisements as part of their daily routines and the casino architecture and (highly visible) material infrastructure including land-based entrances have transformed local neighborhoods.

Goan casinos underscore the interconnectedness between cities and the sea in multifaceted ways. Despite being reluctant and/or unable to venture to sea these casino vessels remain ocean oriented. Their presence on the waterway illustrates the multiple ways in which Lusophone and oceanic imaginaries that emerge from colonial engagements and historical trade networks create new postcolonial maps. The circulation of finance and labor and the encounters and practices that take place in their spaces bring to light new and emerging local and regional networks. But even as these water-based casinos become the site – conceptually and literally – of fluid transregional and translocal relationships, they remain deeply embedded within the social, cultural, and economic life of the city.

Notes

1 I am grateful to Smriti Srinivas, Bettina Ng'weno, Neelima Jeychandran, Brad Jessup, Gina Robinson, Penny Jones and the participants of the "Reimagining Indian Ocean Worlds" workshop for helpful comments on earlier versions of this chapter. My research was funded by the University of California, the "Reimagining Indian Ocean Worlds" Mellon Research Initiative at the University of California, Davis and the Social Science Research Council.

Ethnographic data for this chapter has been generated from several sources, including journalistic accounts, news sources and recent fieldwork undertaken in Panaji over 18 months.

2 Prior to 1961, Panaji was known as Panjim, the anglicized version of its Portuguese name *Pangim*, but the official name of the city is now "Panaji." However, many local residents still refer to the city as Panjim and the Corporation of the City of Panaji (CCP) website uses both names. In this chapter, I refer to the city as Panaji, but also as Panjim (depending on context).

3 There have been a number of cases before the High Court of Bombay to compel the casinos to relocate (see Botelho 2018; Costa-Pinto 2019). For more on the multiple ways of conceptualizing "the offshore" see Appel (2012).

4 Although initially on instructions from the National Green Tribunal, the Goa State Pollution Control Board (GSPCB) monitored and penalized the casinos, in recent years the GSPCB has stated that the casinos are not the culprits and are depositing waste responsibly (see Botelho 2018: 59). However many residents remained unconvinced and in June 2019, the government announced that the GSPCB would conduct a water audit of the casinos in order to monitor the raw water pumped into the vessels and the waste water released into the tanks (*Times of India* 2019b).

5 Routledge (2000: 2651) notes that this representation of Goa privileges that of the "Catholic upper caste elites."

6 Numerous scholars and writers have noted that there are two versions of Goa: Goa Dourada, which privileges the Portuguese colonial history and influence and Goa Indica which is considered the "Indian bases of Goan culture" (Routledge 2000: 2649, 2001: 224; see also Newman 2001: 56).

7 The Lusofonia Games, a multi-sport event (akin to the Commonwealth Games) involving athletes from Lusophone countries began in 2006. Goa hosted them in 2014.

8 According to Trichur (2013) has been a "gradual decline in demand for low grade minerals during the last quarter of the 20th century" (109). In addition, in 2018, the Supreme Court ordered the cancellation of 88 mining leases.

9 I have used a pseudonym to protect the identity of the individual. Fieldwork was completed in September 2017, prior to the announcement by the Chief Minister of Goa in early 2020 that Goans would be banned from entering casinos.

10 *Chor* translates to *thief* in Hindi, Marathi and Konkani. Chor *Bazaar* is a market in south Mumbai.

11 A card game akin to Poker.

12 A form of Indian Rummy.

13 Indian-made foreign liquor (IMFL) refers to hard liquor that is manufactured in India – excluding alcoholic beverages such as fenny and toddy (among others), which are indigenous to India.

14 A *Times of India* investigation into the casino workforce noted that the Goans work as chefs, in the front office, in security, guest relations and in the food and beverages area. Nepalis and employees from India's northeastern states work as "pit bosses", operations, and dealers. Non-Goans (including foreign nationals) work in the most "high level" positions (*Times of India* 2014).

15 The article also noted that women's activists were highly critical of the casino industry. (See Navgenkar and Rodrigues 2013).

References

Alvares, Claude. 2002. *Fish Curry and Rice: A Sourcebook on Goa, its Ecology and Lifestyle*. Mapusa: The Goa Foundation.

Appel, Hannah. 2012. "Offshore Work: Oil, Modularity, and the How of Capitalism in Equatorial Guinea." *American Ethnologist* 39(4): 692–709.

Botelho, Afonso. 2018. "Casinos in Goa: The Challenge Ahead is to Implement Sustainable Strategies to Minimize Their Ill-Effects." *International Journal of Hospitality & Tourism Systems* 11(2): 56–62.

Boxer, Charles R. 1969. "A Note on Portuguese Reactions to the Revival of the Red Sea Spice Trade and the Rise of Atjeh, 1540–1600." *Journal of Southeast Asian History* 10(3): 415–428.

Cameron, Angus and Ronen Palan. 2004. *The Imagined Economies of Globalization.* London: Sage Publications.

Costa-Pinto, Maya. 2019. *The City in Flux: Navigating Urbanism(s) through Waterways in Goa, India.* PhD Diss., University of California, Davis.

Das, Goutam. 2015. "The Riverboat Gamblers." *Business Today.* September 13. Accessed 23 September 2019. www.businesstoday.in/magazine/cover-story/inside-asia-largest-luxury-offshore-gaming-den/story/222989.html

D'Mello, Pamela. 2016. "Enraged by an Ownership Change, Passionate FC Goa fans are Celebrating the Team's Recent Dismal Form." *Scroll.in.* 27 November. Accessed 23 September 2019. https://scroll.in/field/822623/enragedby-an-ownership-change-passionate-fc-goa-fans-are-celebrating-the-teams-recent-dismalform.

Dolan, Catherine and Dinah Rajak. 2016. "Introduction Toward the Anthropology of Corporate Social Responsibility." In *The Anthropology of Corporate Social Responsibility*, edited by Catherine Dolan and Dinah Rajak, 1–28. New York, NY: Berghahn.

D'Souza, Dielle. 2016. "Floating Fantasy." *Viva Goa.* July–August 2016, 10–20.

Fernandes, Agnelo. [1989] 2002. "Goa in the International Trade: 16th–17th Centuries." In *Essays in Goan History*, edited by Teotonio R. de Souza, 61–68. New Delhi: Concept Publishing Company.

Fernandes, Jason K. 2007. "Panjim: Realms of Law and Imagination." In *Law and the City*, edited by Andreas Philippopoulos-Mihapoulos, 113–130. London and New York: Routledge.

Foucault, Michel. 1979. *Discipline and Punish: The Birth of the Prison.* New York: Vintage Books

Foucault, Michel. 1986. "Of Other Spaces." *Diacritics* 16(1): 22–27.

Gatty, Harsha Raj. 2016. "Offshore Casinos May Stay Afloat in Goa: State Budget Suggests." *Indian Express.* 17 March. Accessed 23 September 2019. https://indianexpress. com/article/india/india-news-india/goa-offshore-casinos-state-budget/

Goncalves, Arnaldo M.A. 2003. "Macau, Timor and Portuguese India in the Context of Portugal's Recent Decolonization." In *The Last Empire: Thirty Years of Portuguese Decolonization*, edited by Stewart Lloyd-Jones and Antonio Costa Pinto, 53–66. Bristol, UK and Portland, OR, USA: Intellect Books.

Grant-Smith, Deanna and Robyn Mayes. 2017. "Freedom, Part-time Pirates, and Poo Police: Regulating the Heterotopic Space of the Recreational Boat." *Environment and Planning A* 49(6): 1379–1395.

Hao, Zhidong. 2011. *Macau History and Society.* Hong Kong: Hong Kong University Press.

Hashmi, Sameer. 2015. "Goa's Casino Industry Comes Under Pressure." *BBC News.* 20 November. Accessed 23 September 2019. www.bbc.com/news/business-34871124

Hoek, Lotte. 2016. "Urban Wallpaper: Film Posters, City Walls and the Cinematic Public in South Asia." *South Asia: Journal of South Asian Studies.* 39(1): 73–92.

Jaschke, Karin. 2003. "Casinos Inside Out." In *Stripping Las Vegas: A Contextual Review of Casino Resort Architecture*, edited by Karin Jaschke and Silke Otsch. 109–132. Weimar: University of Weimar Press.

Johnson, Peter. 2013. "The Geographies of Heterotopia." *Geography Compass* 7(11): 790–803.

Jouhki, Jukka and Kenneth Bo Nielsen. 2016. Gambling as Development in Goa and Macau. 31 October. Accessed September 23, 2019. Poverty and Development Research Centre. Department of History and Ethnology, University of Jyväskylä, Finland. http://povdev.blog.jyu.fi/2016/10/gambling-as-development-cases-of-goa.html

Kamat, Prakash. 2014a. "Offshore Casinos to go by 2015, assures Parrikar." *The Hindu.* 5 March 2014. Accessed 23 September 2019. www.thehindu.com/news/national/other-states/offshore-casinos-to-go-by-2015-assures-parrikar/article5753139.ece

Kamat, Prakash. 2014b. "Parrikar Urged to Drop Casinos, Massage Parlours from Goa Tourism Plan." *The Hindu.* 6 August 2014. Accessed 23 September 2019. www.thehindu.com/news/national/other-states/parrikar-urged-to-drop-casinos-massage-parlours-from-goa-tourism-plan/article6287053.ece

Kamat, Prakash. 2017. "Panaji Mayor gets casino ads removed." *The Hindu.* 9 February 2017. Accessed 23 September 2019. www.thehindu.com/news/cities/mumbai/Panaji-Mayor-gets-casino-ads-removed/article17264411.ece

Karlsson, Bengt G and Dolly Kikon. 2017. "Wayfinding: Indigenous Migrants in the Service Sector of Metropolitan India." *South Asia: Journal of South Asian Studies* 40(3): 447–462.

Kaushik, Divya. 2016. "Vegas, Lanka, Macau, Goa – Hot Diwali Party Spots." *Times of India.* 30 October 2016. Accessed 23 September 2019. https://timesofindia.indiatimes.com/city/delhi/Vegas-Lanka-Macau-Goa-Hot-Diwali-party-spots/articleshow/55130175.cms

Kingma, Sytze F. 2008. "Dutch Casino Space or the Spatial Organization of Entertainment." *Culture and Organization* 14(1): 31–48.

Kingma, Sytze F. 2011. "Waterfront Rise. Urban Casino Space and Boundary Construction in the Netherlands." In *Gambling, Space, and Time. Shifting Boundaries and Cultures*, edited by Pauliina Raento and David Schwartz. 83–107. Reno & Las Vegas: University of Nevada Press.

Klein, Norman M. 2002. "Scripting Las Vegas: Noir Naïf, Junking Up, and the Strip." In *The Grit Beneath the Glitter: Tales from the Real Las Vegas*, edited by Mike Davis and Hal Rothman, 17–29. Berkeley: University of California Press.

MacNaughten Phil and John Urry. 2000. "Bodies of Nature: Introduction." *Body and Society.* 6(3–4): 1–11.

Mathew, K.M. 1988. *History of the Portuguese Navigation in India, 1497–1600.* Delhi, India: Mittal Publications.

Mora, Amalia. 2016. *Dancing Where the River Meets the Sea.* PhD. Diss., University of California, Los Angeles. Retrieved from http://escholarship.org/uc/item/2zh7p1rk

Murteira, Andre. 2014. "Dutch Attacks Against the Goa–Macao–Japan Route, 1603–1618." In *Macao – The Formation of a Global City*, edited by C.X. George Wei, 95–106. London and New York. Routledge.

Nagvenkar, Mayabhushan. 2014. "Babies on Board: Goa's Casinos Warm Up to the Idea of Great Indian Family". *Firstpost.* 26 June 2014. Accessed 23 September 2019. www.firstpost.com/living/babies-board-goas-casinos-warm-idea-great-indian-family-1590487.html

Nagvenkar, Mayabhushan and Francisca Rodrigues. 2013. "Women in Casinos: The Best Job on Earth? Certainly Not This One." *Firstpost.* 20 May 2013. Accessed 23 September 2019. www.firstpost.com/living/women-in-casinos-the-best-job-on-earth-certainly-not-this-one-798825.html

Navhind Times. 2017. "Government Won't Issue Fresh Casino Licenses." 25 July 2017.

Newman, Robert. 2001. *Of Umbrellas, Goddesses, and Dreams: Essays on Goan Culture and Society.* Mapusa, Goa: Other India Press.

Pearson, Michael N. 1981. *Coastal Western India: Studies from the Portuguese Records.* New Delhi: Concept.

Pearson, Michael N. 2003. *The Indian Ocean.* London and New York: Routledge.

Routledge, Paul. 2000. "Consuming Goa: Tourist Site as Dispensable Space." *Economic and Political Weekly.* 35(30): 2647–2656.

Routledge, Paul. 2001. "Selling the Rain', Resisting the Sale: Resistant Identities and the Conflict Over Tourism in Goa." *Social & Cultural Geography.* 2(2): 221–240.

Saldanha, Arun. 2002. "Identity, Spatiality and Post-colonial Resistance: Geographies of the Tourism Critique in Goa." *Current Issues in Tourism* 5(2): 94–111.

Sequiera, Devika. 2017. "After Fighting Against Goa's Casinos, Parrikar Gives Them What They Want." *The Wire.* 7 August 2017. Accessed 6 November 2017. https://thewire.in/politics/parrikar-gives-casinos-always-wanted-permanent-base-goa

Sharma, Aasheesh. 2014. "Casino Nights in Goa." *Hindustan Times.* 3 November 2014. Accessed 24 September 2019. www.hindustantimes.com/brunch/casino-nights-in-goa/story-414NCFyZpY9rspIWJUr9PJ.html

Shetye, Murari. 2014. "Workers from Northeast Voice Out Against 'Exploitation'". *Times of India.* 6 September 2014. Accessed 24 September 2019. https://timesofindia.india times.com/city/goa/Workers-from-northeast-voice-out-against-exploitation/article show/41813120.cms

Steinberg, Phillip. 2001. *The Social Construction of the Ocean.* Cambridge: Cambridge University Press.

Subrahmanyam, Sanjay. 2011. *Three Ways to be Alien: Travails and Encounters in the Early Modern World.* Waltham, Massachusetts: Brandeis University Press.

Tare, Kiran. 2017. "Why Chips are Down for Goa Chief Minister Manohar Parrikar in Row Over Offshore Casinos". India Today. 5 June 2017. Accessed 6 November 2017. www.indiatoday.in/magazine/nation/story/20170612-goa-manohar-parrikar-government-offshore-casino-licences-986498-2017-06-05

Times of India. 2014 "The Players Table." 23 May 2014.

Times of India. 2019a. "Monserrate Hints at Moving Offshore Casinos Onshore." 13 May 2019.

Times of India. 2019b. "Pollution Board to Audit Water of Casinos." 14 June 2019.

Trichur, Raghuraman S. 2013. *Refiguring Goa: From Trading Post to Tourism Destination.* Saligao: Goa 1556.

Unnithan, Sandeep. 2011. "Indians Feel at Home in Gambling Hotspots." *India Today.* 22 October 2011. Accessed 25 September 2019. www.indiatoday.in/magazine/cover-story/story/20111031-indian-gamblers-diwali-2011-macau-asia-china-asia-hottest-casinos-749402-2011-10-22

Zandonai, Sheyla. 2015. "Casino Development and Urban Transformation in Macao." *IIAS Newsletters.* 72: 10–11.

Zalik, Anna. 2009. "Zones of Exclusion: Offshore Extraction, the Contestation of Space and Physical Displacement in the Nigerian Delta and the Mexican Gulf." *Antipode* 41(3): 557–582.

7 Improvising Juba

Productive precarity and making the present at the edge of the Indian Ocean world

Christian J. Doll

In August of 2012, I travelled on the newly opened road running from the town of Torit west and crossed the South Sudan–Uganda border.[1] On the other side, I met Omony, a Ugandan border control officer. While answering some questions about his work, Omony said of Uganda's northern neighbor, "The only thing they export is rubble and dead bodies." This hyperbolic statement reflected a widely-shared Ugandan perception: that while Uganda exported a great deal to South Sudan and a lot of Ugandans made good money selling produce and other items in South Sudan, South Sudan had sent little back in the past decades other than displaced citizens and waste. Trucks passing in both directions attested to Omony's broader point: those densely packed with food, construction materials, and plastic products were driving into South Sudan with far less commercial transport passing the other direction. Further, on the South Sudanese side of the border, meanwhile, sat the built-up town of Nimule, with luxury hotels and an immaculately paved road. There was no equivalent on the Ugandan side of the border, a fact that attested to the relative importance of the border region to both countries. While hyperbolic, Omony's statement was not merely a reflection of the attitude many Ugandans had toward their neighbor: it spoke to the deep and continued interdependence of the South Sudanese economy on the region, and the world, and the extent to which South Sudan remains highly import-dependent.

Broader descriptions of South Sudan parallel Omony's sense that South Sudan produce nothing but waste and death, foreign onlookers have described South Sudan's capital, Juba, in terms parallel to dismissals of South Sudan as a "failed state." They claim the city to be a total wasteland, a hollowed-out war zone, or more akin to a refugee camp than a city (see Kurc 2009, in Shuichiro 2013). Such descriptions, in rendering Juba as a closed space of bare survival, reduce lived experience to passive victimhood. This ignores the vibrancy and creativity of urbanites who use Juba's contours and international intersections to their advantage while remaking the city. Their actions produce regularity that formal systems and nascent government programming rarely have and perhaps never will. The experiences of those remaking their worlds in the capital city of the world's newest nation suggests the ways urban space and mobilities shift the contours of action beyond the local and outside the bounds of the nation-state. In improvising Juba, urbanites engage the global embeddedness of the landlocked city to foster new possibilities. Diverse global investments and entanglements range from the economic investment in oil infrastructure by China, political intervention by the United States and African uber-states South Africa and Ethiopia, and funding of state directed projects by actors as diverse as Morocco, Norway, and South Korea. On the streets of Juba, one daily encounters evidence of these international connections. It is visible in the recent build-up of high-end hotels and towering offices buildings in the years following South Sudan's independence and in the influx of foreign aid workers, diplomats, and entrepreneurs from across the globe who, alongside South Sudanese from across the country and the diaspora, have swelled the city's terrestrial bounds. Such engagements create a dynamic economic and social life in the physically isolated city at the spatial limits of the Indian Ocean world, turning it into a vibrant space for creating new possibilities, opportunities, and futures.

Through a series of ethnographic vignettes, I suggest that in this far-flung space in the world's newest country, people use urban space and the transregional crossings made possible by the city to forge new realities that both confront the limits of state-directed infrastructures and build a present and future of possibility. I demonstrate the need to focus on quotidian practices of remaking and reimagining space and place for contemporary studies of the Indian Ocean. I argue that the varied ways that people improvise Juba constitute informal, invisible, and social infrastructures which create possibilities to forge normality and predictability from the tumult of urban life, ongoing conflict, and arcane government and international interventions rooted in the city. To discuss these remakings of Juba, I begin by discussing the way two small social networks produce a regularity of service delivery and income in the face of urban precarity. I then turn to a discussion of how an enterprising money changer, a landowner, and land occupiers convert unstable exchange rates and "empty" space to craft perpetual social and monetary gain. I last turn to a discussion of the Juban use of the term "company," which indexes the lack of distinction between business and humanitarian ventures from the view of most South Sudanese. One young man's use of this term to describe his growing money-transfer network offers a final demonstration of how urbanites forge value, cohesion, and predictability through strategic engagement with urban global situatedness and crossings.

Several lines of thinking have inspired my account of quotidian urban remaking in the face of uncertainty. In their endeavors, Jubans, like urbanites throughout the Indian Ocean world, are engaged in what AbdouMaliq Simone (2001) calls "worlding." While African cities are still instrumentally used as points of resource extraction (as they were under colonialism) (ibid., 18), contemporary urban Africans, Simone argues, "engage the city as a resource for reaching and operating at the level of 'the world.'" (ibid., 22) Such "worlding" makes the city a productive site from which to build international networks and attain opportunities that exist beyond the territorial confines of the city and the nation-state. Urbanites' acts of worlding allow cities that are not as obviously linked as ports or global financial hubs to be dynamic nodes for global action and connection.

Simone identifies a similarly active stance of urbanites creating alternative infrastructures and possibilities "people as infrastructure," which he defines as "tentative and often precarious process of remaking the inner city" through new social cohesions which prevent broader economic and political forces from wholly defining people's work and lives (Simone 2004: 411). Simone's sense of the remaking of the city and the particulars of social action confronting seemingly insurmountable economic and political realities is similar to the dynamic Filip De Boeck calls "the urban politics of the possible" (De Boeck 2011: 269)[2] in Africa and Asef Bayat's notions of "nonmovements," "the art of presence," and "quiet encroachment" in cities in the middle east (Bayat 2013). Bayat contends that urbanites "strive to affect the contours of social change in their societies" by "discovering and generating new spaces within which they can voice their dissent and assert their presence in pursuit of bettering their lives" not through direct protest or large-scale social movements but through diffuse, small-scale actions (ibid., ix). In Juba, the dynamic of commanding space and creating more livable realities occurs in the accumulation of a variety of small, strategic everyday actions. While Africa-focused, these scholars' insights are similar to those of scholars writing on the Indian Ocean and they offer frames for reading urban actions as productive and continuous. As Hancock and Srinivas similarly argue about remaking urban life through spiritual and religious practices, "[t]he often-aggressive verticality of modern urban spaces" abandons spaces which "in turn, may be claimed through habitation or use for new, improvisational, or precarious forms of life" (2018: 464). I draw on all of these theorizations of urban remakings in demonstrating how layers of regional and international convergence in cities – and the uncertainty of intervention and infrastructure – are engaged with by urbanites to create new ventures, new communities, and new "companies" that achieve more predictable, reliable, and real outcomes than those promised by capitalism or by state-directed ventures.

The Minister of Darkness

In 2011, then-editor of South Sudan's newspaper, *The Citizen*, Nhial Bol Aken, began calling then-Minister of Electricity and Dams, David Deng Abethorbei, the "Minister of Darkness" and his office the "Ministry of Darkness." Capturing sentiments about the government's handling of infrastructure in Juba and beyond as they did, the names would come to stick to both Abethorbei and the ministry itself. Speaking on the much-listened-to Radio Miraya, Abethorbei maintained his composure, even as it was suggested that perhaps it would be most appropriate to call him the "Minister of Generators." The event which had stoked Nhial's ire was the shutdown of Juba's main hospital following South Sudan's 2013 oil crisis. The city had been enveloped in darkness when the government couldn't negotiate to supply more fuel and run its petroleum-based power plant. The plant and the hospital's shutdown, was, to Nhial, the ultimate symbol of waste, neglect, and incompetence. What were these well-paid officials and their staffs doing in a Ministry of Electricity, he asked, when no electricity was being supplied? The bitter humor in Nhial's framing reflected a resilience and seizing of control in the face of unmet expectations that has come to characterize life in Juba.

Nhial's biting commentary is but one of the strategies of defiance and perseverance in the face of uncertain and disappointing state infrastructure. With government and city-supplied power electrifying only a few blocks of Juba, many Jubans have created regularity through small networks and agreements that share the costs and upkeep of electricity across interlinked compounds. One such Juban is Amira, a single mother living with her sister and their children in a compound built on land she inherited from her Moru family in one of the fastest growing parts of the city. Amira had familial ties that gave her formalized ownership of land in the highly contested city. For much of my time in Juba, I lived on a compound next door to hers and became close to her son, an industrious student at the University of Juba. At the NGO-rented compound where I stayed, a large, humming generator was turned on for a few hours of light and computer usage at night. As I realized during my increasingly frequent visits, Amira's household ran their satellite-connected TV, fans, and refrigerator day and night, offering them respite from Juba's stifling heat. To achieve just a few hours of power at my compound, meanwhile, two logistics officers working for the NGO expended days acquiring fuel from various sources throughout the city or waiting for one of the overworked generator repairmen to come by. While they attempted to keep two drums of diesel on hand, refilling the drums required members of the NGO's staff to find government workers or government-connected people willing to sell off stockpiled fuel or wait in long lines at gas stations when word got out that these stations were selling rationed-out amounts of newly imported fuel.

While this chasing down of fuel to run generators and cars was common in Juba, Amira and her family, despite their always-on electricity, never wasted time chasing down erratic supplies of fuel. With no power lines being run to her house from the so-called "Ministry of Darkness," Amira instead paid a small fee to an Ethiopian man who ran power lines to her compound and about ten others surrounding them. This small web of electrified homes never suffered the blackouts or uncertainty of availability of electricity that many Jubans, rich and poor, tended to take for granted. Amira's family, because of their formal ownership of land in Juba, were not as badly off as many in the city, but they were hardly well-off. That they had more stable access to electricity than a well-funded NGO was due to their being socially and materially linked to their neighbors. Such predictability through socially built systems and small-scale entrepreneurship has similarly allowed for a reliable system of water delivery, waste management, and transportation throughout Juba. Water delivery and sewage removal is conducted through privately owned, city licensed tanker trucks whose widely known, regular schedules and routes are regulated not by city officials but the personal relationships that maintain them throughout the city. These alternative infrastructures are buttressed by social linkages and low-barrier-to-entry but quite profitable business which allow water to reach parts of the city that are far from the river or from public bore holes and which allow easy, reliable transport across the city just as small networks allowed generator-less people to have electrified compounds. These socially driven systems offer a regularity never offered by government institutions and business opportunities for entrepreneurs able to invest in a tanker truck or willing to run a large generator as a full-time job. Such systems create a dynamic and layered web of infrastructures that can respond to the perpetual needs of urbanites better than the centralized, top-down system in Juba ever had.

Another decentralized, ordered system is the social grid organizing and self-regulating motorcycle taxis, or "boda bodas" within Juba. Knowing that he had largely covered his school fees by working as a boda boda driver in Juba, I asked James, one of my University of Juba anthropology students what his experience had been like. He had begun driving right at a moment where the boda boda space had been opened up for ambitious young South Sudanese, he explained. In an uncharacteristically protectivist move, in August 2013, the South Sudanese government unilaterally banned all foreigners from operating boda boda taxis in Juba. This created a minor international incident as Ugandan drivers caravanned *en masse* across the border and a number of South Sudanese in Kampala were assaulted in retaliation for the order. James noted that the policy had created a sudden massive opportunity for people like him. Not only did many Ugandans quickly sell off their motorcycles to South Sudanese who otherwise would have paid massively to import them, but James and other South Sudanese could now turn their deep knowledge of the city into fairly reliable income. In the time James started riding, a handful of powerful boda boda driver associations had made deals with the government, which was happy to outsource managing Juba's many newly minted boda boda drivers.

These associations were little more than extortion rackets, James explained, enforcing fees with no services returned in exchange from them. Instead, James explained, his social ties offered the needed regularity and protection of that the associations had promised but never delivered. He had come to share and defend control of a boda boda "stage" with a group of ten other men. Their consistent physical presence in their spot and their internal regulations gave them consistent work and pay. They had a rotating order for taking customers, allowing them to share profits on days they had business. It helped that their stage was in a highly desirable location on a main road just a few steps from the embassies of the United States and European Union a few feet from the passport and visa office for the Government of South Sudan. This location, explained James, meant that his customers were generally people who could and would pay him upon arrival at their destination, something that was not a certainty in his line of work. Not only was the location good because people filing visa and passport applications had to carry cash but also because the nearby embassies and offices all had heavy security. While many people viewed boda boda drivers as criminals, James explained, it was drivers who faced the most danger, for passengers were known to lure drivers to desolate parts of the city and police saw them as easy targets for issuing fines or requesting bribes, especially as authorities constantly shifted which streets boda bodas were banned from without notice. James and his partners continually monitored these risks to their lives and livelihoods. Maintaining their space and sharing both opportunities and information, they were able to make a stable living from what was otherwise unstable and dangerous work. Like Amira's compound's electricity and the other peopled infrastructures, James and his colleagues' improvised pragmatic systems of regularity forged generative urban futures from a precarious present.

Dealing with dollars and making sense of the pound

The streets leading in and out of Juba town center (or "Juba Dit," as my Dinka interlocutors called it, using a term of endearment used to designate someone of importance or prominence in a community) are filled with offices offering money-changing services and young South Sudanese men holding large stacks of colorful bills while clamoring to change money with anyone passing by. These street-level money changers, whether waking down the street waving cash or seated at tables in Juba's many markets, like the formalized exchanges offices, are a prominent feature across Juba's markets. The business of changing money is enormous and multiscalar, and despite a few moments of crackdown on black market exchange that has led street money changers to disappear for days at a time, black-market money changing and formalized, institutionalized money exchanges continue to live alongside each other. The perpetual existence of two exchange rates, the official one sanctioned by the government and used in formal exchange institutions and the "black market" rate operative between individuals and with unlicensed money changers, is often decried by foreign interventionists as emblematic of South Sudan's economic woes and its deepening disorder. When the government has intervened to flatten the divide by bringing the official rate closer to the black-market rate and cracking down on unlicensed exchanges, the demand for dollars and their still-limited supply has swiftly pushed the two rates back into existence. Jubans continue to navigate the system in order to move around, do business, go to school, and support family members living across the country, the region, and the globe. For those able to instrumentalize the tumult of the South Sudanese pound and the two-tiered exchange rate of the US dollar against the pound, the complex system of money change has become a social and financial opportunity. Their work creates new possibilities not only from the uncertain economic reality but by accessing and intervening in the crossings and convergences found in urban space.

On one visit to Juba Dit, I met with a particularly adept entrepreneur of money exchange named Mayen, a Ciec Dinka who transitioned from running a construction material transportation business to changing money full time. Giving me context for how he launched his business, Mayen explained how his opportunity was created by the fact that the South Sudanese government exchanged US dollars for South Sudanese pounds at a fixed rate. Only the South Sudanese Central Bank with its main branch in Juba exchanged at these rates and only to those with the proper paperwork – typically well-connected business people, heads of NGOs, and government officials – were able to make such exchanges, but even these actors were limited in the amount they could exchange. Mayen's former business had won several government contracts, and this had given him access to changing money at the so-called "government rate." While the heads of the Ministry of Finance and the Central Bank aimed to offset total dollarization, the dollar was still heavily valued and sought after in Juba. So, after changing South Sudanese pounds for dollars, Mayen then exchanged these dollars with money changers working on the street or with people needing to change large numbers of pounds for dollars but who lacked access to local banks. At the most extreme and profitable point, Mayen could buy $100 from the central bank for 300 SSP, and then sell that $100 for 2000 SSP or more.

Mayen and others like him were doing a more grounded and direct version of the value creation done by futures traders and exchange rate speculators in banks and investment firms around the world. Mayen's particular niche, though, comes from his unique ability to mediate between otherwise mutually inaccessible and untransferable domains of value. His exchange work relies on the convergence of several types of currency and domains of value converging within worlded Juba. Most of Mayen's clients come to him because they were crossing borders. Neighboring Kenya, Uganda, and Ethiopia so devalued the pound that anyone who had to send money to family or was traveling was willing to pay exorbitant rates to travel with dollars instead of pounds. Mayen's work, though, extends far beyond the large exchanges he would make with people who met him in his office. He acts as a node connecting disparate networks groups of people that would have no means of crossing otherwise. This urban density is only possible in cities which, whether they are landlocked ports or true ports, link up diverse people, and stitch them together into an otherwise impossible network. All the street-level money changers Mayen worked with were Dinkas and Nuers based in rural areas and moving in and out of Juba quickly. Usually they had come to multiply their money before transforming it into the socially salient currency of cattle upon return to their homes. Mayen often settled disputes between these money changers, helped them on the occasions that police chased them off the streets or out of markets. He even used his extensive cashflow to extinguish disputes between street-level money changers and their clients. Typically, Mayen told me, it was worth it for him to hand over the amount the aggrieved party was demanding because maintaining his reputation with customers and with money changers and keeping peace between them was good for business.

In doing this, Mayen was implementing an urbanized iteration of dispute settlement familiar throughout South Sudan, where justice is based in the mutual satisfaction of all parties for the sake of ending conflict rather than meting out punishment to a "guilty" party. This social infrastructure fills a gap for people for whom "official" authorities would offer more harm than help. To the street-level money changers, their clients, and those changing large sums in the safety of Mayen's office, Mayen was seen as a fair and impartial arbiter and authority figure. He noted one instance in which a street-level money changer had come into conflict with a client. who claimed he had given him counterfeit dollars in exchange for pounds. Mayen had both the changer and the client meet him in his office and express their views on what had happened. After hearing them out, Mayen stayed neutral rather than accepting that one version of events was more true than the other. He then gave the client dollars of his own and cautioned the changer to check his dollars more carefully to make sure he was not in possession of fakes before making any further exchanges. The payment, Mayen explained, was not a loss but a cost he had calculated into his business operation. Keeping both sides happy and willing to work together and with him was ultimately far more important for his bottom line than the amount he had paid to the client, he explained. Smoothing over the bonds in his network meant that his enterprise could run smoothly going forward. His mediation, he explained to me, prevented an escalation and involvement of "formal" law enforcement: police and government workers in Juba who were happy to find a bad actor among the street-level money changers that they generally tolerated and only occasionally made a performative act of cracking down on by arresting a few or chasing them out of their hubs in Juba Dit and other markets.

The work of Mayen and others like him creates a stable infrastructure in an otherwise deeply unstable context. With government and official commercial

Figure 7.1 Coffee, tea and *shisha* being sold in a partially completed tower near Juba International airport, Juba, South Sudan.

Image credit: Christian J. Doll.

offices unable to meet the need for dollars, less official money exchange creates a system that is constant and reliable and more directly and nimbly able to link disparate actors. Foreigners, cattle keepers, and business owners could, through Mayen's enterprise, make smooth transitions between distinct realms of value – dollars, pounds valued at different exchange rates, and cattle – all of which reached their thickest convergence in Juba. Juba's import-reliant economy, while the subject of complaint by South Sudanese and concern by foreign policy-makers, offered Mayen and his whole network of clients and partners an opportunity: not *in spite* of the exchange fluctuations and the two dollar-to-pound rates, but *through* them.

The hundred-year lease and the usefulness of unused space

Speaking to Noah, one of my anthropology students at the University of Juba about his research on land disputes in Juba, I heard of one of the most extreme examples of land being turned into present-day and potential future profit by landowners in Juba. A Bari man had signed a lease for his land in the Atlabara neighborhood of Juba. The neighborhood's proximity to the center of town, its long history as a "high class" area and its well-maintained roads had made it a valuable place, making leases to foreigners developing hotels while the title-holders of these properties rented space in other parts of the city relatively common. But unlike the leases lasting five or even ten years in much of the more valuable parts of the city, this man had leased his land for 100 years. He, like many titleholders, had collected all the money up front. He had negotiated the monthly price, drawn up a contract and collected the hefty sum directly from the Eritrean entrepreneur happy to open one of many profitable hotel-bars in the area. At the end of such a lease, land is to revert to the titleholder, and they would then possess any physical buildings on their land. These leases, then, are a long-term investment and an outsourcing of costly and cumbersome construction. But this particularly long lease period, while giving the man a useful influx of cash and a solid possibility of earning more money through his land in the very long term, was causing problems between his two sons, the presumed inheritors of the land, in the short term. It had worsened an already tense dynamic of competition among sons from different wives.

As Noah explained, the 100-year lease was the product of the byzantine and dysfunctional system of land allocation in Juba, complicated by the multiple legal jurisdictions operating simultaneously as well as by concerted efforts to keep a tight control over the granting of titles following the population booms in 2005 and 2011, after the end of the second civil war and South Sudanese independence. The man and his sons had different ideas of the best way to extract value from the land, Noah learned: while the father welcomed an immediate profit from his land title, his sons saw their hope of continual profit deferred for far longer than they felt comfortable with. The terms of the lease meant that their children or grandchildren were more likely to make use of the land, and whatever had been built upon it, than them. The patriarch's offer of a 100-year lease may have aimed at just such a deferral, preventing himself from having to oversee any inheritance fights between his sons in his lifetime while ensuring his land would still generate value for his ancestors. Whatever his reasons for drawing up such far-reaching terms in the contract, the lease was hedged on the perception of the perpetual value of land in the new state into the far future.

Other plans and activities make equally strategic use of "empty" space in Juba, turning vacant space and stalled construction sites into hubs of continual commercial use. I became interested in one partially built building on a prominent commercial road near the airport. Its lack of completion has not prevented it from becoming a continuous space of commerce. I had expected to see the tea and *shisha* cafe moved out as the building was sold, but in successive years visiting Juba, I continually saw the uses unused space was put to, turning hollowed towers into crowded and recognizable spaces of sociality, allowing foreigners to build and run hotels with the anticipation of eventual future profit, and otherwise making Juba's most valuable resource, its land, work. In another part of Atlabara, the paving of a main road called Tumbura quickly generated a hum of commercial activity. While many of the new construction businesses, hotels, and stores there made use of their land in conventional ways by setting up contained buildings offering food and lodging, far more were created on the steps in front of the many unused storefronts built in the construction boom following South Sudan's independence but which had largely remained vacant. The women who daily generated restaurants and coffee shops in front of these empty shells by placing plastic tables and chairs on the roadside and offering consistent products to a stream of regular customers seemed poised to outlast the concrete structures that housed them. Just like the man who had drawn up the 100-year lease, these women managed to turn "undeveloped" land into stable income and otherwise closed spaces into open-ended, generative hubs of social and commercial activity. These reimaginings of stalled development and empty space into new loci for extracting value and allowing social connections to thrive reflects the dynamic Srinivas (2015) demonstrates among urbanites who rework space in ways unimagined by the linear (liberal) development of cities. Through such acts, she argues, urbanites "make sense of, control or direct the shifting, dangerous, painful, or uneven dimensions of their habitations and bodies" (Srinivas 2015: 144).

Building "companies"

In 2015, I sat down with one of my University of Juba anthropology students, Simon, to discuss his post-graduation plans. "As I finish my university now," he told me, "I'm thinking of a lot of things to do. Currently I'm thinking of how and where to start.... But my interest is on private sector: being a business enterprise or non-governmental organization. So, I'm thinking of looking for those things now specifically." He explained that most people he knew were thinking about the public sector but are not thinking about business. To clarify, I asked if business and NGO work were the same type of work, and he explained that one should work between them, taking the money one earns at an NGO job and then launching businesses with that money. To Simon, "private sector" referred to anything that was not the government, so both business and humanitarian organizations fit under this label. Simon added that raising money and getting all the paperwork to start an NGO or a business were nearly identical. Simon's own work reflected the interweaving of these seemingly distinct sectors. During some of the University of Juba's closures, he co-founded an NGO that straddled the two levels NGOs operated on in South Sudan: the cash-strapped service-delivery done by national NGOs and the grant-rich, implementation and bureaucratic work that international NGOs tended to operate within. This made Simon and his co-workers an anomaly in South Sudan: rarely were South Sudanese NGO founders both implementers with ties to the community and effective fundraisers.

Simon's work, and his placing of NGOs and businesses into one category and the South Sudanese government in the other was not particular to him. In the Juba lexicon in general, few people drew a distinction between businesses and NGOs: both tended to be referred to as "companies." This usage points to the way these two seemingly distinct domains converge. In Juba, one could easily recognize the slippage between the entities that the term "companies" universally referred to. Companies are avenues for capturing money and putting it toward one's own goals. Companies are owned by and benefit particular communities even if they outwardly state otherwise. Larger companies tend to have their home base in Juba and satellite offices throughout the country. An over simple reading would call this conflation an acquiescence to the reality of rampant corruption, but the word "company" does not imply diverting humanitarian funds into personal financial gain. The term instead makes sense of the complex web of foreign intervention, investment, and imposition in the emerging South Sudanese state that is visible on the main thoroughfares in Juba, and which remained staggeringly difficult to understand, intervene in, or disentangle from governance and everyday life. A neoliberal normative framework would place governments and aid organizations on one side and for-profit ventures on the other: seeing them as interconnected but separate entities, one responding to the market, the other regulating that market for the sake of enabling it.

To Jubans like Simon, a foreign aid worker, a foreign businessperson, and a foreign diplomat are indistinguishable in sight and in action. They all inhabit the same spaces in Juba and have achieved similar levels of enrichment as a result. Juba is a convergence point for these indistinguishable forces, and in launching his projects, Simon was using Juba's layerings and the myriad of financial investments and social connections to build opportunities and possibilities spanning social change and personal financial gains. Simon's and other Jubans' collapsing of these distinctions, then, is both a more accurate depiction of the South Sudanese state and of the convergence between humanitarianism and capitalism that characterizes contemporary intervention across the globe. Their use of the word English word "companies" is a keen, perceptive, and more fundamentally honest reading of the global political world order, where politics, influence, and profit have never been as separate as is often imagined. This lexical work and its attendant actions subvert neoliberal logics and categorizations. It both makes sense of the international crossings within Juba and creates openings for building new connections outward, unimpeded by any limitations that being merely for-profit or aimed at a social good.

Such a deft reading of the intertwined economic and geopolitical realities surrounding Juba allowed Simon to dream up and build a business that met his goal of offering a needed service to people from war-affected communities like his own, earn a stable income, and help others like him potentially earn a livable income and by launching their own ventures. His company was inspired by experiences similar to many Nuers living in Juba following the outbreak of violence in 2013. He had lived for a time in one of the UN-run Protection of Civilian camps in Juba and later relocated his mother, his wife, and his children to Kenya. Sending them money was challenging, and Simon worked with a few friends to start a money transfer company that would serve several war-affected towns in South Sudan and allow people to cheaply and easily send money throughout the country and the region. The company, BAB for General Trading and Investment, takes its name from the Arabic word for "door," a reflection of their sense that it offered several entranceways to opportunity. BAB is one of a spate of small money transfer networks employing ubiquitous cell phone usage and coverage to allow people to send money around the country. Money transfer is run entirely on cellular phone networks, with agents on either end using log books and issuing transfer codes to the senders and recipients, allowing people to send and receive money in locations where there are no banks or other financial institutions and between "unbanked" people. A small fee is charged on each transfer on the sender's end. This money in turn pays the one or two staff members at each center and the office's rent and security. Enough money generally flows through each center to keep each one flush with cash to pay out to recipients and channel funds back to the Juba home office.

Simon and his partners aimed for BAB to confront the fact that the only banks in South Sudan operate only in large towns and cater to the professional class of government workers and humanitarian aid professionals. Banks thus remain inaccessible to the majority of South Sudanese people, especially those from the war-torn northeastern region that Simon and most of his partners are from. BAB's money transfer network was meant to link up displaced people employed family members based in in Juba or soldiers stationed throughout the country to help pay school fees for children living across the country. Based within Juba and networked into the massive aid industry and the local business community, BAB's founders have been able to bend a variety of resources and opportunities into bringing their expansive vision into being. In their promiscuous approach to fundraising from both business investment and humanitarian sources and their strategic playing up of their being a multiethnic team (and in particular, Simon's ability, as an ethnic Nuer, to navigate and network within the war-torn northeastern region of South Sudan), they have created the seemingly impossible: an integrated regional money transfer network accessible to people at every income level. BAB's network, then, connects parts of South Sudan to each other in ways the country's network of roads and grid of domestic flight paths has rarely managed. As Simon's notion of companies doing social intervention as well as being profitable enterprises suggests, BAB has vast goals for the impact of their network. They claim to they have dampened the impacts of war and displacement and combatted the over-reliance on humanitarian aid that has become especially acute in recent years. Their grant proposals and strategy documents note that their primary goal is to curb the reliance on humanitarian aid by training young people in financial literacy and encouraging them to run small businesses.

Just after I finished my fieldwork in Juba, Simon and I won a poverty alleviation innovation research grant from the University of California, Davis, which we used to help BAB set up four new transfer points in South Sudan and link the network to the two major money transfer systems in the region: MTN Mobile Money in Uganda and the Kenya-based Mpesa. These links allow anyone near any of BAB's centers to stop relying on the costly and risky methods most people had employed previously to send money to their widespread friends and family: sending cash with someone traveling between the countries or exchanging their pounds for dollars to use one of the other money transfer companies operating in the major towns in South Sudan. Since launching these links, Simon and his partners had seen extensive use of BAB's linkages to these more robust money transfer networks, reflecting the growing needs of the many South Sudanese studying and working in the neighboring east African countries and the steady number of Kenyans and Ugandans living and working in South Sudan. The steady use of these new linkages demonstrated just how dense the social web was within the region. Their ambitions, like the infrastructure they had built and the growing reality of people in South Sudan, the region, and the global south in general, was unimpeded by national borders. Simon and others' framing of all types of Juba-based initiatives under the mantle of "companies" cuts through the logics of neoliberal capital, offering a more accurate and actionable framework for engaging the geopolitical reality where intervention and capitalism are fundamentally intertwined. Like the initiatives and socially rooted ventures of building boda boda driver collectives, linking different actors through money exchange, and running an independent electrical grid, BAB has become a social infrastructure that manages the present into something less precarious and more predictable.

Conclusion

In telling these stories of improvising Juba, I have suggested how people manage to make precarity productive and the ways Jubans seize control of the resources and people around them to create predictability that state systems and aid regimes have never managed to. Such spatial remakings, innovations, and "nonmovements" (Bayat 2010) use the city's dense social grid and the convergence of diversely situated people to create new connections within and beyond the borders of the state and stretching out far beyond the city's, and the state's, limits. In doing so, these actors remake space in the city and alter the contours of possibility. Their actions are active responses to contexts and situations that are all-too-often under-read as failed or chaotic. In precarity, these urbanites find avenues for new ventures, and in the urban milieu they find new ways of connecting. By recognizing the intricate, globe-spanning, rhizomic webs through which people actively remake urban realities to make places livable, predictable, and generative, we see not a dangerous and disordered urban ruin but a dynamic incubator of care and connection, of new communities and "companies." In recognizing how uncertainty can be reframed into opportunity, and by understanding the various forms of infrastructures that are perpetually produced, reworked, remade, and reoriented both in the face of – and through – precarity, we can see how distinct domains of power and value and disparate people can be sewn together in ways only possible in urban space. These examples of dynamic actions in a landlocked but port-like city demonstrate the necessity of reading the quotidian to recognize the distinct lifeways, dynamic mobilities, creative economic ventures, and subaltern remakings daily emerging across the Indian Ocean world.

Notes

1 This chapter is based on ethnographic research conducted in South Sudan between 2012 and 2016. This research was funded by grants from the Departments of Anthropology and African and African American Studies at the University of California, Davis; the National Science Foundation; the "Reimagining Indian Ocean Worlds" Mellon Research Initiative, and the Wenner-Gren Foundation.
2 See also his discussion of invisible infrastructure (De Boeck 2012).

References

Bayat, Asef. 2013. *Life as Politics: How Ordinary People Change the Middle East*. Stanford, CA: Stanford University Press.

De Boeck, Filip. 2011. "Inhabiting Ocular Ground: Kinshasa's Future in the Light of Congo's Spectral Urban Politics." *Cultural Anthropology* 26 (2): 263–286. doi:10.1111/j.1548-1360.2011.01099.x.

De Boeck, Filip. 2012. "Infrastructure: Commentary from Filip De Boeck." Curated Collections, Cultural Anthropology [Online] 26 November 2012, www.culanth.org/curated_collections/11-infrastructure/discussions/7-infrastructure-commentary-fromfilip-de-boeck.

Hancock, Mary and Smriti Srinivas. 2018. "Ordinary Cities and Milieus of Innovation." *Journal of the American Academy of Religion*. Vol. 86, No. 2, pp. 454–472.

Kurc, Maciej. 2009. "How to Survive in an African City?: A Migrant in the Face of Urbanization Processes in the South Sudanese Juba," paper presented at *3rd European Conference on African Studies*, The University of Leipzig, Leipzig. June 4–7.

Schuichiro, Nakao. 2013. "A History from Below: Malakia in Juba, South Sudan, c.1927–1954." *The Journal of Sophia Asian Studies*. No. 31: 139–160.

Simone, AbdouMaliq. 2004. "People as Infrastructure: Intersecting Fragments in Johannesburg" *Public Culture* 16 (3): 407–429.

Simone, AbdouMaliq. 2001. "On the Worlding of African Cities." *African Studies Review*. 44 (2): 15–41.

Srinivas, Smriti. 2015. *A Place for Utopia: Urban Designs from South Asia*. Seattle and London: University of Washington Press.

8 Displacemaking with *shutki*

Living with dead, dried fish as companions

Bidita Jawher Tithi

Shutki and displacemaking: an introduction[1]

How does one introduce *shutki*? It is an acquired taste – that is often the first line one feels obligated to say. *Shutki* (pronounced shoot-key) is the generic name of dried fish[2] in Bangladesh and is an important part of the Bangladeshi regional cuisine. There are myriad ways of preparing it, particularly in the southeastern division of Chittagong with which it is closely associated. But what makes *shutki* notorious is its smell. There is an intense "fishy smell," and for the first-time eaters, the smell can be overwhelming, and "peculiar." First time eaters are asked to get past the smell to enjoy the dish. But for many, it is a smell that is associated with a favorite food. And, for some who work in the thriving *shutki*

Figure 8.1 Shutki drying on scaffolds at Nazirartek, Bangladesh.
Image Credit: Bidita Jawher Tithi.

business, particularly in the Indian Ocean world of Cox's Bazar, in southeast Bangladesh, it is a familiar smell of their lives. Although there can be various opinions about the smell of *shutki*, there is consensus about one thing regarding the smell – it is a smell that spreads and lingers. Like a shroud, the smell of cooking *shutki* covers not only the kitchen where it is being cooked, but sometimes the entire house or even nearby places so that one can walk into a neighborhood and know that *shutki* is being cooked in a house there.

Perhaps that is why I was surprised when I first encountered *shutki* in Kutubdia Para, Cox's Bazar. After catching a glimpse of the dried fish yard in the distance from Kutubdia Para, I had expected the smell to be a punch in the face as I got closer to the dried fish yard. But the smell was surprisingly light. I asked questions and my colleagues explained that the intense smell is "released" during cooking. I pointed out that it was probably because there were coastal breezes blowing in the opposite direction. We agreed to disagree.[3] I took pictures and walked away – eager to explore other more interesting places. But I found out that like its smell, *shutki* lingers in other ways in the story of displacement that looms large in the Kutubdia Para.

Situated right at the precarious margins of the Indian Ocean, Kutubdia Para is a lively settlement of 40,000 people that dates back to early 1990s. This neighborhood emerged when the displaced people from the neighboring Kutubdia Island moved to this location after their island home was devasted by a cyclone in 1991. Kutubdia Para continues to face a number of different environmental hazards, such as cyclones and storm surges during which the inhabitants of this place move to safer sites (such as multi-purpose shelters). The inhabitants also face anxieties about future displacement, as their low-lying neighborhood is likely to fall victim to sea level rise due to climate change. Moreover, there is anxiety that the community will be evicted from their present location as the government land or *khas* land where the settlement is located is likely to be developed into an extension of the airport.

Kutubdia Para thus fits the dystopic imagination of today's changing world with growing anxiety of the future when "climate change … is projected to increase displacement of people" (UNHCR 2015: 4). Displacement[4] is generally analyzed with an alarmist viewpoint that is associated with "metaphors of submersion used as *torrents, streams, tides*, and *waves*" (Piguet 2013: 154; emphasis in original). The predominant response to this projection of future displacements has been to seek ways to prevent it (e.g., UNFCC 2015). But what does it mean to live while displaced? How is the process of becoming displaced connected with other processes, particularly with the process of placemaking, a term that is gaining increasing attention in relation to precarity and displacement in anthropology (Hinkson 2017)? Here I propose a worlding that takes the complexities that come from the process of displacement. Call it displacemaking. Instead of treating displacement as a threat to placemaking (e.g., Davidson 2009), this chapter imagines placemaking and displacement as deeply connected. This term favors a messy continuance – where displacement is never a done deal.

To think with the concept of displacemaking, I focus on three connected ideas of possible becomings, fluidity or movement, and contaminations that are implied in this displacemaking, which, I argue, make an important contribution to Indian Oceans studies. Becoming, in the Deleuzian sense, opposes the static and fixed aspects of the term "being" (Dovey 2010: 6), and helps to open up the world to allow for an understanding of interspecies and material connectivities (Massumi 1996). The concept of becoming aids in thinking about the placemaking that is imagined and produced in the communities of today through a variety of quotidian practices. Ideas of movement, non-fixity and mobility are also central to this chapter (Sheller and Urry 2006; Faulconbridge and Hui 2016) as I treat the connections created by people moving and *shutki* becoming a source of livelihood or a source of placemaking for those on the move. Instead of focusing on the fixity of the traditional borders of the Indian Ocean, this chapter strives to elaborate on contemporary and emerging transnational connections between different communities in Bangladesh, Myanmar, and the United States. Further, this chapter discusses issues of contamination such as the inclusion of pesticides and harmful preservatives in the preparation of *shutki*. At the same time, as cultures in Bangladesh and elsewhere have started highly valuing purity, even in terms of maintaining social divisions in terms of gender, class, caste and religion (Rozario 1992), I explore here how displacemaking has led to contaminated in-betweens in the Indian Ocean and discuss the anxiety and tensions that exist over social and food-related impure contaminations. In addition, being in the precarious margins, this chapter brings Indian Ocean Studies into conversation about climate change as the chapter imagines the new possibilities of life adrift (Baldwin and Bettini 2017) in the Indian Ocean Worlds through *shutki* as a companion in Kutubdia Para.

Dead and smelly, *shutki*, our companion, by its very state is a story of death and decomposition. How do we benefit from connecting it with the lively world of displacemaking? First, life and death go hand in hand in this world of displacemaking. As we see in the picture in this chapter, (dead) fish are dried in the bamboo racks right next to huts where people reside. And, more importantly, the dead, smelly fish is a way of living for many. While there can be lively companions that we need to understand the world, such as Donna Haraway's dog (Haraway 2004), and Tsing's mushroom (Tsing 2012), this chapter takes seriously the simultaneously deathly, dead, and rotting connections between non-humans and our own living in today's world.

Second, making *shutki* is a multi-step process involving different people. The (broad) steps are catching the fish, salting it, drying it, selling and then cooking it. The investigation of the *shutki* making means that one can study the possible connections as well as the ruptures in this becoming that can be positive and empowering but also problematic and exploitative.

Third, *shutki* also helps to understand the complex relations of food, socio-economic status and shifting regional identities. In Bangladesh, *shutki* is associated most closely with Chittagong, one of the divisions of Bangladesh renowned for its coasts. It is a *"chaat-gaya"* (Chittagongian) food, not only for the people living in the coastal regions but also those who live in the hills, including the indigenous groups. For the people of Chittagong, *shutki* is part of their regular cuisine, while for most other places, especially those that are at a distance from the coastal regions, *shutki* is a specialty food, cooked occasionally. But this is not the only relation that can be drawn. There are other relations possible. In the state of West Bengal in India, *shutki* is associated with the region and the people of Bangladesh or the *"Opar Bangla"*, the Bengal of the other side – and the families from that side who had migrated to West Bengal during the partition of 1947 or after. Whether one eats *shutki* or not is thus a test of the origins of one's family. Another possible relation of eating *shutki* is the socioeconomic status. Until recently, *shutki* was associated with poverty – only those who could not afford fresh fish bought *shutki*. In one memorable scene from the magical realist film *Goynar Baksho* (Jewelry Box), these dynamics are highlighted. The character of the ghost of Pishima (who had migrated to West Bengal after partition) reprimands Somlata (whose family is from West Bengal) for not eating *shutki*. "Think you are royalty?" the ghost scolds- as if only royalty can be excused for giving up the pleasure of eating *shutki* because of their high status in society. After scolding Somlata some more, the character of the ghost engages in a nostalgic remembrance of her childhood in Faridpur, a region in southern Bangladesh, and her memories of eating hot, spicy *shutki*. *Shutki*[5] therefore highlights the complex relations and conflicts that exist in these communities. It both divides and joins – separating people into distinct groups of eaters and non-eaters, but the lingering memories of *shutki* helps to connect those in the diasporas with their imaginary homelands.

Shutki in Nazirartek: the process of becoming

Situated next to Kutubdia Para is the dried-fish yard called Nazirartek. According to the local communities in Cox's Bazar, it is said to be the largest dried-fish yard, *shutki mohol* or *shutkipotti* in Bengali. Walking there, one can see almost all the different stages of making *shutki*. In the mornings and evening, the fish arrives in Nazirartek in wooden vans pulled by men and sometimes in smaller baskets. These are fish that have been just brought in from the nearby beach where the returning trawlers from the sea bring in huge hauls of fish. There are different varieties, including *chhuri* (hairtail), *loitya* (Bombay duck[6]), *poa* (panna croaker), *phaisa* (gangetic anchovy), shrimp and *rupchanda* (Chinese silver pomfret). Sometimes the small fish are mixed together in the same containers, in which case they are separated before the processing begins. Each fish is first gutted and then cleaned.

After that, the fish is sometimes treated with salt, although recently, due to customer preference for *shutki* with no salt, this step is avoided. Then the fish are put out to dry in the sun. The smaller fish are laid out on a large slab to dry. The larger ones are hung on bamboo racks, locally called *bara*, that can be used to carry the (drying) fish from one place to another and also hung on bamboo poles to dry. The drying time differs from one species to the other depending on the limpid composition of the fish. The ribbon fish and Bombay duck, two of the most common types of *shutki* dried in Nazirartek, take the least amount of time. Other types like the silver pomfret take much longer. After the fish has dried, they are tied together, and, a small portion is sold at the markets there; the rest is put into large trucks and transported to other markets. One of the main places where the *shutki* is taken is the Asadgang wholesale market in the port city of Chittagong which is 130 kilometers to the north (Belton, Hossain, and Thilsted 2018). But over the years, the demand for *shutki* has increased so that there are now five such dried-fish yard/markets in Cox's Bazar and a total of 10,000 separately owned dry fish processing small scale businesses in these yards/markets (Bangladesh Bureau of Statistics 2011).

Shutki for different usages is prepared at different times. There is *shutki* that is prepared right after catching the fish in the boats. This is the *shutki* that is used as food for the days when the fishermen are out in the ocean. The fish are gutted right after being caught and then salted and left on the boat's bow to dry. The *shutki* that are not eaten during the trip are taken home and consumed by the family. The fish chosen for this is generally the fish that is perceived to be of low quality which would not fetch a good price if converted into expensive *shutki*. These fish then never reach the dried fish yards of Nazirartek. At the same time, the more expensive *shutki* are also prepared and sold mostly in places that are more inland than Nazirartek. In many places, the fish are sun dried on top of buildings. My friends from those areas explained that rooftops are chosen because those places are safer. But I wondered – safer from what? It is not only stealing that one fears (although there are sometimes incidents of crime), but also the unpredictability of the natural elements. The more expensive fish can be easily stored away in the *pucca* buildings in case of a storm surge or cyclone.

These activities of gutting, cleaning, (sometimes) salting, and hanging out the fish on scaffolds to dry goes on from early morning till evening, for the post-monsoon seasons of the year, approximately from October to March when the average rainfall is the lowest. Women, men and young children all work for long hours in mostly unhygienic conditions with poor pay. Men (who are not supervisors) make about 300 BD Taka (US$3.85) per day and women make about 200 BD Taka (US$2.55) per day.[7]

The business of Nazirartek has a liveliness of its own. This liveliness is also deeply entangled with the location. As the process of *shutki* making needs to be done as soon as possible in order to preserve as much of the taste of the fish as possible, the process of drying is carried out very close to the seashore. The process is dependent therefore on the availability of land near the sea. At the same time, Nazirartek is connected by roads to the other markets that makes the transport of *shutki* easier. And, the salt that is used is obtained readily as well as there are 38 salt processing small-scale cottage industries in the same sub-district (Cox's Bazar Sadar) and three in the neighboring Maheshkhali sub-district (Bangladesh Bureau of Statistics 2011).

And how do we connect this liveliness of the Nazirartek dried fish yard/ market in respect of today's world of changes and displacemaking? First, Nazirartek has been possible because of displacemaking. The *khas* land or government land was utilized for the industry because of the movement of the people from Kutubdia Island. *Shutki* has been a major source of income for many people of Kutubdia island. But according to several people that I interviewed, *shutki* making used to be a secondary livelihood in Kutubdia Island while their primary occupation was fishing. *Shutki* making was not prioritized as they were not able to earn enough money from this business. Before they were displaced, they used to dry the fish in the island and then transport to the *shutki* markets in other places, including Cox's Bazar. Moving to the area near Cox's Bazar Airport, has connected the dried fish yards more closely with the rest of the country. "Now we do not need to bring the fish to Cox's Bazar. It used to be costly for us," Rashid,[8] one Kutubdia Para resident confided in a focus group meeting. To date, most of the small businesses in Nazirartek are owned by people from Kutubdia Para.

With time, there have been flows of people into the area from different parts of Bangladesh, particularly from the other sub-districts of Cox's Bazar. Another group that has also joined the labor force are the Rohingya refugees from neighboring Myanmar.[9] Many of the workers, including the Rohingya people are seasonal workers who mostly come and stay near the Nazirartek during the fish drying season. But the people from Kutubdia are permanently settled there and see Nazirartek as their own place.

Shutki on the move

Dried fish has historically been a companion of those on the move (Fagan 2017). Today, it is also a food that is being transported to those who have moved elsewhere globally. *Shutki* is a popular food that is exported outside of Bangladesh for the Bangladeshi diaspora in the United States, UK and in the Middle East. I first encountered this in my own experiences in the United States when I had *shutki* in an intimate dinner with some friends at a Bangladeshi friend's house in California. Unlike other items, it was not brought to the dining table itself. Our host asked whether we objected to having some *shutki*, and then she brought in the prepared *shutki* that her mother had sent from Bangladesh. On many occasions, I have encountered cooked *shutki* paste that is brought to the United States by friends and family, with its distinctive smell and its spicy make-up. It is treasured as a food that is shared only in intimate gatherings. The *shutki* brought from Bangladesh is treated almost like smuggled goods. There is no consensus about whether the food, especially when brought in prepared, is legal to bring into United States or not. "The trick is not to declare it at the immigration," I am advised. Unprepared *shutki* is also available in many South Asian markets but many do not prepare it in their home because they are worried about the lingering smell. Some even advise against heating it – "Be careful, remember the microwave will stink if you heat it there," I was once told.

What can we make of this transnational practices of eating *shutki*? While we tried *shutki* in California, a Bangladeshi news channel was playing on the television. Although the news generally focused on current affairs in Bangladesh, it was evident that the news channel was inclusive of the people watching the news from outside of Bangladesh – during intervals, there were advertisements about spices with "*aschol deshi moja*" (real taste of Bangladesh), or of markets selling Bangladeshi products in Jackson Heights. The ads featured familiar faces from Bangladesh, those who have been models or actors in Bangladesh and are now immigrants themselves. These everyday placemaking are part of a particular form of making home (Jennings et al. 2014) of the immigrant community of Bangladesh in California who can be said to be "transnationals: people with emotional, social, political, economic, and spiritual commitments in two places, and with the ability to move back and forth [in today's world] in order to make use of each to compensate for what the other lacks" (Brown 1999: 80) and who can stay in touch with Bangladesh via television and food while sitting in their houses in California and elsewhere.

Besides the transnational communities of Bangladesh, another group that are the main customers of *shutki* are the inhabitants of the Rohingya-registered refugee camps in Cox's Bazar. Since mid-2014, the World Food Programme has changed the food distribution from in-kind food rations to e-vouchers. Every month the beneficiaries of this program can purchase items such as rice, lentils, spinach, spices and *shutki* with their "value-recharged FoodCard" at three shops located within the camps (World Food Programme, and Government of Bangladesh 2016). Besides the fact that *shutki* is readily available at a cheap rate, *shutki* has also been chosen as it is a food that is a part of the regular diet of the Rohingya people. While *shutki* is considered a regional food of Chittagong in Bangladesh, it also has strong roots in the Rakhine state (previously Arakan) in Myanmar (Duguid 2012). In discussions with Rohingya people, the story of *shutki* is entangled with the story of the time before the region was divided into parts of nations. Abdul, a 50-year-old Rohingya man, told us in a tea stall in the market outside one of the refugee camps, "Once this place was part of Arakan. All this was actually part of our homeland, once. And then it was broken." Indeed, the history of Bengal and Arakan is filled with one kingdom conquering the other, and then the kingdom becoming fragmented again (Ramachandra 1981). But at one point in time the Rohingyas could have been free to live in the country without having to carry the burden of being a refugee with limited rights. Abdul shared his theory that the similarity in language and food habits shows that actually there are not too much differences between the host communities of Bengali people of today and the Rohingyas, who are the descendants of those who used to also belong here. This was in 2014, before the recent destruction of Rohingya villages (Human Rights Watch 2016) and before the new group of Rohingya refugees started coming to the area. When we discussed the issues of being a refugee, Abdul shared his wish to go back one day but stated that at present he was happy. His placemaking of Bangladesh was also through food – "there are not too much differences here – we eat the same thing here."

The two communities discussed above share certain similarities. *Shutki* evokes memories of a past (real and imaginary) mapping of placemaking for both communities. But there are also differences. While the two communities clearly differ in socioeconomic classes, I draw attention to the non-movement or fixity of one and the transnational mobility of the other. Unlike the Bangladeshi transnationals in California, the community of refugees are extremely restricted in their current location with little chances of maintaining their connections in both Myanmar and Bangladesh. Moreover, the immigrants choose to eat or share *shutki* as a food while for the refugee community, the food "choice" is made by others for them that, as we shall see later in this chapter, can also be removed from their diet through decisions of others. At the same time, the practice of eating shukti also helps to uncover the everyday practices via which the people of the two communities cope with the uncertainity and anxiety and make sense of their positions in the current world (Srinivas 2016). Besides forming a connection with the past, *shutki* helps Abdul from the refugee community draw familiar connections with the host communities in the region and with the place where he currently lives. Their occasional reluctance to bring the food to the table and reminders to not heat it in the microwave hint at the anxieties of the transnational Bangladeshi immigrant community regarding their uncertain positions as immigrants in the post-9–11 world and the pressure to ensure that that they are not seen or smelled as different.

Shutki gone bad: contemplating contamination

Given that there are different groups, such as the Bangladeshi immigrants abroad and the beneficiaries in the refugee camps, that are customers of *shutki*, the price of *shutki* is going up. From what used to be a staple food item for people of low-income groups, it is now a luxury food item that is found in South Asian grocery stores in different parts of the world. In other parts of Bangladesh as well, there is a growing acceptance of the food. But with this popularity, there is also anxiety about the food. One of the main concerns is the *shutki*-making practices; in discussions, one of the most common complaints is that *shutki* is not prepared hygienically ("they use their hands"), or that the fish is not cleaned properly. But there is greater anxiety about pesticides that are added to the fish to shorten the drying time or to make the dried fish last longer.

My interviewees stated that before 2015, pesticides had to be added to *shutki* to prevent fly infestation. This, they claimed, was due to a greater demand for *shutki*. As a result, *shutki* is prepared during all nine non-monsoon months and not only during the winter months when it customarily was prepared. Due to the humid weather, *shutki* gets spoilt very easily, especially when in storage. Pesticides are added mostly to the *shutki* in summer, but not in winter, I was told.

This was shared openly, and the added 'medicine' was highlighted as a reason why the fish was "high quality" as it would keep fresh longer. Since 2015, there has been a drastic change in discussions about *shutki* preparation: no longer are these "medicines" openly discussed but instead there are discussions of "fresh" *shutki* with "no added salt or anything."

The shift is based on the anxiety about food contamination that has gripped the Bangladeshi imagination due to multiple reports on how pesticides and preservatives are being added to food, even to brands that are widely respected. Eating such food could cause cancer or even death, according to several videos found on social media about food contamination. The worst culprit is "formalin," a colorless solution of formaldehyde used as a disinfectant allegedly added to many fruits, vegetables and fish in order to extend its shelf life (FAO 2015). Formalin is said to be "a few hundred times worse than poison"[10] and reportedly has been added to fruits, vegetables, and fish. In reaction to this, there are sign-boards outside grocery stores that claim that the vegetables and fruits sold are "formalin free." The topic captured the public imagination so vividly that during the period from 2014 to 2015 there were several *natoks* ("drama") specials,[11] a popular form of entertainment on television, that had names containing the word Formalin and included jokes about the anxiety over formalin. The anxiety has led many people to stop eating certain fruits (such as mangoes and apples) and this in turn has led the Bangladesh Food Safety Authority to make a formal announcement that no formalin has been found in these fruits (The Daily Star Report 2017).

It is within this context that the discourse of quality and freshness of *shutki* must be located. Since Nazirartek has gained recognition recently as (allegedly) the largest dried fish yard in Bangladesh, there have been a number of documentaries[12] and newspaper coverage regarding the quality of *shutki* there (Zinnat 2015; Zinnat and Huq 2017). The topic has also been covered by people doing documentary style "vlogs" on their own social media channels. "Better to prepare your own *shutki* at home" we are told in these vlogs. Scientific studies have found the main form of "contaminant" in *shutki* to be DDT (dichlorodiphenyltrichloroethane), that, although banned in Bangladesh, is readily available and has been found to be present in many different types of *shutki* (Haque et al. 2013).

The notoriety regarding contaminations has led to less willingness to admit that pesticides are added. There is a fear that the *shutki* will not be sold. In fact, WFP temporarily stopped buying *shutki* as a source of food for the refugee camps for a few months in 2014 as the *shutki* that had been bought had tested positive for DDT (World Food Programme, and Government of Bangladesh 2016). An informant from Cox's Bazar told me that when he spotted the mixing of DDT or any pesticide fix, he was told that it was just "soap" for washing the *shutki* – in a way altering the discourse. The *shutki*-makers want to assure us that the *shutki* is not contaminated, that it is clean; after all it has been washed with soap for better hygiene.

While there has been increasing awareness and anxiety about the contamination in *shutki* in Bangladesh, there has been also anxieties in Kutubdia Para about other forms of mixing related to *shutki*. This thinking about purity and exclusion of others is driven by politics both local and transnational. While the business of *shutki* making has grown, there are fears that the development of the Cox's Bazar airport will lead to evacuation of the people from Kutubdia Para. In the past, they have used their pioneering action in the *shutki* business as a way to argue for their right to stay in the area. But with the influx of more people from other regions, there is rising fear that their political identities and rights might be wearing away.

In conversations with people from Kutubdia Para, I found that there is growing resentment about people from other regions, particularly the Rohingya people. In the past, most of the workers were seasonal and used to leave at the end of the *shutki* season. But recently, there have been more people settling as permanent residents in the area. This is leading to tension between the groups. Although the Rohingya people were part of the *shutki* business from the very beginning of Nazirartek (Belton, Hossain, and Thilsted 2018), their contributions are not readily recognized by the people from Kutubdia Para who feel that the *shutki* business and Kutubdia Para should remain a place for the people from Kutudia Para. Ayesha, a 23-year-old resident from Kutubdia Para, shared that one of the main reasons for this is that now they have to compete with people from other places for jobs. But she also elaborated that "We want our community to last. The others are different. They have their different culture. We want our own culture." This resentment towards the "others" was not only expressed by those who were in the *shutki* business but also by shopkeepers who are not directly connected with the *shutki* business. The efforts to avoid any form of mixing are likely to be challenged as more changes come in the near future.

Shutki and future challenges

This chapter has explored the possible "becomings," contamination, and movement of people and non-humans/materials to discuss how the changing relations to food, socioeconomic status and connections across borders have led to complexities of placemaking and lived experiences of displacement in the Indian Ocean worlds. The *shutki* in Cox's Bazar shows how placemaking and quotidian practices are valuable frames for understanding relationality in the Indian Ocean. By foregrounding the non-fixity of this placemaking, this chapter also emphasizes the need to consider how the contemporary 'becomings' are likely to change in the near future.

One of the sources of change that is already affecting the *shutki* business is the fluctuations in the weather patterns. In 2015, for example, unexpected rainfall during the *shutki*-making period of September and October led to a fall in profit of 1500 million BDT (US$19 million) for the *shutki* business in Cox's Bazar (Khan 2015). Although compared to other months (especially June and July), the rainfall in drier months like December is very low, but there is a trend of more rain on average per year since 1973. This trend is likely to continue with climate change (IPCC 2007). More rainfall also means that there is greater humidity in the air and more chances of (dried) *shutki* absorbing the moisture and getting infested with flies and maggots.

Some of the shopkeepers have come up with many new ways to combat the humidity. One is a "neat trick" that a shopkeeper shared with us to make sure that the fish stays fresh. The *shutki* is put in a polythene bag – this keeps them fresh and prevents them from rotting away. In the humid weather of Bangladesh there is a race to defeat the infestation by flies and maggots. The usage of the plastic bags is one step in the race. But another is the drying time and the "ray" radiation that can help to kill the germs. In discussions, the *shutki* sellers lament that they have no access to the infrastructure to build an industry for drying the fish.

What would such an industry look like? I wondered. A quick search on YouTube, as suggested in discussion with one of my interviewees, led me to a YouTube video from a dried fish factory in Thailand. "The latest technology is used there," I was told. In the video, I see men in factory overalls, with gloves, gutting and cleaning fish and then putting the fish in trays that are then put on racks of a shelf by a robot arm, and then the racks are moved to a "drying room" where they are machine-dried. Robot arms working in collaboration with humans. Is that the future? I asked my friends. Perhaps one day, I was told. For now, there were easier goals. There was excitement about a big fair that was organized by Palli Karma-Sahayak Foundation (PKSF), a development organization established by the Government of Bangladesh in 1990 that works towards poverty reduction by creating employment opportunities. In this fair, the stall of dried fish made with a new drying method won one of the "Best Stall" prizes. This is a low-cost fish drier that is being piloted right now but may be widely available through microcredit. This is an "organic" drying method, in which fish are placed in a large box-like structure and dried quickly. There is no need for mixing preservatives, salt, or even the sun – the drying can be done at night too. Other attempts are also being tried to ensure that the *shutki* is of export quality – one of which is to educate the *shutki*-makers about the harms of the DDT and to teach them how to use spices such as turmeric and chili as preservatives.

According to the IPCC (2007), climate change will also increase the intensity and number of cyclones and storms. So far, this area has not suffered from extensive damage in terms of human life due to cyclone protection programs. But the world of *shutki* and its connections are changing – the threat of sea level rise will likely affect the area that is being used as the dried fish yards.

There are other changes happening as well. Fishing done through trawlers leads to overfishing and many types of fish are becoming extinct. With expanding markets across oceans, the demands and preferences are likely to change and these in turn may lead to shukti making being outsourced elsewhere. The influx of Rohingya refugees in recent years will likely also affect the *shutki* business. While previously many of the Rohingya refugees had openly worked in the dried fish yards, recently their position has become hazardous – if they are found out to be Rohingya then they are no longer allowed to work.[13]

These and other concerns populate the discussion of *shutki* and displace-making. It is a way of thinking and connecting that helps to understand the everyday (dis)placemaking in the contemporary precarious world. There are many reasons to think about the future, to worry and to mourn the possible loss of a thriving industry. But at the same time, it is also important to recognize the fact that the very market of *shutki* is a product of the connections and the ruptures that have happened because of displacement. For now, *shutki* as our companion in displacemaking, like its smell, lingers.

Notes

1 The fieldwork and writing of this chapter were supported by the "Reimagining Indian Ocean Worlds" Mellon Research Initiative at the University of California, Davis.
2 There are some exceptions to the rule. Dried hilsa fish (called *ilish* in Bengali) has its own name, *nona ilish* (salted hilsa).
3 Since then I have come to the realization that the intensity of the smell varies. We still have not reached a consensus regarding the reasons for this.
4 This is not to deny the troubles that can come from displacement. I agree that displacement can be a traumatizing experience and there are often losses of lives and livelihoods because of displacement. But the challenge taken in this chapter is to also consider alternate and more complex stories.
5 Following the vibrant field of assemblage theorization in geography and anthropology (e.g., West 2016), I use the concept to understand how *shutki* is an entanglement of multiple and (inter)connected materials, meaning and capacities (Deleuze and Guattari 1988) that can be used to explore the continual processes involved with displacemaking, particularly those of becoming, moving (dis)connections and contaminating in-betweens.
6 The English name of this fish is itself entangled in the colonial lore of the region. The lore goes that the fish was named Bombay "dak" (mail train) after the cargo trains that used to carry the dried fish from what was Bombay (now Mumbai), another region where the dried version of the fish is made and eaten; another origin story for the name is that the British gave this name as the smell of the dried fish reminded them of the damp odor of the wooden floors of Bombay Dak trains (Sen 2012).
7 The exchange rate was US$1 = 78.5 BDT in December 2016 when the data was collected. I was not able to ascertain the exact rate for the amount paid to children as the numbers reported varied widely. According to the study conducted by Belton, Hossain, and Thilsted (2018), the workers who are younger than 15 years get about US$0.40 to 0.60.
8 All names have been changed to protect the privacy of the individuals.
9 During my study, I met mostly Rohingya women in the dried fish yard. In interviews, I found that most of the Rohingya men work in the fishing boats as labor.
10 Part of the report, regarding a popular food brand, in Bengali can be viewed at www.youtube.com/watch?v=vUgBtPmeHRQ&t=16s (accessed on 19 September 2017)
11 Examples include "Formalin," "Formalin Reaction," "Formalin Plus." Source: Amarnatok.com (accessed on 19 September 2017)
12 One such documentary is the Talash episode titled *Shutkite Bish* (Poison in *Shutki*) at www.youtube.com/watch?v=NRjZwW-Yrdw (accessed on December 2, 2017)
13 From personal correspondence with two informants on 10 December 2016 and 12 December 2016.

References

Baldwin, Andrew and Giovanni Bettini. 2017. *Life Adrift: Climate Change, Migration, Critique*. London: Rowman & Littlefield Publishers.

Bangladesh Bureau of Statistics. 2011. *District Statistics 2011: Cox's Bazar*. (Dhaka).

Belton, Ben, Mostafa A.R. Hossain, and Shakuntala H. Thilsted. 2018. "Labour, Identity and Wellbeing in Bangladesh's Dried Fish Value Chains." In *Social Wellbeing and the Values of Small-scale Fisheries*, edited by Derek S. Johnson, Tim G. Acott, Natasha Stacey, and Julie Urquhart, 217–241. Cham, Switzerland: Springer International Publishing.

Brown, Karen McCarthy. 1999. "Staying Grounded in a High-Rise Building: Ecological Dissonance and Ritual Accommodation in Haitian Vodou." In *Gods of the City: Religion and the American Urban Landscape*, edited by Robert A. Orsi, 79–102. Bloomington and Indianapolis: Indiana University Press.

Davidson, Mark. 2009. "Displacement, Space and Dwelling: Placing Gentrification Debate." *Ethics, Place & Environment* 12 (2): 219–234.

Deleuze, Gilles, and Félix Guattari. 1988. *A Thousand Plateaus: Capitalism and Schizophrenia*. London: Bloomsbury Publishing.

Dovey, Kim. 2010. *Becoming Places: Urbanism/Architecture/Identity/Power*. New York: Routledge.

Duguid, Naomi. 2012. *Burma: Rivers of Flavor*. New York: Artisan Books.

Fagan, Brian M. 2017. Fishing: how the sea fed civilization. New Haven: Yale University Press.

FAO. 2015. "What is Formalin?" Improving Food Safety in Bangladesh. Accessed 18 September 2017. www.fao.org/in-action/food-safety-bangladesh/resources/did-you-know/detail/en/c/380816/.

Faulconbridge, James, and Allison Hui. 2016. "Traces of a Mobile Field: Ten Years of Mobilities Research." *Mobilities* 11 (1): 1–14.

Haque, Enamul, M Kamruzzaman, Md Shofikul Islam, Tanvir Sarwar, Shaikh Shahinur Rahman, and Md Rezaul Karim. 2013. "Assessment and Comparison of Quality of Solar Tunnel Dried Bombay Duck and Silver Pomfret with Traditional Sun Dried Samples." *International Journal of Nutrition and Food Sciences* 2 (4): 187–195.

Haraway, Donna. 2004. *The Haraway Reader*. New York: Routledge.

Hinkson, Melinda. 2017. "Precarious Placemaking." *Annual Review of Anthropology* 46: 49–64.

Human Rights Watch. 2016. "Burma: Massive Destruction in Rohingya Villages." Human Rights Watch. Last Modified 13 November 2017. Accessed 17 January 2017. www.hrw.org/news/2016/11/13/burma-massive-destruction-rohingya-villages.

IPCC. 2007. Synthesis Report. Contribution of Working Groups I, II and III to the Fourth Assessment Report of the Intergovernmental Panel on Climate Change. Geneva, Switzerland: Intergovernmental Panel on Climate Change.

Jennings, Hannah Maria, Janice L Thompson, Joy Merrell, Barry Bogin, and Michael Heinrich. 2014. "Food, Home and Health: The Meanings of Food Amongst Bengali Women in London." *Journal of ethnobiology and ethnomedicine* 10 (1): 44.

Khan, Mohammad Jamil. 2015. "Dried Fish Traders see Tk150cr Profit Fall this Year." *Dhaka Tribune*, 16 December 2015.

Massumi, Brian. 1996. "Becoming-deleuzian." *Environment and Planning D: Society and Space* 14 (4): 395–406.

Piguet, Etienne. 2013. "From 'Primitive Migration' to 'Climate Refugees': The Curious Fate of the Natural Environment in Migration Studies." *Annals of the Association of American Geographers* 103 (1): 148–162.

Ramachandra, GP. 1981. "Captain Hiram Cox's Mission to Burma, 1796–1798: A Case of Irrational Behaviour in Diplomacy." *Journal of Southeast Asian Studies* 12 (2): 433–451.

Rozario, Santi. 1992. *Purity and Communal Boundaries: Women and Social Change in a Bangladeshi Village*. London: Zed Books.

Sen, Rajyashree. 2012. "The Making of Bombay Duck." *The Wall Street Journal* (Online), 6 December 2012, India Real Time.

Sheller, Mimi, and John Urry. 2006. "The New Mobilities Paradigm." *Environment and planning A* 38 (2): 207–226.

Srinivas, Smriti. 2016. "Roadside Shrines, Storefront Saints, and Twenty-First Century Lifestyles: The Cultural and Spatial Thresholds of Indian Urbanism." In *Place/No-Place in Urban Asian Religiosity*, edited by J.P. Waghorne, 131–147, New York: Springer.

The Daily Star Report. 2017. "No formalin in vegetable, fruits:BFSA." *Daily Star*, August 17, 2017. Accessed September 20, 2017. www.thedailystar.net/country/no-formalin-vegetable-fruits-bangladesh-food-safety-authority-adulteration-artificial-eggs-1450948.

Tsing, Anna Lowenhaupt. 2012. "Unruly Edges: Mushrooms as Companion Species: for Donna Haraway." *Environmental Humanities* 1 (1): 141–154.

UNFCC. 2015. "Tast Force on Displacement." UNFCC. Accessed 18 September 2017. http://unfccc.int/adaptation/groups_committees/loss_and_damage_executive_committee/items/9978.php.

UNHCR. 2015. *UNHCR, The Environment and Climate Change*. Geneva: UNHCR.

West, Paige. 2016. "An Anthropology for 'the Assemblage of the Now'." *Anthropological Forum* 26 (4): 438–445.

World Food Programme, and Government of Bangladesh. 2016. *Assistance to Refugees from Myanmar: Standard Project Report 2016*. World Food Programme (Dhaka).

Zinnat, Mohammad Ali. 2015. "Dry fish trade thriving in Cox's Bazar of Bangladeah." *Daily Star*, 10 December 2015.

Zinnat, Mohammad Ali and Enamul Huq. 2017. "Huge potential, problems untouched." *Daily Star*, 2 February 2017.

Part III
Memory and maps

Part III
Memory and maps

9 Memory, memorialization, and "heritage" in the Indian Ocean

Pedro Machado

Introduction

The long centuries of interaction in the vast waters of the Indian Ocean have produced cultural forms and commercial structures of great complexity and layering, involving multi-directional engagements that informed religious, intellectual, legal, and political life across the ocean (e.g., Bishara 2016; Machado 2014; Tagliacozzo 2013). The legacies and histories of these engagements are multifaceted and have left indelible marks and traces that are visible among the populations and landscapes scattered across the lands and islands of this maritime basin. They have also been remembered and represented in different ways that can reflect, and in turn inform, any number of cultural, social, economic, and political dynamics and considerations. Crucially, the processes and forms that remembering takes can be central to the shaping of group identities and to ideas of national or ethnic belonging. They are implicated, moreover, in how historical memory and the retelling of the past can be cast to privilege one version over another, instantiate claims about authenticity, or actively silence contentious and difficult pasts.

In this chapter, I explore how select aspects of Indian Ocean pasts have been excavated through processes of memory-making, memorialization and heritage discourses to understand how communities and individuals have sought to come to terms with the weight of history. I do so by considering acts of remembrance as imagined through sites and landscapes that have been marked historically by community structures (such as religious shrines) or become marked through processes of heritage-making that may often include the use of public space or museums. However, as pasts can be elided or actively forgotten, the chapter also explores how memories can be suppressed within communities or marginalized by the intervention of state institutions.

My exploration of historical memory is centered around the theme of slavery that constituted a central element in the shaping of Indian Ocean histories of unfreedom and forced migration. Thousands of individuals were dislocated from their homes over centuries of slave trading across a range of distances and locales that established the parameters of this vast sea of slavery. Framed around an idea of the ocean as a scape of slavery, labor, marine extraction, and sacred geographies, I examine the materiality and practices of remembering pasts in particular sites in East and South Africa, the Gulf and India, as establishing ways of knowing and identification that can align with state-sanctioned views of the past or transcend them to create alternative forms of memory.

Sacred geographies

Islam occupies a significant place in the history of the Indian Ocean, with networks of religious affinity often spurring the extension of commercial exchange and groups (and vice versa) along the many littorals and islands of the ocean. The multiple crossings and circulations of Muslims in the ocean created a vast seascape of "familiar strangers" whose contours were ever-shifting according to different political, commercial, and social imperatives (Kresse and Simpson 2011; Trivellato 2012).

While the materiality of Muslim presences in the ocean is visible, for instance, in the many mosques of varying styles and sizes that were constructed from a range of materials along the ocean's littorals – often incorporating local design idioms and aesthetics – the sacred geography of Islam was rendered equally visible through other structures that have tended to be under-studied. I refer here to *keramats*, the ubiquitous popular shrines that are found throughout the landscapes of much of Muslim Southeast Asia and the Indian Ocean region as a whole. The venerated graves of notable figures, *keramats* (a Malay word for popular sites of prayer, derived from the Arabic noun *karāmāt* used to refer to miracles performed by a *walī*, a revered spiritual figure or "saint") trace their establishment to the emergence of Muslim social networks and Islam in the ocean as a transregional cultural framework from the fifteenth to the eighteenth centuries (Mandal 2012). While, as recently noted, these sites are comprised of the graves of individuals from a variety of ethnic backgrounds, histories and faiths – and therefore involve socially and culturally diverse practices – they are mostly associated with Muslims and frequently with Hadrami migrants or their descendants (Mandal 2012).

Those commemorated in *keramats* were in many instances Sayyids (sometimes rendered as "Syed"), male descendants from the Prophet Muhammad, with visitors being drawn to *keramats* by the possibility of deepening their connection to God through the miraculous workings of the *walī* channeled through his grave shrine (Mandal 2012). Significant factors in the making of *keramats* were scholarship and piety of the deceased saints, but an individual could become a *keramat* if they had distinguished themselves in some way within a particular community. In Singapore, for instance, the *maqam* ('tomb shrine') of Habib Noh (b. 1788), born at sea to Hadrami parents en route from Penang to Palembang and settled in Singapore as a young man, recognizes a lifetime of work among the poor along with his spiritual gifts. Soon after his death in 1866 his shrine became a place of local and regional *ziarah* (pilgrimage). Tied intimately to the oceanic itineraries of travel and trade, and the cosmopolitan port cities through which pilgrimage and migration were channeled and organized, many prominent *keramat* emerged in such places as Aceh, Penang, Melaka, Jakarta, and Surabaya.

Keramats emerged also in other regional settings where they evoked the power of the sea as a living and expansive arena through the praxis of pilgrimage and prayer. In the context of post-apartheid South Africa, for instance, *keramats* (locally rendered as *kramats*)[1] have assumed particular importance in the invocation of memories associated with oceanic linkages, and been spaces for the contestation over heritage claims, identities, and the meaning of Islam in the country. In the region of the Western Cape roughly two dozen *kramats* mark the resting places of pioneering ancestors of the local Muslim community, several of whom were brought to the area as political exiles and convicts through VOC (Dutch East India Company) carceral networks of empire (Ward 2009). Figures such as the political convict, Imam 'Abd Allah bin Qādi 'Abd al-Salam (known locally as Tuan Guru; d. 1807), brought to the Cape from Tidore in the Moluccas, eastern Indonesia, and buried in the Bo-Kaap, were shipped across thousands of miles of the Indian Ocean as Dutch officials sought to tame opposition and resistance to their rule in the "East Indies" by sending individuals into state-sanctioned exile. Believed to have first spread Islam at the Cape, such figures became integral to the formation of an early Muslim community in South Africa.

As the burial sites of significant historical figures, *kramats* marked the landscape as material manifestations of linkages to the beginnings of Islam in South Africa. But they also marked a particular sacred geography, for their placement in the area of greater Cape Town was said to form a "Circle of Islam" that protected the city and its inhabitants from natural and other disasters. The work of Saarah Jappie in particular has highlighted how *kramats* were and remain "spiritually potent sites" where the interaction of the physical and spiritual worlds is seen to take place. *Kramats* thus define a particular historical and spiritual geography that link the pious deceased to the establishment of Islam at the Cape, and to the broader histories of forced migrations from around the Indian Ocean (Jappie 2018).

Among those who were forcibly taken to the Cape, arguably the most famous of all is the Indonesian Sufi scholar and exile, Shaykh Yusuf. Born in Makassar in the eastern reaches of the Indonesian archipelago in 1626, Shaykh Yusuf became a religious leader in the independent polity of Banten, Java, and was brought to the Cape as a Dutch political prisoner where he died in 1699. Believed by some to have been the first Muslim to read the Qur'an in South Africa, Shaykh Yusuf has assumed a central place in the memorialization of Islam at the Cape. While his memory was initially kept alive through collective sharing and annual visitations to the *kramat* at Easter as part of the traditions of people who visited the site, his history was not actually attached to the site. Over the course of the twentieth century, however, Shaykh Yusuf's biography was promoted as a foundational narrative of Cape Islam – due in part to efforts by the Hajee Sullaiman Shahmahomed Trust that assumed ownership of the *kramat* in 1908 and had this narrative engraved at the site itself for visitors to read – and

Figure 9.1 Kramat Shaykh Yusuf, Macassar, Cape Town.
Image credit: Pedro Machado.

romanticized (and exoticized) as a noble Muslim's opposition to imperial oppression in the Indian Ocean.[2]

Shaykh Yusuf's centrality to the memory of Islam was powerfully marked with a signal event that coincided with South Africa's first post-apartheid election in 1994: the tricentenary celebration of Shaykh's arrival at the Cape ("Sheikh Yusuf Tricentenary Commemoration").[3] It marked also the beginnings of a significant reorientation of Muslim identity and public memory in Cape Town. During the apartheid-era while Islam had been seen as something of an elite religious practice mostly of the Bo-Kaap quarter of the city, in the post-apartheid period it became a catalyst of identification for a much broader sector of the city's population. Despite the fact that slaves and convicts had actually played a larger role in the transmission of Islam in Cape, as noted by Kerry Ward and Nigel Worden, Shaykh Yusuf was regarded by many as the "bearer of Islam" (Witz, Minkley, and Rassool 2017: 108) to the Cape and as a "spiritual liberator" (Ward and Worden 1998: 213; Worden 2019) Shaykh Yusuf thus represented an indelible link to the oceanic currents of Islam; his memory shaped the sacred and geographical imaginaries for Muslims at the Cape in compelling ways as a transnational community of global belonging. Significantly, the tricentenary celebrations included an event, a "Muslim Arts and Crafts" exhibition, that took place at the Castle of the Cape of Good Hope in the center of the city. A powerful symbol of white rule during the years of apartheid, the

Castle was built by the VOC as its military headquarters in the region in the seventeenth and eighteenth centuries, and remained as a structure that symbolized state and military authority throughout apartheid. The Sheikh Yusuf Tricentenary Commemoration coordinating committee sought to challenge the use of this space and to reclaim the Castle for Cape Muslim history, specifically within a context of slave heritage, that I will discuss later (Ward 1995).

The tricentenary celebrations also laid bare the fraught nature of geographical imaginaries and how their embeddedness in the cultural lives of Cape Muslims linking them to a broader Muslim world worked to influence the politics of memory recall. The tricentenary highlighted the re-emergence of a "Malay" identity as part of a "Malay" diaspora that had been the product of the VOC's forced migration of "Malay" exiles during its rule at the Cape (Haron 2005; Jeppie 2001). The idea of "Cape Malay" identity has long been mobilized in South Africa for different ends – for the apartheid state in the 1940s and 1950s, for instance, support for a distinctive (archetypal and romanticized) "Malay" identity and the demarcation of a specific "Malay Quarter" (today's Bo-Kaap) for Cape Town's Muslims with Southeast Asian origins contributed to the racialization of Muslim identity. For the Cape Coloured population, who made up the vast majority of Muslims in the city, it had served as a marker of distinction in a racially stratified society in the 1950s and 1960s in which " 'Coloured' was stigmatized as collaboration with the racial classificatory system of the Population Registration Act (1950)" (Worden 2009: 26, 2019).

The memorialization of a particular pre-apartheid past that Shaykh Yusuf had been important in fostering was enthusiastically endorsed by the Malaysian government during the apartheid years, and after the 1994 South African general election, they began promoting "roots" tours to the Southeast Asian country. Eager to explore business possibilities in a democratic South Africa, a Malaysian business delegation proclaimed a year later that "the people of Malay descent in Cape Town are of some interest to use – it is good to re-establish the links broken many years ago" (Rossouw 1995).

This idea of a "Malay" past was celebrated publicly also by then Deputy President, Thabo Mbeki, at the adoption of a new constitution in 1996, and in service of pleas for unity: "In my veins courses the blood of the Malay slaves who came from the East. Their proud dignity informs my bearing, their culture a part of my essence. The stripes they bore on their bodies from the lash of the slave master are a reminder embossed on my consciousness of what should not be done" (*Cape Times* 1996, quoted in Ward and Worden 1998: 215). But, as Kerry Ward and Nigel Worden have argued, this essentialization of "Cape Malay" obscures the reality that only a small number of exiles and slaves sent to the Cape actually came from what is today the state of Malaysia. Rather, the overwhelming majority shipped from the "Indies" were actually brought from the Indonesian archipelago, while India and Madagascar were main sources of supply for Cape slaves (Ward and Worden 1998; Worden 2016). This diversity remains lost in popular memory, though, for even the category of "Coloured" excludes the variety of people subsumed by it. Moreover, the popular celebrations of Cape

Malay cuisine evoke a singular identity whose performative aspects – the preparation of food, for instance – work to deepen a historical memory with a purported "homeland" in Southeast Asia.[4]

As sites of religious visitation and remembering, the stories of *kramats* both create linkages across the Indian Ocean to particular lines of descent and signal their place within a sacred geography of Islam. The *kramats* are a material manifestation of the multiple histories that have constituted Cape Town's oceanic pasts, even as they have at times been sites of contestation for Muslims (Jappie 2018). They also provide a framework for communities and various stakeholders to conceptualize a liminal space that is neither strictly bound by land or sea but rather connected to both in defining a sacred topography across the Indian Ocean, and against which can be read the contours and complexities of belonging and place (cf. Sivasundaram 2017: 59; Winichakul 1994; and also Govinden 2012).

Coerced pasts

The *kramats* also represent an awareness of Muslim links with a slave past in Cape Town that have developed over the years since the end of apartheid. Slave heritage in particular has been elaborated around an idea – stressed especially by certain leaders in the early years of the new political dispensation – that the liberation of South Africa from its apartheid past required also recognition of the experiences and struggles of those who were brought to its shores as slaves or under coercion. The liberation struggle, in other words, should not necessarily stand apart from a deeper history of suffering and displacement, and should be read in tandem with the struggles of slaves that included various attempts to liberate themselves from the control of white masters through acts of resistance, such as fleeing (Ward and Worden 1998).

In a variety of ways, slave heritage has become a powerful avenue through which to articulate both a renewed sense of "Colouredness" as well as distinctive belonging in post-apartheid South Africa for many Cape Muslims. Moreover, it has been mobilized in compelling ways to address issues such as land use, for instance in galvanizing support for opposition to property developments on land containing the grave sites of Muslim slaves and of religious leaders from the Dutch period (Worden 2009).[5]

But, as is often the case with the memorialization of slave pasts, tensions have arisen over how these pasts are remembered and represented, and by whom. Competing claims in particular have demonstrated, as elsewhere (e.g., the United States) the fraught terrain of recalling and commemorating a slave past. An instructive example is the 1 December Movement that was founded by middle-class Coloureds in 1996 as a forum to address political and economic issues that the community was facing at the time in the Western Cape (Worden 2001; Worden 2009). The launch of the movement included laying a wreath at the "Old Slave Tree" in central Cape Town, a site that had been memorialized as a place where it was popularly believed slave auctions had taken place (Worden 2009: 28).[6] The movement thus utilized slavery and slave emancipation consciously as a unifying image for activating certain memories and, as a local newspaper articulated, to "serve to unlock the door of memory and knowledge of who we (coloured people) truly are, where we came from and where we belong" (*Cape Times* 1996, quoted in Worden 2009: 28).

Named for the day of slave emancipation that had been commemorated by freed slaves throughout the nineteenth century but subsequently forgotten, the 1 December Movement justified its existence by claiming that "the coloured community needed a movement which recognized that the particular slave experiences and history of coloured people had ongoing consequences in the way that coloured community perceived itself and how it responded to key moments in its history" (Ward and Worden 1998: 215–216; Worden 2001). However, because in the eyes of many African activists and politicians it evoked a "separatist ethnic identity" that was seen as divisive at a time when building a "unified" new country was being stressed, it was vehemently attacked and denigrated. The effort, in this instance, of invoking a slave past to further a particular political agenda was ultimately a failure – the movement attracted very little funding and subsequently folded (Worden 2001).

Among other moments that reflect the vexed nature of the memorialization of slavery in Cape Town as part of its Indian Ocean past, was the erection of several marble blocks in Church Square, site of the "Old Slave Tree" in 2008. Each marble block commemorated an aspect of the slave experience, such as how slaves were identified by imperial officials and masters (e.g., Abraham van Malabar; Aron van Ternate; Hoop van Mozambique, and so on are engraved on two of the blocks), and the work they did at the Cape. In the words of then-Mayor of Cape Town, Helen Zille, the blocks were "to preserve the memory of the enslaved, to prevent their contribution from being lost" (*Cape Times* 2008, quoted in Worden 2009: 39). Clearly drawing on the visual elements of the public memory of the Holocaust – as many of the monuments and memorials to slavery have done in places such as Senegal and Ghana – the monument was meant also to convey a somber tone, yet was criticized for its lack of contextual information that limited its interpretive potential. Additionally, opposition to it reflected a deepening distrust over official state control over slave heritage in a city that continues to be divided deeply both racially and politically (Araujo 2014; Worden 2009).

The memorialization of slavery as a central narrative of Cape Town's oceanic past has not been only mired in criticism or controversy, for it has become an important component of popular assertions of identity. This was recognized early in the post-apartheid years, with the National Heritage Resources Act of 1999 recognizing the "special value" of the "sites of significance relating to the history of slavery in South Africa" (National Heritage Resources Act No. 25 of 1999, quoted in Worden 2009: 30). One of the key spaces in which this past has come to be represented is the Slave Lodge, formerly the Cultural History Museum that in 1998 was renamed "in honour of the ... slaves who lived in bondage over a period of 179 years" (Big Issue 1998, quoted in Worden 2009: 31). Since its opening, and amidst continued robust engagement by community leaders, academics, and the broader public, the Slave Lodge has regularly hosted workshops, lectures, and cultural performances about slavery and its legacy. Permanent exhibitions evoke the multi-locality from which slaves in the Indian Ocean were brought to the Cape, and incorporate the most current academic scholarship to tell the stories of slaves' lives at the Lodge (where the VOC had housed slaves) and the experiences of the enslaved during the oceanic crossing. The success of the Lodge as a museum space dedicated to the memory of slavery reflects the extent to which public awareness of slave heritage has grown within the city and more broadly across the country (Worden 2009).

Additionally, the slave heritage represented by the Slave Lodge, perhaps inadvertently, also plays into the broader appeal that an image of a "creolized" Cape Town has for the tourist market. International tourists regularly visit the Lodge and spend considerable time exploring the exhibits. While Cape slavery does not fit the model and images of Atlantic slavery that UNESCO have emphasized in their Slave Route project, it appeals nonetheless to slave heritage tourism that especially in Ghana and elsewhere in West Africa has resulted, for example, in significant numbers of African American visitors going to the country to visit sites such as "slave castles" and the "door of no return" (Worden 2009). But a recent archaeological discovery off the coast of Cape Town, however, has re-located its slave history more firmly within the larger Trans-Atlantic histories of slavery, as I discuss later.

When one turns away from South Africa and looks more broadly across the Indian Ocean, though, the memorialization and representation of slave pasts have tended to be complicated because of intentional or active forgetting by former slaves and their descendants who sought to reintegrate themselves by creating new social identities in post-emancipation societies as opportunities presented themselves. This took place often in contexts where paternal descent rather than phenotype was a marker of status – or where slave pasts became elided by other histories of labor migration such as indenture, that I will discuss later in the chapter.[7] Yet, even when slave pasts have been forgotten or occluded, the performative dynamics of cultural praxis undeniably reflect that past (even if unconsciously). We see this, for instance, in the songs that communities of African descent in Gujarat have performed that identify their places of origin in present-day Mozambique and Somalia. In some cases, song lyrics are sung in Shambaa, a Bantu language from northeastern mainland Tanzania, while musical and dance performances in Gujarat and North Kannada, equally, have drawn on African idioms (Alpers 2000).

In all, the "nondiscursive bodily practices" of performance form a body of social memory in environments where the history of slavery has been forgotten (Argenti 2007). These embodied musical traditions are, therefore, sites of memory in a contemporary context of social marginalization for most African descent communities in South Asia. The "social relations of inequity and exploitation" that many endure today are present too in other contexts such as the Grassfields of northwest Cameroon, where Nicolas Argenti has argued they "perpetually recall the past by reinscribing its social polarization in the present, giving to long-standing embodied practices a contemporaneity that makes of them not merely a body of social memory but the site of an ongoing struggle between the generations – a struggle in which contemporary oppression is inscribed and reified in the bodies of the people by means of dances that were first inspired by the extreme violence of the eras of the slave trade and forced labor" (Argenti 2007: 6, 2010). It is increasingly recognized that repressed histories can be embedded in everyday habits and practices in which "the body is implicitly recognized as a mnemonic entity" and where we can identify tacit apprehensions of practical memory "forgotten as history ... because they are embedded in habits, social practices, ritual processes and embodied experiences," as Rosalind Shaw (2002) has argued for Sierra Leone. Remembrances of slave pasts, in other words, emerge through these nondiscursive forms of memory that can have "at least as much importance as those that are discursively 'about' the past" (Shaw 2002: 7).

Slave pasts in the Indian Ocean at times have been elided also by being overwritten by histories of other coerced labor migrations. In Mauritius, for example, indenture histories have dominated popular memory in a reflection of the large numbers of indentured laborers who arrived on the island in the second half of the nineteenth century after the abolition of slavery in the early 1830s, and dominated the post-emancipation economy, as their descendants shaped the politics of independence in the 1960s and subsequent political culture of the island nation. Former African slaves, after having served a six-year apprenticeship, became small-holders of land before becoming a marginalized or "creolized" community (Vaughan 2005). With Indian Mauritians at the forefront of island politics, slavery was forgotten and silenced in popular memory in ways that accord with Michel-Rolph Trouillot's understanding of "silencing" as an "active and transitive process: one 'silences' a fact or an individual as one silences a gun. One engages in the practice of silencing" (Trouillot 1997: 48–49). Indenture and its histories effectively silenced the memories of African and Asian slavery that once were the dominant forms of labor organization on the island.

Acts of silencing included Mauritian Creoles (descendants of the island's largely African and Malagasy slave populations) being identified as part of the "General Population" in the ethnically-determined electoral classification system in contradistinction to the distinctive categories of "Hindu" and "Moslem" (Worden 2001). Indentured history has been memorialized and represented prominently in the island, most potently perhaps at the Aapravasi Ghat site in Port Louis on the site of the remains of an immigration depot that had been built in the late 1840s to receive indentured laborers to work in the plantation economy. Declared a World Heritage site by UNESCO in 2006 – the organization states that it "stands as a major historic testimony of indenture in the nineteenth century and is the sole surviving example of this unique modern diaspora" – the Aapravasi Ghat and its foundation members have been instrumental in mobilizing indenture memory both as central to Mauritian life and to understandings of global labor migrations (UNESCO World Heritage Centre a).

There have been moments when slavery was recognized, for instance, during the 150th anniversary of its abolition in 1985; but the continued social, economic and political exclusion of many slave descendants mobilized oppositional politics in the 1990s to redress these inequalities and the "Hinduization" of society that contributed to the marginalization of Creoles (Alpers 2000). This politics included ceremonies by Creole artists from Mauritius and Reunion marking the memory of slaves at sites of significance to their slave heritage, as occurred in 1998 when the government held major celebrations to commemorate the 400th anniversary of the Dutch "discovery" of Mauritius. In the same year, Port Louis also hosted a UNESCO Slave Route project conference aimed at drawing attention to the history of slavery and its impact on modern Mauritius, which resulted in the unveiling of a monument to the "Unknown Slave" and the passing of several resolutions, among which was the replacement of the "General Population" category by one of "Creoles" only; the inclusion in the school curriculum of materials on slavery; and the establishment of a slavery museum in the capital (Worden 2001).

These proposed measures reflected greater recognition of a Mauritian slave heritage, the commitment to the memory of this past clear also with the declaration of a national holiday on 1 February in commemoration of emancipation, and the inscription of the Le Morne Cultural Landscape (an area located around a mountain in the southwestern part of the island where it was believed slave runaways – maroons – escaped in the eighteenth and nineteenth centuries and were buried) as a UNESCO World Heritage site in 2008. Yet, progress has been slow on the actual delivery of promises (Calaon and Forest 2018; Eichmann 2012; UNESCO World Heritage Centre b; Worden 2001). Plans are still in the works, for example, for the construction of what has now become the "Intercontinental Slavery Museum" following a recommendation by the Truth and Justice Commission in 2011 (Le Mauricien 2018). The guiding idea is that this will be a museum linking Mauritius, Mozambique, and Madagascar "as they all formed part of the slave trade network in the eighteenth and nineteenth centuries" (Le Mauricien 2016).

Notions of slave heritage through community or individual memorialization acts have been increasingly influenced by the particularities of how slavery is framed by the UNESCO Slave Route project that for more than 20 years has sought to promote research and understanding of slavery and its legacy. In Mozambique, where the memorialization and representation of its slave past was practically non-existent, a recent initiative under the Slave Wrecks Project has sought integration into the "Slave Route" project. It highlights an awareness of its slave past through the medium of the trade's materiality. This awareness is oriented also towards "heritage tourism development" in ways that echo the Mauritian government's approach to socioeconomic development, and can be found also in the endorsement of African American heritage tourism to West African sites of embarkation of the Middle Passage (Calaon and Forest 2018; Smithsonian Global).

The recent discovery by a team of maritime archaeologists of the remnants of a slave ship that had shipwrecked off the coast of Cape Town in the 1790s en route to Brazil from Mozambique Island with a cargo of slaves, the São José, demonstrates the possibilities of such a strategy specifically to assist with the funding of development initiatives for local communities in northern Mozambique that have been marginalized by the central government. That the materials recovered from the sea floor – such as ballast blocks and copper fastenings (nails) – represent the first physical objects known to come from a vessel that sank with African slaves still on board, gave the São José a potent symbolism highlighting the global dimensions of the African slave trade. The recovery project was broadly collaborative, and its preservation included work by researchers from Iziko Museums of South Africa and Eduardo Mondlane University where a new archaeological museum that opened in late 2017 featured a display of the discovery of the São José.

While the story of the São José, established through painstaking archival and archaeological research, is compelling, it risks flattening understandings of slave heritage by privileging its connections to the Trans-Atlantic slave trade and to the memorialization of slavery tied to the brutalities of the Middle Passage, where the "experiences of enslavement and racial oppression are key to African identities in the Americas" (Larson 1999: 360, 2008). This risk is clear in the loan of artefacts from the São José to the Smithsonian, which are currently on display at the National Museum of African American History and Culture in Washington, D.C., where they occupy a prominent place in representations of slavery as central to African American history. Atlantic slavery is thus taken to stand in for all slavery.

This is especially problematic for the memories of slavery in the Indian Ocean where, in a place such as Cape Town, the majority of slaves were Asian and not African, and the oceanic exchange of slaves followed multiple trajectories that were not financed or centered on any particular region. Even as scholarship has increasingly recognized the plurality of the slave experience when viewed through a global lens, the politics of representation into which the São José artefacts have been enfolded occludes this broader history and ultimately offers us a narrow reading of the slave past.

Extractive pasts

While slave heritage in the Indian Ocean has been shaped by particular politics of representation, identity, and the social and cultural praxis of its myriad communities, the memorialization of other pasts linked more directly to the materiality of the ocean itself has tended to be marginalized or occluded, especially in state discourses and national narratives. This is perhaps most evident in the case of marine product extraction in which vast amounts of natural resources were harvested by a range of peoples across the waters of the Indian Ocean. Yet, recently, there have been notable exceptions suggesting a broader acknowledgement of how natural resources shaped history in this oceanic space. These have focused on pearls and shell, which for centuries were collected and dived for along the littorals, sea beds, and reefs of the Indian Ocean, especially among

Gulf states. The oil wealth that began to flood into the Gulf and southern Arabia from the 1940s and 1950s remade regional economies tied to the sea and gave the region a heightened international importance to a global economy that was reliant overwhelmingly on fossil fuels. Moreover, that the oil period coincided with the precipitous decline of pearling in the Gulf as a result of competition from cultured pearls, resulted both in an overly determined interest in this fossil fuel as a precursor of Gulf modernity and the occlusion of other histories that did not fit state narratives of nation-building.

But Gulf states have begun recently to support the representation of pre-oil pasts and the creation of pearling heritage through museum representations and other sites of public memory (Hightower 2011; Lawson and al-Nabbodah 2008). Yet, its place in Gulf heritage, constructed usually around such symbols as the date palm, the *dhow* and the camel, is at best ambiguous. Thus, while pearl imagery and aspects of the pearling past are marketed as emblematic of Gulf history in brochures and the pearl itself is rendered in large sculptures in public spaces in Abu Dhabi, Ras al-Khaimah, and elsewhere – and recently heritage organizations such as the Pearl Diving Heritage Revival Festival in Kuwait have sought to revive the "tradition" of pearling – they are shorn of deeper historical meaning (Hightower 2011).

Rather, the pearling past is mostly represented in highly romanticized terms that recall some of the ways in which the "*dhow*" and its imagery have been mobilized along the East African coast to evoke a timeless Indian Ocean world.[8] These representations produce sanitized accounts more reflective of the contemporary state project of nation-building than they are of the possibilities of a more meaningful past for a greater number of Gulf residents. In the United Arab Emirates, heavy state involvement in the creation of heritage narratives is designed to shape Emirati identity along particular contours; thus, while the Dubai Museum located in the Fahidi Fort in the heart of Bur Dubai (one of the three historic zones of Dubai Town) has a large and quite dramatic pearling display, there is almost no mention of a cornerstone of pearl extraction – African slaves who dived in large numbers for pearls throughout the pearl "boom" of the second half of the nineteenth and early twentieth centuries (Hightower 2011). This is true too of other pearl-diving exhibits, such as those at the Bahrain National Museum (Hopper 2015).

While the reasons for the omission of slavery and the slave trade in museum and other official representations of Gulf history are not entirely clear, it serves official discourse in (re)presenting simplified histories of oceanic intercourse that brought different peoples from Africa and elsewhere to Gulf shores. Matthew Hopper has written about the effacement of slave pasts in Oman, where even presentations of music and dance widely regarded as African in origin, Al-Laiwa, are vague on how it came to Oman. One is thus left with "the impression that Omani traders witnessed the dances from the safe distances of their ships rather than the truth – that they carried back thousands of young Africans to labor on their shores" (Hopper 2015: 214). The particular complexities of how race and genealogy figure in the construction of identities in the Gulf, where remembrances of slave pasts have been forgotten in ways that resemble but are quite distinct from the Mauritian case, together with a variety of recent political, social, and economic factors (such as the extension by Gulf states of national citizenship to descendants of slaves) have made memorializing slavery for those of servile ancestry of little to no interest. This is a function, in large part, of the success of their cooption into the project of nation-building (Hopper 2015).

Conclusion

Indian Ocean memories are not, of course, defined by understandings of the ocean as a singular scape of labor and bondage. The variety of experiences over its vast landscapes, islands and littorals is too rich to be encompassed by any one framework. Yet, the movement of thousands of coerced laborers to work in a range of oceanic settings makes grappling with their pasts – especially its representation and related processes of remembering and forgetting – critically important to our understandings of the place of memory in the making and remaking of the Indian Ocean as a space of innumerable dimensionality.[9] What makes a past a distinctly oceanic one and the seascapes across which its memory is produced through memorialization, or as "heritage," further opens up possibilities for larger questions of who should or should not represent that past or assert truth claims about its interpretation.[10]

The exploration of these memory practices – rather than reflecting a view of the Indian Ocean as constituting a coherent, singular unit – reinforces a view of its plurality and the many dense imbrications that shaped, and in turn were shaped by, the particularities of social geographies mapped along shifting and mutable spaces of interrelation. Therefore, instead of assuming some sort of coherence to the ocean, it is more useful intellectually to map the Indian Ocean's material pasts manifested through social, religious, legal, and commercial geographies as they took shape at different times, for they reveal a disaggregated picture that is less than the sum of its parts (Sivasundaram 2017). In other words, we do well to "follow" the material, social, and intellectual trajectories of movement and circulation along sub-oceanic currents and sea tracks, for they can give us a clearer sense of an ocean that was made up of intricately braided and distinctive "segments." By exploring the remembrances and representations of some of these interrelated but distinctive pasts, we can gain insights into memory work, performed by a variety of actors that inform Indian Ocean imaginaries.

Notes

1 Jappie (2018) notes that in the context of Cape Town, the shrine is itself referred to as a kramats, whereas in Malay-Indonesian contexts it is at times referred to as a *makam karamat* or "sacred grave."
2 Ownership by the trust of the land on which the Shaykh Yusuf kramat is located, which imposed certain limitations on access, has been controversial, as detailed by Jappie (2018).

3 My discussion here relies extensively on Ward (2009); and Ward and Worden (1998).
4 Numerous cookbooks are now available on a variety of aspects of "Cape Malay" cuisine.
5 Worden discusses an early example covered in a local newspaper: "Moslems Versper Pad by Oudekraal," *Die Burger*, 16 September 1996. The opposition campaign to the building of housing and a hotel at Oudekraal, on the Atlantic seaboard slopes of Table Mountain, succeeded in stopping the development and the area was ultimately incorporated into the protected Table Mountain National Park.
6 Similarly, in Sierra Leone, the "Cotton Tree" has held a significant place in slave memory, with versions about its historical existence being associated both with a slave market and its affording protection for the first freed slaves that were sent to settle Sierra Leone in 1787, and it having been planted by freed slaves (Basu 2007: 235).
7 These themes have been fruitfully explored for the social life of Zanzibar, for which see, for example, Fair (2001); and Prestholdt (2008).
8 The *"dhow"* also encapsulates a certain nostalgia for an idealized past that does appear less present in the case of pearling (cf. Gilbert 2011).
9 I could have included another labor category in this chapter, that of seamen and their oceanic remembrances, but due to space constraints I am unable to do so.
10 For a discussion of truth claims by historians, see Machado (2016).

References

Alpers, Edward A. 2000. "Recollecting Africa: Diasporic Memory in the Indian Ocean World," *African Studies Review*, 43, 1 (April): 83–99.

Araujo, Ana Lucia. 2014. *Shadows of the Slave Past: Memory, Heritage and Slavery*, New York: Routledge.

Argenti, Nicolas. 2007. *Intestines of the State: Youth, Violence and Belated Histories in the Cameroon Grassfields*, London: University of Chicago Press.

Argenti, Nicolas. 2010."Things That Don't Come by the Road: Folktales, Fosterage and Memories of Slavery in the Cameroon Grassfields," *Comparative Studies in Society and History*, 52, 2 (April): 224–254.

Basu, Paul. 2007. "Palimpsest Memoryscapes: Materializing and Mediating War and Peace in Sierra Leone," in Ferdinand de Jong and Michael J. Rowlands (eds.), *Reclaiming Heritage: Alternative Imaginaries of Memory in West Africa*. Walnut Creek, CA: Left Coast Press.

Bishara, Fahad. 2016. *A Sea of Debt: Law and Economic Life in the Western Indian Ocean, 1780–1950*, Cambridge: Cambridge University Press.

Calaon, Diego and Corinne Forest. 2018. "Archaeology and the Process of Heritage Construction in Mauritius," in Krish Sheetah (ed.), *Connecting Continents: Archaeology and History in the Indian Ocean World*, Athens, OH: Ohio University Press: 253–290.

Eichmann, Anne. 2012. "From Slave to Maroon: The Present-Centredness of Mauritian Slave Heritage," *Atlantic Studies*, 9, 3: 319–335.

Fair, Laura. 2001. *Pastimes & Politics: Culture, Community, and Identity in Post-Abolition Urban Zanzibar, 1890–1945*, Athens, OH: Ohio University Press.

Gilbert, Erik. 2011."The Dhow as Cultural Icon: Heritage and Regional Identity in the Western Indian Ocean," *International Journal of Heritage Studies*, 17, 1: 62–80.

Govinden, V. 2012. "Subjects of History: Gokoola and Jhumun Giri Gosye, Indentured Migrants to Mauritius," *Man in India*, 92: 333–352.

Haron, Muhamma. 2005. "Gapena and the Cape Malays: Initiating Connections, Constructing Images," *Sari*, 23: 47–66.

Hightower, Victoria Penziner. 2011. "In the Time Before Oil: A History and Heritage of Pearling in the United Arab Emirates," PhD dissertation, Florida State University.

Hopper, Matthew S. 2015. *Slaves of One Master: Globalization and Slavery in the Age of Empire*, New Haven and London: Yale University Press.

Jappie, Sarah. 2018."Between Makassars: Site, Story, and the Transoceanic Afterlives of Shaykh Yusuf of Makassar," PhD dissertation, Princeton University.

Jeppie, Shamil. 2001."Reclassifications: Coloured, Malay, Muslim," in Zimitri Erasmus (ed.), *Coloured by History, Shaped by Place*, Kwela Books, 2001: 80–96

Kresse, Kai and Edward Simpson. 2011. "Between Africa and India: Thinking Comparatively Across the Western Indian Ocean," *ZMO Working Papers*, 5.

Larson, Pier. 2001."Reconsidering Trauma, Identity, and the African Diaspora: Enslavement and Historical Memory in Nineteenth-Century Highland Madagascar," *William and Mary Quarterly*, 56, 2 (April): 335–362.

Larson, Pier. 2008. "Horrid Journeying: Narratives of Enslavement and the Global African Diaspora," *Journal of World History*, 19, 4 (December): 431–464.

Lawson, Fred and Hassan al-Nabbodah. 2008. "Heritage and Cultural Nationalism in the United Arab Emirates," in Alanaod Alsharekh and Robert Springborg (eds.), *Popular Culture and Political Identity in the Arab Gulf States*, Saqi, in association with Middle East Institute, London: SOAS.

Le Mauricien. 2016. "Musée des Esclaves a Port-Louis: Mémoire, Réparation et Dialogue." (6 February 2016)

Le Mauricien. 2018. "Cabinet Decision no. 2 of 5th January 2018, Museum: Where the Matter ... Stands? ... Ends?" (8 January)

Machado, Pedro. 2014. *Ocean of Trade: South Asian Merchants, Africa and the Indian Ocean, c. 1750–1850*, Cambridge: Cambridge University Press.

Machado, Pedro. 2016."Views from Other Boats: On Amitav Ghosh's Indian Ocean Worlds," *American Historical Review*, 121, 5 (December): 1545–1551.

Mandal, Sumit. 2012."Popular Sites of Prayer, Transoceanic Migration, and Cultural Diversity: Exploring the Significance of Keramat in Southeast Asia," *Modern Asian Studies*, 46, 2: 355–372.

Prestholdt, Jeremy. 2008. *Domesticating the World: African Consumerism and the Genealogies of Globalization*, Berkeley, CA and Los Angeles/London: University of California Press.

Rossouw, Rehana. 1995. "Malaysia Rediscovers Links with SA Malays," *Mail & Guardian* (25 August)

Shaw, Rosalind. 2002. *Memories of the Slave Trade: Ritual and the Historical Imagination in Sierra Leone*, London: University of Chicago Press.

Sivasundaram, Sujit. 2017."The Indian Ocean," in David Armitage, Alison Bashford and Sivasundaram (eds.), *Oceanic Histories*, Cambridge: Cambridge University Press: 31–61

Smithsonian Global. "Where We Work." https://global.si.edu/where-we-work [accessed 28 October 2019]

Tagliacozzo, Eric. 2013. *The Longest Journey: Southeast Asians and the Pilgrimage to Mecca*, New York: Oxford University Press.

Trivellato, Francesca. 2012. *The Familiarity of Strangers: The Sephardic Diaspora, Livorno, and Cross-Cultural Trade in the Early Modern Period*, New Haven and London: Yale University Press.

Trouillot, Michel-Rolph. 1997. *Silencing the Past: Power and the Production of History*, Boston: Beacon Press.

UNESCO World Heritage Centre a. "Aapravasi Ghat." https://whc.unesco.org/en/list/1227/ [accessed 28 October 2019]

UNESCO World Heritage Centre b. "Le Morne Cultural Landscape." https://whc.unesco.org/en/list/1259 [accessed 28 October 2019]

Vaughan, Megan. 2005. *Creating the Creole Island: Slavery in Eighteenth-Century Mauritius*, Durham and London: Duke University Press.

Ward, Kerry. 1995. "The '300 Years: Making of Cape Muslim Culture' Exhibition, Cape Town, April 1994: Liberating the Castle?" *Social Dynamics* 21, 1: 96–131.

Ward, Kerry. 2009. *Networks of Empire: Forced Migration in the Dutch East India Company*, New York: Cambridge University Press.

Ward, Kerry and Nigel Worden. 1998. "Commemorating, Suppressing, and Invoking Cape Slavery," in Sarah Nuttall and Carli Coetzee (eds.), *Negotiating the Past: The Making of Memory in South Africa*, Oxford: Oxford University Press: 201–217.

Winichakul, Thongchai. 1994. *Siam Mapped: A History of the Geo-Body of a Nation*, Honolulu: University of Hawai'i Press.

Witz, Leslie, Gary Minkley and Ciraj Rassool. 2017. *Unsettled History: Making South African Public Pasts*, Ann Arbor: University of Michigan Press.

Worden, Nigel. 2001."The Forgotten Region: Commemorations of Slavery in Mauritius and South Africa," in Gert Oostindie (ed.), *Facing Up to the Past: Perspectives on the Commemoration of Slavery from Africa, the Americas and Europe*, Kingston: Ian Randle Publishers, 2001: 48–54.

Worden, Nigel. 2009. "The Changing Politics of Slave Heritage in the Western Cape, South Africa," *Journal of African History*, 50: 23–40.

Worden, Nigel. 2016. "Indian Ocean Slaves in Cape Town, 1695–1807," *Journal of Southern African Studies*, 42, 3: 389–408.

Worden, Nigel. 2019. "Ambiguous Pasts: The Indian Ocean World in Cape Town's Public History," in Burkhardt Schnepel and Tansen Sen (eds.), *Traveling Pasts: The Politics of Cultural Heritage in the Indian Ocean World*, Leiden and Boston: Brill: 110–130.

10 Shorelines of memory and ports of desire

Geography, identity, and the memory of oceanic trade in Mekran Coast (Balochistan)

Hafeez Ahmed Jamali

A seaward perspective?

The growing scholarly interest in Indian Ocean studies and South Asian borderlands in recent years has served to de-center the privileged focus on the nation-state and its imagined heartlands. In the case of scholarship on Pakistan, this task has proved much more difficult because the events of the partition of 1947 not only make up the foundational narrative of Pakistani nationalism but also continue to cast their long shadow into the present. For instance, at a recent literary gathering on Karachi's history, veteran Pakistani journalist Imran Aslam remarked that after 1947, the people of Karachi had turned their backs on the sea! He was criticizing the inward-looking attitude of the Urdu-speaking Mohajir elites, mostly from the landed gentry, who had migrated from North India to Karachi and continue to dominate the cultural and political landscape of the city. In contrast to the orientation of Punjabi and Mohajir elites, people from Baloch, Sindhi, and Gujarati ethnic groups living in Karachi and elsewhere along Pakistan's coastline found more significant commercial, genealogical, and imaginative horizons facing seawards towards Bharuch, Bombay, Calicut, Muscat, Dubai, Bahrain, Mombasa, and Zanzibar rather than looking landwards to Lahore and Delhi.

In this chapter, I trace the overlapping geographies of the Mekran Coast and Gwadar town in Balochistan Province, Pakistan with the larger Indian Ocean world to unsettle received ideas of imperial frontiers and national borderlands as isolated "savage spaces." The territorial boundaries of ethnic Baloch people inhabiting the Mekran Coast are confined to the sovereign states of Pakistan and Iran. Their lived and imagined geographies, however, traverse the vast oceanic expanse via Muscat (Oman) all the way to Mombasa and Zanzibar. Despite decades of Pakistani rule and immigration restrictions set up by Gulf Arab countries in the wake of the oil boom of the 1970s, fragments of these geographies trace an arc over the Indian Ocean through memory, nostalgia, and diasporic networks. Unearthing these fragments and the connections they point towards enables us to imagine Indian Ocean worlds as layered places whose social fabric and identity have been constituted by entanglements with significant "else-wheres," real and imagined. As Patricia Spyer points out in her ethnography of Aru Islanders of Indonesia, emphasizing the significance of these elsewheres, so central to the self-identity of maritime communities, allows us to question and displace the strict dichotomy between "self" and "other," "inside" and "outside," and "us" and "them" that nationalist discourse poses and the nation-state tries to enforce (Spyer 2000: 7). We realize that maritime enclaves like Gwadar that presently lie at the real and imagined margins of the nation-state, occupied a more central place in other social geographies whose fractured pieces continue to structure the everyday lives of people, serve as mnemonic maps, and provide anchors for their senses of belonging.

Blending oral narratives of Baloch fishermen and African-descent laborers with accounts from the colonial archive, this chapter traces these remembered and lived geographies. I follow the memories of the historical movement of Baloch and African-descent bodies across the ocean between Zanzibar, Muscat, Gwadar, and Karachi as well as their contemporary placemaking practices to show the layered social geography of the Mekran Coast. I suggest that this seaward perspective allows us to re-imagine and reframe Pakistan's social and historical geography beyond the dominant nationalist narratives. It is also a per-spective that enables local Baloch fishermen to critique Pakistani governments' plans for shaping their present and future.

Gwadar, a small harbor town located on the Mekran Coast, caught the atten-tion of Pakistani policy-makers due to its pivotal location near the entrance to the Persian Gulf and for its potential as a terminal for North–South transportation of oil and gas from the landlocked Central Asian countries and western parts of China. Since the early 1990s, Pakistan's political and military leadership has con-sidered Gwadar a cornerstone of their strategy to increase their country's eco-nomic and military clout in the Middle East and Southwest Asia (Government of Pakistan 2005). The first phase of Gwadar Port was completed in 2007 and its operation and maintenance were handed over to the Port Authority of Singapore (PSA). In 2013, the port's operations were taken over by a Chinese company, the China Overseas Port Holding Company (COPHC), as a prelude to the start of the China-Pakistan Economic Corridor (CPEC).

However, before Gwadar was annexed to the newly established Pakistani state in 1958, it was a small but significant node in the maritime empire of Sultanate of Oman. The Al-Busaidi Sultans of Oman "owned" the small enclave of Gwadar for well over 200 years, including 150 years of Indirect Rule by the British Raj in India. They eventually "sold" it to Pakistan for 8.4 million dollars under a treaty agreement between the two countries (*Time Magazine* 1958). The Omani Sultan's possessions on the Mekran Coast stretched from Gwadar to Bandar Abbas in Iran. Baloch soldiers from Gwadar and elsewhere in Mekran region formed the backbone of this maritime empire and Baloch sailors worked as boat-captains (*nakhuda*) and navigators (*maalim*) on Arab *dhows* sailing on the ocean between Zanzibar, Muscat, Gwadar, Diu, and Calicut. These soldiers and sailors helped the Omani Sultan in establishing his sovereignty over the entire Swahili Coast in Africa from Somalia to Tanzania. Along with Omani Arabs, they were also overseeing the lucrative trade in ivory, spices, and enslaved Africans (Nicolini 2006, 2007). More than 200 years of Omani rule have left an indelible mark on the physical and cultural landscape of Gwadar Town and the outlook of its residents.

Pakistani and international discourse about Gwadar, however, tends to portray the town as a small, isolated, fishing settlement inhabited by presumably insular tribesmen who have little contact with or knowledge of the outside world. Pakistani discourse about the Gwadar and Mekran region thus involves the suppression or exclusion of alternate histories and social geographies, a form of nationalist amnesia that serves to produce a coherent narrative of modernity for a nation desperately searching for economic revival and enhanced collective self-esteem. Through this process of elision, metropolitan Pakistani subjects from Punjabi and Urdu-speaking ethnic groups and Western observers can construct an authentic discourse of Baloch tribalism, primitivism, and underdevelopment. This discourse not only justifies the exploitation of their abundant natural resources and strategically important places, such as Gwadar, but also legitimizes the repeated use of military force in "scorched earth" campaigns to impose the writ of the state in Balochistan Province. The marginality of the Gwadar and Mekran region, therefore, is an outcome of the way this region has been represented in Pakistani history books and maps which tend to justify and naturalize the subordinate position of Baloch people in the country's social and political hierarchy.

Barring a few nuanced and sympathetic accounts (Axmann 2008; Swidler 1992, 2003; Titus and Swidler 2000), the tropes of "tribalism" and "primitivism," and the image of Balochistan as a largely empty, distant, and limitrophe place have also dominated the sociological and anthropological imagination of Balochistan (Salzman 2000; Spooner 1975). On the one hand, this imagination informs public opinion and cultivates political attitudes, lending itself easily to the service of imperialist military adventures. It is used by political analysts to justify Western interventions for or against "the tribes" in order to prevent otherwise gloomy scenarios of tribesmen running amok (Kaplan 2009).[1] On the other hand, ethnic Baloch political activists resisting Pakistani state's development agenda advance a counter-narrative of their own. They claim that Gwadar is an integral part of a historic Baloch homeland extending from the banks of the river Indus in the east to the town of Bampur in Iran in the west. There is some historical evidence to support this argument and it serves as an important challenge to counter the hegemonic ambitions of state authorities. Nevertheless, on the whole, this claim is a mirror image of the Pakistani version in that it ignores the interpenetration of distant times and places that have informed the outlook of subjects in Gwadar over centuries of trade and contact with the outside world. In collapsing distinct time-spaces into a linear rendering of Gwadar's history and a stable narrative of Baloch identity, the nationalist version ignores the complex skein of trajectories the people in Gawdar have traced in the Indian Ocean.

Figure 10.1 Nakhuda Noor Muhammad reminiscing about Omani rule in Gwadar.
Image credit: Hafeez Jamali.

Slaves, tribesmen, and the transformation of the Mekran Coast

The oppressive present that Gwadar's residents critique through overt protests and nostalgic recollection has been shaped by their discursive framing into tribal subjects by colonial and postcolonial state authorities and their insertion into colonial regimes of infrastructure and imperial connections in late nineteenth century. As I have suggested earlier, these tropes inform the attitudes and opinions of metropolitan Pakistani subjects towards Balochistan regardless of whether they are of liberal, conservative (religious), or socialist persuasions. In the following pages, I trace the genealogy of this discourse in the colonial era, its tensions with the rhetoric of abolition, and its entanglement with new imperial infrastructures to show how the social geography of Gwadar and the Mekran Coast was influenced by their slave pasts.

The methods of rule and the reach of colonial authority in India were uneven in general, including, for instance, the territories ruled directly by the British and the Princely States under Indirect Rule. Balochistan, or Kalat State as it was then called, belonged to the latter category. Its legal and administrative status was further complicated or shadowed by the long borders that it shared with Persia (Iran) in the west, Afghanistan in the north, and the Arabian Sea in the south. In territories like Kalat that were appended to the empire as its "frontiers," the question of protecting imperial interests from the unhealthy influence of rival European powers such as Russia and France and the defense of British India haunted the imperial imagination constantly. Gwadar Town and the Mekran region were situated at the confluence of two colonial frontiers of the British Raj: the Persian frontier in the west and the Arabian Frontier in the south.[2] Colonial authorities were faced with the problem of securing the attachment of reluctant Baloch tribesmen to their cause on these "wild and lawless" frontiers. These people had historically shown only nominal allegiance to any central authority, whether it was Persia, India, or Afghanistan. They defied it openly whenever the opportunity was offered.

British difficulties with Baloch tribesmen in Mekran arose out of their insistence on implementing the abolition of slavery policy in Gwadar, which was physically located on the Mekran Coast but was under the sovereignty of the Sultan of Muscat. Further, colonial authorities were worried about Gwadar and the Mekran Coast more broadly on account of the raids on trade caravans traveling upcountry to Gwadar, purported measures for stopping the Indian Ocean slave trade, and the protection of the Indo-European Telegraph Line. The Indo-European Telegraph was hailed as a technological and administrative miracle of its time and formed one of the mainstays of imperial control over the Indian subcontinent in the aftermath of the Sepoy Revolt of 1857.

In May 1876, three slaves belonging to one Dad Mahomed of Rind tribe and others escaped from their masters' houses along the Mekran-Persia border and took refuge in Gwadar Town. The Omani Wali or Governor of Gwadar was bound by the treaty of 1873 with the British not to return any slave to their masters against their will (Aitchison 1933 [1865]). When Dad Mahomed approached the Wali of Gwadar about the return of his slaves, he refused to entertain the request without the permission of British authorities. Dad Mahomed then appealed to Captain Mockler, at that time the assistant political agent in Gwadar, who again refused to interfere in the matter. Dad Mohammad left the town vowing revenge on both Omani and British authorities. Later that evening, he cut the British telegraph wire, burnt the Telegraph Line Guards' house, and carried off a local employee of the Telegraph Department. Captain Mockler approached the representative of the Khan of Kalat in Mekran to gain the return of the captive employee and stolen property and to punish Dad Mahomed. While Rind tribesmen returned some of the stolen property and the captive Telegraph employee was freed, the demand for punishing Dad Mahomed was not met. These troubles renewed in 1892 when the Rind tribesmen demanded the return of some 70 runaway slaves who they alleged had absconded to Gwadar (Lorimer 1986 [1908]: 620). This incident led to a series of skirmishes between the British and Omani authorities on the one hand and the Rind tribe on the other in and around Gwadar Town for next three decades.

Over a cup of tea in Captain Rahim's Café in the old *bazaar*, my friend Nasir Sohrabi recounted the details of the dispute between residents of Gwadar and the irate Rind tribesmen over the runaway slaves as told by his mother and his grandfather. Nasir is a social and political activist who belongs to a leading family in Gwadar who have lived there for the past several generations.

> The families of runaway slaves came to Gwadar to take refuge from the cruelty of their masters in Persian Balochistan. Our people had their own slaves and servants, but we didn't treat them harshly like the Rinds did, so they didn't have a reason to run away and take refuge with other people. These Baloch slaves settled in Toobag Ward and a few families are still there. But they don't like to talk about their past or accept that they are descendants of former slaves. They claim that they belong to Rind and Hoth tribes but, of course, people know better. We called them *koheeg* or mountain folks because they spoke Balochi in a thick accent and their masters from Rind and Hoth tribes lived in mountains in Persian Mekran.

When I tried to broach the subject with one of the leading men from the self-emancipated community Nasir was referring to, there was reluctance on his part. Even when the gentleman I spoke to acknowledged this oppressive part of his family's history, he did not seem to remember any significant events or historical details. While initially perplexing, this appears to be a common survival strategy among fugitive slaves who had escaped their masters and found refuge in another community. As Lydia Marshall and others have argued in the case of Kenya, freedmen on the Swahili coast integrated themselves into local indigenous communities by adopting local ethnic affiliations. This absorption necessitated a certain amnesia about their slave past which represented the final step away from the social marginality of enslavement (Marshall 2015). Thus, the Indian Ocean provides a different and more complex narrative of slavery and its aftermath in contrast to the Atlantic slave trade.

Since the Rind tribesmen quarrelling with the Wali of Gwadar were considered the subjects of the Khan of Kalat, the responsibility for settling this dispute fell on the shoulders of Robert Sandeman, the Agent to the Governor General (A.G.G.) and the most senior British political officer in the newly created Balochistan Agency that comprised the Kalat Khanate. Having "pacified" the Afghan frontier, Sandeman now turned his attention to the southwestern border with Persia (Iran). During his first tour in Mekran in 1883, he took upon himself the task of settling the "Rind Disturbances" and other similar disputes then brewing in the Mekran region. In a series of visits beginning in 1884, during which Sandeman held durbars, tribal jirgas, and conducted negotiations with the Rinds, he tried to settle the Rind affair. Unlike his predecessors who advocated using an iron fist in dealing with Rinds, Sandeman struck a more conciliatory tone and ascribed the belligerence of Rinds to British ignorance of Baloch customs pertaining to slavery. In a dispatch to the Foreign Secretary in Calcutta, he noted:

> A system of this kind, which has the sanction of centuries, cannot be upset in a day without disturbing effects; and this is especially the case when the change involves serious pecuniary loss to individuals. It is necessary to insist on this, truism though it be. It is then hardly a subject for wonder that the rude Biluch who dwells in the country near Gwadar is slow to appreciate the motives which have led the English people to strive so earnestly for the abolition of slavery.
>
> (Agent to the Governor General in Balochistan 1890: 11)

Sandeman's attempt at condoning slavery as a peculiar custom of purportedly savage Baloch tribesmen appears to be patently hypocritical and self-serving. In 1842, for example, the Honorable East India Company had occupied and annexed the neighboring princely state of Sindh on the basis of the charges of engaging in slavery and encouraging the slave trade, among other things (Outram 1846: 492). This is an example of the selective use of the definition and label of slavery. Commenting on the issue of slavery in colonial Balochistan, anthropologist Nina Swidler observes that Sandeman's statement craftily occluded the plight of fugitive slaves by wrapping it in the garb of a benign indigenous institution (Swidler 2003). The designation of slavery as an indigenous Baloch cultural institution and the status of Kalat as a purportedly independent ally of the British Empire in India provided the rationale for Sandeman's approach. Sandeman's opinion on the slavery question was also a "paradigmatic statement of 19th century European views about cultural difference," contrasting the "civilized" Englishmen with the "rude" Baloch (Swidler 2003: 347).

The complicity of Dutch, French, and American trading companies in introducing plantation slavery in the coastal communities in the Indian Ocean in the late eighteenth and nineteenth centuries have been documented extensively in the historical literature on slavery and abolition (Campbell 2004; Sheriff 1987). In particular, Sheriff (1987) points out how the intervention of colonial powers in the affairs of Zanzibar, the main emporium of trade on the East African Coast and the principal town in the Swahili-speaking world, increased the quantum of slave trade and intensified the exploitation of enslaved Africans. Through the integration of the Omani commercial empire into the larger Atlantic-based trade, this enterprise increased the number of enslaved Africans being transported to the Arabian Peninsula and onwards to South and Southeast Asia. It also intensified the exploitation of enslaved Africans on the Swahili Coast itself through the introduction of plantation slavery on the islands of Zanzibar, Pemba, and Madagascar with whom the British, French, and American companies enjoyed special trading relations and privileges.

Similarly, the British East India Company's subsequent attempts to maintain control over native society under the purportedly humanitarian motives of abolishing the "East African Slave Trade" have been treated more fully by historians of South Asia. For instance, Indrani Chatterjee points out that British abolition policy did not achieve much by way of ensuring the emancipation of slaves, especially female slaves. However, the discourse or rhetoric of abolition did add another weapon to the arsenal of British political officers, such as Sandeman, in colonial India. They could use this sledgehammer against rulers and influential persons in Princely States when they threatened colonial interests and ignore it conveniently when it was otherwise (Chatterjee 2005: 144).

In the case of Kalat State or Balochistan, the colonial officers chose to do the latter and this policy continued up until 1921. In several such incidents that were brought to the attention of colonial officers, discretion was considered the better part of valor. In 1897, the Khan of Kalat, Mir Mahmood Khan, wrote a long letter to the A.G.G. in Balochistan, specifically linking the construction of the Quetta-Kalat road to the unrest among domestic slaves in that part of Balochistan. The Government of India's reply to the A.G.G. in Balochistan on this subject was emphatic. He was to steer clear of any controversial action while paying lip service to the rhetoric of abolition back home in Britain.

> There is no desire whatever to move hastily in the matter, and at the present juncture it would probably be inopportune to take any action whatever. The subject is, however, one which receives close attention at home, and the desirability of making known the policy of the British Government has to be borne in mind.
>
> (Agent to the Governor General in Balochistan, Essential Records Basta No. 9, File No. 292 Vol. I pg. no. 4 1898)

As a result, Kalat State would be one of the last regions in British India to abolish slavery. Slavery was formally abolished in 1926 by virtue of a royal edict (*Farman*) issued by the Khan of Kalat under British pressure. Other forms of bondage such as *Begar* (forced labor) continued to be practiced while British officers looked the other way in the name of tradition and local customs well into the 1930s.

While Sandeman's efforts to carve an imperial margin by creating order out of chaos on a "wild and lawless" Persian frontier were one end of the story, the misreading of British intentions by Dad Mohammed's slaves formed the other end of the emerging colonial geography in coastal Balochistan. As the most profitable "cargo" travelling on Arab *dhows* headed from Zanzibar, Mombasa, and Lamu to the ports of Sur, Basrah, Bandar Abbas, Gwadar, Sonmeani, Karachi, and Bombay, the bodies of enslaved East Africans connected the Baloch of Gwadar and the Mekran region to the Omani commercial empire in the Indian Ocean. Gwadar was not an emporium of trade like Calicut, Muscat, or Zanzibar but it functioned as an important node in the Omani commercial empire as an intermediate port and a staging ground for recruitment of Mekrani Baloch soldiers who served the Omani empire.[3]

The circulation of Baloch and African-descent bodies through raids, trade, and migration between Zanzibar, Muscat, and Gwadar threads together the logics of Indirect Rule, extension of colonial infrastructures, and peopling of new cities. In particular, the construction of the Indo-European Telegraph Line (in 1862), the introduction of steam navigation into the Persian Gulf (in 1857), and the aggressive patrolling of Indian Ocean waters by British warships in the second half of nineteenth century induced fundamental changes in the lives of people inhabiting the Persian Gulf and Mekran coasts.

It led to the decline of intermediate port towns like Gwadar and the transformation of the bodies of African descent Baloch people from a site of servitude to a site of "free" colonial labor. For the most part, this movement was from the Mekran and Persian Gulf coast in the west to Karachi and Bombay in the east where they would form several of the Mekrani Baloch neighborhoods or Paras that survive today.

The unnamed slaves of Dad Mohammed, as mentioned earlier, were part of a trickle of Mekrani Baloch of African descent who had been escaping their masters' cruelty by seeking refuge in British-protected territories in the aftermath of abolition treaties signed by the Sultan of Oman. Dad Mohammad's slaves had joined a small community of about 300 freedmen in Gwadar who were already settled there. By the 1890s, the number of fugitive slaves in Gwadar had become very large, and the management of their angry masters from the Rind tribe a serious problem for the colonial government. According to the Gazetteer of the Persian Gulf:

> During the cold weather of 1892–93, fugitive slaves continued to collect at Gwadar, where their number in May 1893 amounted to several hundred; and so strained was the situation thus created that it was found advisable to induce the refugees to remove to British India, and some of them were even provided with the means of reaching that destination.
>
> (Lorimer 1915: 620)

Eventually, these freedmen were moved to Karachi as part of a compromise the British officers had mediated between the Rind tribesmen and the Wali of Gwadar. The methods of "inducing" the fugitive slaves to go to British India included their detention at Gwadar and their consequent deportation to Karachi and Bombay. The colonial archive shows that the expense of detaining and deporting the fugitive slaves continued to be a contentious issue between various bureaucrats in the Persian Gulf and Balochistan Political Agencies. (A Revenue Commissioner in Baluchistan 1910: 1–5)

Nostalgia and madness as critique of the present

Karimok's teahouse is a typical establishment in the old town area where I used to spend time with local fishermen during my fieldwork in 2009–2010. It is an old rickety shop in the back of Gwadar's old *bazaar* along the East Bay that is colloquially dubbed the "General Headquarters" (GHQ) by local people. My host Kaleemullah, a local boat captain, and I were sipping tea and debating the day's happenings with other fishermen at the teahouse when my attention was drawn towards a frail old man sitting nearby. It was the old man's persistence in the face of rude questioning and boisterous laughter from a group of young men that had attracted me towards him. He kept making emphatic declarations that according to the Pakistani constitution, we were all mad (*Ayeen kay mutabiq ham sab pagal hain*)! When asked to comment on his own sanity, he calmly replied that although no one followed the law anymore, he strictly abided by the law and demanded of others to do the same. But as the young men became more aggressive and disruptive, the old man started to lose his cool. Addressing the general audience beyond the young men he warned them that they better watch their words. He explained that although he may appear to be at the teahouse at that moment, in reality he was walking seven feet under the sea and, if his hand was forced, he might summon his seven and a half djinns to set the naughty kids right! Some onlookers laughed while others got annoyed by the noisy exchange and his nonsensical comments. Alarmed that this crazy man might turn away his customers, Karimok's waiter duly appeared at the "table" – a worn out wooden bench attached to a desk—and told the eccentric man to get the hell out of there. The gentleman, however, did not take this intervention kindly: "Mind your own business, Mister! You clean tables for these people here, your father cleaned them for the British, and before them your grandfather did the same for the Arabs of Muscat!" This evoked a roar of approval and laughter from the audience. The waiter had to beat a sheepish retreat, muttering indignantly that the local authorities needed to do a better job of locking up such "mental cases" in Gwadar.

The eccentric man's answer and the audience's approving laughter point towards the absence of the rule of law in contemporary Pakistan while evoking Gwadar's entanglements with Oman. In the minds of many residents of Gwadar, Omani rule was associated with stability, the rule of law, and swift justice. These were qualities that they felt were lacking in the Pakistani state and its relationship to them. It was this contradiction that appeared so bewildering to the old man and seemed to be driving him crazy. Rumor had it that the late Karimok, the teahouse owner, fancied himself a citizen of Muscat and he would keep his shop open on Pakistani national holidays or, for that matter, during the numerous protest rallies, strikes, shutter-down, and wheel-jam calls given by Baloch ethnic nationalist parties. Folks at the teahouse recalled that even at the peak of the Baloch Students Organization's (BSO) movement against General Zia's dictatorship in the 1980s, old Karimok refused to budge from his position. The agitating youth were then demanding that he shut down his teahouse in solidarity with their shutter-down strike against the military government. He calmly told them he was a subject of His Majesty Sultan Qaboos Al-Busaidi and wanted no part in their quarrel with the Pakistani government.

Nakhuda Noor Mohammad, a veteran seafarer then in his nineties, vividly recalled the period of Omani rule. He spent most of his time praying and meditating in the local mosque next to the beach and his long flowing beard had turned completely white and threadbare. Noor Mohammad had worked as Navigator (*maalim*) on a local *dhow* in his younger days. Using a pen and his bare hands, he draws a perfect circle on a piece of paper and explains to me how he navigated with the help of compass, chart, and a few sticks of wood that they used to mark the direction of the ocean's current. In reply to my question, he answers that he had not worked on a sail-only boat because none were left by the time he grew up. When he was a child though, a few sailboats were still anchored in the West Bay harbor. His friend Hatum, another veteran seafarer, chimed in and said that their fathers and grandfathers would go out on those long journeys to Zanzibar and back. He says that the coconuts of Zanzibar were very famous in Gwadar. They had a saying attributed to his grandfather, Kia. *"Kia went to Zanzibar and brought coconuts with him."* These sailors would sometime be out in the ocean for years on end and when they returned home, their children had already grown up. When the long-gone sailor would return home, his children could not recognize their father!

He recalled Omani rule as a peaceful time when justice was swift and cheap under the Arab *Wali* or Governor of Gwadar.

> The *Wali* would greet you in person and order the soldiers to arrest the suspects. The suspects would then be produced and tried in front of a Muslim judge (*qadi*) who would decide the case according to Sharia law. You didn't have to go to the police or register a FIR (a written complaint called the First Information Report).

Hatum and Noor Muhammad wistfully recall the lamplighter from the local Town Committee who would come out in the evening to pour oil and light the streetlamps at night. Indeed, during a recent protest against the frequent electricity outages in town, the protestors chanted slogans that they were fed up with the Pakistani electricity and wanted the old lamplighter from Omani time back.

These anecdotes and other remains of Omani rule are fragments of memory that evoke different kinds of nostalgias among Gwadar's resident. As Kathleen Stewart reminds us, nostalgia is not a desire to return to the past or hang on to the present by a more natural or localized people who are unable to function efficiently under late capitalism (Stewart 1988). Indeed, the condition of nostalgia requires the object of nostalgia to be out of reach: nostalgia for the past can only be felt once it has receded or become distant enough not to come back. Instead, this "nostalgia of the oppressed" provides a narrative frame and argument for Gwadar's residents to critique the present, a present that they are dissatisfied with. It has everything to do with the corrupt police officers, unreliable electric power, lack of water supplies, and unfamiliar faces in Gwadar.

Ghosts of memory: djinns, winds, and placemaking

These fragments of memory and the places that evoke them dot the landscape of Gwadar Town like pieces of pottery, bone, and ashes strewn around an archaeological site. These include a host of places such as the old rope ladder path cut into the cliff facing the beach on the West Bay, the remains of a stone masonry dam on the top of the mountain attributed to Portuguese conquerors, and the dungeon below the Omani watch-tower where hardened criminals would be thrown on the orders of the Arab *Wali*. In a sense, the old town and its immediate surroundings serve as a large-scale mnemonic device where the memory of colonial and pre-colonial pasts latches on to familiar objects and is evoked by them. While one aspect of this memory is to serve as a powerful critique of the present, in other ways it is phantasmagoric and invokes oceanic connections without obvious physical referents.

Few material objects and relations evoke these deeper connections more powerfully than djinns and other spectral presences in the old town, especially for the fishermen and other working-class people in Gwadar. During a routine conversation by the beach, I asked *Nako* Dur Muhammad, a septuagenarian boat captain in the Gazrawan neighborhood, whether he had considered sending his kids to Muscat for employment like many other people in Gwadar had done. *Nako* reacted to my question in a rather dramatic fashion. Grabbing my right hand with his frail hands and shaking it vigorously, he exclaimed: "don't you really know?" When I shook my head, he declared emphatically that the city of Muscat and its surroundings were full of supernatural beings such as djinns, *Jaatig*, and *Gwats*.[4] How could he, in good conscience, send his kids into the belly of monsters! He went on to narrate that until recently, it was quite common to encounter these spectral beings in Gwadar and people had to take good care to avoid becoming their victim.

Nako was expressing the belief, widespread in Gwadar and elsewhere on the Mekran coast, that the toughest evil spirits, referred to in Balochi as *Gwat* or wind, were of animistic origins and came from the Arab coast of the Persian Gulf, especially Muscat, and Africa (During 1997; Sultana 2013).[5] Unlike the local djinns, these spirits are believed to be non-Muslim and the afflicted person cannot be cured through the intervention of a local *Mullah* or *Syed*.[6] They require intervention by a special healer called *Gwati Mat* (literally, mother of the Wind), usually of African Baloch descent. The healer cures the afflicted person through an elaborate ritual called *Gwat-i-Leb* (literally, play of the Wind), which includes trance sessions to the accompaniment of a particular repertoire of music called *Gwati-Damali* (During 1997; Sultana 1995). The continuing after-lives of *Gwats* or African winds in Gwadar points to the deeper significance of Indian Ocean connections in psychological and spiritual realms and the social lives of the people of the Mekran Coast. It is not difficult to surmise that these evil winds most likely accompanied the soldiers, sailors, and slaves as they travelled between Gwadar, Muscat, and Zanzibar.

Beyond the particularities of spirits and rituals, townsfolk's belief in these spectral beings reveals the seams of stories and layers of dwelling that constitute the city and hold it together as a lived and imagined space for its residents. Much like William Darlymple's Delhi, the architecture of old town and remains of Omani rule in Gwadar retain their physical and affective presence despite the onslaught of modernity and capitalist development in the twenty-first century

(Darlymple 1993). This belief is not only shared by the fishermen but also the members of the Ismailia community who live in the heart of the old town next to the crumbled remains of the Omani Fort and the Portuguese watch-tower.

Although altered and reworked by more than 60 years of Pakistani rule, shards of these earlier geographies trace an arc through memory, nostalgia, arts, and architecture. These arcs are also re-traced through the ongoing movement of Baloch and East African descent people between Zanzibar (East Africa), Muscat, and Gwadar. They are reflected in the large Baloch diaspora in Oman who constitute the second largest ethnic group in the Sultanate after its Arab population. They are inscribed in the intricate wooden tapestries and lattice work of houses in old town of Gwadar, in the immaculate gold jewelry and graceful saris worn by the elderly women from the Ismailia community, in its narrow lanes and alleyways, in the boat-making style and designs of Wado craftsmen, and the decaying remains of Omani forts and watchtowers that overlook the townscapes of Gwadar, Muscat, Zanzibar, and Mombasa.

Conclusion

In reconstructing the history of Gwadar and invocation and remembrance by the town's residents in the face of the oppressive conditions and dilemmas facing them, I have shown how colonial and postcolonial discourses framed the town and its inhabitants as an isolated and lawless space home to uncivilized tribes-men. This representation and the accompanying production of a postcolonial geography rub against the self-understanding, experiences, and senses of belonging of Gwadar's residents in a wider Indian Ocean world. These senses of being and belonging are structured by the paths that self-emancipated slave communities traced on the Mekran and Sindh Coasts as they fled their masters in the hinterland, the experience of Omani rule that provides a reference point for criticizing the absence of rule of law in the present, and cultivation of an intimate relationship with the spectral beings, such as *Gwat* and *Jaatig*, from across the ocean. Although these appear fragmented and disparate, these threads of memory, nostalgia, and spirit rituals offers a different frame for imagining Gwadar and Mekran's past (and perhaps its future) than the dreams of global connectivity and national integration offered by Pakistani state authorities.

Notes

1 This is not to say that the scholars who write these articles and books themselves approve of military intervention and human rights abuses.
2 On British role in the Arab Gulf region during this period, see James Onley, *The Arabian Frontier of the British Raj: Merchants, Rulers, and the British in the Nineteenth-Century Gulf* (Oxford University Press, 2007).
3 During his political mission to Mekran in 1861, Lieutenant-Colonel F.J. Goldsmid, the Assistant Commissioner in Sindh, observed that there were 30 large and 70 small long-distance sailboats anchored in the Gwadar Harbor in 1861 (Goldsmid 1862: 17).

4 People in Gwadar believe in many types of supernatural spirits and beings. Djinns are the well-known spirits mentioned in the Holy Quran and Arabic and Persian lore. A *Gwat* spirit is an evil "wind" that possess its victim. *Jatig* (singular, *Jatu*) are human beings who are believed to have sold their souls to the devil in return for possessing evil knowledge or *Sehir*.

5 As mentioned earlier, *Gwati* spirits are only one of many types of supernatural beings which people believe in and there is no presumption of exoticness about them.

6 A *Syed* or *Sayyid* is a descendent of Prophet Muhammad. They are commonly believed to have spiritual powers because of their genealogy and piety.

References

Agent to the Governor General in Baluchistan. 1890. *Sir Robert Sandeman's Policy in Connection with the Rinds and other tribes of Mekran.* AGG/V.I. 38. Directorate of Archives, Government of Balochistan, Quetta, Pakistan.

Agent to the Governor General in Baluchistan. 1898. *Slavery in Baluchistan.* AGG/V.I. 164. Directorate of Archives, Government of Balochistan, Quetta, Pakistan.

Aitchison, C.U. 1933 [1865] *A Collection of Treaties, Engagements, and Sunnuds Relating to India and Neighbouring Countries.* Calcutta: Government Printing Press.

Axmann, Martin. 2008. *Back to the Future: The Khanate of Kalat and the Genesis of Baloch Nationalism, 1915–1955.* USA: Oxford University Press.

Campbell, Gwen. 2004. *Structure of Slavery in Indian Ocean Africa and Asia.* Portland, OR: Frank Cass.

Chatterjee, Indrani. 2005. "Abolition by Denial: The South Asian Example." *Abolition and its Aftermath in Indian Ocean Asia and Africa: Studies in Slave and Post-Slave Societies and Cultures.* New York: Routledge.

Dalrymple, William. 1993. *City of Djinns: A Year in Delhi.* New Delhi: Harper-Collins.

During, Jean. 1997. African Winds and Muslim Djinns. Trance, Healing, and Devotion in Baluchistan. *Yearbook for Traditional Music,* 29: 39–56.

Goldsmid, F.J. 1862. *Mission to Mekran.* IOR/L/PS/20/MEMO39/7. India Office Records (IOR), British Library, London.

Government of Pakistan. 2005. Report of the Parliamentary Committee on Balochistan. Islamabad: Senate of Pakistan.

Kaplan, Robert. D. 2009. Pakistan's Fatal Shore. *The Atlantic,* May 2009.

Lorimer, J.G. 1986. [1908] *Gazetteer of the Persian Gulf, Oman and Central Arabia.* Gerrard's Cross, UK: Archive Editions.

Lorimer, J.G. 1915. *Gazetteer of the Persian Gulf, Oman, and Central Arabia, Vol I, Part I.* Calcutta: Superintendent Government Printing Press.

Marshall, Lydia Wilson. 2015. "Marronage and the Politics of Memory: Fugitive Slaves, Interaction, and Integration in Nineteenth-Century Kenya." In *The Archaeology of Slavery: A Comparative Approach to Captivity and Coercion,* 276–299. Carbondale: Southern Illinois University Press.

Nicolini, Beatrice. 2006. The Makran–Baluch–African Network in Zanzibar and East Africa During the XIXth Century. *African and Asian Studies,* 5(3–4): 347–370.

Nicolini, Beatrice. 2007. Baluch Role in the Persian Gulf During the Nineteenth and Twentieth Centuries. *Comparative Studies of South Asia, Africa and The Middle East,* 27 (2): 384–396.

Outram, James. 1846. *The Conquest of Scinde: A Commentary.* Edinburgh: W. Blackwood.

Revenue Commissioner in Baluchistan. 1910. Orders Regarding Adjustment of Charges in Connectin with Deportation of Fugitive Slaves Who May Take Refuge in Gawadar. RCG 2013. Directorate of Archives, Government of Balochistan, Quetta, Pakistan.

Salzman, Philip Carl. 2000. *Black Tents of Baluchistan.* Washington, DC: Smithsonian Institution Press.

Sheriff, Abdul. 1987. *Slaves, Spices and Ivory in Zanzibar: Integration of an East African Commercial Empire into the World Economy, 1770–1873.* Athens, OH: Ohio University Press.

Spooner, Brian. 1975. "Nomadism in Baluchistan." In L.S. Leshnik and G.D. Sontheime (Eds.), *Pastoralists and Nomads in South Asia,* 171–182. Wiesbaden, Germany: Harrassowitz.

Spyer, Patricia. 2000. *The Memory of Trade: Modernity's Entanglements on an Eastern Indonesian Island.* Durham: Duke University Press.

Stewart, Kathleen. 1988. "Nostalgia – A Polemic." *Cultural Anthropology,* 3.3: 227–241.

Sultana, Farhat. 1995. "Gwat and Gwat-i-Leb: Spirit Healing and Social Change in Makran." In Paul Titus Ed. *Marginality and Modernity: Ethnicity and Change in Post-Colonial Balochistan,* 28–50. Karachi: Oxford University Press.

Sultana, Farhat. 2013. "Ethnicity and Healing Rituals in Gwadar, Balochistan, Pakistan." *The Journal of the Middle East and Africa,* 4(2): 169–185.

Swidler, Nina. 1992. "Kalat: the political economy of a tribal chiefdom." *American Ethnologist,* 19(3): 553–570.

Swidler, Nina. 2003. "On The Difficulty of Telling a Slave from a Wife." In Jahani, K. and A. Korn Eds. *The Baloch and Their Neighbours: Ethnic and Linguistic Contact in Balochistan in Historical and Modern Times,* 343–356. Weisbaden, Germany: Reichert Publishing.

Time Magazine 1958. Gwadar: the Sons of Sinbad. September 22 1958.

Titus, Paul and Nina Swidler. 2000. "Knights, Not Pawns: Ethno-Nationalism and Regional Dynamics in Post-Colonial Balochistan." *International Journal of Middle East Studies,* 32(1): 47–69.

11 The ship and the anchor

Shifting cartographies of affinity and belonging among Sikhs in Fiji

Nicole Ranganath

Two boys were born in international waters aboard a cargo ship on the Indian Ocean on the month-long journey from Calcutta to Fiji in 1936. The Captain named the Sikh boy "Ganges Singh" and the Muslim boy "Ganges Khan" after his ship, the SS *Ganges*. The oral histories passed down by Ganges Singh's family emphasize the life-long bonds of *jihajis* (ship brothers and sisters) forged on the voyage across the Indian Ocean. The ties of mutual dependence between shipmates could be even stronger than ties among Sikhs.[1] Jihajis considered each other family members who could be relied on for help in times of distress, and these bonds transcended religious, caste, class and regional boundaries persisting over generations. The lasting influence of his passage by sea was reflected in Ganges Singh's life. Due to his birth in international waters, Ganges easily obtained legal status to relocate from Fiji to New Zealand in the 1960s and he dedicated his adult life to fostering cooperation among diverse South Asian faith communities.[2] Jihaji narratives illustrate the importance of the Indian Ocean as a critical transient site in which new and enduring transcultural affinities were formed. Despite their longevity and importance, these seafaring bonds are often neglected by scholars interested in the formation of overseas communities and intra-community dynamics in ports of calls across the Indian Ocean.

This chapter explores the seafaring narratives and sacred geography of Sikhs who migrated from northwest British India to Calcutta by land and eventually to Fiji by ship from the early twentieth century onwards. It uncovers the hidden history of Sikhs in a remote archipelago in the South Pacific situated over 7000 miles southeast of India. The chapter's core focus is the tension between two defining features in the lives of Fijian Sikhs – *the ship* and *the anchor* – considered in their material manifestations and their symbolic importance as well as how they changed across the twentieth century. The ship refers to the bonds of fellow jihajis formed at sea, as well as their contemporary and historical links to India and the Indian Ocean region during the height of the British Empire; the anchor represents the prodigious efforts of the Fijian Sikh community to set down roots and create sites of permanency in Fiji through the construction of *Gurdwaras* (Sikh houses of worship). The *Gurdwara* is examined as a material edifice and as a primary source for unearthing the religious and social history of Sikhs in Fiji; it is also analyzed as a crucial site of sovereignty for one of the most portable communities in the world. As this chapter shows, this anchor remained tenuously moored in Fiji due to the ongoing insecurity of land tenure and the inability of Sikhs to gain social acceptance, economic independence, and political representation in Fiji's racialized society. As a result of the increasingly unfavorable environment for South Asians since Fiji's Independence in 1970, the majority of Sikhs have mobilized global kin networks to pursue greater opportunities in New Zealand, Australia, the United States and elsewhere in the world. In the absence of textual sources created by Sikhs, this study relies on original oral history research and a careful examination of the material edifice of the *Gurdwara* in Fiji in order to obtain a rich community history.

Although there is considerable research about Islamic and Hindu sacred geography and pilgrimage in Indian Ocean worlds, there is a paucity of research about Sikhism: a historical study of the imaginaries and placemaking practices of Fijian Sikhs enriches Indian Ocean studies. A unique and fascinating aspect of the Sikh faith is its *portability*: the founder Guru Nanak traveled in all four directions of the known world, establishing the importance of *udasi* (sacred journeys) in the Sikh tradition from its inception. Another factor in the hypermobility of Sikhs is the primacy of the scriptures. After the end of the succession of ten Gurus in 1707, Sikhs have worshipped the *Guru Granth Sahib* (sacred scriptures) as the Eternal Living Guru. Even though Sikhs continue to attach importance to sacred sites in South Asia, a critical result of the portability of the sacred scriptures is that the faith is largely unbounded by territoriality; Sikhs see themselves as cosmic citizens who belong nowhere and everywhere and the lack of caste prohibitions among Sikhs has allowed so many to leave the Indian subcontinent to settle globally. The history of the Sikhs living in transit in the South Pacific also informs the amorphous boundaries of Indian Ocean worlds. During the period of intense overseas migration from the mid-nineteenth to the mid-twentieth century, Sikhs formed the backbone of the British Empire, maintaining law and order as soldiers, watchmen, and police officers. As they traveled vast distances across and beyond the Indian Ocean, Sikhs' imaginaries of self, place, and community shed light on the fluid borders of these worlds.

South Asians in Fiji

Between 1830 and 1930, approximately 29 million Indians dispersed across the British empire: over a million of them arrived in British colonies in the Caribbean, Guyana, Mauritius, Natal, and Fiji as indentured laborers to work on sugar plantations after the abolition of slavery (Tinker 1974). From 1879 to 1916, over 60,000 Indians migrated to Fiji as part of the indentured labor system to work on sugar plantations owned by the Colonial Sugar Refinery of Australia (Lal 1992). In 1874, Fiji became a British colony when the indigenous Fijian chiefs signed the Deed of Cession and Indians were brought to Fiji to meet the rapidly expanding need for labor in the sugar industry.

When Punjab was annexed in 1849, it was one of the last areas of the Indian subcontinent to come under British control. Due to poverty and oppressive land tenure conditions, Sikhs sought employment in the British Army and security forces in Shanghai, Hong Kong, and Singapore beginning in the mid-nineteenth century. The British gave the Sikh *Jat* (farming) community preferential recruitment into the colonial army and police forces. Most of the Punjabis were Sikh *Jats* from congested rural areas in the Doaba region of Punjab, but there were other castes and Muslims as well. Once abroad, the Sikhs heard about and then pursued greater economic opportunities in Canada, the United States, Argentina, Fiji, and elsewhere. Sikhs who came to Fiji intended to stay temporarily in order to pay off their debts before returning to Punjab or moving on to places that offered greater prosperity. Fiji was reputed to be one of the least desirable destinations in the indentured diaspora; however, most indentured laborers remained in Fiji after their five-year contracts ended due to low wages and debt and exclusionary immigration policies introduced in the West in the early 1900s. Their descendants form the bulk of the South Asian Fijian population today.

The construction of racial identity in Fijian society that formed under British colonial rule created unique dilemmas for Punjabi Sikhs: in India and throughout much of the British Empire, the British gave Sikhs preferential recruitment into the British Indian Army and security forces due to their perceived qualities as a so-called "martial race." In fact, British colonial officials in Fiji made extensive efforts to recruit the first ten Sikh police officers from Hong Kong to Fiji in 1911.[3] However, in Fiji, native Fijians were cast as the loyal martial race and caretakers of the land while South Asians were viewed as docile coolie laborers.

The current political predicament in Fiji, as Vijay Mishra and Devleena Ghosh suggest, was partially fueled by South Asian Fijians' drive for independence both in India and in Fiji (Ghosh 2004; Lal and Pretes 2001; Mishra 2007). The native Fijian chiefs had no interest in the anti-colonial struggle. After Fiji's Independence, many native Fijians feared that the numerically dominant South Asian population would take control of their country and remove the political and economic protections for native Fijians created by the British. Instead of forging a regional solidarity based on their shared colonial pasts, the native Fijians feared that they would lose their country to another migrant race just as the Maori and Aboriginal peoples had in nearby New Zealand and Australia. In Fiji's unique land sharing arrangement, 83 percent of the land was set aside for ownership by native Fijians according to the 1874 Deed of Cession. South Asian Fijians have never enjoyed security of land tenure in Fiji, most lease land from native Fijians. At the time of Fiji's first coup in 1987, South Asian Fijians only owned 1/60 of the land even though they comprised 49 percent of the population.[4] Due to their lack of protection from rent increases when their long-term leases from native Fijians expired, the majority of Sikhs became convinced that it was necessary to leave Fiji in order to secure a better future for their children. The backlash among native Fijians in the 1987, 2000, and 2006 coups marginalized South Asian Fijians by further limiting their political and economic advancement and land rights. The Sikh community in Fiji had already mobilized global kin networks since the 1950s, but their departure accelerated, beginning in the 1980s.

The scholarship about South Asians in Fiji focuses almost exclusively on the history of indentured laborers and their descendants as "coolies" (these include Kelly and Kaplan 2001; and Lal and Gillion 1977). The experiences of the small but significant communities of Punjabis and Gujaratis who arrived in Fiji as voluntary migrants beginning in the 1920s do not figure into the master narratives of South Asian Fijian scholarship, and the history of Punjabi Sikhs in Fiji has been almost entirely ignored by scholars.[5] Although the Sikh community has only formed 3 percent of the South Asian Fijian population, their history is worthy of scholarly attention since it offers a productive vantage point into the placemaking practices and transnational networks of Sikh communities that were deeply connected to but spilled over beyond the Indian Ocean. This chapter places the seafaring journeys and sacred geography of Sikhs in Fiji within shifting transnational networks in which the notion of home is continually reimagined, unsettled, and elusive.

This study builds on recent scholarship emphasizing the importance of historical specificity in understanding the migration of South Asians in the Indian Ocean region and beyond unsettling classic and static ideas of diaspora (Aiyar 2011; Amrith 2013; Bose 2006). New histories of modern Indian migrancy across the Indian Ocean emphasize the ease of return to the homeland, circular migratory patterns, and the diaspora's continued cultural, political, and economic simultaneous and changing engagements with both the homeland and the hostlands.[6] Fiji's geographical distance from India and the Indian Ocean region – combined with the tumultuous ruptures the community experienced during the 1980s in India and in Fiji – contributed to the de-centering of India and the Indian Ocean in the lives of Sikhs by the late twentieth century. In contrast to the migrants who engaged in circular migration in the Indian Ocean closer to India, the experiences of South Asians in Fiji were better characterized by isolation, distance, and a state of finding themselves marooned in a remote archipelago. Since the 1980s, however, Sikhs in Fiji have increasingly mobilized global Sikh diasporic networks and imaginaries. Amidst a global movement to establish a Sikh homeland, the global network of *Gurdwaras* assumed new meanings and significance as sites of sovereignty, refuge, and collective identity.

The study of the global network of *Gurdwaras* is a fruitful object of analysis to better understand the Sikh diaspora within the colonial and post-independence contexts. During the late nineteenth and early twentieth centuries, Thomas Metcalf posits that India formed the central nodal point within the British Empire and the Indian Ocean world (Metcalf 2007). However, as Tony Ballantyne theorizes, the relationship between overseas Sikh diasporic communities and the homeland is best conceptualized as "webs of Empire." Sikh kinship structures and religious institutions and networks formed the backbone of British colonial ties, and they responded simultaneously to developments in India, in places where they settled overseas, and in colonial settlements across vast distances (Ballantyne 2006). In recent decades, diasporic Sikh communities in Vancouver, Singapore, and Yuba City have increasingly competed with sites in

Punjab due to the accelerated velocity of mobility and communications, political alienation of Sikhs from India, and the wealth and influence of diasporic Sikhs.[7] Fiji *Gurdwaras* have shown remarkable adaptability and resilience, and they have provided religious, financial, political, social and emotional anchors for the Fijian Sikh community in the midst of dramatic societal and political changes in India and in the diaspora.

The historical record about Fiji's Sikh community is fragmentary with many silences. Given the limited information about Sikhs in the National Archives of Fiji, it was necessary to gather unofficial community sources, such as *Gurdwara* committee records and community histories, as well as oral history and visual culture. Over the last two years, the author has also conducted oral histories with Sikhs in Fiji, as well as with Fijian Sikhs in California.

The ship: the portability of Sikhs and Indian Ocean affinities

Travel lies at the core of Sikh identity. Guru Nanak was one of the most traveled historical figures in the sixteenth century. He spent half of his life traveling in all four directions, engaging with peoples of different faiths, cultures, and languages. Since the colonial period, Sikhs have migrated throughout the British Empire as soldiers and police officers, as well as preachers, merchants, farmers, and laborers. Of interest here is the significance of the memory of the Indian Ocean journeys to the remote archipelago of Fiji in the early twentieth century. Sikh travel narratives enrich the study of the complex identities, affinities, and placemaking practices of highly mobile communities in transit with shifting ties to the Indian Ocean region. Unlike the famous memoir of Totaram Sanadhya, *My Twenty-Two Years in the Fiji Islands*, Sikh narratives were never incorporated into anti-colonial debates, efforts to reform or eradicate indenture, or other public discourses in India or Fiji.[8] In the absence of published autobiographical sources by Sikhs (most of whom were illiterate), the Indian Ocean journeys of the Sikh community are gleaned from the colonial archive and original oral history research.

The earliest accounts of Sikhs in the South Pacific highlight their experiences of disorientation, distress and disappointment upon arrival. Although the vast majority of Punjabis arrived as voluntary migrants, it does appear that a small number of Sikhs were indentured laborers in Fiji. C.F. Andrews' influential report on indenture in Fiji includes this brief passage about Sikhs:

> A whole group of Punjabis was once recruited ... under false pretenses. When they found out on arrival how they had been cheated, they broke out into open mutiny... until Government separated them ... and distributed them among different coolie 'lines.'

> (Andrews 1916: 6)

The first group of Punjabi voluntary migrants in Fiji in 1904 also felt deceived by false promises of high wages after they landed in New Caledonia. Unable to secure work, 70 Punjabis continued their journey to Fiji. Disappointed by the low wages in Fiji, they returned to New Caledonia and were eventually repatriated to India. A letter from 46 Punjabis in 1914 sought compensation for the false promises of recruiters (Gillion 1962). In the early 1900s, a group of Sikhs were desperate after being deceived into paying large fees to leave for South America: "We would like to go to the Argentine Republic in South America. We have heard we will get many jobs there. But no steamer goes to South America from Fiji. What shall we do? How shall we go?" (Sanadhya 1991: 57). The overall impression from the early days of the community is that the Sikhs were marooned in Fiji.

As Sikhs arrived in Fiji in greater numbers in the 1920s, they traveled aboard regular immigrant ships and their sea journeys were similar to those of Indian indentured laborers. By the 1920s, the journey from Calcutta to Suva by steamship lasted one month. The conditions on board were cramped and uncomfortable, and many suffered from seasickness. Sometimes immigrants like Ganges Singh arrived on cargo ships. Rations on board were limited and the *jihajis* would share communal meals. Upon arrival, the immigrants were transferred to barges to the island of Nukulau where they were quarantined before disembarking in the town of Suva. Sikhs first lived near Suva before eventually settling into sugarcane farming on the western side of Viti Levu (the main island) in Ba, Tagi Tagi, and the surrounding areas. Most remained tenant sugar farmers working for CSR or on land owned by native Fijians. Sikhs contributed a great deal to the country's economic development in farming, transport, and the kava and timber businesses. They also occupied the professions as police officers, teachers, and priests; many migrated from other locations in Singapore, Malaysia, and East Asia.

The Sikhs were more willing to travel overseas partly due to economic pressures, as well as their relative freedom from caste restrictions and overseas experience in the British Army and security forces. The community had long engaged in migrations to earn money and then returning to their home villages, especially in heavily populated districts. As previously mentioned, Fiji was one of the least desirable options and most sought greater opportunities in the West (Gillion 1962). Many arrived in Fiji in the 1920s largely because they were barred from legally entering their preferred destinations. Sikhs began to leave Fiji beginning in the 1950s for more desirable countries as soon as the immigration policy allowed migration from Asia on a limited basis.[9] By 1966 there were 3000 Sikhs in Fiji (out of 476,727 Indians) and Punjabi was spoken in only 175 households in Fiji, according to the Fiji Census.

Joginder Singh Ratendra's family history illustrates the fortuitous sequence of events and journeys that culminated in their arrival in Fiji. Joginder only arrived in Fiji due to an unlikely series of events in which his father was deported back to Punjab from California after traveling from Mexico, Panama and Argentina. The family arrived in Fiji abroad the *SS Ganges IV* in 1938 where his father worked as a laborer. Joginder's sons achieved financial success by building Fiji's largest kava business and eventually owned over 35 acres of land.[10]

Sikh narratives in Fiji reflect their complex ties to India. They continued to send remittances to their families in Punjab, and they engaged in anti-colonial agitation leading up to India's Independence in 1947. As communication and travel increased in recent decades, there was an increased flow of religious leaders from Punjab to Fiji and greater knowledge of traditional religious practices. In addition, recently Sikhs in Fiji have married more often with women from Punjab, thus increasing knowledge of Punjabi cultural and religious customs in Fiji.

Fiji's remote location far from India also led to the unusual development of language, culture, and politics among Fijian South Asians. Due to its isolation, South Asian Fijian culture developed a high degree of hybridity and innovation in religion, cultural forms, and language (including the creation of a distinct Fijian Hindi dialect). After their ruptures with both the Indian and Fijian governments in the 1980s, Sikhs increasingly strengthened their material and imaginary ties with the global Sikh diaspora. It is within this historical context that *Gurdwaras* assumed greater significance as imaginary islands of sovereignty globally in the absence of a Sikh homeland.

The anchor: Sikh sacred geography in the Fiji Archipelago

Gurdwaras serve as valuable primary sources for understanding the historical presence of Sikhs in Fiji, their shifting ties to India and the Indian Ocean world, and their relationship to local communities and power structures. The *Gurdwara* has served a critical role in the Sikh diaspora that helps to preserve the identity and self-reliance of Sikhs regardless of where they live in the world. *Gurdwaras* reflect the core values of Sikhs, including financial independence, hard work, equality, and community service.

Fiji *Gurdwaras* share a number of similar functions with mosques in the Indian Ocean region, but they also reflect the unique portability and the significance of sovereignty in the Sikh tradition.[11] Devotional worship at *Gurdwaras* involved reciting, singing, and explaining the *bani* (verses) of the *Guru Granth Sahib* in the presence of the *sangat* (congregation). Another core feature of this institution is the *langar* hall (community kitchen) where volunteers prepare free vegetarian food to anyone in need. *Langar* exemplifies the emphasis on social equality: Sikhs believe that the most powerful way to eradicate social barriers is by sharing a common meal. These aspects were particularly important in the early days of settlement when the *Gurdwara* provided free room and board for new arrivals until they could find work.[12] *Gurdwaras* are also inter-faith institutions that not only serve the Sikh community but also Hindus and Muslims, some of whom had intermarried with Sikhs. Sports also formed an integral part of the life of Fiji *Gurdwaras*. Following the long-standing tradition in Sikh culture, there was great emphasis placed on physical strength, especially in wrestling competitions.

As Sikhs arrived in Fiji in greater numbers in the 1920s, their first and highest priority was to build a *Gurdwara* as a place of worship and as a site of security and sustenance. Sikhs secured permission from the British colonial government to obtain Crown Land on which the *Gurdwaras* were built. The first *Gurdwara* in the South Pacific was built in Samabula near the port city of Suva in 1923 on the Old King's Highway. The excavation and construction of the *Gurdwara* was completed manually by volunteers: "many Sikh labourers, working in the city [of Suva], used to carry one or two bags of cement ... on their shoulders every day after work from the city to the *Gurdwara*" (Rana 2011: 161). When restrictions to immigration were put in place during the 1930s, the *Gurdwara* took legal responsibility for Sikhs arriving in Fiji. Additional *Gurdwaras* were built to serve the growing community in the western districts in Tagi Tagi (1926) and Lautoka (1933), and in Nasina near Suva in the 1940s. No *Gurdwaras* were built in Fiji after the 1940s.

Gurdwaras have served as islands of sovereignty carrying new and greater significance abroad as Sikhs began migrating overseas in greater numbers in the late nineteenth century. For Sikhs, the institution of the *Gurdwara* is a space for honoring the supreme power of God and preserving the core values of the Sikh community. The most prominent symbol of Sikh sovereignty is the *nishan sahib* (Sikh flag) that flies prominently at every *Gurdwara*. The flag is a symbol of the Sikh *qom* (nation or people), faith and culture. It serves as a beacon for anyone in need of shelter and sustenance. In the flag's center, there is a *khanda* (double-edged sword) symbolizing the importance of both spiritual and material prosperity. The khanda also reflects the martial tradition in Sikh history in which the community has fought for self-preservation and survival for centuries. As Sikhs settled all over the world, the *nishan sahib* has served as an index of the community's power vis-à-vis local authorities and as a lightning rod for tensions with local communities. There is no record of local opposition to erecting the *nishan sahib* in Fiji, however, reflecting the community's relatively positive relationship with the British colonial government and local communities in the early twentieth century.

The *Gurdwara* has also served as a sanctuary for the people of Fiji, not only the Sikh community. This reflects the emphasis in the Sikh faith on serving all of humanity. The city of Suva has experienced disruptions in the water supply historically. The early Sikh settlers built one of the few wells in the Suva area on the grounds of the Samabula *Gurdwara* in order to benefit the surrounding community. During World War II, the Sikh community built two bunkers in the Suva *Gurdwara* to protect the broader community during the threat of a Japanese invasion. Similarly, during the devastating floods in the early 1960s, the Samabula *Gurdwara* provided a disaster relief shelter for Fijians of all backgrounds.

Festivals honoring birth anniversaries of the ten Sikh Gurus were important occasions in which Fijian Sikhs publicly asserted their identity and faith. The first surviving account of a Sikh festival was the celebration of the birth anniversary of Guru Nanak on 1–2 November 1933. The festival was celebrated by devotional singing, speeches, and lectures about Guru Nanak's life and teachings, and a communal meal. Another major festival was the 300th birth anniversary of Guru

Gobind Singh in 1967 (Rana 2011: 153). The devotional hymns for this important festival were broadcast for the entire South Asian community on Fiji Radio.

Sikh *Gurdwaras* were characterized by greater diversity of religious practice and sectarian heterodoxy. There was a small private *Gurdwara* in Ba that predated the Suva *Gurdwara* that was owned by the Ganga Singh family that followed a different sect of Sikhism (Gillion 1977: 115). During the 1960s, the Fiji *Gurdwaras* became sites of heated contestation over religious orthopraxy. As Sikh priests from India started to visit Fiji, there was an effort to restore traditional religious practices. The visiting Sikh priests would instruct members of the congregation to keep their heads covered inside the Gurdwara, and to abstain from smoking or drinking alcohol at the *Gurdwara*. In 1965, multiple conflicts arose at the *Gurdwaras* in western Fiji that led to violence, injuries, and legal action. These disputes arose between followers of mainstream Sikhi and the followers of the Namdhari sect.[13] Interestingly, the controversies that animated *Gurdwaras* in the West in recent decades are almost completely absent in Fiji. For instance, the decision to allow chairs inside Fijian *Gurdwaras* was never contested (some Sikhs believe that everyone should sit on the floor in the *Gurdwara* to reflect the importance of equality while others favor accommodations for the elderly).

The 1980s marked a turning point for the Fijian Sikh community's relationship to Fiji, as well as to the global Sikh diaspora. Mr Dalabar Singh (a Ba sugarcane farmer) describes the harrowing days during the 1987 coup in which Lt Colonel Rabuka, a native Fijian, ousted the previous government in a backlash against the political influence of South Asian Fijians. In the months that followed, South Asian Fijians and their property were targeted in numerous violent attacks. One of the most disturbing incidents was the arson at the Lautoka *Gurdwara*.[14] The fire destroyed the *Gurdwara*. Mr Dalabar Singh described how he and other Sikhs decided how they should ritually cremate the Holy Books that were badly damaged during the arson:

> There were about seven or eight Holy Books …which were badly damaged by the fire. According to our Sikh religion, ritually the Holy Books … had to be cremated like they cremate a human being because we regard the Holy Book as the holy Guru of the Sikhs. It contains all of the writings of the Sikh Gurus and also of some Hindu and Muslim saints.[15]

Dalabar Singh and others in Fiji did not know the correct rituals for cremating the Holy Books. Rather than consulting with religious authorities in Punjab, Mr Singh contacted leading figures in the Khalistan movement for advice, including Dr. Gurmit Singh Aulukh in the United States.

This traumatic incident highlighted the precarious position of Punjabi Sikhs in Fiji. In the same decade that Sikhs were grappling with a traumatic decade in India marked by violence and alienation from the Indian government, many Sikhs no longer felt that Fiji was their home. A hypermobile community, Sikhs increasingly left Fiji to join kin in other countries. Sikhs in distant parts of the

Figure 11.1 Memorial for the cremated Sikh holy books, Lautoka Gurdwara, 2017.
Image credit: Nicole Ranganath.

world were reminded that they did not have a homeland, so they mobilized global family networks to uproot themselves in order to rebuild their lives once again.

Conclusion: the emergence of a global *Gurdwara* imaginary and uncertain futures in Fiji

Recent Indian Ocean historians have explored the significance of the mosque in the region as a historical gauge of a community's mobility, placemaking practices, inter-community relations, and expectations of a future in any given locality. In similar ways, a study of the *Gurdwara* in Fiji highlights the complex negotiations and new imaginaries of Sikhs in the South Pacific with changing ties to the Indian Ocean region. A careful analysis of community narratives and the material and symbolic significance of *Gurdwaras* offer a window into the rich, multi-layered emotional dimensions of Sikhs' attachment to Fiji. The history of Sikhs in Fiji reveals the amorphous and shifting boundaries of Indian Ocean worlds; their lives were shaped by a rapidly changing interplay between local, regional, and global influences.

In this global context of dispersal and transit, the ambitious restoration project of the Suva *Gurdwara* raises questions about what it means to journey, drop anchor, or make meaningful maps of habitation in Indian Ocean worlds. According to the Fiji Census, the number of Sikhs in Fiji declined from 3076 in 1996 to 2577 in 2007. Community leaders estimated that only 700 Sikhs remain in Fiji as of 2017. As a result of the departure of Sikhs, the congregations of Fiji *Gurdwaras* have dwindled (Mann, Numrich, and Williams 2001; Singh 2006). Recently there were vacancies in the posts of the head priests at all the Fiji *Gurdwaras*. The major Sikh religious functions require five initiated Sikhs to be present. Only a handful of Sikhs in Fiji can perform these functions today, and therefore, generally the same five individuals must travel from across the main island of Fiji in order to perform the rites.[16]

Given the uncertain future of Sikhs in Fiji, it is surprising that a major remodel of the Suva *Gurdwara* was completed in 2019. The projected cost of the remodel is approximately US$400,000.[17] According to the planning committee, the project aims to "upgrade the *Gurdwara* so that it can be one of the most attractive in the South Pacific Region."[18] The new design pulls features from an eclectic array of transnational *Gurdwaras*, including the Golden Temple in Amitsar, Punjab. Other transnational *Gurdwaras* referenced in the planning document are located where they are supported by large and wealthy Sikh communities in England, Australia, the United States, and Canada. The Southhall *Gurdwara* outside London is highlighted as a role model. The Suva *Gurdwara* restoration planning committee aimed to correct a perceived design flaw: "the building does not give a normal *Gurdwara*."[19] The missing defining feature of a so-called normal transnational *Gurdwara* was the onion dome. The committee's aim is to add onion domes to the Suva *Gurdwara* in order to align its design with other modern transnational *Gurdwaras* without detracting from its neo-Greek aesthetic. The new onion dome serves a religious purpose by increasing natural light over the Sikh Scripture, emphasizing its importance.

Until recently, Sikhi in Fiji was known for its heterodoxy and hybridity. However, since the 1990s, the Fijian Sikh community has been increasingly reconnected with South Asia through greater ease of travel and communications with Punjab, and Fiji *Gurdwaras* also adopted mainstream Sikh religious practices. Due to a complex series of events that unfolded in the 1980s in Punjab and in Fiji, the Fijian Sikh community uprooted itself once again by mobilizing kin networks throughout the global diaspora. The vast majority of the highly mobile Sikh community have already left their homes and *Gurdwaras* behind in Fiji. In the midst of the many challenges in Fiji, the Suva *Gurdwara* restoration project is evidence that the small number of remaining Sikhs there have continued to invest in creating an enduring sacred geography. The future of the Fiji *Gurdwaras* is precarious, however, as they approach a tipping point as their congregations continue to disperse around the world.

Notes

1 Sikhism, the fifth largest world religion, originated in the Punjab region in north India in the fifteenth century. I also wish to express my appreciation for the generous

support of the UC Davis "Reimagining Indian Ocean Worlds" Mellon Research Initiative and a travel grant from the Dean's Office, College of Letters and Sciences, University of California, Davis.

2 Gurmej Singh Virk, Interview, Sacramento, CA, US, October 30, 2017.

3 Minutes, "Recruiting Sikh Police From Hong Kong," National Archives of Fiji, 1910.

4 For an extensive history of Fiji's land policy and its effects on South Asians, see Lal (1992) and Brown (1989).

5 The notable exception is K.L. Gillion's *Fiji's Indian Migrants: A History to the End of Indenture in 1920* (1962). There are two valuable published community histories of the Sikhs in Fiji, which are Gajraj Singh, *The Sikhs of Fiji* (Suva: South Pacific Series, undated); and, Hardayal Singh Rana, *Shabad Simran* (2011).

6 In her study of anti-colonial agitation among Indians in Kenya, Sana Aiyar (2011) suggests that Indian diaspora scholars assume a static relationship between the homeland and hostland in which migrants' idealization of the homeland leads them to reproduce religious and cultural traditions wherever they reside. In the classic definition of diaspora, the study of migrants emphasizes the themes of dispersal, involuntary exile, and a desire but inability to return to the homeland.

7 For resources about the Sikh diaspora, see Barrier and Dusenbery (1989); Dusenbery and Tatla (2009); McCann (2011); Talbot and Thandi (2004) and Tatla (1999).

8 Sanadhya (1991). For other valuable oral histories of indentured laborers, see Ali (1980); Andrews and Pearson (1916); and Lal (2000).

9 Balbir Singh Johl, Interview, Yuba City, CA, December 1916. His father, Khazan Singh Johl, was one of the first Sikhs to emigrate to the US from Fiji in 1955.

10 Joginder Singh Ratendra, Interview, Tamavua, Fiji, July 27, 2017.

11 Sebastian Prange's study of historical mosques along the Malabar coast identifies many core features of Indian Ocean mosques. There are many similar functions shared by both Indian Ocean mosques and *Gurdwaras*, including the importance of providing food and shelter for travelers, places of communal prayer, and the anomalous architectural features of religious institutions in distant locations. One prominent feature of mosques that was largely absent in Fiji was that *Gurdwaras* did not serve as important institutions of learning. See Prange (2018).

12 Sikh Gurudwara Prabandhak Committee Application as a Corporate Body for Religious Purposes, Suva, Fiji, October 22, 1992; "Sikhs Make Fiji Their Home," *Fiji Times* (May 4, 2017); and, Balbir Singh Johl, Interview, Yuba City, CA, US, December 2016.

13 Namdharis are part of a sect of Sikhism that emerged in the nineteenth century. Renowned as fierce warriors, the sect is generally not considered part of the mainstream Sikh faith. (Rana 2011: 317–318).

14 The Lautoka Hindu temple was also seriously damaged during the 1987 arson.

15 Dalabar Singh, Interview, *Gurdwara*, Lautoka, Fiji, July 9, 2017.

16 Preetam Shokar Singh, Interview, Suva, Fiji, July 28, 2017.

17 Joginder Singh Ratendra, Interview, Suva, Fiji, July 27, 2017.

18 Sikh Gurudwara Prabandhak Committee Suva *Gurdwara* Report, Suva, Fiji, April 14, 2016.

19 Sikh Gurudwara Prabandhak Committee Report,

References

Aiyar, Sana. 2011. "Anticolonial Homelands across the Indian Ocean: The Politics of the Indian Diaspora in Kenya, *c.*1930–1950." *American Historical Review* 116(4): 987–1013.

Ali, Ahmed. 1980. *Plantation to Politics: Studies of Fiji Indians*. Suva: University of the Pacific.

Amrith, Sunil. 2013. *Crossing the Bay of Bengal: The Furies of Nature and the Fortunes of Migrants*. Cambridge: Harvard University.

Andrews, C.F. and W.W. Pearson. 1916. *Indentured Labour in Fiji: An Independent Enquiry.* Calcutta, Star Printing Works.

Ballantyne, Tony. 2006. *Between Colonialism and Diaspora: Sikh Cultural Formations in an Imperial World.* Durham: Duke University.

Barrier, Gerald N. and Verne A Dusenbery. 1989. *The Sikh Diaspora: Migration and the Experience Beyond Punjab.* Columbia: South Asia Publications.

Bose, Sugata. 2006. *A Hundred Horizons: The Indian Ocean in the age of Global Empire.* Cambridge: Harvard University.

Brown, Carolyn Henning. 1989. "The Social Background of Fiji's 1987 Coup." *Sociological Bulletin* 38(1), 95–117.

Dusenbery, Verne and Darshan S Tatla. 2009. *Sikh Diaspora Philanthropy in Punjab: Global Giving for Local Good.* Oxford: Oxford University.

Ghosh, Devleena. 2004. "Re-Crossing a Different Water: Colonialism and Third World-ism in Fiji." *Third World Quarterly* 25(1), 111–130.

Gillion, K.L. 1962. *Fiji's Indian Migrants: A History to the End of Indenture in 1920.* Melbourne: Oxford University.

Gillion, K.L. 1977. *The Fiji Indians: Challenge to European Dominance, 1920–1946.* Canberra: Australian National University.

Kelly, John D. and Martha Kaplan. 2001. *Represented Communities: Fiji and World Decolonization.* Chicago: Chicago University.

Lal, Brij V. 1992. *Broken Waves: A History of the Fiji Islands in the Twentieth Century.* Honolulu: Hawaii University.

Lal, Brij V. 2000. *Chalo Jahaji: On a Journey Through Indenture in Fiji.* Canberra: Australian National University.

Lal, Brij V and M Pretes, Editors. 2001. *Coup: Reflections on the Political Crisis in Fiji.* Canberra: Pandanus Books.

Mann, Gurinder Singh, Paul David Numrich, and Raymond B Williams. 2001. *Buddhists, Hindus, and Sikhs in America.* Oxford: Oxford University.

McCann, Gerard. 2011. "Sikhs and the City: Sikh History and Diasporic Practice in Singapore." *Modern Asian Studies* 45(6), 1465–1498.

Metcalf, Thomas R. 2007. *Imperial Connections: India in the Indian Ocean Arena, 1860–1920.* Berkeley: University of California.

Mishra, Vijay. 2007. *The Literature of the Indian Diaspora: Theorizing the Diasporic Imaginary.* London: Routledge University.

Prange, Sebastian. 2018. *Monsoon Islam: Trade and Faith on the Medieval Malabar Coast.* Cambridge: Cambridge University Press.

Rana, Hardayal Singh. 2011. *Shabad Simran.* Suva: Quality Print.

Sanadhya, Totaram. 1991. *My Twenty-Two Years in the Fiji Islands & The Story of the Haunted Line,* Translated and Edited by John Dunham Kelly and Uttra Kumari Singh. Suva: Fiji Museum.

Singh, Gajraj. Nd. *The Sikhs of Fiji.* Suva: South Pacific Series.

Singh, Gurharpal. 2006. "*Gurdwaras* and Community-Building among British Sikhs." *Contemporary South Asia* 15(2), 147–164.

Talbot, Ian and Shinder Thandi, eds. 2004. *People on the Move: Punjabi Colonial and Post-Colonial Migration.* Karachi: Oxford University.

Tatla, Darshan S. 1999. *The Sikh Diaspora: The Search for Statehood.* London: Routledge University.

Tinker, Hugh. 1974. *A New System of Slavery: The Export of Indian Labour Overseas, 1830–1920.* Oxford: Oxford University.

Unpublished Sources

Fiji Times.
Balbir Singh Johl, Interview, Yuba City, CA, December 1916.
National Archives of Fiji.
Joginder Singh Ratendra, Interview, Tamavua, Fiji, 27 July 2017.
Sikh Gurudwara Prabandhak Committee Report, Suva, Fiji, 14 April 2016.
Dalabar Singh, Interview, Lautoka, Fiji, 9 July 2017.
Gurmej Singh Virk, Interview, Sacramento, CA, US, 30 October 2017.
Preetam Shokar Singh, Interview, Suva, Fiji, 28 July 2017.

Part IV
Methods and disciplines

12 Bibi's *uchungu*

Eating, bitterness, and relationality across Indian Ocean worlds

Laura A. Meek

In December of 2014, Bibi, her adult daughter Mrs. Muro, and I were all cramped into a small room at Hitech Sai Healthcare Centre, a private health clinic in Dar es Salaam, Tanzania that is advertised as a "diagnostic and specialty clinic."[1] We had traveled nine hours by car from our home in the Southern Highlands of Tanzania to come here so that Bibi could have an upper endoscopy to check for ulcers. Bibi, who was 77-years old at the time, is the great-grandmother with whom I had lived for the past year and a half. Since the time she moved in with us, Bibi had been suffering immensely from chronic stomach pain, a condition that had plagued her for many years. After hours of waiting at this clinic, we were finally called into a small back room where a young technician told Bibi to lay on a cot. He then turned on a machine, and without asking for any patient history, led the narrow lighted tube down Bibi's throat. Her whole body was tense during the procedure, her fists tightly balled up and tears rolling slowly down her cheeks.

We waited again for a doctor to explain the results, and when he did, he addressed me in English – which neither Bibi nor her daughter understood. He did not translate the results to them until I insisted upon it and, by all indications, he had no intention of doing so. This dynamic is quite common in Tanzania (and beyond), where doctors do not routinely review diagnoses with their patients; frequently, they tell the patient nothing at all after examining them and just simply hand them a prescription (Feinstein and D'Errico 2010). When I inquired as to why this was the case, doctors usually explained to me that their patients would not be able to understand any of it, anyway. What the doctor told me – in English – was that Bibi had "gastritis," indicated by red spots on her stomach and intestinal walls. Crucially, the endoscopy did not reveal any ulcers. When the doctor spoke to Bibi and Mrs. Muro at my urging, he translated "gastritis" into Swahili as "*michumbuku*," which means scratches.

That translation ended up being critical to the discourses and practices around Bibi's "ulcers" that developed over the subsequent year. Everyone in the Muro household took those *michumbuku* as evidence for what they already understood the problem to be and so they all continued to refer to Bibi's ailment as "ulcers" (using the English term). For Bibi, "ulcers" were a manifestation of her grief over the loss of her husband and two of her children; for her daughter, they were signs indexing Bibi's vulnerability to being "eaten" by maleficent spiritual forces; and for Mr. Muro (Bibi's son-in-law), the scratches were damage caused by Bibi's continued use of chewing tobacco, a poisonous substance that "ate" at her stomach lining. In all cases, Bibi's body was portrayed as being consumed by something or someone, but who or what was highly contested. I learned an important lesson after this: that "ulcers" are not ulcers, as I understood them to be – hence my decision to refer to them as "ulcers" throughout this chapter. Before our trip to Dar es Salaam, I had misunderstood what it meant when everyone in the Muro household referred to Bibi's problem as "ulcers," and so I had mistakenly assumed that the endoscopy would produce definite knowledge through the idiom of the biomedical diagnosis.[2]

In what follows, I elaborate on Bibi's *uchungu*, focusing especially on how the chronic "ulcers" she suffered from are also openings into her life history and speak to larger formations of embodiment and healing across Indian Ocean worlds. I propose that what makes Indian Ocean worlds into "worlds" in this context is a set of (divergent yet resonant) practices, which – sustained and repeated – produce the embodied qualities that enable well-being or sickness. I understand these embodied qualities as "qualia" (Munn 1986), a concept which refers to how the qualities of things, relations, or places become materialized in bodies, such that experience can be understood as a semiotically informed aspect of the world, rather than simply an individual subjective state. In this chapter, I elaborate on the quale of bitterness (*uchungu* in Swahili) as one such worlding practice.

In my focus on qualia and embodiment here, I depart from the dominant tropes of medicine and healing in the Indian Ocean to date, which have largely focused on the movement of medical knowledges, practitioners, and treatments across trade routes and networks of migration (see for instance Dilger, Kane, and Langwick 2012; Winterbottom and Tesfaye 2016a, 2016b). While such approaches focus on the ways in which geographically distant locals are connected physically across space, my work reveals how the qualia that comprise a world may also inhere in a single place, home, family, and even, body.

In proposing this alternative approach, I am deeply influenced by feminist methodologies which prioritize the quotidian and intimate over epic, grand narratives, as well as by recent ethnographies of bodily afflictions that focus on small acts of everyday life (Garcia 2010; Han 2012; Povinelli 2011). Elizabeth Povinelli, for instance, chooses to follow accounts of suffering that are "ordinary, chronic and cruddy rather than catastrophic, crisis-laden and sublime" (2011: 132). Veena Das (2013) compares Povinelli's concern with "quasi-events" to Han's interest in "critical moments" in which "what we are led to see is how quotidian, everyday acts – perhaps unremarkable in terms of their dramatic import – nevertheless provide the subtle means for life to be knitted together in slow rhythms, pair by pair" (2013: 219). Informed by such methods of apprehending lifeworlds, I also dwell on small, everyday encounters and consider how they are in Indian Ocean worlds and how Indian Ocean worlds inhere in them.

I argue that properties as seemingly banal as bitterness can hold together a shared world; that Indian Ocean worlds exists as much – and even perhaps more so – through the practices and bodies worlding them than as a physical space whose boundaries could be drawn on a map. In this sense, then, Indian Ocean worlds are not merely containers within which people, things, and ideas circulate. The worlds of the Indian Ocean can and do move, appearing not only along coastal communities, but also – as here – materializing in inland communities like the Southern Highlands of Tanzania.[3]

Bibi's grief (*uchungu*)

As Bibi continued to suffer intensively from *vidonda vya tumbo* (stomach wounds), she was often admonished by her relatives that she should try not to cry so much about the deaths of her husband and two of her children, as this was causing more *nyongo* (a bile-like substance) to accumulate in her stomach. The *nyongo* was in turn understood to eat away at her stomach lining, leading over time to the formation of "ulcers." My interlocuters explained to me that grief is felt primarily in the stomach, the seat of all social relations. For this reason, at funerals, women closest to the deceased frequently tie a piece of cloth around their waists to stabilize and strengthen this wounded area of their bodies; wounded because, as one friend put it to me, "the network has been cut." Bibi knew that her grief increased the *nyongo* in her body, so when I went into town, she would often ask me to buy her Rabeloc, a proton pump inhibitor that works by reducing the production of acid in the stomach. Her daughter and son-in-law, however, were concerned that Rabeloc was turning poisonous after reacting with the chewing tobacco that Bibi stubbornly refused to give up. They worried that the Rabeloc was "*kula*" (eating) Bibi's stomach lining as well.

To understand Bibi's *uchungu*, it is important to grasp something of the significance of bitterness more generally. The Swahili term "*uchungu*" is used to refer to bitter tastes and was originally of interest to me during fieldwork because it was used to index powerful medicines – both herbal and pharmaceutical. A classic example of this is the very bitter tasting tree called *mwarobaini*, from the word "forty" (*arobaini* in Swahili), so-called because its leaves, bark, and roots are said to treat 40 illnesses. I think about the taste of such medicines in connection with Judith Farquhar's (1994) work on traditional medicine in China, where tastes like bitterness are also understood to index a substance's embodied effects. Additionally, tasting, insofar as it involves eating, is of both moral and social significance, because acts of consuming the labor of others are the foundation of forming relations and becoming persons in Tanzania. Across Africa, the "stomach is considered the site of human personality and agency. Social relations are considered in terms of eating" (Stoller 1997: 7). My increasing awareness of how fundamental tasting and eating were to notions of well-being among my interlocuters helped attune me to other uses of the term "*uchungu*," which, besides meaning bitterness, is also evoked to speak of certain types of pain, including chronic suffering, child birth, and grief. By contrast, the

Swahili term "*maumivu*" refers to physical pain, like that caused by an injury or wound, and does not carry the same moral and social significance.

Bibi understood her "ulcers" to be a result of *uchungu* (grief). By employing this term, she was not only referring to her "ulcers" as a kind of chronic suffering, though this connotation was surely evoked. Rather, Bibi specifically referenced the loss of her husband and two of her children as experiences which caused and/or exacerbated her "ulcers." With increasing frequency during my fieldwork, she would lay in bed crying and say that she was in so much pain that she would be better off dying. She would implore God to take her. This is what precipitated our trip to Hitech Sai Healthcare Center in Dar es Salaam in December 2014, where the technician performed the endoscopy and found some red spots (indicative of gastritis), but no ulcers, and left Bibi with the explanation that he saw *michumbuku* (scratches). As noted above, this diagnosis only reinforced Bibi's perception of having the wounds of grief in her stomach.

When we saw the doctor at Hitech Sai Healthcare Center, he prescribed Bibi two months of Rabeloc (rabeprazole sodium – 20mg) to be taken twice a day, 30 minutes before eating. Rabeloc is a proton-pump inhibitor (PPI) that reduces stomach acid and that is used to treat duodenal ulcers and gastroesophageal reflux disease. Although this drug never seemed to make any significant difference for Bibi's overall condition – and although I now "knew" that she did not have ulcers (as I understood them) – I continued to purchase it for her, at her request, for the following year, long after the original two months prescription had run out. Bibi also sometimes requested omeprazole capsules, which, biomedically, is prescribed for gastroesophageal reflux and peptic ulcers.

Meanwhile, the source of Bibi's stomach pain was a topic of much debate and conflict in the Muro household: her daughter and son-in-law frequently insisted that Bibi's "ulcers" were in some way of her own doing. At one point, Mrs. Muro even implored us (the other women living in the household) not to buy any more ulcer medicine for Bibi. And yet, Bibi was very wily. After that, Bibi would tell me that her throat hurt and that she wanted me to buy her those omeprazole capsules to help treat her throat "like amoxicillin." Sometimes Bibi would cajole me into getting her some pills and then hide the little brown envelope of pills in a windowsill or in the pantry off the kitchen. When I finally asked her, "Bibi, what's this *really* for?", she said, "for *nyongo*" (bile), and reassured me that she does not take the pills every day, but just when she really needs them. She really needed them on the days when her grief became too much, causing an over-production of *nyongo* in her stomach; that acidic substance then "ate" her insides, as revealed by the scratches the doctor saw that day.

In addition to consuming pharmaceuticals, the other practice that Bibi frequently engaged in to reduce her *nyongo* was forcing herself to throw up. I frequently awoke to the sounds of her doing this in the morning, in the bathroom across the hallway from my bedroom. She would say: "*kutapika ni safi*," to throw up is clean/good. She lamented the fact that one could no longer find a certain pharmaceutical which used to be commonly available around 40 years ago and that folks used to consume to induce vomiting. Instead, the drugs these days just add more poison to the body, rather than removing it, she would complain. One of my research assistants, George, would also tell me that he knew his malaria medicine was working well and that he was getting better if it caused him to vomit. Here, vomiting is not a "side-effect," as we may be accustomed to knowing it, but, rather, it is an essential element of the treatment and cure (see Etkin 1992).

Much "traditional" medical treatments in Tanzania (herbal and/or spiritual) work by inducing vomiting and diarrhea, which clean out the body and remove poisons – including poisons caused by witchcraft and by the *mazingira* (social/ physical environment). Sometimes when Bibi knew I was going to interview a traditional healer, she would also ask me to purchase this kind of medicine for her, too. Once when I gave her Maasai herbs that I was instructed would give her severe diarrhea, I asked, "Bibi, isn't this *mateso* (torture)?", to which she replied emphatically, "*Hapana, hata leo, nilikuwa na nyongo njano, njano, njano! Kuharisha ni safi!*" ("No, even today, I had yellow, yellow, yellow bile! To have diarrhea is clean!").[4] Below, I will go into more detail about Bibi's life and the history of purging as health intervention, but for now I want to highlight how PPIs were incorporated into local bodily schema and notions of well-being.

As medical anthropologists have long argued, Western medical knowledges and objects, far from being value-free phenomena, are grounded in local cultural conditions, becoming something new as they travel and enter into different worlds, where they are reshaped by geographically and historically situated processes (Etkin 1992; Petryna, Lakoff, and Kleinman 2006). Moreover, in plural medical contexts, the boundaries between discrete categories of knowledge and practices are often blurred and purposefully left ambiguous by patients and healers alike (Dilger, Kane, and Langwick 2012; Ecks 2013). This requires us to move beyond the notion of distinct epistemic categories sustained by earlier ethno-medical studies of local medical systems that sought to understand interpretive systems of illness in isolation.

Indeed, Indian Ocean scholarship reveals how biomedicine and "traditional" medicine have been coproduced through encounters such as colonization, missionization, trade and commerce, and international development (Winterbottom and Tesfaye 2016a, 2016b). As I demonstrated in this section, Bibi's self-fashioned treatment – which involved the somewhat interchangible use of PPI pharmaceuticals, periodic vomiting, and herbal remedies – reveals how healing regimes comingle and produce new entanglements in ways that cannot adequately be captured by appeals to "medical pluralism" or "hybridity". In the following two sections, I expand upon the significance of eating and bitterness across multiple, entangled healing regimes, arguing that Bibi's embodied practices construct Indian Ocean worlds in and through her body, even when separated through time and space from some of the places they call forth.

Land and personhood

In October 2015, about ten months after our trip to Hitech Sai Healthcare Centre, I was walking home from the town market and came upon Bibi sitting outside the property on a large bolder at the side of the road, about one house down from ours. I surmised that she was chewing *ugoro* (tobacco) and trying to do so in secret as both Mr. and Mrs. Muro chastised her for using the substance. While her daughter seemed primarily concerned with how Bibi's desire (*hamu*) for tobacco could leave her vulnerable to nefarious forces like jinn (a perennial concern for members of their Evangelical congregation), Mr. Muro tended to stress more how chewing tobacco was a traditionally male activity and that Bibi's use of it was thus improper. Thus, her choice to sit on the boulder off the property – seemingly the most banal practice – is actually quite significant as it reflects the broader strains of changing religious, gender, and generational norms in this family and in Tanzanian society more broadly. While men may have *hamu* for cigarettes and chewing tobacco, women – when enacting proper gender norms – are expected to have *hamu* for other kinds of substances, such as *udongo* (soil), which is often eaten by pregnant women. As I have elaborated more elsewhere (Meek 2019), Bibi's masculine *hamu* may index in some ways Mr. Muro's lost control and authority in the home.

When I sat down next to Bibi on an adjacent boulder, she immediately asked me what I had in my bag from the market. I pulled out two bananas and we chatted as we each ate one. I asked her what she misses from her village in the Manyara Region of northern Tanzania; she told me about her banana trees, many other fruit trees like guava and avocados, vegetables, and her family's large plot of corn. Bibi explained that she had been a farmer (*mkulima*) all her life and that her family cultivates over four acres of crops. It was during this conversation that I realized that Bibi's grief was not only over the loss of her husband and children, but also over the loss of the land to which she was deeply connected. As I explore in this section, her connection to land – and her ties to her deceased kin – materialized in her body through the quale of bitterness. I came to understand her *uchungu* as a present-absence, a relation with that loss which was taking a piece of her with it, but without which she could not be.

Bibi was born in 1937, the second of six children, and was very proud of the fact that her father had recorded this in the front of their family Bible – as her parents had both converted to become Lutheran. Her family is ethnically Chagga, from the Manyara Region in northern Tanzania, an area that is well known for growing bananas as a staple crop and for having received missionary education early on, with a legacy that today many Chagga are employed in business and government positions.

When I asked about what medicine was like when Bibi was young, she first told me that "there was no medicine." She said: "*sikujua sindano*," meaning "I didn't know the syringe." This phrasing is significant as injections are widely considered to epitomize the dangers of biomedicine (White 2000). Bibi said that she never had malaria until just a few years ago and that there were no mosquitos

Figure 12.1 Bibi with her great-granddaughter.
Image credit: Laura Meek.

in Manyara when she was younger. A big smile lit up her face as she recalled that the government started insisting that they use mosquito nets anyway; when they were distributed in her community, people "used them for the chickens." Nets were laid over the chicks to keep them together in one place. Other times people repurposed them into ropes to tie up goats, Bibi added.

The most important treatment that existed during Bibi's youth was a preventive technique practiced annually when the corn (*mahindi*) reached maturity. Everyone in the community would eat a certain medicine that caused diarrhea and cleaned out the intestines. After a hospital was built in their region, they would go there to buy medicines that had this same medicinal capacity, especially "*salti na kastor oli*" (salt and castor oil) – both of which could be used to induce diarrhea. Bibi lamented that these medicines no longer exist in Tanzania today. She explained that if one's stomach was clean, one would never need medicine; one could simply ingest these substances two or three times a year to cleanse the stomach and maintain a state of well-being. This same logic of purifying the body was at work, of course, when Bibi vomited to remove excess *nyongo* (bile) from her stomach. Part of the perceived danger of pharmaceuticals, I was often told – by elders, youth, and doctors of all kinds – was that they *add* poisons to the body, rather than cleansing it as medicine is supposed to do.

When I asked Bibi what she thought was making people less well these days than in the past, she answered, like many elders do, that "things coming from outside the country are causing disease." Such globalization has affected all aspects of life, but there are two areas in which changes are seen as especially deleterious: *hali ya hewa* (weather) and *vyakula* (diet). As an example of the latter, Bibi mentioned "*mafuta*" (oil), especially Korie, a brand of refined palm oil produced by Murzah Oil Mills in Dar es Salaam, Tanzania. Before such products began flooding the market during the time of structural adjustment (1980s–1990s), people in Manyara typically used animal fat for cooking. When Bibi was a young girl, her father "went to a place and saw a slaughtered cow; got the fat of the cow and took it home to her mom, who would boil it and put it aside to use for cooking." Now, Bibi does not know where the oil in the shops is coming from. Crucially, not knowing from *where* a food comes also means not knowing from *whom*. Thus, the Korie oil comes from "outside," not in the sense that it is literally manufactured in another country, but in that its production and circulation transpire outside the productive relationships between people that make certain foods nourishing.

As my conversations with Bibi continued, I learned more about the significance of food and eating in producing and nurturing people. Bibi and her husband had seven children, of which only the last child was born in a hospital. All the previous births took place at home, with a midwife and other women present, including her mother-in-law, mother, and neighbors. After each birth, Bibi gave the umbilical cord to her mother-in-law to plant beneath a banana tree for the child. The adult child now owns that tree, "so Mama Muro has a tree there!", Bibi exclaimed. This practice creates a material connection between the life of the child and the land, such that what it means to be a person is to be in relation to and connected to a specific place. This helps elucidate why returning bodies home to that land for burial is such a crucially important practice in Tanzania. I understood Bibi's longing for her land through this lens as well, as more than just boredom or restlessness in the absence of meaningful activity to occupy her time (though it was also that). I understood her desire to return home as symptomatic of her alienation from kin and land, the very relations that make someone a person. And yet, perhaps ironically, it was her kin who prohibited her return – for her daughter feared that if Bibi returned home, she would give in to her *uchungu* and pass away there. It sometimes seemed that the physical presence of Mrs. Muro caught Bibi in a relational obligation, in a form of care which was perhaps also violent in its refusal to let her go.

When we discussed the origins of Bibi's current health problems, she explained that her "ulcers" came to her due to the shock (*mshtuko*) of the death of loved ones. Although the acid started "coming" in 1992, it only became severe after the death of her young son in 1994. Her sixth child, this boy was living with Mrs. Muro, his sister, while he attended grade school, when one day he was suddenly overcome with intense stomach pain. Although his condition required surgery, it was too late when he finally arrived at the hospital. Maybe his appendix burst, Bibi speculated.[5] His family brought his body back to Manyara to be buried.

Then, less than two years later, in 1996, Bibi's husband died, causing her to feel "*moto*" (fire or burning) in her stomach. Her husband had received an operation at a major regional hospital because "his intestines were twisting." He survived the surgery and returned home, but then fell ill again and passed away about one month later. Only a few years after this, in 2002, Bibi's first child was taken by uterine cancer. This last death caused Bibi to experience "*mawazo*" – a condition which is loosely akin to severe "stress" – and it was this *mawazo* which inflamed the "ulcers" until they became unbearable.

Bibi's narrative reveals the intercorporeality of kinship: her "ulcers" changed over time in dynamic relation to transformations in the bodies of her husband and children. Additionally, her life history illuminates the ways in which people are in and of the land – forged in "their place" (*mahali kwao*). In ordinary conversation, this is often connoted with the word for "place" left implicit – i.e., one says, "she has returned to their" (*amerudi kwao*). People grow out of a particular place – even a particular tree, as we have seen – and it is to that land that they must return when they become ancestors. There they can continue their relations, receiving *sadaka* (sacrifice/offerings) from their living kin. As I write this, I imagine that this is what Bibi is doing these days, now that *amerudi kwao*.

Eating as relationality across Indian Ocean worlds

This account of Bibi's *uchungu* demonstrates how the chronic "ulcers" she suffered from are openings into her life history and, here I will argue, into Indian Ocean worlds more broadly. As introduced above, one of the key arguments of this chapter is that worlds come into being through embodied practices, thus inverting our oft taken-for-granted assumption that bodies are emplaced within worlds that already pre-exist their enactment. I contend that Indian Ocean worlds are not merely inert containers within which action transpires, but, rather, dynamic and nonlinear spatial-temporal relations which are continually re/produced via intercorporeal and intergenerational becomings, congealing into worlds as certain practices, qualities, and meanings clot over time. Crucial to these becomings are understandings of wellness, the body, and its sensoriums; such understandings are surely multiple and divergent, yet also partially connected across Indian Ocean worlds.

Attention to medicine and healing is just now developing within Indian Ocean Studies; most notably, Anna Winterbottom and Facil Tesfaye published two volumes to explicitly conceptualize the interconnections of medical treatments (2016a, 2016b). They argue for the Indian Ocean as a coherent region based upon a shared physical geography (i.e., monsoon season, contagious diseases), which they posit in turn enabled a common set of therapies and medicines to have circulated along trade routes in the region for centuries. My approach here differs from their contribution in that I conceptualize the embodiment of qualia like bitterness as worlding practices which can re/produce Indian Ocean worlds in any region or geographical locale. Might we then think of Indian Ocean worlds as connected to – but not simply isomorphic with – the Indian Ocean as a geographical area or region?

Far from being antagonistic to Winterbottom and Tesfaye's proposal, I think this methodological intervention builds upon an argument that they make in their introduction when they allude to Merleau-Ponty's notion of the "world of perception" (2016a: 27). They point out that "[m]any of the societies around the Indian Ocean shared some form of "humoral" theory, based on ideas of the balance of hot, cold, wet, and dry elements in the body and the environment and healing according to the theory of opposites" (2016a: 11). It is this shared humoral conceptualization of the body – in terms of balance, opposites, and/or in relation to the environment/elements (2016a: 11) – that allows scholars to speak of a shared "world," based upon such phenomenological similarities. I, too, am interested in forms of embodiment across Indian Ocean worlds, but from a somewhat different point of departure: the alimentary.

In her writing on the alimentary in India, Parama Roy (2010) explores how the sensorium around eating involves desires, tastes, disgusts, and appetites which constitute a kind of "bodily grammar" that can be read to understand colonial and postcolonial relations in South Asia and beyond. Broadly speaking, her work investigates how violent colonial relations transformed habitus for both the colonized and colonizer. The resonances between the eating Roy writes about in India and the kinds of eating I have explored here do not necessarily lie in the similarity of the practices themselves, but in an attunement to the intercorporeality of bodies and their mutual consumption of each other as a framework for articulating forms of relationality. Roy notes that eating is "more than an exercise in self-augmentation or self-possession; it can be an experience of vulnerability, uncertainty, and dependence … the body in alimentation stages the fraught relationship between an inside and an outside whose boundaries are not always known or fixed, and between subject and object status" (2010: 194). Her approach offers a conceptual opening for understanding the varied power relationships within practices of eating, as tasting and eating can be simultaneously forms of both care and violence.

By approaching Bibi's *uchungu* in this way, we can recognize the multiple valences of consumption in her story: when pregnant, she ate *udongo* (earth) in order to produce the right types of transformations – ones that enable and strengthen kin relations – as the land nourishes the developing child; later, when those relations were torn apart, in grief, the wounds of that loss manifested in her body as *uchungu*, its acidic bile violently eating at her stomach to form "ulcers." Even *uchungu* itself is multiple in Bibi's account: *uchungu* long ago provided Bibi the strength to give birth: recall that *uchungu* also refers to the painful and transformative power of child labor. This power has now turned caustic as a result of her children dying before her, reversing the proper relations between generations. The violent presence of wrenched, deceased children ate away at Bibi's stomach, inverting the manner in which their earlier presence was nurtured by the earth (*udongo*) they ate through her. Eating, as a form of relating, thus defies alimentary binaries like nourishing or poisonous, nurturing or caustic.

A methodological proposal

The methodology I have pursued here – involving sustained relations not just of long-term research but also of care and obligation – can open up new ways of apprehending and thinking about connections across Indian Ocean worlds. It was only through being caught (see endnote 2) that I came to learn that "ulcers" were not ulcers, that *uchungu* is not simply bitterness (but also grief and child labor), and that stomachs can be connected through intercorporeal formations of kinship and land. These insights may also provide new avenues of research for understanding Afro-Asian connections today: for instance, might part of the appeal of Chinese remedies in East Africa stem from shared (divergent and yet partially connected) humoral understandings of the body and/or attributions of medicinal potency to the quale of bitterness?

Certainly, the importance of bitterness is clear in Bibi's account – both as the condition that afflicted her (*uchungu*) and as a quale of its treatment. This resonates with traditional Chinese medicine in which "flavors are also an expression of the roles of drugs, different flavors having different functions" (Farquhar 1994: 472). Judith Farquhar notes that there is no sharp demarcation between food and medicine in China; they are embodied through a similar "aesthetics of habitus" (1994: 481). Such similitudes between Chinese and Tanzanian notions of medical effectiveness and bodily experience have arisen amidst recent and longer histories of Afro-Asian connections. From the 1960s to 1980s, the non-aligned socialist Tanzanian state explicitly sought to model its healthcare policies after China, whose approach to integrating traditional medicine and biomedicine served as a model of self-reliance for the new nation. The two countries formed the Joint Tanzanian and Chinese Project on Traditional Medicine and sent delegates of students and doctors back and forth between their respective countries to learn from each other (Langwick 2010). These relations continued even after the economic liberalization of the 1990s, in part because the Tanzanian state began to view China as again a model – this time for turning traditional herbal remedies into marketable commodities (Langwick 2010: 29).

In accounting for the popularity of Chinese traditional remedies within Tanzania, Elisabeth Hsu posited that Chinese medical clinics appear to

Tanzanians to exist in a middle ground between "Western"/"scientific" and "traditional"/"magical," thus infusing them with multivalent symbolic capital. For instance, she notes that some of her interviewees in Tanzania mentioned that Chinese remedies were made from herbs, but that their appearance, "in pill or tablet form, aluminum foil or plastic packages, made them similar to biomedical drugs" (Hsu 2002: 307). One limitation I see to such approaches, however, is that the researcher here has predetermined in advance what categories come to matter in the use of such medicines: traditional, modern, scientific, local, and so on. Such methodologies – based on formal interviews, for instance – may delimit the possible responses in advance, precluding the existence of embodied resonances which operate in ways that cannot be captured by such Western binaries.

The methodological proposal I suggest here allows us to apprehend how Indian Ocean worlds are produced via bodily sensoriums for which Euro-American understandings of the senses as the passive recipients of data are insufficient. Work on sensoriums across Indian Ocean worlds demonstrates how tasting and eating figure centrally as embodied epistemological, aesthetic, and moral practices – from across the African continent (Geurts 2002; Stoller 1997) to India (Ecks 2013; Roy 2010) and China (Farquhar 1994). In these sites, senses participate in the active construction of knowledge, relations, bodies, kin, and their worlds. Scholarly attunement – including our own embodied attunement – to these sensoriums may therefore open new avenues for theorizing relationality across Indian Ocean worlds. Meanwhile, the insights this generates within Indian Ocean Studies are poised to offer crucial contributions to broader theoretical trends in the humanities and social sciences which increasingly approach eating as a way to theorize relationality (Mol 2008; Strathern 2012; Wilson 2015).

Conclusion

This chapter offers a methodological provocation – to think of Indian Ocean worlds as connected to, but not simply isomorphic with, the Indian Ocean as a geographical region. Not only does this approach offer something new to Indian Ocean Studies; it simultaneously brings the insights of that field to bear on concerns within my primary field – medical anthropology. For instance, we might consider anew Arthur Kleinman's reflections in his seminal work on illness narratives, including his poignant observation that the "trajectory of chronic illness assimilates to a life course, contributing so intimately to the development of a particular life that illness becomes inseparable from life history" (1988: 8). I propose extending this insight beyond life history to ask how Bibi's *uchungu* may also be understood as a worlding practice. Bibi's "ulcers" enact changing Indian Ocean worlds at many different scales simultaneously. To provide just a few examples, her *uchungu* bespeaks:

- the economic liberalization of healthcare in the region, where it is increasingly necessary for patients to travel great distance to receive the care they seek – evidenced here by the nine hours we drove for Bibi's endoscopy;

- tensions from changing gender roles as Bibi is blamed for exacerbating her *uchungu* by chewing tobacco, an accusation which also reminds her of her place in the home and forces her to leave it to chew in secret;
- phenomenological experiences of grief and loss, which stem not only from physical deaths, but also from a longing for land, home, and proximity to a distant yet viscerally embodied lifeworld;
- the interactions of intertwined, yet incongruent, healing regimes – as demonstrated here through Bibi's interchangible use of PPI pharmaceuticals, periodic vomiting, and herbal remedies;
- and, finally, deeply rooted notions of personhood as formed in and through embodied connections to place and kin.

Many of these themes appear in the other contributions to this text, but I would argue that fine-grained scholarship on the body, well-being, and illness can illuminate contemporary socio-cultural and political-economic formations of Indian Ocean worlds in a unique way. Analyzing such quotidian and embodied practices requires a different kind of methodology – one that starts from the most minute details of a life and then asks what worlds such forms of life call forth.

I propose that Indian Ocean worlds are held together by divergent yet resonant practices, which – sustained and repeated – produce the embodied qualities that enable certain forms of life and well-being. While much Indian Ocean scholarship focuses on the ways in which geographically distant locals are connected physically across space, my work reveals how the qualia that comprise a world may also inhere in a single place, home, family, and even, body. Indeed, I argue that properties as seemingly banal as bitterness can hold together a shared world; that Indian Ocean worlds exist through the practices and bodies worlding them. In this sense, Indian Ocean worlds are not merely containers within which people, things, and ideas circulate; these worlds can and do move, appearing not only along coastal communities, but also – as here – materializing in inland communities like the Southern Highlands of Tanzania. Indian Ocean worlds are made through worlding practices in and across diverse geographical locations, as bodies carry worlds within them, producing worlds as, in, and through, embodied qualities that call forth diverse yet partially connected forms of life.

Notes

1 I have used pseudonyms to protect the identities of my interlocuters. Everyone mentioned herein has consented to participate in my research and to their stories and experiences being written about by me. This material is based on over two years of ethnographic fieldwork I conducted in Tanzania from 2013–2016. My larger research project concerned the uses and understandings of pharmaceuticals among biomedical practitioners, traditional healers, and lay people in a semi-urban area of the Southern Highlands. I would like to express my gratitude to the National Science Foundation, the "Reimagining Indian Ocean Worlds" Mellon Research Initiative, the University of California, and the Wenner-Gren Foundation for funding that supported this project.

2 As I developed close ties in the community, I frequently became caught in the ethical obligations that illness demands of one's relations, especially when I fell sick or when a family member I lived with did. Following Favret-Saada, I understand being "caught" as a form of participation that attunes one to a particular experience through being affected by it (1990: 194).

3 This method for approaching Indian Ocean Studies in terms of theoretical relationality rather than geographically grew out of dialogues which took place at the Reimagining Indian Ocean Worlds Mellon Research Initiative at the University of California, Davis. I am indebted to Neelima Jeychandran, Bettina Ng'weno, and Smriti Srinivas for proposing this innovative rethinking of what makes a "world."

4 This word for "clean," *safi*, is also commonly used to mean "good" more generally.

5 Bibi had her own appendix removed in the 1960s and considered her back pain to be a result of the spinal cord injection of anesthesia that she received for that operation, again signifying the dangers of syringes (see White 2000).

References

Das, Veena. 2013. Neighbors and Acts of Silent Kindness. *HAU: Journal of Ethnographic Theory* 3(1): 217–20.

Dilger, Hansjoerg, Abdoulaye Kane, and Stacey Langwick, eds. 2012. *Medicine, Mobility & Power in Global Africa*. Bloomington, IN: Indiana University Press.

Ecks, Stefan. 2013. *Eating Drugs: Psychopharmaceutical Pluralism in India*. New York, NY: New York University Press.

Etkin, Nina L. 1992. "Side Effects": Cultural Constructions and Reinterpretations of Western Pharmaceuticals. *Medical Anthropology Quarterly, New Series* 6(2): 99–113.

Farquhar, Judith. 1994. Eating Chinese Medicine. *Cultural Anthropology* 9(4): 471–497.

Favret-Saada, Jeanne. 1990. About Participation. *Culture, Medicine and Psychiatry* 14: 189–199.

Feinstein, Sheryl and Nicole C. D'Errico. 2010. *Tanzanian Women in their Own Words: Stories of Disability and Illness*. New York, NY: Lexington Books.

Garcia, Angela. 2010. *The Pastoral Clinic: Addiction and Dispossession Along the Rio Grande*. Berkeley, CA: University of California Press.

Geurts, Kathryn Linn. 2002. *Culture and the Senses: Bodily Ways of Knowing in an African Community*. Berkeley, CA: University of California Press.

Han, Clara. 2012. *Life in Debt: Times of Care and Violence in Neoliberal Chile*. Berkeley, CA: University of California Press.

Hsu, Elisabeth. 2002. "The Medicine from China Has Rapid Effects": Chinese Medicine Patients in Tanzania. *Anthropology & Medicine* 9(3): 291–313.

Kleinman, Arthur. 1988. *Illness Narratives: Suffering, Healing, and the Human Condition*. New York, NY: Basic Books.

Langwick, Stacey. 2010. From Non-Aligned Medicines to Market-Based Herbals: China's Relationship to the Shifting Politics of Traditional Medicine in Tanzania. *Medical Anthropology* 29(1): 15–43.

Meek, Laura. 2019. Pharmaceuticals in Divergence: Embodied Experiments and World-Making Tastes in Tanzania. *PhD Dissertation*. University of California, Davis. ProQuest (18883).

Mol, Annemarie. 2008. I Eat an Apple: On Theorizing Subjectivities. *Subjectivity* 22: 28–37.

Munn, Nancy. 1986. *The Fame of Gawa: A Symbolic Study of Value Transformation in a Massim (Papua New Guinea) Society*. Durham, NC: Duke University Press.

Petryna, Adriana, Andrew Lakoff, and Arthur Kleinman, eds. 2006. *Global Pharmaceuticals: Ethics, Markets, Practices*. Durham, NC: Duke University Press.

Povinelli, Elizabeth. 2011. *Economies of Abandonment: Social Belonging and Endurance in Late Liberalism*. Durham, NC: Duke University Press.

Roy, Parama. 2010. *Alimentary Tracts: Appetites, Aversions and the Postcolonial*. Durham, NC: Duke University Press.

Stoller, Paul. 1997. *Sensuous Scholarship*. Philadelphia, PA: University of Pennsylvania Press.

Strathern, Marilyn. 2012. Eating (and Feeding). *Cambridge Anthropology* 30(2): 1–14.

White, Luise. 2000. *Speaking with Vampires: Rumor and History in Colonial Africa*. Berkeley, CA: University of California Press.

Wilson, Elizabeth. 2015. *Gut Feminism*. Durham, NC: Duke University Press.

Winterbottom, Anna and Facil Tesfaye, eds. 2016a. *Histories of Medicine and Healing in the Indian Ocean World, Volume One: The Medieval and Early Modern Period*. New York, NY: Palgrave Macmillan.

Winterbottom, Anna and Facil Tesfaye. 2016b. *Histories of Medicine and Healing in the Indian Ocean World, Volume Two: The Modern Period*. New York, NY: Palgrave Macmillan.

13 *Marfa masti*

Performing shifting Indian Ocean geographies

Pallavi Sriram

In a narrow courtyard, a bright retro red and yellow speaker-mobile frames a semi-circle of young men playing large double-sided barrel dhol drums with their hands, steel pots, one keyboard, and the essential wide mouth marfa *(kettle drum). Kids and men surround them and with the resounding opening beats of the band's signature nagin (snake-charmer) tune, they stream into the open space between them. A chubby young boy bursts in with his arms up, back and forth with the beat, shoulders popping, a cheeky grin on his face *dinka chika dink achika din*. A young man looking suave in suit and tie – in this case, the groom of the wedding of which this band is playing in the courtyard of – showers rupee notes into the group, towards the boy. Jabri Bin, the leader of the band, turns and plays, beckoning, pulling the man in and ... all of a sudden, the man too dives into the beat with arms up as everyone cheers. As more people start dancing, sweaty crowded and cheering, another man pops into the frame with two short jambiya daggers extending his waving-circling arms precariously into the space over bopping heads, sometimes between, taking notes in his mouth as he dances to cheers and hugs. The clip, like most YouTube videos of* marfa *bands/parties, ends abruptly in the midst of noise, color, drumming, sweaty bodies and waving daggers, leaving us to imagine the rest of the event and its aftermaths ... or to look for the next clip.*

Marfa dance and music are distinctly Hyderabadi and yet far more complicated in their located-ness than the term implies. *Marfa* is a social dance and music form in Hyderabad, South India, adapted from Afro-Arabic music through the Hadramawt region in Yemen. Simultaneously complicating notions of (South) Indian-ness, African-ness, and Arab-ness, the spaces and gestures of *marfa* or daff parties allow us to think not about "cultural identities" as static markers – a distinctly (post)colonial construction – but about networks of relationality. Drawing together African diasporic culture, South Indian Muslim self-representation, popular entertainment, and displaced histories of Afro-South Asian connectivity, *marfa* is a relational choreography of Indian Ocean connections that are processual, historically contingent, and dynamic.

Scholarship on African diaspora in India has focused on ritual practices in western India, especially associated with the African Sufi saint Bava Gor in Gujarat and Karnataka. Amy Catlin-Jairazbhoy, Helene Basu, and Beheroze

Shroff have documented music as part of spirit possession and ritual ceremonies with explicit or submerged Africana religious roots – particularly
roots in East Africa (Basu 2008; Catlin-Jairazbhoy 2010, 2002, 2003, 2004;
Shroff 2013). Sidi communities on the western coast have been seen and
staged in ways that are legible as African in part because of their proximity to
the Indian Ocean littoral.[1] Their visibility as African is due in part to Indian
national interest in sports recruitment from the 1980s. The Sports Authority of
India started the Special Area Games (SAG) scheme to identify and train
those considered to exhibit "natural physical aptitude" for sporting events in
communities in the tribal, rural, hilly, and coastal regions of the country,
which centrally included identifying African-origin people in the rural parts of
western India.

However, little attention has been paid to African presence further east, particularly in the South Indian state of Telangana. The communities discussed here
are not recognizably framed and performed as "African" in the way those of
western India are. Afro-Indian communities in Hyderabad reflect complex histories of movement mediated through the Arabic world. African diaspora known
as Sidi, and Hadrami diaspora (from the Hadramawt region in Yemen) known as
Chaush both have a long and deeply intertwined history in the city. Hyderabad,
the capital city of Telangana, reflects a western Indian Ocean site far from
the littoral – thus offering a different kind of insight into movement beyond the
oceanic. In this chapter, I turn to connections between the horn of Africa, the
Hadramawt and the central part of South Asia known as the Deccan, of which
Hyderabad is a part.

Historically, the Deccan has been a significant space of cultural exchange and
hybrid milieus. Though African presence in Hyderabad is colloquially traced
back to the late eighteenth century regime known as the Nizamate, there is a
longer history in which those from East Africa were central to the geopolitics
and cultural milieu of the Deccan, especially from the fifteenth century. Changing imperial geographies – the decline of the Mughal empire and increasing
British East India Company presence from the late eighteenth century –
however, changed the Deccan's relationship to Indian Ocean circulations and
the role that East Africans played in Deccani public spheres. Hyderabad's relationship to Indian Ocean circulations weren't eradicated by colonial histories,
however. Today, Sidi and Hadrami men move to the Gulf to work while families
remain in Hyderabad. Beyond networks of labor and economy, there are additional connections – specifically popular dance and music. Young people create
new circulations and connected social imaginaries in popular dance and music,
through the possibilities of new media online. M*arfa* dance and music practices
are not explicitly associated with ritual and religion. They are social practices,
occurring at weddings, public celebrations, and the digital social sphere. The
question remains open – what are *marfa*'s relationship to these longue duree histories of circulation?

This chapter starts in the seventeenth century Deccan with representations of
performing Afro-Indian bodies in poetry-inscribed miniature paintings. I tease

apart the relationship between African performance presence, military, and urban spaces of Sultanate fort cities. Then, framed by Mughal and colonial histories which shifted the ethnic geography of Hyderabad and its relations to the broader Indian Ocean, I turn to *marfa* performance in the present. Referencing Sidi and Chaush military histories, *marfa* physicalizes older points of military in the Deccan through its rhythms and gestures. More importantly, I suggest that *marfa* as a social dynamic which traverses physical and virtual spaces, enlivens older logics of circulation and relationality across the Indian Ocean. Turning specifically to YouTube videos and the self-fashioning of *marfa* youth on other social medias, the analytic of geo-tagging is central to understanding the way young people choreograph identity and place in surprising innovative ways. While the digital media they utilize are relatively new, the relationship between performance and media is neither entirely new nor fully understandable through existing Western-centric studies of media and globalization. In this study, both early modern painting and twenty-first century YouTube are understood as media – forms of assemblage and visual codes of translocation, drawing together not just bodily gesture but frames of meaning-making around performance.

While "diaspora" assumes a shared notion of homeland,[2] and "transnational" presumes the political and performative configuration of the nation, this chapter proposes the translocal as key. Ayona Datta and Katherine Brickell define translocality as the "simultaneous situated-ness across different locales" (Brickell and Datta 2011: 4). While I am not interested in simultaneity, I am interested in relationships across specific cities and regions – an important question in the Indian Ocean context. *Marfa* or *daff* elide easy originary locations and instead choreograph the slippages between "African," "Arabic," "Muslim," and "Hyderabadi" as identity formations. Rather than searching for origins through the gestures and rhythms of *marfa*, I am interested in how performing bodies mediate multiple sets of circulation and belonging, producing cultures of relationalities.

Sitting at the intersection of dance studies and critical cultural studies, I hope this work opens new methodological possibilities for understanding the contemporary Indian Ocean world. Dance as corporeal practice, Hyderabad as site, and an attention to the longue duree through multiple media offer a distinct set of entry points. I consider dance as process or as acts of coming-into-relation through gesture, rhythm, orientation to space, and participation (Dils and Albright 2001; Foster 1996; Hamera 2006a). I propose that dance and music choreograph place and media into translocal imaginaries – at once local and operating beyond the local – constituting shifting "performative geographies" over time. Often lying outside official archives of the state and perhaps not even easily narrativized in terms of personal life-stories, dance offers fragmentary and contingent engagements with pasts and other places. Attending to these dynamics allow us to de-essentialize cultural identities, including South Asian notions of blackness. We can move towards new understandings of identity, locatedness, and mobility across the contemporary Indian Ocean.

Figure 13.1 "An African Lyre Player" (recto), calligraphy (verso).

Image credit: Unknown Artist, *c*.1640–1660. Cleveland Museum of Art (www.clevelandart.org/art/2013.289, accessed June 3, 2016).

Afro-Asia in the seventeenth century Deccan – courtly elite and a Sufi lyre player

Dense networks of political, economic, and material movements have shaped multiple urban milieus across the Indian Ocean littoral over centuries – from Mombasa and Zanzibar, the Mediterranean basin, both coasts of the South Asian subcontinent (Gujarat, Malabar, Coromandel, Bengal) to Southeast Asia with Malacca, Jakarta, and Penang. Men from the Eastern and horn of Africa came to South Asia as sailors, traders, and soldiers – both as independent agents and through systems of slavery. In the vertical system of military dynasties, (Cairo, Ghaznavids, Delhi, Abbasid), primarily foreign-origin men thus recruited could become kings and members of the ruling elite (Chatterjee and Eaton 2006).[3] Men from not just east Africa – from the Christian kingdom of Abyssinia – but eastern Europe and central Asia moved this way. For example, Jacob Young was a Hungarian taken by Turks as a slave and became part of the retinue of Khodja Murad, a seventeenth-century diplomat to the Mughal court from the Ethiopian court (Foster 1921).

From the sixteenth century, Abyssinian men centrally helped define the politics and culture of the Deccan– as political leaders, king-makers, and city founders (Ali 1996; Alpers 2009; Robbins and McLeod 2006). Malik Ambar, born in Harar (in Ethiopia) to an Oromo family, was brought through Baghdad to an Abyssinian statesman in the Deccan and became one of the most successful generals in the early-seventeenth century. He created an independent army, became Prime Minister of the Ahmadnagar Sultanate, and led highly successful military campaigns against the expanding Mughal empire (Ali 2016). A half century earlier, Malik Raihan Habshi, later given the title Ikhlas Khan, was prime minister of the Adil Shahi Bijapur sultanate. Sidi statesmen Farhad Khan was part of the Golconda political milieu. It is no surprise that whether Chaush, a Turkish military term for officer or guard, or Sidi, derived from the Arabic term sayiddi for sea captain, military identities are deeply embedded in Afro-Arab presence in the subcontinent.

While the military history of African presence in the subcontinent has been better recorded, cultural presence has been barely so. The absence of African-diasporic performance histories is due in part to the paucity of the archive as well as difficulty in pinpointing who might have had African origins. Early modern Africans were sometimes referred to as Deccani along with local South Indians, while Turkic and Persian elites were referred to as foreign. In Mughal sources, "South Indian" (those from south of the Vindhya mountain range) and "African" were often both described in similar terms on the basis of dark skin and political opposition. Ali Khan Karori was a legendary figure in South Asian classical music histories – architect of the modern *khayal* and icon of the rudra vina. He was granted the title Naubat Khan by Mughal emperor Jahangir in the sixteenth century. The *naubat* refers to an orchestra with kettledrums and *shehnai*-style (double-reed wind) instrument found across Arabic-influenced parts of the Indian Ocean, including South and Southeast Asia. The *naubat khana* simultaneously indexed an occasion, a band, and a place – (1) the ceremony which officially marked time (*naubat* in Persian), (2) the drum and brass band which played it, and (3) the drum-house in the entrance tower to the main palace where the band played (Jahangir, Rogers, and Beveridge 1909: 111).[4] Paintings of Naubat Khan consistently portray him as dark-skinned, similarly to those whose titles includes Sidi or Al-Habash. Naubat Khan's dark skin, South Indian links, and Arabic military instrumental associations leave us to untangle the intersection of location, cultural production (music, dance), and physical space.

In this period, new genres of language, poetry, painting, courtly dance and music, and architectural motifs emerged in the Deccan. It is no coincidence that this was also the period of heightened African importance here. The confluence of African presence and new flourishing South Indian vernacular sensibilities produced a distinct cosmopolitan cultural legacy. The cities of the Deccan were contact zones or translocal spaces between Eastern and Western Indian Ocean influences. There wasn't an a priori Decani or South Asian culture into which African diaspora entered as "others." Instead, multiple sets of "foreign" and "local" elite defined a shifting cultural and geopolitical landscape.

A rare painting from the mid-seventeenth century Deccan, by a Golconda court painter, portrays an African lyre player.[5] A man dressed in the current fashion of Decani nobility – with embroidered white *jamma* robe, green *pyjama*, a *kalamkari* turban, an areca-nut satchel and short dagger hanging from his waist – launches into motion, the clouds ambling behind him and a glimpse of turquoise sky visible above. The instrument he plays is the five-stringed East African lyre known variously as *kisser, barbaryeh, tanbour, enganga,* or *krar.* The instrument has a shallow round wood bowl body, sheepskin soundboard, and widening string board. It is still used in northern Egypt but no longer played in Sidi communities in India today.[6] The back of the painting is inscribed with a Persian poem in nasta'liq (Arabic) script:

> *It is springtime friends! Time to celebrate sensual pleasure:*
> *wine, a bard, a pretty face, a secluded corner in a garden.*
> *What would I have done given my lack of means,*
> *if my heart did not have a cure for searing longings?*
> *My heart derives from the bounteous Sea of Compassion,*
> *its self-abnegation otherworldliness, an ever-radiant gem glowing in the*
> *night.*[7]

The painting brings together Ethiopian lyre, Decani clothing, and portraiture style from Mughal Delhi. It draws together multiple representational strategies to choreograph a hybrid elite African identity in the subcontinent. The poetic verse operates on two registers to frame the performing figure in-motion: the first celebrating material pleasure, the second underlying evincing the mystical realm of Sufism. Genres of poetry-painting bringing together dance and music, courtly eroticism, and devotion were emerging in this period from the Deccani courts, making this painting quintessentially Deccani (Haidar and Sardar 2011).[8] Sartorial choices are distinctly Deccani, marking the confluence of Mughal fashion trends with increasingly popular South Indian textiles. There are a number of paintings of Abyssinian courtiers, ministers, and commanders.[9] On another level however, the instrument, the short dagger, and the nature of his body-in-motion, are not common. The instrument and dagger mark this figure as linked to East Africa and the Hadramawt. Perhaps his motion too is telling – launching him into the space of slippage between Afro-Arabic and South Indian locations? Aspects of the painting located in an "elsewhere" are interlocked with markers which locate the painting in a Decani "here." What first seems simply an African musician in a Decani painting in fact reflects an entire constellation of placed markers and imaginaries that choreographs seventeenth-century movements, relationships, and bodily sensibilities.

Golconda to Hyderabad: the Deccan's changing locatedness

Other seventeenth-century paintings portray the main *bazaar* of the Deccani city of Golconda filled with Persian, Abyssinian, and South Indian men along with vendors, performers, and others interacting, mingling, jostling in bustling market-places. The Persianate Shia Qutb Shahi sultanate had expanded the existing city of Golconda into a fortified cultural and political hub in the sixteenth century – a maze of tiered walls, mosques, gardens, and living spaces spiraling up a granite hill leading up to the main *bazaar* and ultimately the main palace and audience hall at the top.[10] One of the four entrances opening into the main fort – the south-eastern gate which leads into the *bazaar* – is known as the Abyssinian gate (*kammans*). Above the gate are the rooms in which the officers of the Qutb Shahi army would stay, including the *naubat khana* or Mughal-style drum house. African presence was central, not marginal to the cosmopolitan city space of early modern Golconda.

In the eighteenth century, the Mughal empire expanded south and established a Sunni Turkic dynasty with roots in modern-day Uzbekistan, the Asaf Jahis, in the eastern Deccan. The new rulers moved their capital from Golconda to nearby Hyderabad. As the Mughal empire declined by the end of the eighteenth century, the Asaf Jahi dynasty entered into alliance with a newer political power in the subcontinent – the British East India Company. The British were concerned about the Asaf Jahi's relationship with the Hadramawt, fearing an Arab takeover in Hyderabad, and clamped down on Afro-Arab migration. Yet, many Africans continued to be brought through Bombay through unofficial channels (Arab families returning from the Hajj). The Nizam recruited men for a cavalry which came to be known as the African Cavalry Guard (Eaton 2006). The Nizamate continued as a princely state under British rule and after Indian Independence, ending only with State Reorganization in 1956. The last Nizam is said to have granted a new neighborhood, A.C. Guards (African Cavalry Guards) to the African diasporic community while the Hadrami diaspora remained in the neighborhood known as Barkas (Arabization of barracks). The neighborhoods continue to be linked to the Arab world, through food, dance and music. Both communities formed a small minority of the city and hold onto community identities rooted in military history of the Nizam and links to the Arab world (Khader 2017; Yimene 2007).

Under colonial-Nizamate rule, with the shift from Golconda to Hyderabad, African presence shifted from rulers and political agents to soldiers and domestic help, from the center of cultural political milieus to the margins. European company trade and plantation-slavery redefined the nature of movement and labor across the Indian Ocean world from the nineteenth century. While Arab-driven slave trade was unarguably brutal, the scale and style of European slavery left little room for the subjectivity of enslaved people. More importantly, the cultural and racial discourses of colonial power created a specific narrative: the tribal African or Indian who was fixed to one locality, a primordial reflection of ancient origins.[11] In effect, the logics of colonial cultural discourse rendered impossible the idea of shared or connected cultural spheres of Afro-Arab-South Indian.

The twentieth-century construction of the Indian nation as a coherent cultural configuration served to further marginalize and invisiblize Afro-Arab presence in the subcontinent while simultaneously shifting focus away from cultural and political ties across the Indian Ocean world. Post-colonial diplomatic efforts to bring together Afro-Asian countries through the Bandung Conference, ASEAN, and the New Asian-African Strategic Partnership (NAASP), left little room for the fluid, translocal relationalities that had defined older Indian Ocean logics. The kinds of translocal movement and political mobility once definitive of Deccani public spheres was rendered all but impossible – in practice as well as imagination. Yet, if we look beyond official nationalist cultural representations to less discussed social dance, music, and media, we might see new navigations of belonging and connectivity.

Marfa masti – twenty-first century choreographic translocations

Today *marfa*, or daff parties, operate as a center of social congregations, namely around Muslim weddings and other celebratory occasions in Hyderabad. *Marfa* has been co-opted into celebrations of state, for example, into the national Indian Independence Day celebrations at Red Fort in New Delhi as part of the national guard's band march. However, unlike the official performance of state, *marfa* in Hyderabad and the social media sphere perform translocal, rather than national, belonging. Through its gestures and the configuration of the brass and drum band, *marfa* is often described in association with the military history of Afro-Arab links to the Nizam and military service. Yet, I suggest that as younger generations make *marfa* popular in the public sphere in new and unprecedented ways, these military associations recede somewhat as quotidian associations with Hyderabadi youth culture, cross-cultural linkages, Sidi city-space, and broader Islamicate Indian Ocean legibility become more important. I suggest that *marfa's* public presence is more akin to but also redefines older circulatory logics of the Indian Ocean world, particularly by mobilizing new media.

In *marfa*, or daff parties, band members play the *marfa* kettle drum alongside *dhol* and other south Indian percussion. The kettle drum widely is played in the Hadramawt but with roots in East Africa. The instruments, but also the rhythms they play, reference the Hadramawt and East Africa. In Hyderabad, they come together with the popular rhythms of *teenmaar* or *dapankuthu*, South Indian folk- dance and music with Dalit origins.[12] Finally, there are a number of tunes that are part of the fluid repertoire of *marfa* bands, played by a keyboard player who is an essential part of the band along with the percussionists. While there are signature Arabic tunes which most bands play, bands also have their own signature tunes which locate it within the spheres of popular music in South India, including popular (South) Indian film songs and folk tunes.

Marfa's dance moves locate it within shifting geographies. A *daff* party is not complete without a guest of the party finding their way into the midst of a chaotic crowd, brandishing the signature short daggers and the quintessential shoulder-popping, arm-waving moves. The curved dagger, known as the *jambiya*, comes from Yemen. Even today, Yemeni men in the Haraz mountains and Sana'a dance in a circle with the *jambiya* to the accompaniment of kettle drums on the occasion of weddings or other celebrations. The signature arm moves and the distinction of a single main dancer, however, embody ambiguous origins. From one angle, we might link the circular motion of arms, the swing of shoulders, the deep bounce echo, to the dance of Ogun, the Yoruba god of Iron, known as a warrior and spirit of metal work.[13] While the circulation of Yoruba spirits and influence of their practice on broader social practices has been addressed in the Trans-Atlantic context, it has barely been explored in the Indian Ocean context. From another perspective, however, the signature movement of arms could index a number of social dance forms, South Asian or otherwise, not limited to Yoruba practice.

If we look at the configuration of people in space, bands perform in a semi-circle and participants from the wedding party or celebration enter into the middle of the space soon surrounded by others. This dynamic is more reminiscent of *ngoma* performance with East African roots than the Yemeni *jambiya* dance which involves men dancing in a snaking line. We could call forth the Africanist cipher which American scholars of African diasporic performance practices have found so central to Hip Hop and Afro-Caribbean forms. However, we would also have to contend with South Indian folk performance which have similar configurations, centralize drumming, and call-and-response. In Hyderabad today, bands bring together popular rhythms and gestures of South Indian folk dance, for example. This kind of ambiguity, far from an inconvenient point, lies at the heart of Indian Ocean identities and cultural practices – the impossibility of searches for origins. Indian Ocean practices, and those of Hyderabad specifically, are a product of layers of innumerable crossovers of cultures in the longue duree – we can only begin to tease apart when and how they have overlapped, been incorporated, adopted, and transformed.

There are many *marfa* bands in the A.C. Guards. In fact, the daff parties are one of the primary ways that people in A.C. Guards define their identities and economic resource since jobs have been hard to come by for many. One of the bands making a big presence today is led by a young man named Jabri Bin. Jabri is a fifth-generation Sidi *marfa* musician, and he leads the band started by his grandfather, one of the few Hyderabadi Sidis well known on a national level – a member of the national hockey team. In the last five years, Jabri Bin has posted many videos of their performances to YouTube – for weddings, festivals, or other events – with an ever-growing following. His most popular video has over seven million views and hundreds of people commenting.[14] Jabri Bin has been particularly adept at adapting popular film tunes, qawwali (Sufi devotional music), and more to his band's signature sound. Most conversations about African diaspora in Hyderabad have been about identities and cultural practices dying out or being lost. Jabri Bin, however, has redefined *marfa* at the center of Hyderabadi popular culture, particularly by centering the Sidi neighborhood of A.C. Guards.

Jabri Bin's performances incorporate multiple musical and performative elements across Afro-Asian performance but are almost always framed by the A.C. Guards streets and venue alleys, surrounded by crowds of men and flanked by their brightly colored van with built in speakers, the band plays *marfa* by incorporating much of pop culture into their tunes. There have been a number of critical discussions about popular social dance and urban placemaking. Work on hip hop in the United States has led the way, tracing the tension between dance as neighborhood or city dynamic and popular circulations. With a more global focus, dance scholar SanSan Kwan provides an important articulation of how identity is embodied in and as cities – in her case "Chineseness" in different global cities (Kwan 2013). I am doing almost an inverse study here – of how Indian Ocean circulation-identities converge and exist in the city of Hyderabad. Recent scholarship on nightlife, moving beyond paradigms of concert dance or experimental performance, explore dance as a social, impromptu, physically located dynamic – addressing issues of masculinity, homosociality, queerness, class, multi-culturalism, interpersonal bodies and more (Hamera 2006b; Khubchandani 2014; Muñoz 1997; Suriano 2011; Thomas 1997).[15] This work presents social dance as both cosmopolitan and highly specific to place. Jabri's band doesn't just popularize *marfa*, it makes visible the streets and spaces of the Sidi neighborhood as central to *marfa's* identity.

Jabri Bin's band doesn't just play and video their performances in the urban spaces of Hyderabad. They mobilize digital media in strategic ways, both strengthening *marfa's* relationship to Sidi identity and the A.C. Guards and making it is successful through new circulations. Dance scholars have increasingly begun to address the distinct kinds of questions raised by the popular screen beyond film and TV – the many screens associated with the internet – computer, tablet, phone, smart watch (Dodds 2001). They draw attention to how popular culture is constructed and moves through the possibilities of these new media.[16] For Jabri, popular media doesn't just allow for a de-localized circulation of *marfa*. Rather, it offers a way to simultaneously center place-ness even in, or especially in, the digital sphere. Almost every video Jabri Bin has uploaded to YouTube is geo-tagged – to A.C. Guards – unless the performance is for an out-of-town invitation. Not just the YouTube videos, but Jabri Bin's public Instagram account are also consistently geo-tagged to the neighborhood. These digital moves consciously and consistently identify *marfa* with these spaces and these spaces with *marfa* – colliding digital and physical space or, put differently, anchoring the digital in the physical.

Sidi *daff* parties thus perform a distinctly local identity, but one which is legible across the Islamicate world. *Marfa* and its mediated participatory circulations are distinctly translocal. Jabri's WhatsApp sign-off warns those in the "Old City," "Kabhi copy math karna, kyunki Xerox kabhi original nahi hua karte hain" ("Don't try to copy because a copy can never be as original as 'original'"). At the same time, the band is invited to play for weddings in the gulf states of Saudi and Yemen. In part due to Jabri Bin's distinct popularization of *marfa*, including his signature "*nagin*" (snake-charmer) tune, *marfa* has become a visible choreography of Hyderabadi youth culture that then travels back across the western Indian Ocean world.

Marfa has turned into a popular social media sensation, traveling back to the Gulf and beyond. Young people make videos in their homes, bedrooms, parties, cars, public parks, or anywhere else. A number of YouTube channels like Hyderabad My Heart and *Marfa* Diaries and celebrities like Baseer Ali have taken on *marfa* in one way or another. Many of the videos are reminiscent of other viral dances such as the Harlem shake videos. They primarily take the signature wave of the arms, signature kettle drum, plus Arabic melody, and transpose across them informal public and private spaces (Shifman 2012). The videos find their way to young women as well as young men in Saudi Arabia and other parts of the Arab world doing the "real" Hyderabadi *marfa*. Popular dance and music in the digital social sphere blur conventional demarcations of producers and consumers of culture.

Marfa is not just African or Arabic of Indian or any hyphenated combination of the three. Rather, it is a set of embodied affiliations specifically between east Africa and south India, of dark skin and rhythmic resonance, of shoulder bounces and the community of the social-dance circle – all converging in the brass band space of chaotic mid-celebration. *Marfa* brings together the sociality of Hadrami male authority, the nineteenth-century military histories of Sidi and Chaush in Hyderabad, and the gestures and rhythms of African practices, together with the distinctly South Indian flavor of teen mar or dapankuthu. Whether in a wedding hall, a public street, or courtyard the participating bodies take up and redefine space as both social and translocal. Copying, physically translating *marfa*'s moves into new spaces, commenting on and sharing its videos, are also quintessentially relational acts or choreographic moves. They define a network not just of participation but identity-construction, of positioning in a wider shared world. What does it mean to perform Hyderabadi *masti* (fun) or *kiraak* (awesomeness) and is it the same as performing Sidi identity? Do *marfa*'s new social/media circulations reach as far as the East African world? Does *marfa* as mediated, bodily assemblage bring together the same geographies as the early modern miniature painting or have they fundamentally altered? The band leaders, the young people making their own videos, commenting on Jabri's posts, and those participating without digital trace all move beyond the boundaries of presumed cultural identities. In this context, Jabri's insistence on A.C. Guards, a Sidi space, as the heart of *marfa* is a radical act, even as he and other Sidi artists make *marfa*'s moves widely accessible to a generation of young people, connecting across lines of color or shared Islamicate cultural sphere.

Performative geographies of the Indian Ocean: past, present, future?

In his seminal work about performance and the circum-Atlantic world which connects Europe, Africa, and the Americas, Joseph Roach argues performance embodies memory but also reinvention – that any act of remembering involves a partial forgetting, an erasure, and a surrogation (Roach 1996). Seen in theatrical terms, he is thinking especially about the surrogation of people into "roles," performative and social, just as European colonialism enacts a surrogation in the invention of a "new world" in the Americas. While the modern circum-Atlantic world can perhaps be understood in terms of an originary moment with Spanish "discovery" and the slave trade, the Indian Ocean world is one connected by multiple waves of movement in multiple directions and over many historical moments, often without single dominant centers, or by extension, peripheries. In this context, what does it mean to think about bodies, memory, performance, and place? Is it possible or sufficient to think about surrogation when so many re-place-ments and reinventions have taken place? After all, these are linear processes and assume a cultural dialectic. The Indian Ocean forces us to think multi-directionally and non-linearly even in our conceptions of reinvention of practices and cultures. I believe popular social dance and music as bodily and spatially mediated dynamics uniquely allow us to understand the Indian Ocean world as relational choreographies – ones defined by translation and assemblage as much as by surrogation. We have barely begun to really think through these possibilities – what more can performance and popular culture tell us about Indian Ocean movement? Can it offer new ideas about hybridity which more centrally take into consideration physical location and social space? Can it link different pasts to the present in new ways? This chapter perhaps raises more questions than it answers, but that seems inevitable and is perhaps the real work of approaching corporeal histories of the Indian Ocean world.

In proposing performative geographies, I ask us to think of the Indian Ocean world as sets of relationalities, constantly constituted and practiced through dynamics of popular social performance – bodily, contingent, and iterative. *Marfa* and other popular social dance and music – their lexicons, rhythms, and social configurations in space – force us to think more deeply about the boundaries between "there" and "here," between foreign and local. This is particularly important given the position of blackness in South Asia today, the position of Arab-ness in the global sphere and the presumed cultural isolation of Afro-Asian worlds generally. The ways in which popular culture "move" are slippery and unfaithful to imagined or real origins. This is true not only through practices and trends like *marfa* but through cinema, club cultures, and other forms of danced translation. Forms like the *taarab chakacha* dance in Mombasa, South Indian *dapankuthu* in Tamil films, for example, offer a means to better understand the complicated layers along which translocal public spheres are constructed. Importantly, they open up the radical possibility of Afro-Asian connection and dark-skinned coalition. What are the possibilities in thinking further about South India, the Hadramawt, and East Africa together, not just historically but in the present, not just through labor migrations but through popular social dynamics?

Dance was and continues to be situated in a broader set of exchanges vis-à-vis urban cosmopolitanism and performance that crisscross the Indian Ocean world, connecting it in more ways than one. From *bedaya beksan putri* (women's dance) in the *istanas* and *kratons* (royal houses) of Suryakarta and Yogyakarta to music and dance in urban centers like Mombasa of the Swahili coast – gestures, rhythms, aesthetic registers, representations, broader spheres of debate about the performing arts, and spaces of performance continue to make visible intersecting conceptions of urban place, translocal vocabularies, commerciality and politics of authority. One of the primary violences of colonialism was the silo-ing of cultural, political, social, linguistic, and religious dynamics into ethno-linguistically essential territorial boundaries and identities – of which the nation is living embodiment. Today, discussions of the Indian Ocean are dominated by the language of geopolitics and infrastructure backed by national interests. However, the moves and rhythms of Indian Ocean dance and music, framed by longue durée histories and traversing multiple media, allow us to understand a connected but deeply rooted politics of belonging and relationality, one which exists precisely in the slippages between multiple connected pasts and presents.

Notes

1 When Amy Catlin-Jairozbhoy organized a tour for the goma dancers, she introduced sets, program notes, and specific costuming, framing Afro-Indians in ways made them legible to global – i.e., Western – audiences.

2 William Safran provides a six-point list of criteria for defining diaspora: (1) they, or their ancestors, have been dispersed from a specific original "center" to two or more "peripheral," or foreign, regions; (2) they retain a collective memory, vision, or myth about their original homeland-its physical location, history, and achievements; (3) they believe they are not and perhaps cannot be fully accepted by their host society and therefore feel partly alienated and insulated from it; (4) they regard their ancestral homeland as their true, home and as the place to which they or their descendants would (or should) eventually return when conditions are appropriate; (5) they believe that they should, collectively, be committed to the maintenance or restoration of their original homeland and its safety and prosperity; and (6) they continue to relate, personally or vicariously, to that homeland in one way or another, and their ethnocommunal consciousness and solidarity are importantly defined by the existence of such a relationship.

3 Slavery in the Indian Ocean world was distinct and needs to be understood separately from the plantation slavery of the Atlantic Ocean world driven by European colonial imperialism from the sixteenthcentury onwards.

4 In the *Tuzk-i*-Jahangir (Memoirs of Jahangir), Jahangir writes "On the 14th I gave 'All Khan Karori, who was one of my revered father's old servants and was the darogka of the Naqarakhana (drum-house), the title of Naubat Khan, and promoted him to the rank of 500 personal and 200 horse."

5 Unknown Artist. An African Lyre Player (recto), calligraphy (verso). *c.*1640–1660. Ink, opaque watercolor, and gold on paper. 40.5 × 28.9 cm. Cleveland Museum of Art, Catherine and Ralph Benkaim Collection 2013.289, www.clevelandart.org/art/2013.289, accessed 3 June 2016.

6 Though a rare *kissar* has been found in the Sidi Sufi shrine for Bava Gor near Aurangabad (Maharashtra).

7 Curators of Cleveland Museum of Art with edits by myself in conversation with Professor Sanjay Subrahmanyam.

8 Haidar and Sardar point out "the opulent art of the Deccan courts, invigorated by cultural connections to the Middle East, Africa, and Europe, developed an otherworldly character distinct from that of the contemporary Mughal north: in painting, a poetic lyricism and audacious use of color; in the decorative arts, lively creations of inlaid metal-ware and painted and dyed textiles; and in architecture, a somber grandeur still visible today in breathtaking monuments throughout the plateau."

9 A portrait of Malik Ambar by the painter Hashim, of Jadun Rai Decani currently in the Metropolitan Museum of Arts has the following verse: If the moon were beautiful like you,/Smaller than a crescent were the sun!/In your time, oh friend, who has the strength/To be patient without you at length?/The servant Mir-'Ali the scribe [al-katib], may his sins be forgiven.
   Another single print of a painting of Abyssinian courtier Farhad Khan has been found among Sotheby's collections
10 Tripathy, Arpita. "Golconda Fort of Hyderabad" Photograph. Self-Published. 30 Sep 2017. Wikimedia Commons. https://commons.wikimedia.org/wiki/File:Golconda_fort_of_Hyderabad.jpg (accessed 27 November 2019).
11 Bhabha, Homi K. *The Location of Culture*. Psychology Press, 1994.
12 For more on the Dalit roots of South Indian popular forms like dapankuthu, see forthcoming writing by Kareem Khubchandani.
13 I would like to thank Crystal Sanders, at the Penn State Africana Research Center, and Bettina Ng'weno at UC Davis for their respective provocations about the roots of some of these movement lexicons.
14 Bin, Jabri. "Jabri marfa #nagin #afghan_jalebi..9885938559." YouTube Video, 3:55. 1 January 2017. www.youtube.com/watch?v=jlOd0d33Xq4, accessed 1 August 2016.
15 Relevant scholarship on nightlife in the United Kingdom, Canada, India and United States comes from Urban Studies, Geography, and other disciplines.
16 Scholarship on K-pop has been leading the conversation on the way digital media from the Global South changes understandings of globalization. In particular, the use and consumption of YouTube in ways both official and unofficial has been fruitful – the manufacturing of cover-culture for example.

References

Ali, Omar H. 2016. *Malik Ambar: Power and Slavery across the Indian Ocean*. 1st edition. New York: Oxford University Press.

Ali, Shanti Sadiq. 1996. *The African Dispersal in the Deccan: From Medieval to Modern Times*. Hyderabad: Orient Blackswan.

Alpers, Edward A. 2009. *East Africa and the Indian Ocean*. 1st edition. Princeton, NJ: Markus Wiener.

Basu, Helene. 2008. "Music and the Formation of Sidi Identity in Western India." In *History Workshop Journal*, 65: 161–178. New York: Oxford University Press.

Brickell, Katherine, and Ayona Datta. 2011. *Translocal Geographies*. Ashgate Publishing, Ltd.

Catlin-Jairazbhoy, Amy. 2002. *Sidi Sufi Mystics: Music of African Indians of Gujarat*. Van Nuys: Apsara Media for Intercultural Educational Services.

Catlin-Jairazbhoy, Amy. 2003. "From Africa to India: Sidi Music in the Indian Ocean Diaspora [DVD]." *Van Nuys, CA: Apsara Media for Intercultural Education*.

Catlin-Jairazbhoy, Amy. 2004. "A Sidi CD? Globalization of Music and the Sacred." *Sidis and Scholars: Essays on African Indians*, 178–211. Kochi: Rainbow Publishers.

Catlin-Jairazbhoy, Amy. 2010. "Sidi Music in Western India: Remembering an African Heritage." *Remembered Rhythms: Issues of Music and Diaspora in India*.

Chatterjee, Indrani and Richard M. Eaton. 2006. *Slavery and South Asian History*. Bloomington: Indiana University Press.

Dils, Ann and Ann Cooper Albright. 2001. *Moving History/Dancing Cultures: A Dance History Reader*. Middletown: Wesleyan University Press.

Dodds, S. 2001. *Dance on Screen: Genres and Media from Hollywood to Experimental Art*. Springer.

Eaton, Richard M. 2006. "The Rise and Fall of Military Slavery in the Deccan, 1450–1650." In *Slavery and South Asian History*. Bloomington: Indiana University Press.

Foster, Susan Leigh, ed. 1996. *Corporealities: Dancing, Knowledge, Culture, and Power.* London; New York: Routledge.

Foster, William. 1921. *Early Travels in India, 1583–1619.* London: Oxford University Press. http://archive.org/details/earlytravelsinin00fostuoft.

Haidar, Navina Najat and Marika Sardar. 2011. *Sultans of the South: Arts of India's Deccan Courts, 1323–1687.* New York: Metropolitan Museum of Art.

Hamera, J. 2006a. *Dancing Communities: Performance, Difference and Connection in the Global City.* New York: Springer.

Hamera, Judith. 2006b. *Opening Acts: Performance in/as Communication and Cultural Studies.* Thousand Oaks, CA: Sage.

Jahangir, Emperor of Hindustan, Alexander Rogers, and Henry Beveridge. 1909. *The Tuzuk-i-Jahangiri; or, Memoirs of Jahangir.* Translated by Alexander Rogers. Edited by Henry Beveridge. London Royal Asiatic Society. http://archive.org/details/tuzukijahangirio00jahauoft.

Khader, Khatija. 2017. "Mobile Communities of the Indian Ocean: A Brief Study of Siddi and Hadrami Diaspora in Hyderabad City, India." In *Global Africans*, 88–105. London/New York: Routledge.

Khubchandani, Kareem. 2014. "Ishtyle: Queer Nightlife Performance in India and the South Asian Diaspora." Evanston: Northwestern University.

Kwan, SanSan. 2013. *Kinesthetic City: Dance and Movement in Chinese Urban Spaces.* New York: OUP USA.

Muñoz, José Esteban. 1997. *Everynight Life: Culture and Dance in Latin/o America.* Durham: Duke University Press.

Roach, Joseph R. 1996. *Cities of the Dead: Circum-Atlantic Performance.* New York: Columbia University Press.

Robbins, Kenneth X. and John McLeod, eds. 2006. *African Elites in India: Habshi Amarat.* 1st edition. Ahmedabad: Ocean Township, NJ: Mapin Publishing Gp Pty Ltd.

Shifman, Limor. 2012. "An Anatomy of a YouTube Meme." *New Media & Society* 14 (2): 187–203. https://doi.org/10.1177/1461444811412160.

Shroff, Beheroze. 2013. "'Goma Is Going On': Sidis of Gujarat." *African Arts* 46 (1): 18–25. Cambridge: MIT Press.

Suriano, Maria. 2011. "Hip-Hop and Bongo Flavour Music in Contemporary Tanzania: Youths' Experiences, Agency, Aspirations and Contradictions." *Africa Development* 36 (3–4): 113–126.

Thomas, Helen. 1997. *Dance in the City.* 1997 edition. New York: Palgrave Macmillan.

Yimene, Ababu Minda. 2007. "Dynamics of Ethnic Identity among the Siddis of Hyderabad." *African and Asian Studies* 6 (3): 321–345.

14 Exploring the "unknown"

Indian Ocean materiality as method[1]

Vivian Y. Choi

Introduction

On a grey, drizzly, Pacific Northwest morning in early January 2016, I found myself slowly winding down Sand Point Way toward a large block of white buildings, in Seattle, Washington at the National Oceanic and Atmospheric Administration's (NOAA) Western Regional Center. Built on a former naval air base on the shores of Lake Washington, this sprawling federal facility under the United States Department of Commerce employs the most NOAA staff outside of Washington, D.C. and houses the greatest variety of NOAA programs in a single location in the United States. One of these programs is the Pacific Marine Environmental Laboratory (PMEL),[2] a federal laboratory consisting of approximately 200 scientists, engineers, administrative, and IT professionals, conducting research and making critical short- and long-term observations of the global ocean and its interactions with the earth, atmosphere, ecosystems, and climate.

It was to Building 3, housing PMEL, where I was making my way, to meet with a prominent oceanographer, Michael McPhaden, who was participating in the Second International Indian Ocean Expedition (hereafter referred to as "IIOE-2"), a major global scientific program engaged in oceanographic and atmospheric research from coastal environments to the deep sea to better understand the complexities of the Indian Ocean.

I waited in the lobby. Without security clearance, I was not allowed to wander around the facility unaccompanied by a staff member. Soon, I was being guided through dim corridors, occasionally catching glimpses of labs and offices. As we walked, I briefly explained to my guide that I was interested in the Indian Ocean Expedition and the warming temperatures of the Indian Ocean. My guide assured me that McPhaden was "the Indian Ocean guy," which of course was exciting, but also sent waves of intimidation through my body. In my research for potential contacts to learn more about the Second International Indian Ocean Expedition, I had discovered McPhaden's name and that he was based in Seattle – a manageable location, given my own roots in the Pacific Northwest. I had also glanced at his long list of publications, the first of which was published in 1976. McPhaden is a physical oceanographer, meaning he focuses on the physical properties of oceans. Ocean currents are his specialty, and he is especially interested in large-scale ocean dynamics, ocean-atmosphere interactions, and the ocean's role in climate. McPhaden is one oceanographer out of many scientists working on IIOE-2; studying the Indian Ocean in all its complexities is a multidisciplinary, multidimensional, and, not to mention, expensive endeavor. I return to my meeting and discussions with McPhaden at the end of this chapter.

What prompted my meeting that grey Pacific Northwest morning and continues to intrigue me about the Indian Ocean as an object of scientific interest, discovery, and concern are the following questions: How is it possible to study and understand an ever-changing and vast body of water such as an ocean? How does the materiality and sheer physicality of the ocean guide scientific collaborations and modes of exchange (see, for example, Helmreich 2009)?

I attend to these questions by providing a brief historical sketch of the first International Indian Ocean Expedition (IIOE), which was undertaken from 1959–1965 and spearheaded by the post-World War II established United Nations Educational, Scientific, and Cultural Organization (UNESCO). In broad strokes, I discuss how the "Indian Ocean" emerges and is articulated as an object of scientific study, care, and concern (Callison 2014; de la Bellacasa 2011; Latour 2004; see also Parreñas 2018). I show how the Indian Ocean, in its physical, material and lively characteristics and complexities (Lambert, Martins, and Ogborn 2006: 482) drew together a diverse body of oceanographers, marine biologists, physicists, and local and international governing bodies. I move on, then, to the Second International Indian Ocean (IIOE-2), which began officially in 2015 and will go on through 2020 and into the United Nations Decade of Ocean Science for Sustainable Development (2021–2030). In particular, I highlight how the second expedition builds upon legacies of the first and how the Indian Ocean's dynamics have global implications as a harbinger of climate change, again drawing together a diverse coterie of concerned scientists. The similarities and differences, conjunctions and disjunctions between the two expeditions illustrate the Indian Ocean as an ever-shifting, heterogeneous formation and space. Indeed, studies of, on, and around the Indian Ocean have certainly revealed this protean characteristic of it, examining its productive role in facilitating cultural, political, religious, and economic networks, communities, fractures, and alliances. Further, as a heuristic, the Indian Ocean provides modes of understanding history and social relations beyond the restrictive conceptual framings of continents and nation-states (Ho 2006; authors in this volume). Further still, the Indian Ocean has also been characterized and discussed in more than spatial and cartographic terms, as an imagination and even a consciousness (Prestholdt 2015). Certainly, to engage with the Indian Ocean as an "empirically investigable world-historical space" of possibility and process (Green 2018: 873) obliges us to "extend our axes of investigation" (Hofmeyr 2010: 722). My purpose in this chapter, then, is to add onto this body of work with a view from yet another boat (Ho 2004; Machado 2016; Mahajan this volume): the expedition vessels of Indian Ocean marine sciences and the practices carried out in and with them. This "view" presents what the Indian Ocean *is* for oceanographers and marine scientists. Just as scholars have urged us to consider the unruliness of water (Anand 2017; Amrith 2018) in shaping social and political contexts, pasts and futures (see also Ballestero 2019), I argue that a focus on the physical and material dynamics of the Indian Ocean also serves as a method to gain insights into intellectual, social, political, and global relations, and phenomena of large temporal and spatial scale.

In this paper, Indian Ocean materiality as method is informed by scholarship at the intersections of science and technology studies (STS) and area or regional studies. In particular, I am inspired by the provocation of "Asia as method" (Chen 2010), a project that seeks to decolonize theory and knowledge production, and, as Warwick Anderson (2012) adds, STS. Asia in this methodology is not an essentialized or a fixed geographical region or entity, but rather a location "that is good to think with, and think from" (2012: 448). Fa-ti Fan further reiterates that regional categories such as East Asia are always relational and contextual, existing within specific frames of reference, in specific moments of time, defined differently by different actors: "Hence, we cannot avoid the multiplicity and heterogeneity of what is called "'East Asia'" (2007, 244). It strikes me, then, that we might consider any location as a potential method. My project seeks to plot out the Indian Ocean's multiplicities as method (D'Avella 2019; Mol 2002) in which the materiality of the ocean, as an object of scientific inquiry and study is, as Helmreich describes oceanic waves, "at once material and measured, concrete and conceptual" (2014: 267; Steinberg 2013). Some of these Indian Ocean heterogeneities I have already outlined above. Further possibilities I articulate in the rest of this chapter.

Cooperation and collaboration: marine science, oceanography, and the first International Indian Ocean Expedition (IIOE)

The IIOE as an idea and a plan emerged with the development of several international bodies and scientific committees in the social and political wake of World War II and the intensifying Cold War. From 1957 to 1958, the International Geophysical Year (IGY), set a precedent with the participation of over 60,000 scientists from over 67 countries to promote international scientific data analysis, collection, and exchange (Collis and Dodds 2008). The auspices of the IGY were to promote decidedly "non-political" and uninterrupted *individual* scientific pursuits and to show that science could serve as a universal language regardless of national identities and political differences. The IGY was one of the "boldest" (Doel 2002) scientific undertakings of the twentieth century: it resulted in the establishment of the World Data Centers; it set in motion the start of the space age; and it fostered international scientific knowledge exchange and activity in spite of the Cold War. Though politics was unavoidable (see Hamblin 2011), the IGY did inspire future scientific collaborations, including the International Indian Ocean Expedition.

The Special Committee for Oceanic Research or SCOR ("Special" would later be changed to "Scientific") was one of the IGY's legacies. To continue international cooperation on oceanographic research, prominent oceanographers met in Sweden in 1957 to develop SCOR's mission and agenda. United States oceanographer Roger Revelle, who had also participated in the IGY, took the lead and under his leadership marine science would take on a more development-oriented approach moving toward inter-governmental cooperation – that is, cooperation that would address broader problems of society in addition to the promotion of scientific growth and easing of international tensions (Hamblin 2011). It is significant to note that geopolitics were not the main reasons impeding an international and interdisciplinary marine science endeavor. Rather, it was the reluctance of physical oceanographers to work with marine biologists to create a broader vision of what constituted the marine sciences. As Robert Snider, a former Navy officer, who was appointed to be the IIOE coordinator wrote in *Discovery*:

> The genuine roadblocks to SCOR came from the scientists who saw no need for a new organization incorporating a broader vision ... Danish ocean-ographer Anton Bruun complained that these physical oceanographers were sluggish in supporting the creation of SCOR, whereas marine biologists and meteorologists were anxious to establish a body that would improve the as yet inadequate cooperation between physicists and biologists.
>
> (Snider 1961: 117)

This reluctance was eventually overcome because physical oceanographers conceded that to improve the state of oceanography and to conduct broader research spanning the world's oceans, international and inter-governmental cooperation was necessary.

This "politicization of science" made some oceanographers uncomfortable, as they felt it threatened their own research agendas and the scientific pursuits of oceanography more generally for the good of collaborative research or for developing less advanced oceanography programs elsewhere. Others felt that the humanitarian proposal was disingenuous, merely serving as a cover for the United States' anti-communist agenda. Still, some oceanographers truly believed that oceanography needed to be developed in the countries bordering the Indian Ocean – whether through the development of more advanced research institutions and programs on oceanography or through research that would aid "hungry" countries' development of infrastructures and practices of fishing. The appeal of the Indian Ocean Expedition, however, was that it would be able to address both research and development agendas.[3] If SCOR was to combine a research agenda with a development agenda through the expansion of cooperative relationships through the IIOE, then the politicization of oceanic research was institutionalized and cemented when the Expedition was handed over to UNESCO's Intergovernmental Oceanographic Commission (IOC). In 1959, the IIOE and all future project projects would now be managed by an intergovernmental forum, firmly placing scientific endeavors under the purview and whim of member states rather than individual scientists. On the one hand, SCOR, which was not well-equipped to handle the bureaucracies of a large-scale project such as the IIOE, was happy to hand over those administrative duties to the IOC. On the other, they were concerned about the IOC's interference into personal cooperation and control over scientific initiatives. The Indian Ocean Expedition thus offered the first grand "experiment" in international scientific cooperation and the IIOE was hailed as the first and "the greatest effort in international cooperation ever undertaken in marine science" (Fye 1965). It included the deployment of forty ships from 13 thirteen countries: Australia, France, Federal Republic of Germany, USSR, Indonesia, India, Japan, Pakistan, Portugal, South Africa, Thailand, United States, United Kingdom and participation from: Sri Lanka (Ceylon), Burma, Israel, Sudan, Italy, China, Madagascar, Ethiopia, Malaysia, Mauritius.

There is very little discussion either in IIOE accounts from UNESCO or scientists that discuss decolonization. When looking at the array of countries involved, especially ones who had historically already done some oceanic research in the Indian Ocean basin (Dutch, British, and French powers, for example) colonialism as a force and power cannot of course be cleaved from this oceanic story. An interesting dynamic of the development of these scientific collaborations cannot be considered, in fact, outside of the development of a new international system of nation-states. One oceanographer (Tomzcek 1980), however, was critical of how oceanographers characterized deep sea expeditions and oceanographic discoveries without reference to the colonial and political powers that motivated and enabled them.

Indeed, the Indian Ocean was appropriate for this experiment because at the time it was the least studied and understood ocean and as such every scientist would have a stake in the expedition. According to one marine biologist in the Expedition, the Indian Ocean was an "unknown," "almost a terra incognito" (Humphrey 1961).[4] Daniel Behrman's account, entitled *Assault on the Largest Unknown: The International Indian Ocean Expedition 1959–1965* (see also Hamblin 2011), recounts oceanographer Henry Stommels' anecdote on how the Indian Ocean became the international project for SCOR. SCOR was having their first meeting at Woods Hole Oceanographic Institute in Massachusetts, and Henry Stommels was given the task to create a global map of the world's deep oceans. Then director of Woods Hole, Columbus Iselin, also a member of SCOR, walked into a personal discussion Stommels and his colleague were having. Wanting to change the subject of conversation, Stommels directed Iselin's attention to the map he had put together, to which Iselin's response was: "There have been many more observations since IGY, but there's not much in the Indian Ocean." Stommel's map was literally blank on the east side of Africa. Apparently, Iselin "had a cup of coffee and went back to the SCOR meeting." It is Stommel's opinion that that is how the seed of Indian Ocean Expedition was sown (Behrman 1981: 12). The Indian Ocean was, literally, a blank space on the world map. In a chapter entitled "The Forlorn Ocean," Behrman gestures to the

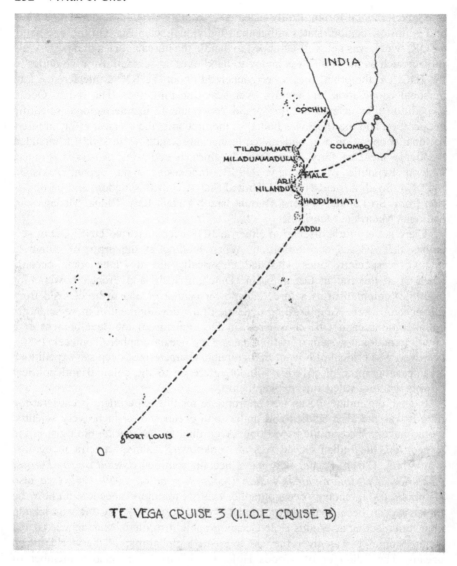

Map 14.1 Route outline of Cruise 3 of the United States vessel Te Vega, as taken from
their cruise reports.

Image credit: https://scor-int.org/project/iioe-1/.

histories (some detailed in this volume) that preceded the expedition and writes
"… it was certainly the Arabs who came closest to the mastery of the science of
the navigation of these waters." (Behrman 1981: 9). Despite its storied significant role historically, in the marine scientific imaginary, the Indian Ocean was
a blank slate.

What little recognized scientific data existed about the Indian Ocean pointed to its alleged unique characteristics that would be worthy of investigation: its biological diversity and potential to be the "most productive" body of water as a source of food; its geography of being almost entirely closed by land, except for its major opening joining it to the South Sea; and of course, its famed monsoons, which at the time, had not been systematically studied or observed by physical oceanographers.[5] As IIOE coordinator Robert Snider laid out in 1961, the international expedition would study the "entire system from below the bottom, through the water itself (with its biological contents and its physical and chemical characteristics), through the boundary between the sea and the atmosphere, and on upwards to the upper atmosphere" (Snider 1961: 114). This all-encompassing study required the participation of many scientific disciplines: geology, geophysics, bathymetry, oceanography, biology, and meteorology. As international coordination and plans developed, however, as Scripps Institute Oceanographer John Knauss wrote, "It becomes apparent that the opportunity to work in the Indian Ocean means different things to different scientists" (Knauss 1961). As confirmed in Behrman's account, it was indeed difficult to get scientists to agree on a research plan. It turned out that the lack of systematic oceanographic research on the ocean made it difficult to identify where to start. After much effort, Roger Revelle, Anton Bruun (of Denmark), and George Deacon (of the UK) agreed on a plan that would prioritize what were identified as research problems and "accommodate conflicting interests for this was a political operation in which people to be persuaded. Coercion could not be used because all efforts were voluntary. Yet we could not compromise as one does in politics. To get everything done, we had to get different people to do different things" (Revelle as quoted in Behrman 1981: 19).

The outcomes of the expedition provided much of the foundations for contemporary scientific practices and understandings of the Indian Ocean and beyond. For example, after the expedition, the first oceanographic atlas of the Indian Ocean basin was published (Wyrtki, Bennett, and Rochford 1971) in addition to a detailed map of Indian Ocean bathymetry that studies the depth and shapes of underwater terrain (Heezen and Tharp 1966). The bathymetry would go on to help establish theories of continental drift and plate tectonics, which at the time of the expedition was still considered a radical theory. An unprecedented number of hydrographic surveys dramatically advanced understandings of monsoon variability and for the first time described the surface ocean circulation that emerges in response to the monsoons. In addition, scientists developed standards for collecting zooplankton samples and carried inter calibration exercises to compare biological and chemical samples. Finally, in concert with its goals to develop scientific capacity in Indian Ocean rim countries, the IIOE helped to establish the Indian Ocean Biological Centre in Cochin (India); later, India would establish its National Institute of Oceanography in Goa. Countries who had participated in the expedition such as Thailand, Indonesia, and Pakistan also created institutions for marine research.

In this abbreviated account of the first International Indian Ocean Expedition, the Indian Ocean takes on many forms: it is a frontier, an unknown space, a body of water filled with biological diversity and "productivity"; a curious force of currents that combined with atmospheric dynamics creates a phenomenon so powerful as to dictate travel and agricultural dependence. It is also, as in so many studies of and about the Indian Ocean (including this volume), an object and force that invites movement, exchange, power, domination, and in the case of the IIOE, international and scientific collaboration and disagreement. As the IIOE illustrates, there was not a unified notion of marine sciences. However, what it would be, and what its politics were, were tied to the physical properties of the Indian Ocean. The interactions and interrelations I have presented in broad strokes here show that, as a heterogeneous object to be scientifically examined, the Indian Ocean draws in multiple actors – scientists, nations, institutions – and thus, it is also a method for Indian Ocean studies and other disciplines to understand the micro- and global social and political relations that form it (Law 1986). How might considering Indian Ocean materiality as method continue to guide ethnographic research in the contemporary?

The second International Indian Ocean Expedition: a "basin-wide research program" with global implications

According to the Fifth Assessment Report of the Intergovernmental Panel on Climate Change (IPCC), the earth is absorbing more heat than it is emitting back into space. 93 percent of the heat produced by the effects of greenhouse gases over the last 40 years has been absorbed in the world's oceans (Rhein et al. 2013). While this warming trend encapsulates all oceans of the world, it has been observed that the Indian Ocean, already the world's warmest ocean basin, has been warming at a rate faster than all of the world's tropical oceans (Roxy et al. 2014) and, more significantly, has been absorbing heat from the Pacific Ocean's warming slowdown through the interplay of trade winds and currents (Lee et al. 2015). The Indian Ocean region hosts more than 25 percent of the world's population, and given the environmental stressors linked to this growing population, combined with the above-mentioned concerns, the changes in the Indian Ocean have potentially grave consequences on life in the air, land, and sea (Hood et al. 2015).

Thus, understanding the Indian Ocean's role in the global oceanic ecosystem has become a priority in oceanographic investigation. Building on the legacies of the first IIOE, 50 years later in 2015, the second began and is slated to continue through 2020. If one of the legacies of the first Indian Ocean Expedition was its (not unproblematic) humanitarian concerns, the IIOE-2 surely follows suit. As stated in IIOE-2's scientific plan, the mission is:

> To advance our understanding of the Indian Ocean and its role in the Earth System in order to enable informed decisions in support of sustainable development and well-being of humankind. IIOE-2 will need to increase

our knowledge of interactions between geologic, oceanic and atmospheric processes that give rise to the complex physical dynamics of the Indian Ocean region, and determine how those dynamics affect climate, extreme events, marine biogeochemical cycles, ecosystems and human populations

(Hood et al. 2015: ix)

Framed in this way, IIOE-2's research plans and motivations situate the Indian Ocean within a broader planetary or Earth ecosystem, in which humans, atmosphere, ocean, currents, biogeochemicals, all relate. It is once again sponsored by the Scientific Committee for Oceanographic Research (SCOR), UNESCO's Intergovernmental Oceanographic Commission (IOC) and also the Indian Ocean Global Ocean Observation System (IOGOOS) established in 2002. The IIOE-2 receives support from numerous oceanographic programs[6] and has endorsed multidisciplinary research projects from at least seventeen countries (including Australia, China, France, Germany, India, Indonesia, Israel, Japan, Kenya, Korea, Mauritius, Russia, Singapore, South Africa, Tanzania, United Kingdom, United States). Many of the oceanographic partner programs represent the observational and technological growth specific to oceanography since the first IIOE in addition to the invention of the internet, easier modes of communication, and data-sharing.[7] As the expedition is still on-going and has been extended, new initiatives, programs, and cruises will surely be added to the plan.

Interestingly, IIOE-2 is framed in terms similar to the first expedition: the Indian Ocean, according to oceanographers is still the most under-researched and least-understood of the world's oceans. Despite the advances and work done during and since the first IIOE, many uncertainties about the Indian Ocean still remain. It is deemed the "last frontier" of oceanography not only because it has been less systematically studied, but also because of its dynamic complexity and its ever-changing characteristics (Hood et al. 2016; Roxy 2018 (personal communication)). With the added dimensions of technological advances since the 1950s and 1960s and the interest and development of more marine research institutions in Indian Ocean countries, the IIOE-2 aims to further strengthen coordinated international and multidisciplinary research and increase scientific capacity and infrastructure within the Indian Ocean rim and neighboring nations.

The plan for the IIOE-2 is structured around six themes that are all dedicated to addressing the first theme and significance of the expedition: Human Impacts. "How are human-induced stressors impacting the biogeochemistry and ecology of the Indian Ocean? How, in turn, are these impacts affecting human populations?"[8] (Hood et al. 2015: X). In the context of climate change, the expedition recognizes that its research will have potentially far-reaching relevance to understand how the "complex dynamics" of the Indian Ocean relate to the other global oceans and the broader ecological Earth System, which is particularly salient in the contemporary moment of climate crisis. The expedition seeks to collect data that inform environmental and oceanic policies. As written into the scientific plan, indeed the "success" of the IIOE-2 will be measured not only by how much the knowledge of the Indian Ocean is advanced, but also by how it "contributes to sustainable development of marine resources, environmental stewardship, ocean and climate forecasting, and training of the next generation of ocean scientists from the region" (Hood et al. 2015: 77).

Back to McPhaden's office a year after IIOE-2 began: I'm seated facing a large window with a view of Lake Washington. It is blustery outside still. Large raindrops pepper and then ooze down the clear glass. I am nervous and he is friendly. I told him that I was interested in some of the broad goals of the IIOE-2 that I listed above – namely how to understand the role of the Indian Ocean amidst a changing climate, amidst climate crisis, and the possibilities for increased extreme weather events. I discussed with him what little knowledge I had acquired about sea-surface warming in the Indian Ocean. I further explained how, as an anthropologist, I was fascinated by the ways in which the Indian Ocean, as such a large, complex body of water could be studied; how did scientists work together to do so in the IIOE-2? McPhaden characterized oceanography today as being fundamentally collaborative. Expeditions are expensive, he explained, and the demand for ship time far exceeds the supply, so cruises often involve many different coordinated projects working side by side on board. Furthermore, advances in technology have enabled more rapid global scientific exchange and communication, especially helpful when dealing with oceanic research and data. He said that if you were to survey oceanography-related publications and research since the 1970s that you would find fewer and fewer single-authored papers. And it is true: looking at his CV online, a quick glance at his list of publications in the last nine years reveals only three single authored papers out of 130 total.

A few months later, over the telephone, I pressed him on the collaborative intentions of the IIOE-2. More specifically I mentioned the explicit humanitarian and social motivations of the expedition and asked if he or anyone in the expedition was working with social scientists. He responded by saying, "No, we are not there yet."

The Indian Ocean as method for an endangered world

I take this moment of "not yet" to meditate on the productive potentials that an Indian Ocean method offers to both Indian Ocean studies and studies of the ocean. Oceans have been incredibly productive in delineating the limitations of area studies and the territorialisms that dictate sites and relations of migration and human interaction. Moreover, as does this volume, oceans have the potential to bring novel and diverse sets of scholars and bodies of knowledge together at many levels (Lewis and Wigen 1999). As I have shown here, the Indian Ocean serves as a framework of investigation, ethnographic, historical, and scientific *and* as something with a "lively and energetic materiality of its own" (Lambert, Martins, and Ogborn 2006: 482; see also Helmreich 2008; Lehman 2016; Steinberg and Peters 2015 on "wet ontologies") that erupts, shapes, intervenes in the lives of communities, nations, and scientific bodies. As the Indian Ocean expeditions have revealed, its materiality has led to novel scientific collaborations and, in the future, hopefully, novel collaborations between the sciences, social sciences and humanities.

After reviewing an earlier draft of this chapter, McPhaden wanted to further elaborate what he meant by "not-yet," which he conceded sounded pessimistic, but actually reflected the long process and pathways by which fundamental research on the oceans makes its way into practical applications of societal value. He described the process as "often circuitous, indirect, and long in being realized. It is the nature of research" (McPhaden, personal communication). Though, eventually, once matured, the hope is to engage with broader communities, and social scientists help scientists understand how to translate research effectively, to know who benefits from it, and what limits its uptake. In turn, he said, social science feeds back into how he and his colleagues process and target information for different audiences. In the nascent stages of his early research on El Niño, for example, he and his colleagues had no idea what the research would yield, and thus, he said, involving other non-specialists would have been difficult and arguably of little benefit in those early stages.

The task of ethnography in our contemporary moment of "late industrialism," Kim Fortun (2012) suggests, is to be creative, to devise experimental ethnographic systems that address complex conditions that resist narration and, in the case of warming oceans, temporal and intellectual boundaries and limits. Large phenomena of scale, such as climate change or the complex dynamics of an entire ocean basin, certainly require methodological openness, urging us to forge relationships and make collaborations that perhaps are unlikely, awkward, or even forced (Ogden et al. 2013; Palsson et al. 2013). In this chapter, I have shown how the "Indian Ocean" emerges as 1) an object of study; 2) an entanglement of social, environmental, and political forces and; 3) a heterogeneous force itself requiring different forms of morphing, changing, and articulated and materialized in both broad and specific scientific imaginaries and practice.[9] In doing so, I propose that a focus on the Indian Ocean's materiality as a harbinger of our "deranged" times (Ghosh 2016) adds more specificity to the global climate crisis. Proposing this kind of methodology is to situate the Indian Ocean within a global, relational, and interdisciplinary framework. The Indian Ocean is one part of the One/Global Ocean, which is not merely a romantic gesture to point to the interconnectedness of the world. Scientists understand the oceans as interconnected waterways that have complex currents and dynamics that feed into each other and cover roughly 70 percent of the earth's surface, and IIOE-2 is explicit about this: "Understanding the connections between the changes that are being observed in the Indian Ocean and other ocean basins is essential to determine the global ocean's response to climate change and potential feedback effects" (Hood et al., 2015: 71).

While we may think of our current era of the Anthropocene as one of ruination, disintegration, decay, and destruction (Moore 2016; Tsing 2016), climate crisis as articulated through the materiality of oceans is characterized by warming, inundation, storms and surges, shifting currents and flows, and, as I propose, ever more needed collaborations. Indeed, the IPCC's most recent report as of September 2019 claimed with ever more urgency the strain of global warming on the world's oceans. An attunement to the ocean and to Indian Ocean science compels us to consider the intricate web of relations (Haraway 2015) between atmosphere,[10] weather, ocean, land, sea, biological life, and even between scientists and social scientists.

Notes

1 I would like to thank the "Re-Imagining Indian Ocean Worlds" workshop at UC Davis in 2018, and the generous comments that greatly improved this chapter. Thanks, especially to Smriti Srinivas for her guidance. I also thank Michael McPhaden and Matthew Roxy, two members of IIOE-2, willing to offer their insight and experiences.
2 www.pmel.noaa.gov/
3 By 1962, UNESCO took over for SCOR and Revelle to manage the IIOE. By that time UNESCO had created International Oceanic Committee (IOC), the umbrella organization under which international marine research would fall.
4 The savior-ish tone of development of the UN and other international aid agencies and projects is apparent and can be found in scientists' accounts as well, in terms of what constitutes knowledge. For example, biologist Humphrey wrote in the *New Scientist*:

> Even though it is a part of the world which supported the earliest civilizations, we had learned little about the natural phenomena that occur there. The charts and sailing directions are some of the most primitive in the entire world. The surrounding countries, which are just now beginning to develop a competence in oceanic research, had lacked the ability to do more than limited surveys in waters immediately adjacent to their coasts. Also, this is a hungry part of the world.... The nations of Asia and Africa which border the Indian Ocean were anxious for assistance and for a better understanding of the environment in which they live. They believed that fuller knowledge of the resources of the Indian Ocean could provide a basis for the solution of some of their problems.
>
> (Humphrey 1961: 36)

5 By 1953, the International Hydrographic Organization (1953) in it *Limits of Oceans and Seas* defined the Indian Ocean's boundaries as delimited from the Atlantic Ocean by the 20° east meridian, running south from Cape Agulhas, and from the Pacific Ocean by the by the meridian of 146°49'E, running south from the southernmost point of Tasmania. Interestingly, according to the IHO's definition, the Indian Ocean's technical boundaries do not include so-called "marginal waterbodies" such as the Arabian Sea and the Bay of Bengal, though, those waterbodies are generally considered to be part of the Indian Ocean, as shown by the cruise tracks of the IIOE.
6 The IIOE-2 also has support from the Integrated Marine Biogeochemistry and Ecosystem Research (IMBER) and the Sustained Indian Ocean Biogeochemistry and Ecosystem Research (SIBER). IIOE-2 also has strong links with the Indian Ocean Panel (IOP) sponsored by the Global Ocean Observing System (GOOS) and Climate Variability and Predictability (CLIVAR) programs, and the Indian Ocean Observing System (IndOOS) Resources Forum (IRF), both under the auspices of IOGOOS. In addition, IIOE-2 will leverage several coastal and open-ocean monitoring programs in the Indian Ocean such as the Indian Ocean Observing System (IndOOS), Australia's

Integrated Marine Observing System (IMOS), the Southern Ocean Observing System (SOOS) etc. (see: https://iioe-2.incois.gov.in/IIOE-2/Partners.jsp).

7 These include, for example: oceanographic and meteorological sensors on earth-observing satellites; new components for the ocean observing system, including the tsunami detection network; developments in ocean modeling in all its various dimensions spatially and temporally; and lastly more accurate techniques of measurement and the improvement of data analyzing software and hardware (Hood et al. 2015).

8 The remaining themes are as follows:

> Theme 2: Boundary current dynamics, upwelling variability and ecosystem impacts (e.g., How are marine biogeochemical cycles, ecosystem processes and fisheries in the Indian Ocean influenced by boundary currents, eddies and upwelling? How does the interaction between local and remote forcing influence these currents and upwelling variability in the Indian Ocean?)
>
> Theme 3: Monsoon Variability and Ecosystem Response *(e.g., What factors control present, past and future monsoon variability? How does this variability impact ocean physics, chemistry and biogeochemistry in the Indian Ocean?)*
>
> Theme 4: Circulation, climate variability and change *(e.g., How has the atmospheric and oceanic circulation of the Indian Ocean changed in the past and how will it change in the future? How do these changes relate to topography and connectivity with the Pacific, Atlantic and Southern oceans?)*
>
> Theme 5: Extreme events and their impacts on ecosystems and human populations *(e.g., How do extreme events in the Indian Ocean impact coastal and open ocean ecosystems? What are the threats of extreme weather events, volcanic eruptions, tsunamis, combined with sea level rise, to human populations in low-lying coastal zones and small island nations of the Indian Ocean region?)*
>
> Theme 6: Unique geological, physical, biogeochemical, and ecological features of the Indian Ocean *(e.g., How do the physical characteristics of the southern Indian Ocean gyre system influence the biogeochemistry and ecology of the Indian Ocean? How do the complex tectonic and geologic processes, and topography of the Indian Ocean influence circulation, mixing and chemistry and therefore also biogeochemical and ecological processes?)*

9 Here I do not seek to replay or reiterate the troubled binary of science and "local" knowledge. The process of such expeditions and explorations makes it possible to highlight the ways that knowledge practices are always embedded within broader systems and institutions and practices of power, even when the intention is to "democratize" knowledge.

10 I am inspired by Choy and Zee (2015), who write that an attunement with air in the Anthropocence "impl[ies] not only an attention to the air but an investment in considering the identification of our long contemporary as a material and existential embroilment in atmospheres" (Choy and Zee 2015: 212) (and I would add an attunement with oceans). See also Choy (2011) and Zee (2017).

References

Amrith, Sunil. 2018. *Unruly Waters: How Rains, Rivers, Coasts, and Seas Have Shaped Asia's History.* New York: Basic Books.

Anand, Nikhil. 2017. *Hydraulic City: Water and the Infrastructures of Citizenship in Mumbai.* Durham: Duke University Press.

Anderson, Warwick. 2012. "Asia as Method in Science and Technology Studies." *East Asian Science, Technology and Society: An International Journal* 6: 445–451.

Ballestero, Andrea. 2019. *A Future History of Water.* Durham: Duke University Press.

Behrman, Daniel. 1981. *Assault on the Largest Unknown*. Paris: UNESCO Press.

de la Bellacasa, Maria Puig. 2011. "Matters of Care in Technoscience: Assembling Neglected Things." *Social Studies of Science* 41(1): 85–106.

Doel, R.E. 2002. "Why Value History?" *Eos* 47(19): 544–545.

Callison, Candis. 2014. *How Climate Change Comes to Matter: The Communal Life of Facts*. Durham: Duke University Press.

Chen, Kuan-hsing. 2010. *Asia as Method: Toward Deimperialization*. Durham, NC: Duke University Press.

Choy, Tim. 2011. *Ecologies of Comparison: An Ethnography of Endangerment in Hong Kong*. Durham: Duke University Press.

Choy, Tim and Jerry Zee. 2015. "Condition – Suspension." *Cultural Anthropology* 30(2): 210–223. https://doi.org/10.14506/ca30.2.04.

Collis, Christy and Klaus Dodds. 2008. "Assault on the unknown: the historical and political geographies of the International Geophysical Year (1957–8)." *Journal of Historical Geography* 34: 555–573.

D'Avella, Nicholas. 2019. *Concrete Dreams: Practice, Value, and Built Environments in Post-Crisis Buenos Aires*. Durham: Duke University Press.

Fan, Fa-ti. 2007. "East Asian STS: Fox or Hedgehog?" *East Asian Science, Technology and Society* 1: 243–247.

Fortun, Kim. 2012. "Ethnography in Late Industrialism." *Cultural Anthropology* 47(3): 446–464.

Fye, P. 1965. The International Indian Ocean Expedition. The Distinguished Lecture Series 1964–1965 Sponsored by Science Bureau, Washington Board of Trade, Georgetown University, January 27, 1965.

Ghosh, Amitav. 2016. *The Great Derangement: Climate Change and the Unthinkable*. Chicago: University of Chicago Press.

Green, Nile. 2018. "Waves of Heterotopia: Toward a Vernacular Intellectual History of the Indian Ocean." *American Historical Review* 123(3): 846–874.

Hamblin, Jacob Darwin. 2011. *Oceanographers and the Cold War: Disciples of Marine Science*. Seattle: University of Washington Press.

Haraway, Donna. 2015. "Anthropocene, Capitalocene, Plantationocene, Chthulucene: Making Kin." *Environmental Humanities* 6: 159–165.

Heezen, B.C. and M. Tharp. 1966. "Physiography of the Indian Ocean." *Philosophical Transactions of the Royal Society of London Series A – Mathematical, Physical and Engineering Sciences* 259: 137–149.

Helmreich, Stefan. 2009. *Alien Ocean: Anthropological Voyages in Microbial Seas*. Oakland, CA: University of California Press.

Helmreich, Stefan. 2014. "Waves: An Anthropology of Scientific Things." *Hau: Journal of Ethnographic Theory* 4(3): 265–284.

Ho, Engseng. 2004. "Empire through Diasporic Eyes: A View from the Other Boat." *Comparative Studies in Society and History* 46(2): 210–246.

Ho, Engseng. 2006. *The Graves of Tarim: Genealogy and Mobility Across the Indian Ocean*. Berkeley: University of California Press.

Hofmeyr, Isabel. 2010. "Universalizing the Indian Ocean." PMLA 125(3): 721–729.

Hood, R.R., Edward R. Urban, Michael J. McPhaden, Danielle Su, and Eric Raes. 2016 "The 2nd International Indian Ocean Expedition (IIOE-2): Motivating New Exploration in a Poorly Understood Basin." Association for the Sciences of Limnology and Oceanography.

Hood, R.R., H.W. Bange, L. Beal, L.E. Beckley, P. Burkill, G.L. Cowie, N. D'Adamo, G. Ganssen, H. Hendon, J. Hermes, M. Honda, M. McPhaden, M. Roberts, S. Singh,

E. Urban, and W. Yu. 2015. "Science Plan of the Second International Indian Ocean Expedition (IIOE-2): A Basin-Wide Research Program." Scientific Committee on Oceanic Research, Newark, Delaware, USA.

Humphrey, G.F. 1961. "The Unknown Indian Ocean: An international investigation." *New Scientist* 9(216): 36–39.

International Hydrographic Organization. 1953. *Limits of the Oceans and Seas*, 3rd edition. Monte-Carlo.

Knauss, J.A. 1961. "The International Indian Ocean Expedition." *Science* 134: 1674–1676.

Lambert, David, Luciana Martins, and Miles Ogborn. 2006. "Currents, Visions, and Voyages: Historical Geographies of the Sea." *Journal of Historical Geography* 32: 479–493.

Latour, Bruno. 2004. "From Matters of Fact to Matters of Concern." *Critical Inquiry* 30 (Winter): 225–248.

Law, John. 1986. "On the Methods of Long-Distance Control: Vessels, Navigation and the Portuguese Route to India." In *Power, Action and Belief: A New Sociology of Knowledge* edited by John Law, 234–263. London: Routledge.

Lee, S.-K., W. Park, M.O. Baringer, A.L. Gordon, B. Huber, and Y. Liu, 2015: "Pacific Origin of the Abrupt Increase in Indian Ocean Heat Content During the Warming Hiatus." *Nature Geosci.* 8: 445–449.

Lehman, Jessica. 2016. "A Sea of Potential: The Politics of Global Ocean Observations." *Political Geography* 55: 113–123.

Lewis, Martin and Karen Wigen. 1999. "A Maritime Response to the Crisis in Area Studies." *Geographical Review* 89: 161–168.

Machado, Pedro. 2016. "Views from Other Boats: On Amitav Ghosh's Indian Ocean 'Worlds.'" *American Historical Review.* 121(5): 1545–1551.

Mol, Annmarie. 2002. *The Body Multiple: Ontology in Medical Practice.* Durham: Duke University Press.

Moore, Jason, ed. 2016. *Anthropocene or Capitalocene? Nature, History, and the Crisis of Capitalism.* Oakland: PM Press.

Ogden, Laura, Ulrich Oskander, Paige West, Karim Aly-Kassam, and Paul Robbins. 2013. "Global Assemblages, Resilience, and Earth Stewardship in the Anthropocene." *Frontiers in Ecology and the Environment* 11: 341–347.

Palsson, Gisli, Bronislaw Szerszynski, Sverker Sorlin, John Marks, Bernard Avril, Carole Crumley, Heide Hackmann, Poul Holm, John Ingram, Alan Kirman, Mercedes Pardo Buendia, and Rifka Weehuizen. 2013. "Reconceptualizing the 'Anthropos' in the Anthropocene: Integrating the Social Sciences and Humanities in Global Environmental Change Research." *Environ. Sci. Policy* 28: 3–13.

Parreñas, Juno Salazar. 2018. *Decolonizing Extinction: The Work of Care in Orangutan Rehabilitation.* Durham: Duke University Press.

Prestholdt, Jeremy. 2015. "Locating the Indian Ocean: Notes on the Postcolonial Reconstitution of Space." *Journal of Eastern African Studies.* 9(3): 440–467.

Rhein, M., S.R. Rintoul, S. Aoki, E. Campos, D. Chambers, R.A. Feely, S. Gulev, G.C. Johnson, S.A. Josey, A. Kostianoy, C. Mauritzen, D. Roemmich, L.D. Talley, and F. Wang. 2013. Observations: Ocean. In: *Climate Change 2013: The Physical Science Basis. Contribution of Working Group I to the Fifth Assessment Report of the Intergovernmental Panel on Climate Change* edited by T.F. Stocker, D. Qin, G.-K. Plattner, M. Tignor, S.K. Allen, J. Boschung, A. Nauels, Y. Xia, V. Bex, and P.M. Midgley. Cambridge: Cambridge University Press.

Roxy, M., K. Ritika, P. Terray, and S. Masson. 2014. "The Curious Case of Indian Ocean Warming." *J. Climate* 27(22): 8501–8509.

Snider, R.G. 1961.The International Indian Ocean Expedition. *Discovery* (March):114–117.

Steinberg, P.E. 2013. "Of Other Seas: Metaphors and Materialities in Maritime Regions." *Atlantic Studies* 10(2): 156e169.

Steinberg, P. and K. Peters. 2015. "Wet Ontologies, Fluid Spaces: Giving Depth to Volume through Oceanic Thinking." *Environment and Planning D: Society and Space* 33(2): 247–264.

Tomzcek, Matthias. 1980. "A Review of Wüst's Classification of the Major Deep-sea Expeditions 1873–1960 and Its Extension to Recent Oceanographic Research Programs." *Oceanography: The Past.*

Tsing, Anna. 2015. *The Mushroom at the End of the World: On the Possibility of Life in Capitalist Ruins.* Princeton: Princeton University Press.

Wyrtki, K., E.B. Bennett, and D.J. Rochford. 1971. *Oceanographic Atlas of the International Indian Ocean Expeditions.* Washington D.C.: National Science Foundation.

Zee, Jerry. 2017. "Holding Patterns: Sand and Political Time at China's Desert Shores." *Cultural Anthropology* 32(2): 215–241.

Index

Page numbers in *italics* denote figures and maps.

Abethorbei, David Deng 120
Abyssinian 215–17, 225n9; courtiers,
  ministers, commanders 215–17; gate 218
Acacia farnesiana 64
A.C. Guards 218, 220–2
affinity 26–8, 30, 32, 33, 35–7, 150,
  180–91
African Cavalry Guard 218
African descent communities 6, 156
African diasporic community 218
African Indians 55
African lyre 215–17
African modernity 52
Afro-Indian communities 213, 215–17
Afro-Asian 215
Alpers, Edward 18, 60–2
alluvial deposit 94
Ambar, Malik 215, 225n9
Amrith, Sunil 2, 18, 75, 90
amphibious 60–2
Anderson, Warwick 229
Andrews, C.F. 184
Anthropocene 237
anti-Asian sentiment 54
anti-Tamil violence in Sri Lanka 3
Arab-driven slave trade 218
Arabian Sea 104
Arabic conceptualizations of Indian
  Ocean 33
Argenti, Nicolas 156
Arusha Declaration 49; and socialist
  belonging 50–3
"Asia as method" 229
Assam 2
Atlantic economy 29
Atlantic slavery 156, 159
Atlantic World 9, 10, 12, 31, 43, 222
Aulukh, Gurmit Singh 188

Bahrain National Museum 160
Ballantyne, Tony 183
Baloch people, territorial boundaries of 165
Baloch Students Organization's (BSO)
  movement 174
Bandung Conference 219
Bangalore 4
Bangladesh Food Safety Authority 141
Baseer Ali 222
Basu, Helene 212
bazaar 170, 173, 217, 218
BBC *see* British Broadcasting
  Corporation (BBC)
bedaya beksan putri see dance, women
Behrman, Daniel 231, 233
Beruwala's traders 89, 98
Bharatiya Janata Party (BJP) 2
bile 199–200, 204
Bille, Franck 70
Bishara, Fahad 65
bitterness 199, 206, 207
BJP *see* Bharatiya Janata Party (BJP)
body *see* embodiment
boat-captains 166, 174; *see* Dhow labor
Bose, Sugata 26, 27
Bremner, Lindsay 70
Brickell, Katherine 214
British Broadcasting Corporation (BBC)
  104, 106–7
British East India Company 171, 213, 218
Bruun, Anton 230, 233
BSO movement *see* Baloch Students
  Organization's (BSO) movement
Buck-Morss, Susan 71
Busaidi Omanis 30
Al-Busaidi, Sultan Qaboos 174
Al-Busaidi Sultans of Oman 166
Byari/Beary community 2, 19n1

Cape Coloured population 153
"Cape Malay" identity 36, 153
Cape slavery 156
Caravela casino 103; ship 103
Casinos, offshore 15, 103, 113
Catlin-Jairazbhoy, Amy 212, 224n1
Centre for Responsible Tourism 111
Ceylon 105
Chatterjee, Indrani 172
Chaudhuri, K.N. 75, 90
China 2, 3, 105
China Overseas Port Holding Company
    (COPHC) 166
China-Pakistan Economic Corridor
    (CPEC) 166
China's Belt and Road Initiative 69
cities 2–5, 13–16, 51–4
Chaush 213–14, 216, 222
Choi, Vivian Y. 17
choreographic translocations 219–22
Choy, T. 239n10
Citizenship Bill, Tanzania 53
'city of gems' 89
Cochin 43–7
colonial authorities 169
colonial-Nizamate rule 218
colonial states 31
Comoros Islands 29
conceptual/theoretical relationality 13
Container Corporation of India
    (CONCOR) 66, 69
Containerization, containers 58–70
contemporary and contemporaneous,
    Indian Ocean worlds 1, 13, 69–70, 91,
    100, 103, 214
COPHC *see* China Overseas Port Holding
    Company (COPHC)
Costa-Pinto, Maya 15
Cox's Bazar 134, 136–9, 141, 142
CPEC *see* China-Pakistan Economic
    Corridor (CPEC)

Dad Mohammed 169, 172, 173
Dadri (Gautam Buddha Nagar) 66–70
daff parties 212, 214, 219–21
dance: men 212–14, 219; women 223;
    courtly dance 216; popular dance
    212–15, 219, 221, 222; identity 218;
    Marfa 212–19
dapankuthu see rhythms
Dar es Salaam 15, 18, 43–5, 49, 51, 51, 53,
    54, 197, 198, 200, 204
Darlymple, William 176
Das, Goutam 107–8

Das, Veena 108, 198
Datta, Ayona 214
Dawdy, Shanon Lee 95
DDT *see* dichlorodiphenyltrichloroethane
Deacon, George 233
De Boeck, Filip 120
decolonization 4, 34, 44, 47, 55, 231
Deed of Cession 181, 182
deeds of debt 65
Delhi 15, 59, 66, 70n7
Delhi School of Economics 4
Dhows, also vahan 73–4, 76, *76*, 78, 82,
    84, 103, 160, 162n8, 166, 172, 175
Dhow labor 73, 80–2; *Nakhuda* and
    Maalim 166, 174
"diaspora" 6, 7, 12, 16, 55, 119, 136, 138,
    153, 157, 177, 182–4, 186, 188, 190,
    191n6, 212–14, 216, 218, 220, 224n2
diasporic Sikh communities 183
Dichlorodiphenyltrichloroethane 141, 143
digital: social sphere 213, 221–2; media
    214, 221, 225n16; space 221
Diocesan Service Center for Social
    Action 111
displacemaking 15, 133, 135, 138
Djinns 1, 174–7, 178n4, 202
D'Mello, Pamela 110
Doll, Christian J. 15, 19
Douglas, Mary 79
dry port 15, 58–70
"D-School" *see* Delhi School of
    Economics
dual articulation 25, 27, 28, 35
dual morphology 74, 77–9, 84
Dubai, UAE 59
Dutch colonization of Cochin 44
Dutch East India Company 30, 151

East Africa 28–31, 172, 215, 217
East African lyre 217
East African Slave Trade 172, 215
Eastern Africa 28–31
Eastern African markets 31
eating 199, 206–7, 208
Earth System, broader ecological 235
El Niño 237
Elyachar, Julia 85n4
embodied musical traditions 156
embodiment 4–5; and gendered
    desire 202; as knowledge 208; as
    method 15–17, 206–9; and worlds 205
    see eating; *see* grief; *see* kinship, as
    intercorporeal; *see* medicine; *see* qualia;
    see sensoriums

emic language of geography 33
Emirati identity 160
Eskimo 79
Baloch people, territorial boundaries of 165
ethnographic perspectives 16, 91, 100
ethnographic vignettes, series of 119
European colonialism 28, 31, 222
European metageographical concepts of
    Indian Ocean 34

Farquhar, Judith 199, 207
Favret-Saada, Jeanne 210n2
FC Goa 110
fieldwork 1, 6, 8, 16, 58, 66, 77, 78, 90,
    114n9, 130, 144n1, 173, 199, 200,
    209n1, 210n2
Fijian Sikh community 180, 183, 184,
    188, 190
Fijian society, racial identity in 182
Fiji Archipelago, Sikh sacred geography
    in 186–9
Fiji Census 190
Fiji *Gurdwaras* 190
Fiji, South Asians in 181–4
First International Indian Ocean
    Expedition (IIOE) 228–35, 238n5
fold, folding 70
foreland 60, 62
Fontainhas 111
formalin 141, 144n11
Fortun, Kim 237

Gandhi, Mahatma 12, 47, 49
"Ganges Khan" 180
"Ganges Singh" 180, 185
gems: mining 92, 93; trading 96, 97, 98
geo-tag 214, 221
Ghosh, Amitav 2, 18, 64
Ghosh, Devleena 182
Goan casinos 103, 107–13
Goan Government 106
Goa, North 105–7, 111
Goa State Pollution Control Board
    (GSPCB) 104, 114n4
Goa South Asia connections 103, 109, 113
Goa transoceanic connections 105
Golconda 216–18, 225n10
Gor, Bava 212, 224n6
Goswami, Chayya 75
Goynar Baksho 136
Green, Nile 18
grief 197–205
GSPCB *see* Goa State Pollution Control
    Board (GSPCB)

Guattari, Felix 46
Gulf modernity 160
gurdwaras 180–1, 183, 184, 186–9;
    Lautoka 188, 189; transnational 190
Gurnah, Abdulrazak 8
Guru Granth Sahib 181, 186
Guru Nanak 181, 184, 187
Gwadar Port 166
Gwat 176, 177, 178n4, 178n5
Gwat-i-Leb 176
Gyanananda/Ghanananda 12

Habshi, Malik Raihan 216
Hadramawt 212, 213, 217–19, 223
Hajee Sullaiman Shahmahomed
    Trust 151
Hanif Latif 1–2
Harar 216
Harris, Mark 79
Hegel 70–1
Helmreich, Stefan 229
Hindu Monastery of Africa 12
Hinterland 60, 62, 70, 91, 94, 95
Hofmeyr, Isabel 34, 42
Hong Kong 2
Hopper, Matthew 160
Hsu, Elisabeth 207
humanistic methodologies 16, 208
Hyderabad 212–14, 218–25
hypermobile community 188

ICD *see* Internal Container Depot (ICD),
    dry port
ICD Baba's shrine *68*
IGY *see* International Geophysical
    Year (IGY)
IIOE *see* First International Indian Ocean
    Expedition (IIOE)
IIOE-2 *see* Second International Indian
    Ocean (IIOE-2)
illama see alluvial deposit
IMFL *see* Indian-made foreign
    liquor (IMFL)
India–Burma border *3*
Indian-made foreign liquor (IMFL) 108,
    114n13
Indian Ocean African societies 30
Indian Ocean circulations 213–14,
    220–2
Indian Ocean Global Ocean Observation
    System (IOGOOS) 235
Indian Ocean materiality 229
Indian Ocean method 1–2, 15–17, 207–8,
    236–8

Indian Ocean ontology: disinterred 54–6; inauthentic Asians 53–4; sensory histories 43–5
Indian Ocean, space of 25–32, 58–70, 222–4
Indian Ocean potentialities 43
Indian Ocean Rim Association for Regional Cooperation 36
Indian Ocean rim societies 30
Indian Ocean sensorium 42, 208
Indian Ocean studies 1, 12–14, 42
Indian tourists, influx of 106
Indo-European Telegraph Line 169, 173
Indonesian archipelago 151, 153
Indonesian government 36
Innovation Lab 18
Intercontinental Slavery Museum 158
interface 58–70
Intergovernmental Panel on Climate Change (IPCC) 143, 234
Internal Container Depot (ICD) *see* dry port
International Geophysical Year (IGY) 229
International Hydrographic Organization 238n5
International Indian Film Awards 106
IOGOOS *see* Indian Ocean Global Ocean Observation System (IOGOOS)
IPCC *see* Intergovernmental Panel on Climate Change (IPCC)
IPK *see* Islamic Party of Kenya (IPK)
Iselin, Columbus 231
Islam 12, 26, 30, 150–2, 154
Islamicate 219, 221–2
Islamic Party of Kenya (IPK) 6, 35, 36
Istanas see royal houses

Jabri Bin 212, 220, 221
Jamal, Ashraf 60–2, 69–70
Jamali, Hafeez Ahmed 16
jambiya 219, 220
Jam Salaya *76*, 76–8, 81
Japanese cotton goods 31
Japanese manufacturers 31
Japanese trade 31
Jappie, Sarah. 161n1, 161n2
Jaschke, Karin 109
Jeychandran, Neelima 8–12, 18
jihajis 180, 185
Jinn *see* Djinns
Joginder Singh Ratendra 185
Joseph, May 15

Juba 118–20, *125*; building "companies" 127–30
Juba-Based initiatives 130

Kachchhi seafaring communities 78
Kalat State 169, 172
kanzus 5
karāmāt 150
Karori, Ali Khan 216
Kaur, Inderjit 18
Kenya 6, 7, 8, 21, 35–7, 48, 50, 54, 55, 124, 129; coastal separatism in 35
keramats 150, 151
Khan, Farhad 216
Khan, Mahmood 172
khas land *see* land, government
King, Martin Luther 49
Kingma, Sytze 104, 109, 112
kinship, as intercorporeal 205, 207
Kleinman, Arthur 208
Klose, Alexander 63–4, 69
Knauss, John 233
Kozhikode 8–9, *9*
kramats 151, 154
Kramat Shaykh Yusuf 151–2, *152*
kratons see royal houses
Kresse, Kai 26
kula see eating
Kull, Christian 64
kutapika see vomiting
Kutubdia Para, Cox's Bazar 134, 142
Kwan, SanSan 221

Al-Laiwa 160
Ladakh 3
land: and soil 202; and personhood 202–5; government land 134, 138
Las Vegas 106–7
Las Vegas of India 106
late industrialism 237
Lautoka *Gurdwara* 188, *189*
Legislative Council 53
Lewis, Martin 26
littoral 30, 58–71
longue durée 25
Luanda, Angola 59, 66
Lumumba, Patrice 49
Lusofonia festivals 106
Lusofonia Games 106, 114n7
Lusophone: networks 105; world 105, 113; former colonies 106; South Asian Lusophone identity 43
Lusophone Society of Goa 106

maalim see navigators
Macao Foundation 106
Macao Government Tourism Office 106
Macau, relationship with Goa 105–7, 112–13
Machado, Pedro 16, 18, 83
Madras 3
Mahajan, Nidhi 15, 91
mahali kwao see place, 'their place'
Mahomed, Dad 169
Malabar Coast 9–11, 43–5, 47, 191n11
Malacca 105, 215
Malaysia 2
Malay Islamic modernity 2
Mandovi river, Goa 103–4, 108–9, 112
Mandovi riverfront 104, 107, 110–12
map: and memory 15–16; of Indian Ocean *32*, 33
maqam see tomb shrine
Marfa 212–15; Afro-Asia in 215–17; Golconda to Hyderabad 217–19; *see* rhythms; *see* dance
Maritime Silk Road 69
maritime zones 27
Marshall, Lydia 170
"martial race" 182
Martin, Craig. 70n10
maumivu see pain
Mauritian case 161
Mauritian slave heritage 158
Mauss, Marcel 74, 79
mawazo see stress
Mbeki, Thabo 153
McPhaden, Michael 227–8, 236, 237
medicine: and Indian Ocean scholarship 198, 206; traditional 199, 201, 203–4, 207; biomedicine 200–1, 202, 204, 209
Meek, Laura A. 17
Mekran Coasts 165, 169, 173, 176
memory 2, 5, 15–16, 42–3
Merleau-Ponty 206
Metcalf, Thomas 183
methodology *see* Indian Ocean method
michumbuku see ulcers
Minister of Darkness *see* Minister of Electricity and Dams
Minister of Electricity and Dams 120–3
Mishra, Vijay 182
Mnazi Mmoja park *51*, 51–2
Mohajir elites 165
Mohammad, Noor 174–5
Mombasa 36, 215, 223
Mombasa Republican Council (MRC) 36

money transfer 129–30; dollars and South Sudanese pounds 123–7
monsoon; pattern 75–9, 81, 82, 85n3; temporality 74, 84–5; relationality 84–5
Moorthy, Shanti 60–2, 69–70
Mota Salaya 78
MRC *see* Mombasa Republican Council (MRC)
Mr. Muro 197, 198, 200, 202, 204
Mrs. Muro 197, 198, 200, 202, 205
Muhammad, Dur 176
multi-vocality 1
Murad, Khodja 215
music 214, 224; Hyderabadi 212; ritual 213; popular/social 213, 218–23; courtly 216, 217
Muslim, materiality of 150

NAASP *see* New Asian-African Strategic Partnership (NAASP)
Nairobi 5, 8, 13, 15, 16, 21
Nairobi City Park 8, 16
Nakhuda see boat-captains
National Capital Region of India (NCR) *see* Delhi, India
National Heritage Resources Act 155
National Institute of Oceanography 104
National Oceanic and Atmospheric Administration's (NOAA) Western Regional Center 227
naubat 216
naubat khana 216, 218
navigators 166, 175
Nazirartek, Bangladesh *133*; *shutki* in 136–8
NCR *see* National Capital Region (NCR)
Ndzuwani Island 29
Nepal 107, 109; Kathmandu 107; Nepali 114n14
Netherlands 109
New Asian-African Strategic Partnership (NAASP) 219
ngoma 50, 55, 220
Ng'weno, Bettina 5, *7*, 17, 18, 21
Nhial Bol Aken 120
nishan sahib 187
Nizamate 213, 218
nomadic identities 43
non-Africans, role of 53
Non-Aligned Movement 35
non-governmental organizations 111
nostalgia 173–5
Nyerere, Julius K. 44, 46–54

Nyerere, Rosemary 52, 55
nyongo see bile

Obama, Barack 52
oceanic ecosystem 227, 234, 235, 238n6
oceanography 235
oceanographic partner programs 235
Omani rule in Gwadar 168, 174, 175, 177
Omani Sultan 166
Omani traders 160
Omani Wali 169
Omony 118
Opar Bangla 136
Ottoman naval 30

Pacific Marine Environmental
    Laboratory (PMEL) 227
Pakistani nationalism, foundational
    narrative of 165
Pakistani rule 165, 177
Palli Karma-Sahayak Foundation
    (PKSF) 143
Panaji, waterways 103–4, 111; impact of
    casinos on 110–12 San Tome 111
Pearl Diving Heritage Revival Festival in
    Kuwait 160
Pearson, Michael 60–5, 69, 90, 91
performative geographies of Indian
    Ocean 222–4
Persia 105
Persian Gulf 33, 73, 76, 77, 166,
    173, 176
pilgrimage 150
PKSF *see* Palli Karma-Sahayak
    Foundation (PKSF)
placemaking, in Indian Ocean worlds 15
place 2; of Indian Ocean worlds 15; "their
    place" 205; of memory 2, 4, 42–3
PMEL *see* Pacific Marine Environmental
    Laboratory (PMEL)
"politicization of science" 230
Population Registration Act, South
    Africa 153
port, port city 2, 58–70
Port Authority of Singapore (PSA) 166
Portuguese-controlled Mozambique 30
Portuguese Goa, nostalgic ideal of 106
Portuguese Asia 105
Portuguese, former colonies 103, 106, 111
post-emergency India 3
Povinelli, Elizabeth 198
PPI *see* proton-pump inhibitor (PPI)
Prange, Sebastian 191n11
Prestholdt, Jeremy 13, 18, 70

primitivism 167
Proterozoic Era 98
proton-pump inhibitor (PPI) 200
PSA *see* Port Authority of Singapore (PSA)

qadi 175
qualia 198, 202, 206, 207, 209
quotidian practices, in Indian Ocean
    worlds 15, 198, 209

Rabeloc 199, 200
racial identity in Fijian society 182
Ranciere, Jacques 50–1
Ranganath, Nicole 16
Rangan, Haripriya 64
Reimagining Indian Ocean Worlds Mellon
    Research Initiative 58
relationality, across Indian Ocean worlds
    13, 28–32, 74, 205–8, 210
ressac 60
Revelle, Roger 230, 233
rhythms: popular 219, 222, 223; African
    214, 219, 222–4; South Indian 220,
    222; Arabic 214, 219, 222–4; Indian
    Ocean 224
"Rind Disturbances" 170
Rind tribe 169, 170, 173
Roach, Joseph 222
Rockel, Stephen 64
Rohingya refugees 139, 142
Roy, Parama 206
royal houses 223

Saba Saba 45–6
Sabaragamuwa 92, 94
sacred geographies 36, 150–4
sacred journeys 181
Safran, William 224n2
SAG scheme *see* Special Area Games
    (SAG) scheme
Samarawickrema, Nethra 15
Sandeman, Robert 170–2
Saraf, Ishani 15
Sathya Sai Baba (1926–011) 5, *14*
Saudi Arabia, racialized labor
    conditions in 1
Sauti Ya Tanu 49
Sayyid 178n6
Schama, Simon 49
science and technology studies (STS) 229
Scientific Committee for Oceanographic
    Research (SCOR) 235
SCOR *see* Special Committee for Oceanic
    Research (SCOR)

scrap/scrap metal 58–9, 66
Second International Indian Ocean
 (IIOE-2) 227, 228, 234–6, 238n6
self-emancipated slave communities 177
Selvadurai, Shyam 4
sensoriums 206, 208
Sepoy Revolt of 1857 169
Sharia law 175
Shaw, Rosalind 157
Sheriff, Abdul 75, 171
shrines, for African saints and spirits
 11–12
Shroff, Beheroze 212–13
shutki 142–4; contamination 140–2; and
 displacemaking 133–6; drying method
 143; on move 138–40; in Nazirartek
 136–8
shutki mohol 136
shutkipotti 136
Sidi: communities 213–14, 217; histories
 216–17; space/neighborhood 219–22,
 224n6; *see* dance; *see* music; *see* rhythm
Sikh community in Fiji 183
Sikh diasporic communities 183
Sikh Gurudwara Prabandhak Committee
 Application 191n12
Sikh identity 184
Sikhism 190n1
Sikh *Jat* (farming) community 182
Sikh kinship structures 183
Sikh sacred geography: in Fiji
 Archipelago 186–9
Sikkim 107
"Silk Road Economic Belt" 69
Simone, AbdouMaliq 119–20, 128, 129
Simpson, Edward 26
Singapore 104, 106–9, 113
Singh, Dalabar 188
Singh, Guru Gobind 187–8
Slave Wrecks Project 158
Snider, Robert 230, 233
social geographies 161
South Asian faith communities 180
South Asian Fijian culture 186
South Asian Fijian population 183
South Asian Fijian scholarship 183
South Asian Lusophone identity 43
South Asian political community 34
South Asians in Fiji 181–4
South China Sea 105
South Sudan 118
South Sudan-Uganda border 118
spatiality, spatial 4–5
Special Area Games (SAG) scheme 213

Special Committee for Oceanic Research
 (SCOR) 230, 231
Sports Authority of India 213
Spyer, Patricia 166
Srinivas, Smriti 1–5, 17, 18
Sriram, Pallavi 17
Sri Lanka 3–4, 89, 107
Stacker, Reach 67
State Reorganization 218
Stewart, Kathleen 175
Stommels, Henry 231
stones' itineraries 89
stress 205
STS *see* science and technology
 studies (STS)
sulaimani chai 9
Suryakarta *223*
Suva *Gurdwara* 189, 190
Swahili Coast 30, 43
Swahili language 33–4
Swahili linkages 28
Swahili-speaking world 171
Swahili terminology for oceanic fields 34
Swidler, Nina 171
Syed 176, 178n6

taarab chakacha 223
Tanzania 3; and medicine and personhood
 197, 199–201, 202–5, 207
Tanzanian African National Union
 (TANU) 54
Tanzanian and Chinese Project on
 Traditional Medicine 207
Tanzanian citizenship 53
Tanzanian identity 50
Tanzanianness 47–50
territorial nationalism 34
Tesfaye, Facil 206
Times of India investigation, into casino
 114n14
Tithi, Bidita Jawher 15
tomb shrine 150
Tourism, Goa 105–7, 109, 111–13
Trans-Atlantic slave trade 159
transcultural 5
translocal 214, 216, 219, 221–4
transnational communities, Bangladesh
 139–40
transoceanic linkages 44
tribalism 167
Trichur, Raghuraman 105, 114n8
Trouillot, Michel-Rolph 7, 157
Truth and Justice Commission 158
Tuan Guru 151

Tumbura 127
Tuzk-i-Jahangir 224n4

udasi see sacred journeys
udongo see land, soil
uchungu see grief
Uhuru na kazi 50
Ujamaa 43, 44, 50, 52, 55–6
"ulcers" 197–200, 205–8
"umland" 60, 62
UNESCAP report *see* United Nations
    Economic and Social Commission for
    Asia and the Pacific (UNESCAP) report
UNESCO *see* United Nations Educational,
    Scientific, and Cultural Organization
    (UNESCO)
unified Indian Ocean 27
United Nations Decade of Ocean Science
    for Sustainable Development 228
United Nations Economic and Social
    Commission for Asia and the Pacific
    (UNESCAP) report 65–6
United Nations Educational, Scientific, and
    Cultural Organization (UNESCO) 157,
    158, 228; Intergovernmental
    Oceanographic Commission (IOC) 230,

235; Slave Route project 158; World
    Heritage site 158
utopian 3, 5

Verne, Julia 91
Vietnam 3
Vink, Markus 27, 33
vomiting 200–201, 204, 209
Vypin, Kerala *11*

Wali of Gwadar 169, 170, 173, 175
waraqa see deeds of debt
Ward, Kerry 152, 153
"webs of Empire" 183
Wigen, Kären 26
Winterbottom, Anna 206
Worden, Nigel 152, 153
World Food Programme 139

Yogyakarta 223
Young, Jacob 215

Zandonai, Sheyla 112
Zanzibar 35, 36, 175, 215
Zee, Jerry. 239n10
ziarah see pilgrimage